Europe in Emerging Asia

Europe in Emerging Asia

*Opportunities and Obstacles
in Political and
Economic Encounters*

Edited by Fredrik Erixon
and Krishnan Srinivasan

ROWMAN &
LITTLEFIELD
────── INTERNATIONAL
London • New York

Published by Rowman & Littlefield International, Ltd.
Unit A, Whitacre Mews, 26-34 Stannary Street, London SE11 4AB
www.rowmaninternational.com

Rowman & Littlefield International, Ltd. is an affiliate of Rowman & Littlefield
4501 Forbes Boulevard, Suite 200, Lanham, Maryland 20706, USA
With additional offices in Boulder, New York, Toronto (Canada), and London (UK)
www.rowman.com

British Library Cataloguing in Publication Information Available
A catalogue record for this book is available from the British Library

ISBN: HB 978-1-783-48226-9
ISBN: PB 978-1-783-48227-6

Library of Congress Cataloging-in-Publication Data

Europe in emerging Asia : opportunities and obstacles in political and economic encounters / edited
by Fredrik Erixon and Krishnan Srinivasan.
pages cm
Includes bibliographical references and index.
ISBN 978-1-78348-226-9 (cloth : alk. paper)—ISBN 978-1-78348-227-6 (pbk. : alk. paper)—ISBN
978-1-78348-228-3 (electronic)
1. Europe—Foreign relations—Asia. 2. Asia—Foreign relations—Europe. 3. Europe—Foreign economic relations—Asia. 4. Asia—Foreign economic relations—Europe. I. Erixon, Fredrik, editor of
compilation. II. Srinivasan, Krishnan, 1937– editor of compilation.
JZ1570.A55.E9774 2015
327.504—dc23

2014048806

Printed in the United States of America

Contents

Abbreviations

AEC	ASEAN Economic Community
APEC	Asia Pacific Economic Cooperation
ARF	ASEAN Regional Forum
ASEAN	Association of Southeast Asian Nations
ASEM	Asia-Europe Meeting
BIT	bilateral investment treaty
BRICS	Brazil, Russia, India, China, South Africa
BTIA	bilateral trade and investment agreement
BTC	Baku-Tiblisi-Ceyhan
CAFTA	China-ASEAN Free Trade Agreement
CIS	Commonwealth of Independent States
CMEA	Council for Mutual Economic Assistance
EaP	Eastern Partnership Programme
EEC	European Economic Community
ENP	European Neighbourhood Policy
EU	European Union
FDI	foreign direct investment
FTA	free trade agreement
FTAAP	Free Trade Area of the Asia Pacific
GATT	General Agreement on Tariffs and Trade
GUAM	Georgia, Ukraine, Azerbaijan, and Moldova
GDP	gross domestic product

GNI	gross national income
GSP	Generalized System of Preferences
HIC	high-income country
HED	high-level economic dialogue
ICT	Information and Communications Technology
IMF	International Monetary Fund
IPCC	Intergovernmental Panel on Climate Change
LIC	low-income country
MIC	middle-income country
MIT	middle-income trap
MDG	Millennium Development Goal
NATO	North Atlantic Treaty Organization
NCPO	National Council for Peace and Order
NGO	non-government organization
NPT	non-proliferation treaty
ODA	official development assist
OECD	Organization for Economic Cooperation and Development
OEM	original equipment manufacturer
OSCE	Organization for Security and Cooperation in Europe
p.a.	per annum
R&D	research and development
R2P	Responsibility to Protect
RCEP	Regional Comprehensive Economic Partnership
RF	Russian Federation
SAARC	South Asian Association for Regional Cooperation
SME	small and medium enterprise
TFA	trade facilitation agreement
TPA	Trade Promotion Authority

TPP	Trans-Pacific Partnership
TTIP	Trans-Atlantic Trade and Investment Partnership
UMIC	upper-middle-income country
UN	United Nations
UNC	UN Command in Korea
UNGA	United Nations General Assembly
UNSC	United Nations Security Council
WTO	World Trade Organization

Preface

Ana Palacio

In *The Man Who Was*, Rudyard Kipling writes of the chance meeting between a wandering Russian journalist named Dirkovitch and officers of an imaginary English regiment stationed in Peshawar at the height of European colonialism in Asia. Dirkovitch, excited to be among his new friends, speaks grandly of the potential for a unified European (Russian and English) approach to civilize Asia. With the mention of this plan, our all-knowing narrator steps in to swiftly dispense with this fantasy. 'Asia', Kipling notes, 'is not going to be civilized after the methods of the West. There is too much Asia, and she is too old'. More than a century after it was published, it remains a reminder for Europeans to prevent slips into ethnocentrism in their approach to Asia.

Europe's relationship with Asia has clearly come a long way since then, though at times there has been a tendency to slip back towards the paternalism of the *mission civilisatrice*. In the European Union's (EU's) strategic approach towards Asia, however, there has been a distinct tendency towards the ignorant optimism of Dirkovitch rather than the knowing scepticism of the narrator, not in content but in outlook.

It has been twenty years since the EU released its first strategy for Asia[1]. In 'Towards a New Asia Strategy', the EU laid out four overarching objectives for its relations with Asia: strengthening the EU's economic presence in Asia, contributing to Asian stability, promoting economic development, and consolidating values (democracy, human rights, and the rule of law) in the region. But from the strategy's very first sentence[2], it was clear that the primary focus was on enhancing economic ties. Incidentally, this tendency to say one thing but do another is present throughout EU policymaking from the Barcelona Declaration to the European Neighbourhood Policy (ENP). Seven years later, when the European Commission moved to revamp the Asia policy, it developed a platform focusing more specifically on building broader partnerships in the region[3]. The strategy's four objectives were reduced to one core goal: 'strengthening the EU's political and economic presence across the region, and raising this to a level commensurate with the growing global weight of an enlarged EU'[4].

Now, two decades and two strategic frameworks later, how successful has the EU been in strengthening its presence in Asia? As is demonstrated throughout this book, the results have been unbalanced at best. The area where there has been the clearest growth is in the realm of economics and trade policy. In the other sectors like security, democratization, promotion of human rights, development, and climate change, the European presence has been either rhetorical or ineffectual, with the most impactful efforts coming from the capitals of EU member states rather than from Brussels.

In its ineffectiveness, the approach to Asia is a microcosm of the broader struggle to craft a meaningful foreign policy at the European level. It is no surprise that where the EU has had the best results, namely commercial policy, is where it enjoys the most consolidation internally. Its difficulty projecting itself abroad in non-commercial areas, other than through the unilateral action of individual member states, carries over into Asia. But beneath these wider structural policymaking failures, Europe is hamstrung by a crucial weakness: It simply does not know Asia well enough.

For Europe, Asia is still an uncertain entity. Indeed, both the 1994 and 2001 strategies devoted space to the question, 'What is Asia?' For sure, certain member states possess a deeper understanding of specific countries or subregions, and most are developing an appreciation of China, but this has not filtered up to the European level. Bridging this knowledge deficit is crucial if Europe is to have any chance of crafting a nuanced approach to Asia that goes beyond mere commerce.

In beginning to address this gap, this book makes an important contribution by bringing together, in one place, a variety of voices from Asia and Europe to highlight the state of play in both individual Asian states and subregions. This essential foundational knowledge of where we are and where we need to be will allow Europe not to engage in a new civilizing mission, but to find plausible partnerships in a region that is poised to shape the global order for years to come.

NOTES

1. European Commission, 'Towards a New Asia Strategy,' COM (1994) 314 final, 13 July 1994.
2. European Commission, 'Europe and Asia: A Strategic Framework for Enhanced Partnership,' COM (2001) 469 final, 4 September 2001.
3. Ibid.
4. Ibid.

Preface

M. K. Narayanan

This volume of twelve chapters, *Europe in Emerging Asia: Opportunities and Obstacles in Political and Economic Encounters*, written by distinguished authors from Europe and Asia fills a long-felt void. The subject is of contemporary relevance, and as the locus of economic power shifts from the West to the East, any interaction between 'new' Asia and 'old' Europe should prove highly riveting.

There are multiple and highly diverse situations across Europe today. Europe is still recovering from the debilitating effects of an economic downturn, and what it most needs today is growth accompanied by greater productivity, reforms, and flexibility to adapt to the new challenges.

Asia, on the other hand, projects an image of surging forward at a time of exponentially accelerating change, and when new paradigms of thought, action, and behaviour are overtaking and replacing old ones. Asia's strengths are many. Asia exudes optimism, a thirst for knowledge, and a desire for success. In recent decades, it has displayed considerable economic dynamism. Among its strengths can be mentioned its policy of 'open regionalism'. The Asian Development Bank anticipates that by 2050 or even earlier, Asia will nearly double its share of global gross domestic product (GDP) to 52 percent. The regional economy of over $19 trillion has become an engine of economic growth[1].

Notwithstanding this, there are many complex variables that could derail the course of events in Asia. Both centrifugal and centripetal forces are at work. Asia's ability to handle environmental and social issues, including pandemics and food safety, is suspect, given its phenomenal demographic and economic growth. Failure to ensure a more egalitarian ethos can also lead to problems.

Many of the old sources of stability in Asia have broken down. In place of earlier ideological divisions, the politics of religion and religious orthodoxy have emerged as a defining factor. This is leading to a new wave of radical Islamist thought and beliefs. Asia is already embroiled in several territorial disputes, but now confronts a widening arc of asymmetric warfare and terrorism. Given the absence of a well-anchored regional security structure, this situation lends itself to geopolitical upheavals.

This volume of essays takes a dispassionate look at how the diversity and complexity of the rise of Asia and the relative decline of Europe could affect the global construct. It examines the strengths and weaknesses of both Europe and emerging Asia. The underlying message for Asia is to try and develop a coherent vision and a meaningful architecture that would require key stakeholders like China, Japan, and India to pare their ambitions and eschew many of their intrinsic rivalries. Unstated is the premise that Asia should try and emulate nineteenth-century Europe and move towards a Concert of Nations in Asia.

The volume does not minimize the difficulties encountered in Europe-Asia strategic and other relations. Nevertheless, the authors feel that the potential for cooperation between Europe and emerging Asia can provide an unprecedented opportunity to shape the future of the world.

NOTE

1. The word dollars used in this book refers to US dollars.

Introduction

Europe in Emerging Asia

Fredrik Erixon and Krishnan Srinivasan

THE GLOBAL SETTING

This book is about economic and political cooperation between the countries of emerging Asia and Europe. The unique contribution of this book is that it brings together the views of former politicians, diplomats, prominent academics, and persons in the public intellectual space in a discussion of Europe's role in a region of Asia where an economic upturn is rearranging the locales of power and influence in a manner that affects the world and calls for reflection and response. Free from doctrinal faith and the jargon from upbeat summit declarations, the book examines the texture of economic integration and the degree to which political preferences converge between the two regions.

An intrinsic theme of the book, however, stretches beyond the ambiguous borders of emerging Asia and Europe, and concerns the search for effective global cooperation in the twenty-first century. Economic integration has evolved remarkably well in the past decades, and even over the past few years if one considers how close the Western world has been to a second Great Depression—a crisis that is by no means yet over for Europe—but political cooperation seems increasingly fragmented and lacking in direction. The global political map is not the same as the global economic map and the differences are, judging by current trends, only growing wider.

Regional cooperation to address common problems is often seen as a plausible alternative to multilateral cooperation if the latter option is not available. But what about region-to-region cooperation between Asia and Europe, or between individual countries in these two areas? Are such forms of cooperation ascending or descending? Can deeper economic and political cooperation between Asia and Europe address shared problems and propel the world in a more cooperative direction?

Headline economic figures will endorse the case for stronger joint leadership by the emerging economies in Asia and in the European continent. The two regions together represent over 60 percent of the world

1

population, 52 percent of the gross domestic product (GDP), and 70 percent of world trade[1]. Both continents have undergone momentous changes in the past century and know the importance of charting viable courses of mutually beneficial cooperation. They also know that economic interaction between the continents has hardly yet been brought to its all-round potential, many aspects in the relationship remain dormant, and as such, they have achieved no basic structural change in bilateral ties except perhaps on the trade front.

In an uncertain international landscape, individual nations and organizations like the European Union (EU) are aspiring to fashion a multipolar world but do not know how to effect it. Polycentrism is still all too evident and the power centres that would constitute the poles in any future multipolar world are not yet certain. Meanwhile, economic growth rates and tables of GDP are a reference point to the currently influential world capitals. If the trends in basic economic indicators continue, Asian political and economic influence in regional and world affairs will increase, but given its diversity, the Asian rise also occasions possible risks that can undermine the transformative process. Emerging Asia is unusually dependent on consistent high growth to address its widening inequalities, mitigate environmental degradation, compete for finite natural resources, and ensure food security, apart from the internal challenges of governance, institutional capacity, and territorial integrity.

Europe's economic slowdown with high employment and debt, and its adverse demographic outlook, give rise to a pessimistic view of the continent's future prospects. Added to this is its energy dependency, lack of natural resources, and declining military prowess. But Europe is still a power in the economic field; it continues to produce innovations in industry, telecommunications, transportation, and renewable energy. The EU is the biggest trader in goods and services and accounts for 16 percent of the world's trade[2]. It ranks first in inbound and outbound investments, has two permanent members of the UN Security Council, and Britain and France still wield significant political and military strength including nuclear weapons.

The unsettled relationship among rising and established world powers, and between the rising powers themselves, may hasten or delay the advent of an 'Asian century'. The rise of emerging Asia does not presume the decline of Europe. Both Europe and emerging Asia are economic heavyweights and regional powers with wide global interests. To safeguard their futures, they should be opposed to instability and welcome a benevolent transition to an equitable world order. This should provide the platform for a common interest in an equal partnership for global peace and security. Asia needs technology and specialized skills to climb the value-added chain and avoid the middle-income trap[3]; Europe needs markets, investments, and a skilled and semiskilled workforce. European exports to Asia are critical in raising Europe's path of economic growth, while its unified market must attract goods, investments, and people from across the globe, helping Asian countries to maintain their growth and development[4]. The Euro is an important reserve currency in Asia, though the Chinese Yuan is starting to make a strong appearance as a medium of commercial exchange; more than 20 percent of China's trade settlements are now in its own currency and the Chinese government is gradually expanding the role of the Yuan in trade, especially by swap agreements with other countries that allow for settlement and clearing of the currency abroad[5]. Equity and equitable benefit are prerequisites for close cooperation, and each side needs correctly to calibrate its relations with the other.

The contributions to this book offer what can be described as two alternative visions—economic idealism and political realism—about the nature of cooperation between emerging Asia and Europe in this century. One school of thought, drawing heavily from growing trade and investment between emerging Asia and Europe, contends that economic interdependence fosters a greater spirit of political cooperation. Even if the balance of economic power is shifting to Asia's advantage, the economic and political benefits of deeper integration are too strong for either side to resist. Inevitably, political cooperation—bilateral and international—between Asia and Europe will grow on the back of economic flows between the regions, leading to more effective policies for peace, security, human rights, and a hospitable environment. It may not be a linear development, but both emerging Asia and Europe have strong enlightened interests to craft a habitable world.

The basic premise of this view is that the political preferences of Asia and Europe, that is, what they perceive as their political priorities, will converge, along with increasing similarities in prosperity and material wellbeing, and perhaps also in societal beliefs. While not an expression of universalism—or necessarily of 'westernization'—economic integration between continents and cultures in past centuries have fostered hierarchies of desires and preferences that are increasingly shared. But an underlying and controversial theme in much of the commentary about economic interdependence is that the economic modernization it purports to represent will lead to political modernization, similar to what the world had witnessed in Europe, the United States, and the developed nations in the Asia-Pacific region. Responsibilities and costs for effective cooperation will then be shared more evenly, and direct as well as indirect cooperation, mediated in global institutions like the United Nations or the Bretton Woods system, will grow stronger.

The contrasting school of thought is less optimistic and takes greater notice of relative shifts in economic power, within emerging Asia and Europe as well as between them, and the conflicting world view that their political representatives project. Their 'habits of the heart' may not be rivals, but to expect closer economic integration automatically to generate a convergence of political interests is a fallacy of hope rather than a shrewd reading of politics. The actual and potential fault-lines in Europe and Asia are many. Countries in the EU have theoretically changed from nation states to member states[6], but essentially they remain both. The EU is nowhere near a unified super-state and nationhood remains important for European political identities. The consensus requirement makes the EU risk-averse and reactive, and it does not elicit loyalty or affection. Unemployment is seemingly ineradicable and the demographic deficit cannot be reversed, with a population used to early retirement and welfare benefits at a time when economic growth is minimal. The situation in Asia is no less fraught. With the largest concentration of population, big increases in an aspirational middle class[7], concerns over terrorism and the proliferation of nuclear weapons, inter-state and intra-state tensions, abject poverty, and climate change fears, the continent enjoys neither political nor economic unity with systems of government ranging from communism to liberal democracy[8].

Emerging Asia and Europe are on two different trajectories. Regardless of the fate of the European Monetary Union, which is at the centre of a prolonged crisis in Europe, the latter is inevitably on course to relative economic decline[9]. Europe may not stagnate in absolute terms, but its share of the global economy is shrinking. Its capacity to lead the world through its economic power has been severely weakened, though the old continent's political psyche and its aspiration to be a normative superpower, largely remains intact[10]. Emerging Asia, on the other hand, is climbing the world economic ladder. It may not yet present a rival ideology to Europe's view of the world, but Asian countries are allergic to any opinion that other powers should prescribe their policy preferences for them. Further support for this approach of Asia-Europe relations can be found in their discrete political personalities. While European countries have invested political and institutional capital in creating pan-European institutions of governance, emerging Asian nations remain anchored in the 'Westphalian' structure of government and power. Asia represents a modern realist political personality, whereas Europe has advanced towards a post-modern character[11], curbing bellicosity and competition for power, and encouraging multilateral international partnership under international law[12].

The institutions of the EU are increasingly challenged on the grounds of democratic illegitimacy, their authority being contested by electorates as well as by governments that place greater emphasis on sovereignty and national integrity, while emerging Asian economies struggle to build effective forms of regional institutions that can help address common issues created or exacerbated by greater prosperity and regional interconnectedness. They too often lack the mutual trust necessary for the emergence of regional structures that can solve problems that national institutions alone cannot. Long-standing border disputes still sour bilateral relations. Sanguine rhetoric about 'win-win' political cooperation and attempts to craft a common narrative for the Asian hemisphere have not provided the commonalities needed for emerging Asian countries to come closer.

Nor have the international multilateral institutions helped much to build a confluence of political preferences and interests. Asia's growing political and economic weight has not yet persuaded the major nations of the region to assume greater responsibilities for global cooperation. It can be debated whether asymmetry between economic size and global leadership exists because they have not been invited to assume leadership roles in global institutions, or because there is uncertainty that they would have any idea what they might wish to use that leadership for, or even whether they would prefer to await the steady demise of the existing institutions that exist for such cooperation. What is clear, however, is that Europe feels that the economic rise of Asia challenges its leadership position inherited from the post–World War II settlement and offers rearguard resistance. European countries have been reluctant to reduce their voting power in the World Bank and their voting strength and management of the International Monetary Fund (IMF), despite support for the principle that power and responsibilities in the Bretton Woods institutions should reflect a country's share of the world economy.

Many of the existing global institutions, including the United Nations and its agencies, carry the post–World War II identity that a few decades of globalization have not managed to alter. The new multilateralism helped European nations to maintain their declining status in the world. The post-war economic system was underwritten by the United States, and European countries conformed, at times reluctantly, to American opinion, because in the final analysis they were the main beneficiaries of the inherited order. Equally important, the new doctrines of European regional integration became a means to remain influential beyond their national borders. To maintain, if not increase, Europe's influence in the world has been a *leitmotif* in many efforts to expand and deepen the European Union.

Yet emerging Asia's rapid economic rise and the aspiration of the new economies to wrest more influence in multilateral institutions has subtly introduced an area of doubt in the European outlook on the utility of multilateralism. Europe's usually unspoken quandary is about whom these organizations really should work for. While its readiness to lend high-minded support to the idea of multilateralism is yet uncontested, Europe, and to a much lesser extent the United States, increasingly excogitate their post-war history because of the widespread recognition that Europe and the United States created multilateral institutions with the purpose of promoting their own concepts of world politics and economics. Europe's hesitation about the benefits of multilateralism, accelerated by the eurozone crisis, is matched by Asia's ambiguity on what it wishes to use these institutions for, or how it should go about deploying its newly acquired economic strength. European doubts are far greater than those on the other side of the Atlantic; while multilateralism was an expedient strategy for influence in the post-war era, Europe now worries about how its relative decline could diminish its multilateral influence.

THE AUTHORS AND THEIR APPROACH

This book originated from a desire to have authors with different backgrounds and scholarly interests discuss the texture and direction of emerging Asia-Europe economic and political cooperation. All the contributions in this anthology are by authors who have either been in government or close to public policy, so what distinguishes this from other books in the field of Asia-Europe relations is that the chapters combine the experience of practitioners with the perspective of the objective observer. While the chapters differ in substance, and often in their conclusions, they represent knowledge and expertise that the authors have gained from the study and conduct of policy both in Europe and Asia.

Books produced in Europe on this subject customarily begin with the premise that Europe is exemplary and emerging Asia has much to derive from Europe. We do not start from this premise. Those works were written by Europeans for Europeans; the contributors to this book are a collection of Asian and European scholars who write as much for Asians as for other peoples of the world who seek to understand the policies of the Europeans and reactions to Europe from engaged circles in the emerging Asian nations. There is an unwitting element of superiority in existing literature; thus, the EU 'should work actively to foster China's emergence', the EU 'has helped to lift millions of Asians out of poverty'[13], 'emerging powers have proved to be irresponsible stakeholders'[14], and 'on balance, Asia has more to learn from Europe than vice versa'[15]. The Republic of Korea is a 'like-minded, responsible member of the international community'[16], the EU offers the 'accolade of a strategic partnership'[17], and 'the [United States] and the EU, given their size in the global economy, are the only two existing global superpowers and . . . Asian countries . . . will have a long way to go to catch up'[18]. By contrast, many writers in the current book make mention of perceived European arrogance and lack of sympathy in dealings with Asians, and we approach the relationship between Europe and emerging Asia from a different optic: not that of donor and recipient, benefactor and supplicant, but that of an engagement of equal parties who must share the credit and the blame for the achievement of success or the lack of understanding.

While the advantage of an anthology is that it offers a plurality of perspectives, its disadvantage is that its contributions may differ too much from each other. This anthology is no exception, but there are several common threads that bind together the chapters of this book. Most contributors agree that there are no clearly valid projections that can be made for emerging Asia-Europe cooperation, even in the foreseeable future. If the reader seeks either Panglossian or Cassandra-like predictions about this relationship, this book will provide neither. What unites the different contributors is the need to eschew the abstractions of scholarly discourse about Asia-Europe and rather take stock of the economic and political realities of how the nations of both regions interact with each other. Various authors offer recommendations on how cooperation could be improved, but all start from the understanding that the future of this relationship can neither be an automatic extrapolation from recent developments nor derived from an academic model.

The contributions accept a positive view of the benefits of highly desirable emerging Asia-Europe cooperation, along with a dispassionate analysis of what may, and may not, be feasible in reconciling the core economic and strategic concerns of nations that are 'unitary self-interested agents' in political science nomenclature. Due to limitations of space, the book cannot deal in any detail with non-state actors and non-traditional threats to security like terrorism, drug trafficking, climate change, money laundering, cybercrime, natural disasters, and pandemics, in all of which Europe has a degree of useful interaction with emerging Asia. But there are ingredients of human security such as human rights and freedoms that have political undertones that can facilitate or obstruct government solutions, and these are mentioned throughout the chapters as one of the main narratives in the Europe-emerging Asia dialogue.

All the chapters weigh the balance between the economic idealism and political realism sketched above or, more precisely, between appreciation of the economic integration achieved hitherto, even if some of it has been on unequal terms, and scepticism about how far economic interdependence could drive political convergence between Asia and Europe in the future. For an appraisal of emerging Asia-Europe relations, which today is dominated by trade and investment policy, it becomes important to observe the interaction of economic ambitions and political realities, which are two separate worlds. The world of economics runs on the assumption that closer ties between entities bring prosperity and economic stability. In other words, economic dependence brings strength. International *realpolitik*, on the other hand, could sometimes view the dependence that trade and investment generate as involving an element of risk for national integrity through weakening a country's ability to defend its borders and preventing it from freely pursuing its national interests. Bestriding the two perceptions is the everyday reality of modern governance.

WHAT IS EUROPE? WHAT IS EMERGING ASIA?

Like other works on Asia and Europe, this anthology suffers from the absence of undisputed definitions of what emerging Asia and Europe comprise as regional entities. These problems arise because Europe and emerging Asia are both uncertain constructs. Europe's administrative, cultural, economic, and social borders are fluid and indeterminate. Most literature conflates Europe, the EU, and the eurozone. Even where there are differences between them, the practical meaning of separating them is not always significant. The eurozone refers to the countries that share a common currency, and references in this book to the eurozone or the European Monetary Union mean this group of countries. However, the eurozone does not have an external policy going beyond the immediate concerns of a central bank, nor does it have institutions tasked to execute an external policy. The European Monetary Union is imbedded in the EU, and in dealing with Europe's 'actorness', in other words, with policies where Europe acts as one, the reference is to the EU of twenty-eight member states. Some refer to Europe as a geographic territory while others will cite the EU as a supranational politicoeconomic entity within Europe.

To complicate the definitions further, there are several countries in Europe that are not members of the EU. Nor is there a common catalogue of policies that all members of the EU have adopted. Nineteen are members of the European Monetary Union and share a common currency; other EU members retain their own currencies. Many, but not all, EU countries are members of the North Atlantic Treaty Organization and share an arrangement for security in Europe with the United States and Canada. Some countries are moving towards deeper political integration in Europe—for example, through new mechanisms of financial surveillance—while others prefer to maintain their sovereign policies. And in many EU member states, there is a lively debate about the benefits and liabilities of continuing in the EU, and Britain may have an in-or-out referendum on this subject in a few years' time.

That there is no single definition of Europe, and no single narrative about the role of Europe in emerging Asia, is reflected in this book. As we are not able to cover every single country in the EU, nor in emerging Asia, we have made selections that we think are of special and general interest. There is no chapter that particularly addresses the role of Germany in emerging Asia. Germany's approach to Asia is dominated by its trade interests; it has other layers of engagement with Asian countries, too, but its prioritized areas of policy integration are by and large extensions or variations of trade policy. Several chapters deal with the commercial aspects of Europe's policy in Asia and discuss the role of Germany in Europe's trade policy. There is a chapter dealing with Britain because, as the leading former imperial power, it has the ability to interpret its erstwhile colonies to Europe and vice versa. In India, especially, Britain rather than the EU is regarded as the spokesman for Europe. Another chapter takes Poland as the leading example of a post-Soviet-era Central and Eastern European country that is growing in influence, partly in consequence of its economic success, and partly because it is a historic entity that had interests beyond its European neighbourhood. Poland is one of a few countries that joined the EU in the 2000s that has enthusiasm for globalization and developed an active foreign policy based on the promotion of human and economic freedoms and democracy. However, the status that Poland and other former Soviet bloc EU countries had enjoyed in India and a few other Asian countries was interrupted with the disintegration of the Soviet Union, and will take time and effort to be restored.

Asia, too, is a portmanteau expression. Asia is a reference to a massive territory with a huge population and vast disparities in income and development. There can be no clear geographical definition of emerging Asia, though the term has entered the lexicon of the international financial organizations. Many economies in Asia today have healthy economic growth and vibrant markets, and have transitioned from being recipients of manufactures to exporters of a competitive variety of goods and services. The decisions and developments in these emerging economies impact the global financial markets, production networks, and pricing of commodities, apart from having an increasing bearing on international politics and global strategies. Small regions like Singapore, Taiwan, Hong Kong, and Macao enjoy developed-nation living standards and impressive growth rates, and as for the major economies of emerging Asia, which lie to the east of the Hindu Kush mountain range, the question of their prominence is not in doubt.

Apart from Japan, which emerged as long ago as the 1960s, four Asian countries are in the top sixteen of the World Bank's GDP table for 2013 — China, India, the Republic of Korea, and Indonesia — and what is even more striking is their growth in terms of percentage of world GDP from 2001 to 2011 — China (154 percent), India (72 percent), South Korea (1.6 percent), and Indonesia (142 percent). Equally remarkable are the rates of decline of certain western economies during the same period: the United States (–32 percent), Germany (–13 percent), the United Kingdom (–24 percent), France (–5 percent), and Italy (–10 percent)[19]. Apart from the GDP criterion, there are many other positive Asian trends to be discerned, political, institutional, cultural, technological, and educational among them. It remains an open question if such developments will lead to emerging Asia constituting a group of newly arrived great powers, though clearly China is already well on the way to that goal. Thus far, the rest of emerging Asia is mainly an economic and cultural phenomenon, but the important aspect is to recognize that there is an ongoing process and not dismiss it as unsustainable or trivial. For this reason, it is timely and useful to examine the two descriptors of the book's title and the quality of their interactions.

China and India are predominant among references to emerging Asia for obvious reasons. They are the leading Asian countries in GDP and the biggest in size and population. Five hundred million citizens of those two countries have moved above the poverty line into modernity in the past twenty years, dramatically changing the world's manufacturing and consumer markets, and this process will continue. Chapters in the book cover the view of Europe from China, India, South Asia, Indonesia, Thailand, and South Korea, while one deals with the push by Europe into Eurasia, and another covers the American 'pivot' to Asia and its implications for Europe and emerging Asia. China views the 'rebalance' as threatening; America's Asian allies welcome it, while the other Asians are alert and agnostic, wary of any revived super-power military presence in East Asia.

THEMES IN THE BOOK

Any speculation on whether the EU is a world power is not useful. Nor is the debate on whether certain economies in Asia are emerging or re-emerging. We are content to state that the EU and emerging Asia are important actors in world affairs, although all the writers draw attention to the EU's infirmities in formulating and executing a common foreign policy. The chapters also do not specifically address the putative decline of the West or rise of Asia except allusively as contingent. It is prudent to postpone any declaration of the 'Asian century', as also of the diminishing global strength of the United States and Europe, despite the current EU crisis in self-confidence. As for emerging Asia, predictions of the implosion of China and the descent of India into dystopia have proved wrong, and there is growing optimism in the capitals of the Asian big economies.

The EU by its very existence has added to the strengths of its individual members. West European maritime nations have traditionally followed a blue-water foreign policy based on historic interest and commercial concerns, and an agenda which stretches beyond their domestic affairs or ties with fellow members of the EU. Many elements in Britain's view of Asia are shared by France and to some extent by the Netherlands and Portugal, two other European countries with an Asian imperial past, and the intensity of their broad-based exposure in Asia is greater than for others in Europe, even if they too have grown more mercantilist and transactional in their attitudes. The non-colonial European states have a different approach to emerging Asia, giving priority mainly to their commercial interests. Germany, for instance, which has no Asian colonial history, has made great strides in its relations with Asia, based less about history and more about business, though as Wang Yiwei suggests in his chapter, the German people appear to be indifferent to their links with emerging Asia. Germany is regarded as the major economic power in Europe, although strategically and culturally, Germany carries little weight in Asia. James Mayall draws attention to the fact that Britain and France have bigger levers to pull: among them, the importance of English as an international language and the connections with Hong Kong for Britain, and respect for the French language and the French tradition of an independent international stance, especially in regard to the United States. On the other hand, Agnieszka Kuszewska suggests in her chapter that the EU's 'new' Central European members have failed to invoke their considerable erstwhile repositories of knowledge and connections in Asia from the Soviet bloc era to bring any valuable resources to the advantage of EU policies towards emerging Asia.

The future political, economic, social, and cultural running will be made by the EU members acting for the most part in their individual capacities. The overall picture from the Brussels viewpoint is therefore less clear-cut than the federal enthusiasts would have us believe. There may eventually be a discernible EU approach to emerging Asia, but this will be dependent largely on political factors in both entities, many of which cannot now be anticipated. But it is safe to conclude, as all the authors assert, that EU policy will be less monolithic and more opportunistic than is implicit in the concept of a European union. The authors are in agreement that the leaders in the main European capitals are far better known in Asia than those of the EU institutions at Brussels. Many chapters such as those of Iftekhar Ahmed Chowdhury, Agnieszka Kuszewska, and Krishnan Srinivasan reveal that the EU's working patterns and competences are regarded as unfathomable by Asians, who are more comfortable with bilateral and historical ties with familiar EU member states.

It is expected that Asian political weight, when not matched against one another or in its own neighbourhood (China/Japan, India/Pakistan) will continue to expand, as will the Asian sensitivity to western criticism regarding pollution, social mobility, freedom of expression, and human rights. China is the most rapidly emerging power, but the rest of the world will be conscious of its drawbacks in regard to population, pollution, gender imbalance, internal unrest, uneasy relations with neighbours, and inadequate material resources. Chinese territorial and maritime claims in the East and South China Seas are a latent flashpoint. China is seen in Europe as a potential big investor, but rather less so in Germany and France whose economies are traditionally less accommodating. The European view of India is more benign, as Agnieskza Kuszewska states, but India and the other emerging economies will not be seen as offering the same opportunities for investment or market openings as China. Reliance on European imports from emerging Asia will grow, with a leaning towards China, as long as the Asian economies maintain price advantage and their currency surpluses are adequately recycled. The EU will scrutinize the level of Asian imports and their effects on European domestic production, and Fredrik Erixon and Zhang Xiaotong draw attention to the rise of protectionist concerns as a consequence.

Obstacles to Engagement

There are innumerable Asian and European profiles, and several issues about each could be noted. How can an increasingly cohesive Europe engage effectively with a diverse Asian continent where rapidly industrializing economies coexist with societies that suffer from exceptional inequality? Europe may have found its apotheosis in the EU, but North-South and East-West divisions exist, and as all the authors point out, the EU generates few uniform viewpoints and its main outfacing profiles are in climate change, World Trade Organization and free trade area negotiations.

In emerging Asia, multilateral institutions for political and security coordination are lacking, and there are few shared international policies other than a sense of victimhood and an entitlement to redress a sense of disenfranchisement arising from the imperial period. There may not be a single 'Asian way', given the cultural and political differences between China, India, and Japan, but pragmatism, emphasis on economic development with modernization, sovereignty, non-interference, top-down benevolent state philosophy, and communitarian values are common concepts throughout emerging Asia. There is a yearning for economic cooperation, as Evi Fitriani states, which in Europe has led to political union, but Asian cooperation, as seen in the Association of Southeast Asian Nations (ASEAN) or the South Asian Association for Regional Cooperation (SAARC), is in the spirit of Asian norms; namely, the absence of confrontation, conscious use of reserve and restraint, respect for consensus-based solutions, and reluctance to afford blame or force any partner to lose face. Typical of an Asian association is the ASEAN Regional Forum (ARF), with its non-intrusive nature, 'soft' institutionalization, and high priority for harmonious conduct and camaraderie. The EU is prone to cavil at the ARF and SAARC for their lack of robust decisions, but this indicates that Europe remains impatient with the Asian style of regionalism and there is a gap in perceptions.

The subsuming of the emerging Asian economies into the globalized world may prove difficult. Fredrik Erixon anticipates a slowdown from the levels of growth in economic exchanges that have already been reached, adding sharpness to the existing disputes between Europe and emerging Asia. He considers that for want of World Trade Organization-driven liberalization, an accelerated reform process in every emerging Asian economy may be needed to engage the EU's interest in mutually

beneficial free trade areas. Zhang Xiaotong agrees, but claims that Europe also needs market reforms as emerging Asia challenges the free market economy philosophy inherited from Europe. China and emerging Asia could eventually opt for a different route with methods similar to the previous colonial masters; the threat or use of force, intimidation, and coercion; and distortion of international instruments to enforce their will[20]. Emerging Asia could over time offer an alternative discourse of modernity, questioning the present order based on Western ideas of free market and democracy, with a form of Sino-style semi free-market model within an authoritarian framework that could sharpen inter-Asian tension, but here again there is little conformity or parallel timelines across the concerned countries. The Asians are busy stressing their differences and not their commonalities, as Iftekhar Ahmed Chowdhury points out, and on the subject of nationalism they are at different points of history in their relationship with the EU. In Europe, supra-nationalism has sought to submerge the sense of nationalism, whereas in Asia national identities are still emphasized, and Asia looks inwards to its own problems and inter-state tensions. A supra-national order may be needed to prevent wars, but even European supra-nationalism has not prevented periodic outbursts of nationalism and parochial interests, as James Mayall shows.

Hari Vasudevan argues that the EU in its eastwards outreach policy projects a stake outside Europe, a strategic development that is not always understood in Asia. The Eastern Partnership policy by Europe anticipates integration through associated partnerships that require an acceptance of the European mission, system, and timetable for the acceptance of European values. The EU believes its principles carry an obligation to project its norms to others, but the proposed agreements come up against the failure of local regimes to construct their own strong institutions, thereby creating a vacuum where the European system is seen as providing soft power alternatives to countries that live by different rules. The Caucasus and Caspian shelf could in time become an intermediate geographical area of contestation between Asia and Europe. Meanwhile, all emerging Asian states view the EU favourably, and that is confirmed by all the Asian contributors taking a positive view of closer ties with Europe, even if they are at times critical of EU policies. Jin Park and Zhang Xiaotong propose that Europe and emerging Asia should aspire to be directly connected by transportation links and pipelines, and Kriengsak Chareonwongsak lists the various elements of interaction with the EU that could enable Thailand to escape the middle income trap. In short, Europe has a highly receptive environment to work in and must carry some responsibility for any lack of substance and delivery in the engagement between Europe and emerging Asia.

Rights and Responsibilities

There has always been an inherent conflict in the EU between the pursuit of material goals and the application of moral and normative principles. The EU sees itself as a unique exemplar and activist in the field of human rights, values, and visions of regional integration, and the manner in which these are pressed upon emerging Asian countries in various negotiations have at times almost constituted a non-tariff barrier. As Jürgen Habermas has written, 'Our values are universally valid values that all other nations should accept in their own best interests. This pseudo universalism is a kind of universalized ethnocentrism'[21]. Even the big and ancient Asian civilizations like India and China do not seek to make other countries like themselves, and have not articulated any worldview apart from the Five Principles of Peaceful Coexistence and Xi Jinping's four principles of major power relations, which are too vague to build upon and which relate to unspecified core interests.

Moving forward from the bilateralism of the early 1990s, fundamental rights and values found increasing resonance in EU policy after the Lisbon Treaty and the establishment of the European External Action Service. The Lisbon Conference declared that values had a symbolic significance and a foundational character and should find expression in the EU's identity, self-perception, and self-projection. It is a matter of interpretation, however, whether these values inform the EU's policy and global policy aspirations, and if they encourage or discourage EU member states acting on the basis of values in their relations with partner countries. This exemplified the capability-expectations gap identified by Christopher Hill[22]. Even with China, EU concerns became more muted, as Wang Yiwei points out, and Zhang Xiaotong claims that China does not yield to outside pressures on fundamental rights. It will always be difficult for Europe and emerging Asia to arrive at a common understanding on norms and values[23]. The former promotes these principles in an absolutist sense, especially where its practical interests are not involved. The latter will wish to reserve its positions to each situational context and lay more stress on the greatest good for the greatest number. There are therefore problems of coherence, and both in Asia and Europe national interests have inevitably taken precedence. In Asia, the colonial state has never fully receded and as all the authors agree, what is construed as European criticism or forceful projection of values is deeply resented. Prescriptive values-based models will not be welcomed by the Asians, and it has taken Europe a considerable time to discover this. However, Europe and emerging Asia have a significant period of human history behind them and can perhaps elicit from mutual interaction new models of human dignity and security that can be applied within the frameworks of their particular societies and commitments to international norms.

The Strategic Dialogues

The varying degrees of cooperation and confrontation between China, Japan, and India, the three Asian giants, make it difficult for the EU to formulate any single strategic plan for emerging Asia. Countries in the EU do not share a common view about what style of political engagement they desire to pursue with Asian countries, nor is there a common understanding of what priority to place upon emerging Asia–Europe relations. The differences between European countries have been reinforced by Europe's prolonged economic contraction. Some countries in Europe, such as Germany, have seen their exports to emerging Asia grow at a fast pace and generally embrace closer economic ties, but other Europeans fear increased competition from Asia and view deeper economic connections with Asia very defensively.

The rise of China has led to a special position for China in all EU policies; countries like India, Indonesia, Thailand, and South Korea, who do not possess the political, military, or economic heft to compete with China, are important but do not compel equal European attention. The EU has four Asian strategic partners: Japan, China, India, and South Korea. Jin Park welcomes the EU-Korean strategic dialogue, but Krishnan Srinivasan and Wang Yiwei are deeply sceptical about its utility for India and China. In Evi Fitriani's opinion, the EU seeks strategic partnerships to remove protectionist obstacles to promote EU industries, and while promoting democracy and human rights, seeks an opportunity to leverage the regional architecture in Asia to its advantage and counterbalance China.

With the exception of Jin Park, the authors from Asia do not regard the EU as a credible strategic actor[24], but Zhang Xiaotong considers that a strategic role for the EU and China is still valid though both parties must make greater efforts to reinforce it. Many Asians, as noted by Krishnan Srinivasan, Wang Yiwei, and Zhang Xiaotong, would like to enlist Europe in promoting a multipolar conception that challenges the dominant role of the United States, but this is hardly likely to appeal to the Europeans. Quite apart from Asian internal divisions, Asian security architecture is weak because all countries keep their options open in a polycentric situation, and not being a member of the East Asian Summit, the EU has been relegated to the position of a not particularly relevant outsider.

The EU has always placed importance on finding a counterpart organization to negotiate with, and has variously engaged with the Asia-Europe Meeting (ASEM), the ARF, and ASEAN, but this produced negligible results because there is no real counterpart body to the EU in emerging Asia. Asians are uncomfortable in dealing with the binding aspects of formal international institutions or EU-type integration, and prefer to resort to bilateralism. Quite often, as in ASEM, they seem content to attend meetings that produce scarcely identifiable results, being content over prolonged periods to await the construction of consensus. ASEM had fifty members in 2014, and more than 60 percent of the world population and GDP, but that does not per se give it much importance; only Agnieszka Kuszewska finds merit in ASEM as a forum for bringing civil society groups together. The EU will continue its quest due to an obsession with its role as an exemplary and unique association, but there is little point in Brussels bemoaning the lack of substantive Asian regionalism without taking into account the different historical and cultural background. Asian sentiments that applauded the EU as a paradigm for regional integration could be outdated. Iftekhar Ahmed Chowdhury and Evi Fitriani acknowledge the debt to the EU of both SAARC and ASEAN, but with ASEAN's economic recovery and the EU's financial crisis, the attraction of the EU model has greatly diminished in emerging Asia.

The American Pivot or Rebalance to Asia

A recurring theme is the role of the United States in emerging Asia and whether it constitutes an obstacle in developing closer EU-Asia ties. While seen by many authors, but not Philip I. Levy, as interdicting a stronger EU role in the political and security dimensions in emerging Asia, the United States considers itself the main security provider, leaving the EU to make routine declarations of cooperation on a bilateral basis. Krishnan Srinivasan and Wang Yiwei mention the desirability, but distinct unlikelihood, of the EU distancing itself from identification with American global strategic policy, a view shared by James Mayall. The United States' 'pivot' to Asia, first mentioned by American Secretary of State Hillary Clinton in 2011[25] and rephrased as 'rebalancing' by National Security Adviser Thomas Donilon in 2013[26], has occasioned little debate or opinion in Europe, but is viewed with interest, and in certain countries in emerging Asia, with considerable concern. A chapter on the United States in the context of the Europe-emerging Asia relationship was therefore necessary to address this aspect. Philip I. Levy's chapter provides an American view about the United States' strategies and the extent to which the much-discussed Asian pivot constitutes an initiative for engagement in Asia. Many authors take stock of the US pivot, but as Levy argues, it is difficult to find evidence of any real pivot to Asia. Due to budgetary and other limitations, the central component of the pivot might comprise the Trans-Pacific Partnership (TPP), a trade agreement negotiation with selected Asian and Pacific Rim countries. Diplomatic and military components of the pivot hit the buffers of political reality, and there were never credible strategies proposed on how to redirect resources from diplomatic and military preoccupations at a time of increasing instability in Europe and the Middle East. The TPP itself has not been cruising towards success; negotiations have been proceeding for more than six years and complications have grown as additional countries such as Japan entered the trade talks. Nor is there much political support for the TPP in the American Congress. The current administration has been cautious in proposing a negotiation mandate for Congressional approval, and attempts by ranking members of the Congress to draft such a mandate have not shown results. The United States is seen in Asia as a much stronger power and presence than the EU, but its capacity to lead the world economy has clearly diminished.

CONCLUSION

Most existing literature deals with China as if it is all of Asia, leaving little time or space for the other emerging Asian countries, whereas this book covers Europe's relations with China and many other parts of emerging Asia. In our discussion of the international order and poly-centricity, the chapters are by four diplomats, two politicians, four academics, and two public figures with close ties to policy formation. The views are recorded of several prominent practitioners who consider the global scene from a personal perspective, having negotiated with, or on behalf of, the EU. Many observations made in each essay will furnish a long-awaited road-map both for Europe and the emerging Asian nations. This book is for the political class and the public, the scholar, and the general reader who has an interest in the world we live in and its future possibilities. The book is for the European and the Asian and those living beyond those two continents. If it stimulates further discussion on the Europe-emerging Asia relationship that is going to be so crucial for the future success of both entities and for the world at large, it will have fully served its purpose.

NOTES

This book owes much to several institutions: the European Centre for International Political Economy at Brussels, the Swedish Collegium in Uppsala, the Maulana Abul Kalam Azad Institute of Asian Studies at Calcutta and the Administrative Staff College of India at Hyderabad. Our profound gratitude to them, and to Anna Reeve, senior commissioning editor at Rowman & Littlefield International.

1. Hamid Ansari, Indian vice president. Speech at Calcutta, 13 September 2014. vicepresidentofindia.nic.in/content.asp?id=505.

2. ec.europa.eu/trade/policy/eu-position-in-world-trade/.

3. World Bank, *China 2030: Building a Modern, Harmonious and Creative High-Income Society* (Washington DC: World Bank, 2012).

4. Vitor Constancio, 'Growth Challenges for Asia and Europe', Asia Europe Economic Forum, 15 May 2014. www.ecb.europa.eu/press/key/date/2014/html/sp140515.en.html.

5. Joseph E. Ganon and Ken Troutman, *Internationalization of the Remninbi: The Role of Trade Settlements*, Peterson Institute Policy Brief Number 14-15, 2015. www.iie.com/publications/pb/pb14-15.pdf.

6. Daniel C. Thomas, *Making EU Foreign Policy* (Basingstoke: Palgrave Macmillan, 2011), 11.

7. Reshma Patil, *Strangers across the Border* (Noida, India: HarperCollins, 2014), 113.

8. Krishnan Srinivasan, 'Asia as a Future Career', the Swedish EU Presidency Conference, Lund University, 7 July 2009. www.vr.se/download/18.227c330c123.

9. David Marsh, *The Euro* (Yale: Yale University Press, 2011), 264.

10. Owen Parker and Ben Rosamund, '"Normative Power Europe" Meets Economic Liberalism: Complicating Cosmopolitanism Inside/Outide the EU', *Cooperation and Conflict* 48, no. 2 (June 2013): 229–46.

11. Robert Cooper, *The Post-Modern State and World Order* (London: Demos, 2002); Christopher Coker, 'Post-Modernity and the End of the Cold War'" *Review of International Studies* 18, no. 3 (July 1992).

12. Tom Ginsburg, "Eastphalia as a Return to Westphalia," University of Chicago Public Law and Legal Theory Working Paper No. 292, 2010. chicagounbound. uchicago.edu/cgi/viewcontent.cgi?article=1106&context=public_law_and_legal_ theory.

13. Thomas Christiansen, Emil Kirchner, and Philomena Murray (eds.), *The Palgrave Handbook of EU-Asia Relations* (Basingstoke: Palgrave Macmillan, 2013); Fraser Cameron, 'The Evolution of EU-Asia Relations: 2001–2011', in ibid., 32 and 39.

14. Knud Erik Jorgensen, 'Prospects for Multipolarity and Multilateralism in World Politics', in ibid., 52.

15. Leslie Holmes, 'Dealing with Terrorism, Corruption and Organised Crime: The EU and Asia', in ibid., 143.

16. Uwe Wissenbach, 'The EU and the Two Koreas-One Strategic Partner, One Strategic Liability', in ibid., 523.

17. David Camroux and Annisa Srikandini, 'EU-Indonesia Relations: No Expectations-Capability Gap?' in ibid., 566.

18. 'Conclusion', in ibid., 630.

19. www.ecominoes.com/2012/11/us-share-of-world-gdp-falls-32-since.html.

20. James B. L. Mayall and Krishnan Srinivasan, *Towards the New Horizon* (New Delhi: Standard Publishers, 2009), 88.

21. Jurgen Habermas, *The Divided West* (Cambridge: Polity, 2006), 103.

22. Christopher Hill, 'The Capability-Expectations Gap or Conceptualizing Europe's International Role', *Journal of Common Market Studies* 31, no. 3 (1993): 305–28.

23. Asle Toje, *The European Union as a Small Power* (Basingstoke: Palgrave Macmillan, 2010).

24. Reimund Seidelmann and Andreas Vasilache (eds.), *European Union and Asia* (Baden-Baden: Nomos, 2009), 208.

25. Hillary Clinton, 'America's Pacific Century', *Foreign Policy*, 11 October 2011. www.foreignpolicy.com/articles/2011/10/11/americas_pacific_century.

26. Thomas Donilon, 'The United States and the Asia-Pacific in 2013', *Asia Society*, 11 March 2013. asiasociety.org/new-york/complete-transcript-thomas-donilon-asia-society-new-york.

ONE

Europe and India

Dialogue Without Intimacy

Krishnan Srinivasan

Despite long historical connections, India was a latecomer on the scene for post–World War II Europe. Only in the mid-1990s was India bestowed with a European Union (EU) 'strategy', and that was due to the modest economic reforms in India that promised to open India's vast consumer market. Despite a high level of dialogue and optimistic statements since then, the relationship has been lacking in real substance. The strategic partnership of 2004 has yielded no result; politically, India bewails the EU's perceived tilt towards China and Pakistan and its lack of understanding of India's non-proliferation credentials. There are splits in the EU on such issues but that only lowers the EU's credibility in India. The blame can be laid equally on India and Europe for the lack of entente. Europe considers India politically and socially incomprehensible, and India feels that Europe fails to recognize India's rightful status as a pole in a multipolar world. The Indian profile in Europe is low compared to other global powers; it struggles with an image problem due to the lack of a strong Indian lobby, and Europe, due to its restrictive visa policies, remains largely unknown to Indian professionals, and its profile in India is largely confined to bilateral dealings with Britain, France, and Germany.

India is one of the big three in Asia along with China and Japan. It has a trillion-dollar economy and joins the other two among the top ten in the world gross domestic product (GDP) table. It has the second highest population after China, both topping the one billion person mark. Along with the other two, it has greater military and human resource strength than any other country in Asia. Japan's economic prowess was apparent even in the 1960s; India was a latecomer and followed China as a high-growth economy after 2003. After the Soviet Union's disintegration, India put in place a 'Look East' policy and associated itself with Asian structures like the Association of Southeast Asian Nations Regional Forum (ARF) and the East Asian Summit. The varying degrees of cooperation and confrontation among the three Asian giants makes it difficult for the EU to formulate any single strategy towards emerging Asia, but it will have to extend a measure of priority towards India despite the general perception that India underperforms on the world stage.

India seeks a stronger stake in the international community; without this, it will continue to be a naysayer in the challenges of change, like climate, energy, and non-proliferation. For the EU, its foreign policy in India is trade policy, and cooperation in political, strategic, and cultural issues is far from optimal. The EU is India's most important trade and investment partner, but the seven-year-long negotiations on a trade and investment agreement have floundered on predictable lines. Both Europe's and India's importance as global players is derived from expectations of future power potential rather than current achievement, and both seem minimally interested in a mutual special relationship despite the commonalities of being the biggest democracies and unions of over twenty-five linguistically, culturally, and ethnically diverse states. They are often at loggerheads in the United Nations (UN) Climate Change conferences and the World Trade Organization (WTO). What is needed is a better understanding of the other's concerns and limitations, and the potential advantages for India as Europe's strategic partner, and for Europe as India's sympathetic supporter in the western world.

EUROPE

Europe is, even for Europeans, a continent difficult to define. Europe has no centre of authority and no fixed territory; its geographical, administrative, economic, and cultural borders diverge[1]. The EU cannot rid itself of a dichotomy; on one hand, it represents itself, and on the other, it represents its twenty-eight member states. The EU's blend of multipolarity, multilateralism, and inter-regionalism is hard to comprehend and 'no one outside a tiny group of Euro-actors and Euro-academics understands how the EU works'[2]. Europe's size and economy as the world's largest exporter and importer of goods makes it globally important, and it is a lifestyle super-power, having as many as twenty places of the top thirty in the UN Human Development Report Index for 2014.

Collectively, the EU has the instruments—capabilities, technology, finances, population—of a great power but lacks the internal cohesion to assume that status. The financial recession after 2008 and the eurozone crisis placed the union project in jeopardy and have led to continent-wide euro-scepticism. The national interests of member countries often override the EU's common foreign policy, leaving Europe without decisive collective action. Europe's aspirations to promote economic progress, human rights, and sustainability through foreign policy are credible, but gaps appear between the EU's espousal of universal norms and the hard reality of international action due to the competing objectives of different national interests. Furthermore, the United States has made it implicit that it wishes the EU to play no autonomous role in security and strategic issues in South, Southeast, and East Asia.

INDIA

India is a continent, a commonwealth, with a diversity of human talent, originality, and spirituality. It uses English as a *lingua franca*. It has the best demographics of any large economy; it has the world's largest student numbers; by 2020, the average Indian will be twenty-nine, the average European forty-nine. In a decade, India will have a workforce surplus of fifty-six million against an anticipated shortage of forty-seven million in Western countries[3]. India is a high savings country; 35 percent of the national income is invested. In India's disorderly democracy, due to its youthful profile, there is entrepreneurial energy which finds expression in investments in the developed world. Its growing middle class is gaining attention from European exporters and investors; the number of Indians watching televised cricket matches exceeds the collective consumer class of Europe and the United States. Its general elections every five years, despite poverty, illiteracy, and inequality, involve an electorate of more than eight hundred million eligible voters. It has multiple competing narratives, many of which are highly divisive. To stay stable and peaceful, India has perforce to be a muddle and a mess, and it has evolved a brand of governance in its own chaotic image. The Indian government had assumed that strong investment and savings rates would maintain high growth, but managers of the Indian economy now face the challenge of restoring it to previous levels. Reforms, so far in homeopathic doses, must be completed, with agriculture decontrolled, taxes simplified; foreign direct investment (FDI) permitted in retail, defence, and insurance; and land and labour legislation reformed and made relevant to Indian growth ambitions.

THE EUROPEAN UNION AND INDIA—THE POTENTIAL

India and the EU have many similarities. Both are bureaucratic, cautious, unwieldy, and slow to decision. They have both wrestled with integration and unity in diversity for over six decades. Both look forward to a multicultural and multipolar world, and face common threats of fundamentalism, terrorism, illegal migration, and climate change. They have the challenge of multiple identities, and India is familiar with the debate that is always engaging Europe—the need for a stronger union. But these affinities have not been translated into any intimacy.

With its tolerant, multireligious, plural complexion and without ideological inhibitions, India might emerge stronger than a more chauvinistic competitor like China; a civilization that accepts the equality of nations may prove stronger than the one based on either isolation or superiority. Close cooperation between the EU and India would give both more prestige and geopolitical leverage in regard to third parties like China and the United States, but the partners are not yet of one mind. The relationship has been likened to a 'loveless arranged marriage . . . between a well-matched couple but with no spark of chemistry'[4]. India needs a 'Look to Europe' policy to supplement its 'Look East' policy, and Europe needs a better understanding of the opportunities that India has to offer[5]. The EU is India's major trade, development, and investment partner, and Europe is becoming increasingly important for Indian companies as a destination for investment and acquisitions. These are positive trends. India and China have been lonely giants, too big to have any close partners, but as they rise, both nations have to assume responsibilities for regional if not global security[6]. India may never bestride the global stage like China, but neither can it be ignored as an insignificant player.

India is interested in the EU's achievement of social justice, economic modernization, regional integration, and the search for a knowledge economy, and the EU could benefit from engagement with India on global issues and forms of global governance, which could include human security, social development, capacity building, democratic reforms, energy consumption, and subnational governance. Europe and India could cooperate in projects in the developing world in a triangular mode, and in naval cooperation in the Indian Ocean, which is a maritime/littoral space of geopolitical, geoeconomic, and geostrategic importance. Being reliant on sea-based commerce, both are important stakeholders in maritime security in this area with its multiple choke points, piracy, terrorism, failed states, rogue states, overfishing, undersea cables, drugs and arms trafficking, and the ever-increasing presence of China by land and sea.

Brussels pushes to broaden the EU-India framework from the European point of view—for example, with respect to the human rights—in which success is hard to achieve, and New Delhi presses for understandings on current issues—for example, with respect to counterterrorism—and is content to leave optimization of the framework to some future date. The EU-India partnership is still a top-down, executive-driven relationship mainly propelled by corporate interests. The links are therefore less than intense, and there is danger that India could underestimate the degree of coherence that already exists within the EU (as can be seen in the free trade agreement (FTA) negotiations, where the EU is the lead actor and not its member states) and thereby disregard the need for closer contacts with the leading EU institutions.

As the predominant country in South Asia, India does not welcome any European political interventions in its backyard, though the EU's potential impact on democratization and social policies in the Indian subcontinent is small. India and other emerging powers and regions, such as Indonesia, Southeast Asia, and South Korea, are neglected in the European public discourse, though a growing interest in Asia is in how the EU will position itself in relation to the United States' strategic focus on Asia. As yet, the American rebalance or 'pivot' to the Asia Pacific has occasioned little comment or reaction in Europe.

EUROPEAN ATTITUDE TO INDIA

The EU is a global economic actor that desires to be a point of reference and a centre of strategic thought, creativity, and innovation. It is economically strong though politically weak, does not have matching military strength, and finds it hard to formulate any coherent foreign policy position. International policies expressed and implemented bilaterally by its members diminish its credibility, and it lacks cultural engagement. On strategic issues, the EU has no clear standing or role, and in areas of security interest to India, the EU has staked out no clear position.

New Delhi could point out that there is no EU defence ministry, army headquarters, or intelligence headquarters, and security cooperation and global issues can best be dealt with bilaterally with the member countries. The EU is reluctant to confront Pakistan on terror-related matters; it wants to be even-handed between India and Pakistan because it is unwilling or unable, due to its internal competences, to deal with India's strategic problems. Europe and India have different security contexts: while the EU lays stress on Indo-Pakistan dialogue, India references Pakistan's support for terror across its border, and is ready for greater coordination against Islamist militancy, but there is a mismatch of expectations. The EU is more concerned with non-traditional threats like cybercrime, illegal immigration, and human trafficking, whereas for India there are anxieties about national integrity, border violations, insurgencies, and separatism.

The EU feels that India is insufficiently entrepreneurial or proactive, that it is mired in its own problems, that its market is too protected, and complains about the absence of intensive engagement. India engages inadequately with the European Commission as well as with the European Parliament. India's democratic polity earns it scant leverage with the EU, which feels uneasy about strategic cooperation, high technology transfers, and defence cooperation with India. The EU is weighed down by legalistic interpretations of non-proliferation, many of its members are uncomfortable with the US-India 2008 Civil Nuclear Accord, and is unable to take a united stand on India's nuclear weapon status. Indian participation in the European Galileo global positioning system project was first mooted in 2003, but was delayed due to some EU members linking India's membership to arms control and dual-use technologies, and India joined the International Thermonuclear Fusion experimental reactor in 2005 in France only after an American clearance when Washington had started negotiations with India on an escape route from the non-proliferation treaty (NPT) in the form of a civil nuclear agreement. Emerging Asia wants changes in international society to reflect its interests, and the United States has appeared more sympathetic to India's rise, whereas the EU is seen by New Delhi as a staunch defender of the existing order. There are other variations as well. Europe has to outsource business and insource skilled labour; it is threatened by a technology gap with the United States and fears of China taking over European manufacturing and India taking over European services. Europe believes in a post-modern world of norms; India in power, realism, and balance of power, with little faith in collective institutions. If India wants to rise and Europe to remain relevant, they have both to exploit their complementarities.

The EU has a low profile in India, and Brussels has little time and political energy for India. In many ways, Europe and India have both come to be perceived as underperforming, struggling to overcome internal divisions and find a space for themselves in the global order[7]. In India's view, the EU does not consider Asia as multipolar and concentrates too much of its attention on China, greatly to India's chagrin.

INDIAN ATTITUDE TO EUROPE

India established diplomatic relations with the European Economic Community in 1962, but it took another thirty-two years for a ministerial-level dialogue to start. On the European Economic Community's part, with regard to all Asian nations apart from Japan, only after 1990 was there greater interest shown in Brussels, and regular India-EU meetings at summit level began only in 2000, after the euro currency was launched in 1999.

India ranks the EU low in its priorities; it regards the EU more as an experiment than as an international organization. It seems uncertain whether the EU is a super-state, a supra-national entity, or a post-modern state. India finds the changing priorities of the EU baffling: The EU seemed to prefer process rather than outcome, with a plethora of forums producing limited results. An Indian viewpoint similar to euro-scepticism is thus evident. For historical reasons, Indians perceive the EU primarily through the British lens and prefer the bilateral route with key EU states like Britain, France, and Germany, and Britain is more or less the spokesman for the EU in India and vice versa. India has found it hard to see value added in the EU as opposed to its individual members, and influential Indians disregard the EU's relevance for India's desired status in the international arena. India has not seen eye to eye with the EU on Myanmar, UN reform, Sri Lanka, climate change, the Doha Round, or non-proliferation. In India's view of geopolitics, the European mind-set of the Cold War has not substantially changed, and the EU has slavishly followed the American lead on too many global issues.

Indians have a dislike to being lectured at, and Europe is inclined to preach. Former Indian diplomat Eric Gonsalves states, 'The European Commission and the EU are a pain in the neck to deal with'[8]. As an older democracy than many EU states, India wants to handle human rights in its own political space. For the EU to insert human rights into a draft FTA as if they were auto emission standards upsets the Indian negotiators. India accepts the concept of multilateralism, but is sceptical about many specific issues promoted by Europe: the International Criminal Court, the Responsibility to Protect (R2P), humanitarian interventions, and the ban on anti-personnel landmines.

EUROPEAN UNION–INDIA PROBLEMS

The EU's moral pretensions are reminiscent of India's posturing after independence in the heyday of Nehruvian non-alignment, but India has since moved to a realist power-oriented attitude. The voting behaviour at the UN General Assembly (UNGA) in the period of 2004 to 2010 is instructive: in the case of full EU cohesion (that is, when all EU member states cast an identical vote), the voting pattern per annual UNGA session between the then twenty-five or twenty-seven EU member states and India varied from 43 percent to 53 percent, which means that in around half of the resolutions voted upon during a UNGA session, EU member states and India cast different votes, reflecting a fundamental difference of approach in world affairs[9].

Both sides appear little interested in pursuing a special relationship and perceive each other as associated with the deficiencies that received wisdom attributes to them without the benefit of any new analysis. The EU is a strong advocate of legally binding commitments and powerful international regimes. It encourages social protection and respect for the environment and human rights, while India is reluctant to limit its economic development by concerns about such issues. India opposes the inclusion of core labour standards in the WTO negotiations or linking trade with environmental issues, child labour, the rights of Dalits, and the death penalty. India differs with the EU in regard to nuclear issues, climate change, agricultural tariffs, trade-related issues, technology transfer restrictions, access for professionals in the labour market, and the complexity of EU policies. Access to the European market and technology, along with the EU's health and sanitary regulations, quality controls, and social restrictions, constitutes a big challenge for India to surmount, and there are disputes on trade-related intellectual property rights and access problems for Indian textiles, spices, automobiles, software, and pharmaceuticals. The EU does not extend to India any noteworthy development assistance, and there is no flagship European project in India, though Operation Flood from 1970 to 1996 was at one time the world's biggest food and development programme, and made India the world's leading milk producer. The Delegation of the European Commission in New Delhi, set up in 1983, is familiar only to a few development activists and non-government organizations (NGOs). The EU-India summits are not newsworthy, achieve little, and get scant media coverage. Indians, and Asians generally, feel that European journalists are obsessed with human rights matters—where India comes off badly—to the exclusion of everything else.

If the EU is accused of being hydra-headed, India should be sympathetic to that predicament: Its federal system has produced several power-broking chief ministers in the states. Both India and the EU, however, do not seem willing to learn from, let alone appreciate, each other. The basis for Indian lack of comprehension of the EU, however, lies elsewhere; there is no country where national sovereignty and use of hard power rank higher. 'Each . . . looks to the most powerful poles . . . rather than towards each other, and spends more time deploring the shortcomings of the other rather than building . . . the future partnership'[10]. This has accordingly become a dialogue of the deaf; the EU hardly makes any conscious effort to understand India. Europe talks about India's political, social, and economic labyrinth; India talks about threats to its security, but Brussels is tolerant of Pakistan's behaviour. The Indian model of growth with democracy is not seen as an alternative to the China model: No one in Brussels will hearken to India in the absence of economic heft, consistently high GDP growth, and a thriving business community.

Indians feel they are talked down to by the EU about prosperity, stability, human rights, and securitized visa regimes, with ignorance about the other party's compulsions. India is affronted when even small member states of the EU, such as the Nordic and Baltic countries, deliver sermons on relations with neighbours, human rights, nuclear non-proliferation, and international law. Nevertheless, on fundamental rights and secularism it is proper for India to demonstrate that it is accountable because the EU through its parliaments and civil society has legitimate concerns and needs to be persuaded about India's good intentions.

India, as the weaker but more moderate country than China, feels it deserves a sympathetic Europe, especially across South Asia where China will exercise more influence in future. In contrast with China, India sees itself as the 'democratic candidate', representing democracy with religion, a common law legal system and the English language. In the 1960s, André Malraux had told India that Europe provided a 'third option' to the United States and the Soviet Union. Is the EU a credible second option for India now? EU foreign policy seems based on the premise of equilibrium between India and Pakistan, terrorism and non-proliferation notwithstanding, and in many trade-related matters, India receives no support from the EU because of serious doubts whether India genuinely believes in open trade.

In information technology, giant companies like IBM and Accenture are expanding rapidly in India to benefit from its low-cost, high-quality labour, and Indian software companies are expanding in the United States to create the closer customer relations essential to compete in high-end consultancy services. This kind of interaction is, however, not happening with Europe, where there is no cross-movement of jobs and labour with firms competing to provide knowledge leadership, breakthroughs, and innovation, and India's information and communications technology (ICT) firms are not able to establish their own 'brands' as vendors and not just as service providers. European sentiment on outsourcing to India creates protectionist attitudes, whereas the lack of good infrastructure in India remains a handicap to European investment.

India was less likely than other emerging nations to be affected by the global slowdown due to the relatively lower factor of its export trade, but the eurozone crisis troubled India because the euro weakened against the dollar, and a stronger dollar pulled down the rupee value. Imports became costlier, fuel prices rose, foreign investors pulled out, and stock markets fell. Indian exports of semi-manufactures, manufactures, and raw materials declined, software earnings were affected and remittances from abroad dropped. Higher imports and lower exports raised the current account deficit and the depletion of Indian foreign exchange reserves. So any shrinkage in the European economy constitutes grim tidings for India. Nevertheless, its growth rate will be far higher than that of the European countries individually, and its GDP is expected to exceed over time all the individual EU member states.

Along with the Association of Southeast Asian Nations, the EU was an exemplar for the founding of the South Asian Association of Regional Cooperation in 1986, but even after three decades, there is little progress in South Asia towards political, economic, or social integration. A South Asian free trade area, customs union, and economic union all have unrealistic timetables, and there is little incentive for greater cohesion when India dominates 70 percent of the South Asian Association of Regional Cooperation market. With growing euro-scepticism as manifested in the

2014 elections for the European Parliament, there is little contemporary invocation in South Asia of the EU as an exemplary model.

In its country paper (2007–2013), the EU provided 470 million euro in development aid to India, mainly in health, education, the Millennium Development Goals, culture, civil society, and academic exchanges. The EU sought to have an impact on the Indian reform process and poverty alleviation, but considering the scale of India's publicly funded welfare programmes, the EU has always been a marginal donor, and traditional overseas development assistance was to be phased out after 2013. There is no discrete European policy towards India, no bilateral trading arrangement, no plan to allocate more European Commission development funds to India, and European-Indian relations have changed in recent years from that of aid donor and recipient to one of partnership. In the European Commission's giant bureaucracy, there is lack of expertise on India, particularly when compared with China.

STRATEGIC PARTNERSHIP

The 1994 Cooperation Agreement laid the initial basis for EU-India cooperation. It fixed annual ministerial meetings and listed broad-ranging areas of cooperation, but with a trade and economic orientation. By 1996, however, a Brussels Communication titled *EU-India Enhanced Partnership* took a somewhat critical stand on India's growth rate, domestic savings and investment, and public sector. Then, the Indian nuclear weapons testing in 1998 led to mixed reactions in Europe, with France leading the opposition to American sanctions. London and Berlin reopened a dialogue with New Delhi, and after the Indo-Pakistan conflict in Kashmir in 1999, when India showed extraordinary restraint, the way was open for the first Indo-EU summit in 2000, when the agenda was opened up to climate change, the environment, and terrorism. By 2004 and the conclusion of a Strategic Partnership between the two entities, the Cooperation Agreement was outdated. The Strategic Partnership in 2004 was supplemented by an EU-India Security Dialogue, but India was disappointed by the EU's response on Sikh Khalistani anti-Indian activities, when Britain, Germany, Netherlands, and others dragged their feet, and the anti-Indian influence of Pakistani and Muslim diaspora voters over European legislatures that inhibits expanded EU partnership.

The EU has strategic partnerships with seven partners, four of them located in Asia. Former EU President Herman van Rompuy summed up the task at hand thus: 'Until now we had strategic partners. Now we also need a strategy'[11]. The strategic partnership is merely a kind of honorary degree conferred by the EU on certain favoured nations: there is no definition from Brussels of what a strategic partnership is[12]. In 2004, India responded to it with its first ever paper on a foreign entity, notably envisaging a relationship 'immune from the vicissitudes of . . . relationship with a third party'; diplomatic shorthand for the United States and China. The strategic Action Plan of 2005 was also the first of its kind for India, but the revised action plan of 2008 is one that leads to more dialogue rather than to any concrete action. For the EU, Indo-Pakistan reconciliation was a priority and it emphasized regional cooperation, but it was too unmindful of India's exposure to an unfriendly neighbourhood and trans-border terrorism. Most EU member countries do not share the same urgency or interest in security as India does, and lay greater stress on values rather than geopolitics.

India and the EU were able to narrow their differences somewhat on nuclear weapons. India said it abided by the NPT though it would not sign up, and would agree to common efforts to contain proliferation of weapons of mass destruction. The EU was split on the US-India civil nuclear cooperation agreement; in principle, it wanted India to join the NPT and the Comprehensive Nuclear Test Ban Treaty. Britain, France, and Germany had some sympathy with the Indian position, but the Nordic states remained unconvinced that India should get a free pass, as they saw it, to nuclear weapon state status.

India relies on hard power capabilities and views multilateral forums primarily as instruments for promoting its national interest, whereas the EU wants to strengthen international organizations and the juridification of international relations. India insists on non-interference and does not innovate in conflict resolution within its neighbourhood or outside it, other than through participating in some UN peacekeeping operations. It does not collaborate in multilateral approaches or working with non-state actors towards conflict resolution, and so is unlikely to work with the EU in international theatres. It is accordingly hard to identify even one example where India and the EU had jointly played a substantial role in resolving any international crisis.

European diplomats express frustration at New Delhi's lacklustre efforts to advance India's strategic partnership with the EU and, conversely, those in the Indian strategic community harbour largely negative perceptions of the importance of the EU as a security actor in the South Asian region. Civilian power is equated in New Delhi with weakness, and the normative-power approach is seen as soft imperialism. So the prospects of security cooperation between India and the EU remain in the realm of the conceptual.

INDIAN DEFENCE TIES WITH EUROPE

At $47.4 billion[13], India has the ninth biggest military budget in the world, which it expends on maintaining the second largest standing army of 1.18 million soldiers and a navy and air force among the top five.

But its armed forces suffer from a poor tooth-to-tail ratio with fighting elements outnumbered by support units, and 60 percent of the expenditure is incurred on recurring costs as opposed to capital investments for modernization and acquisition of new weapon systems. India's failure to build a domestic defence industry results in it being the world's biggest arms importer with 65 percent of its hard and software being sourced from abroad. In addition, most of the acquisitions have been done in a muddled manner with no long-term strategic planning or inter-service prioritization, and delays in procurement have led to huge cost escalations and an aging and obsolescent defence inventory.

Defence manufacturing is a high-cost industry because outlays on advanced technology and research and development are required. Some EU countries maintain big defence industries despite cutting of military budgets. All European countries adhere to technology denial regimes (Missile Technology Control Regime, Nuclear Suppliers Group, Wassenaar Group, and the Australia Group), and the latest generation technology is almost impossible to access. Nevertheless, there is little synergy in the EU between the military sector and security strategy, and in the absence of domestic demand and threat perceptions, export orders become vital to European manufacturers to achieve economies of scale and amortize the cost of development. As a result, complex defence products are seldom purely 'national'. With India as the world's biggest importer, the EU could expect a reasonable share of the $200 billion that India plans to import in the next dozen years.

The prospective, though now aborted, merger between BAE Systems of the United Kingdom and EADS (the French-Spanish-German combine that owns Airbus) could be the way forward to secure Asian markets at a time when European nations are cutting their own expenditures. Britain was concerned that the merger could damage the trans-Atlantic special relationship and was relieved when the arrangement was eventually vetoed by Germany. Despite the BAE/EADS fiasco, consolidation due to mergers and acquisitions has resulted in economies of scale, assisting international competitiveness. Although the defence industry is largely privatized and the obligation to deal with individual governments therefore gets diluted, the commitment at the political level to a contract can be differentiated, and the multinational nature of the European defence industry has facilitated India in some of its defence procurements from Europe.

Transfer of technology is limited for India by the fact that only 49 percent of FDI is so far permitted in this sector. The EU has to contend with an entrenched Russia and growing shares in India's procurement for Israel and the United States, but India's aim is to avoid over-dependence on any one country. For defence contracts, some level of geopolitical understanding must exist, and it is noted in New Delhi that France has eschewed nuclear sanctions against India and is considered a reliable partner. A commercial nuclear deal with the French nuclear giant Areva for nuclear reactors and fuel supply was signed in 2009, which allowed for enrichment and reprocessing rights over the spent nuclear fuel from French reactors under safeguards, and provided assurances of lifetime supply of nuclear fuel for these reactors. In 2011, India declared an intention to place its biggest single arms order, namely $20 billion, for fighter aircraft with the French Rafale for 126 multirole combat planes, and selected Airbus 330 multirole tanker transport over competitors for mid-air fuelling at $1.6 billion. France has also signed the $3 billion Scorpene deal paving the way for naval cooperation, and a $2.4 billion contract was concluded with Dassault Aviation and Thales to upgrade fifty-one Mirage aircrafts. Other projects with France include development of engines for Hindustan Aeronautics Ltd, the Kaveri engine for the light combat aircraft, and the Shakti engine for the Dhruv helicopter. France is negotiating a major project of joint development and manufacture of short-range surface-to-air missiles with India, and both countries are drawing up a plan for long-term cooperation in satellite technology. France has moved to third position in the list of arms suppliers to India, only after the United States and Russia.

India has noted that French and British supplies are not limited by intrusive end-use monitoring as is the case of American supplies. In 2003, India ordered sixty-six Hawk trainer jets from Britain worth $1.7 billion, and in 2010 India placed an order for an additional fifty-seven Hawk aircraft worth $1.1 billion to be built by Hindustan Aeronautics Ltd. While France and Britain have been the major arms suppliers to India from Europe, many other countries such as Germany, Sweden, and Italy have also shared in some modest benefits. This is a field in which greater support from Europe towards Indian strategic concerns could open considerable opportunities of closer cooperation.

CULTURAL PATTERNS

Modern India has taken an active interest in the West during and after European colonization, when the West could no longer be ignored. The situation was different in Europe, where the search for the origins in India of Western civilization or the contemplation of India as the purveyor of unpolluted wisdom, reached its peak with the Romantics and Schopenhauer. At the same time, the West also nurtured the totally opposite sentiment; contempt for everything Indian as 'dark and irrational . . . standing against the light of reason symbolized by Western rationality', and some like Edmund Husserl regarded the Europeanization of the world as a historically predetermined fate[14].

Macaulayism had as its objective the creation of a person 'Indian in blood and in colour, but English in tastes, opinions, morals and intellect[15] ' to keep India in thrall to the British legacy, but India has a resilient core culture; what does not change in India is usually more consequential than what does change. India was able to adopt and absorb many things European, in the same way as it had done in the course of history with local variants of diverse imports from European attire to Chinese food and pizzas from Italy, but its ethos remained quintessentially the same, with Hinduism and caste, and governance with the chaotic characteristic typical of the Indian personality.

Europe believes that human goals and satisfaction are personal and individual; India that belonging to a community is a fundamental human need. There are identity clashes, and both the EU and India are victims of prejudice and stereotyping, with constructed identities of the other. India purports to be considered as an equal and reacts adversely when it is not so treated, and to India's dismay, the EU is not responding fast enough to this assertion. For the Europeans, caste is a repellent aspect of Indian society and they often regard India with the superiority complex befitting a repository of reason and enlightenment. The media play a role in constructing new identities, but the media in Europe and India have usually only reaffirmed and consolidated the old stereotypes.

The cultural divide on how society should perform was evident in several instances of domestic disharmony and forcible family separation when it was felt in India that European ideas are not necessarily valid. Interventions by the European state into the private lives of families are not consistent with Indian culture, and India feels it has been treated insensitively by certain European countries. A few instances will suffice. Twins conceived by a surrogate mother in India were not allowed entry to Norway since its law did not allow surrogate children to become Norwegian nationals. The Indian government took the children's welfare into account and insisted that the Norwegian mother, in Norway, was the best parent possible for the twins. Diplomatic tension arose over two children of an Indian couple in Norway who were placed in a foster home in 2011 despite repeated parental and governmental appeals for a sympathetic and speedy resolution. In a different case in 2012, a married couple was convicted for 'serious child abuse' in dealing with bed-wetting by their seven-year-old son in Norway. The parents had threatened to repatriate their son to India and, hearing of this, the school reported them to the authorities. The parents were accused of 'threats, violence and other wrongs' and sentenced to eighteen months and fifteen months, respectively. Denmark's refusal in 2011 to extradite a person (a mercenary called Niels Holck also known as Kim Davy) involved with airdropping weapons into India due to India's alleged poor jail conditions and poor human rights record was not well received. The Indian government has often had grievances against the activities of European NGOs. It took action in 2012 against local NGOs using foreign money for a people's agitation against the peaceful uses of nuclear energy in Tamil Nadu, and it discovered that funds received from American and Swedish donors and were diverted by the NGOs, including church groups, to anti-nuclear protestors. There are also unspecific reports of fringe elements in Europe rendering financial and material help to the Indian anti-government Maoist underground movement.

INDIAN DIASPORA IN EUROPE

EU-India civil society ties are below optimal; there is a surprising mutual lack of knowledge, unlike between India and the United States, thanks to a successful Indian diaspora. Academic research and tourism are not sufficient to bridge the gap, and expertise on contemporary India is rare in Europe. The situation in India is hardly better: besides a few elite institutions, the EU is not discussed, and the sparse reports in Indian media about the 'old' continent are often of poor quality.

In the twentieth century, migration took place from the colonial periphery to urban centres in the industrialized North. It was not the previous type of imperial-sponsored labour or 'indentured' South-South migration, but that of the largely English-educated middle class, which had the cultural and linguistic background and social contacts to assimilate relatively easily into the new environments. This was followed by a second wave of migration after World War II of skilled and semiskilled Indians to English-speaking countries like the United States, Britain, and Canada. The third ICT wave was another distinct category within the Indian diaspora that moved to multiple destinations in a trans-national space along the networks of companies for which the professionals worked. Europe is India's second largest market for ICT services and accounts for 31 percent of India's ICT exports (the United Kingdom has the dominant share of 19 percent), whereas the United States accounts for 60 percent. Multinational companies look for cost-effective employees, and Britain is the third destination for such Indians after Canada and the United States. The Indian diaspora can and does play a positive role in addressing information and perception deficits, facilitating interactions, and increasing mutual knowledge, but it has not yet gained sociopolitical power within host nations in Europe, and due to its wide dispersion, its overall influence is limited, though it is growing and the persons of Indian origin now number around 1.7 million[16]. The main reasons for issue of residence permits to non-EU citizens in 2009 were family reunification, employment, and education. The highest number of permits relating to education was issued to the Chinese, and the highest number of permits for employment purposes, including researchers, skilled, and seasonal workers, to Indian nationals. Among non-EU citizens, Indians are the largest group to obtain residence permits in the EU for employment (37 percent) and Britain was the main receiver of Indian citizens with 63.2 percent[17].

Skilled migration into Europe boosts competitiveness and economic growth, and there have been increased efforts in the EU to work towards a common policy with a view to making Europe an attractive migration destination like Australia, Canada, and the United States, and to have highly skilled workers change their perception of Europe's labour market as governed by inconsistent admission procedures. All migrants who come to reside and work legally in the EU should theoretically enjoy basic, work-related socioeconomic rights. The Blue Card Directive, adopted in 2009, from which Denmark, the United Kingdom, and Ireland have opted out, would allow the employment of non-Europeans in any country within the EU[18]. Instead of varying national legislations and different visa and work permit requirements, one single permit would be in place. Individual member states could decide how many Blue Cards they wished to grant each year and retained the right to refuse candidates. Unlike the Green Card of the United States, the European Blue Card does not offer permanent residence and is only valid for two years, but is renewable. After five years, it leads to permanent residence, but again unlike the United States, not to citizenship. After eighteen months of legal residence, the holder could move to another member state, but the applicant has to apply for a second Blue Card to comply with nationally determined requirements. In that respect, there is little change from the current situation. The Blue Card offers no substantial added value and does not redress the existing problems for Indian professionals.

EUROPE-INDIA DIFFERENCES: CLIMATE CHANGE

China and India account for 70 percent of the increase in global energy demand, and the two countries are projected to double their energy consumption by 2030. India has 2.4 percent of the world's land and 4 percent of the water resources, but supports 17 percent of the population. Per capita emissions in India are below two tonnes of carbon dioxide a year, one of the least, compared to the United States, which is twenty times higher. But the World Bank says environmental damage accounts for 5.7 percent of India's GDP, meaning that economic growth is largely undermined by environmental loss. India supports some reduction in the intensity of growth of emissions—the carbon released per unit of economic output—and measures to mitigate global warming, but will not agree to any legally binding emission cuts since these are not in line with the Kyoto principle of 'common but differentiated responsibility' on the part of developed and developing countries for global warming. It takes the view that India, like other developing countries, needs 'carbon space' for development, and that clean energy technology must be extended by the

West free of costs and royalties and without the protection of intellectual property rights. Two interests need to be reconciled: the global good of a healthy environment across the world, and India's right to develop and emerge from poverty, which requires energy, which in turn produces emissions. Leaving aside agriculture, Indian emissions intensity to GDP declined from 1994 to 2007 by 25 percent and will do so by another 20 to 25 percent by 2020 compared to 2005.

Big polluters like China and India are aware of the perils of global warming, but see climate change mainly as a Northern agenda to retard their progress, and this is a source of regular friction between India and the EU at climate change conferences where the EU wishes to lead the global debate and hopes that its soft power, in the form of its leadership of an international movement against global warming, would be acknowledged. The EU prepared a global package of commitments for the fifteenth UN Copenhagen Climate Change Conference in December 2009 with an agenda to replace the Kyoto Protocol. The Copenhagen conference proved a failure for the EU; the difference between key participants was so deep that it proved difficult to keep the negotiation going, and its own bargaining strategies were inadequate. The EU can rightly claim to have done more to combat climate change than the United States, China, or India, but at the conference, past achievements and good intentions were of no consequence. Environment and climate change were shared competencies, which meant that the EU had a common negotiating mandate, but member states were also at the table, and the EU proved unable to calibrate negotiating stances because of the member-states' divisions. Finally, Britain, Germany, and France, and not the EU, spoke for Europe, and the EU was absent in the conference's final dealings.

The Copenhagen Accord was accepted by forty-eight countries accounting for 80 percent of global emissions, and endorsed the two degrees Celsius warming benchmark for global progress. Measurement, reporting, and verification were also agreed upon, and $10 billion was to be committed by 2012 for adaptation. Every major economy agreed to identify specific domestic goals and commitments: it being understood that in the absence of any global understanding, the most effective actions had been, and would be, taken at the national and local levels. The same divisions between India and the EU appeared at subsequent UN climate change conferences at Rio, Doha, Warsaw, and Lima, where the EU continued to press in vain for legally binding pledges with timetables and international reviews of intended nationally determined contributions, and the acrimonious debate will be carried forward to the Paris Conference of the Parties in 2015 when the dire warnings in the 2013 report of the Intergovernmental Panel on Climate Change will be considered and a treaty sought to replace the Kyoto one.

In India, it is felt that the Intergovernmental Panel on Climate Change report tried to shift the focus away from the emissions and 'historical responsibilities' of the industrialized countries and the message sought to be given was to forget the past and look only at the future. Thereby, pressure would intensify on the developing world to do more to curb greenhouse emissions. The BASIC (Brazil, South Africa, India, and China) grouping took the view that on the mitigation front, actions by its members were more concrete than the developed world, and that around 60 percent of the cut in emissions had been contributed by the developing countries. This view was contested by the EU which said that the statistics showed an opposite picture: The UN Environmental Programme 2013 report suggested that from 2000 to 2010 developed countries' share in global emissions decreased from 51.8 percent to 40.9 percent whereas developing countries' increased from 48.2 percent to 59.1 percent, with China leading the list of the world's leading carbon emitters, followed by the United States and India. The EU reiterated that it was willing to increase its emissions reductions from 20 percent to 40 percent by 2020 if other major emitting countries would commit to implement their fair share to a global effort.

INDIA, EUROPE, AND GLOBAL FORUMS

Asia and Europe must work together for an effective and legitimate multilateral system with a functioning UN at its core; but it is difficult to justify low Asian permanent representation in the Security Council when the EU, with less than half the population of India alone, is now represented by two, and perhaps by three, members in any future expansion. The EU has too many board seats on all international organizations and this historical legacy crowds out new members from the developing world. The EU's reluctance to relinquish this eccentric power-sharing structure to accommodate new realities is a stumbling block to global governance. The post-war arrangements bestowed a trans-Atlantic monopoly on the International Monetary Fund (IMF) and the World Bank. The managing director of the IMF and the president of the World Bank have always been from Europe and the United States, respectively, which constitutes a fundamental illegitimacy in the selection process. Before 2008, the IMF provided almost no assistance to the EU: It now amounts to about 56 percent or 110 billion euro. The problem of sovereign debt, once considered exclusive to developing countries, has become more serious for the advanced countries, and there is credit risk now attached to sovereign debt in many eurozone countries. The distinction between the givers and takers of liquidity in the world economy has changed, but China with the world's second largest economy, and India with the tenth[19], have only 3.8 percent and 2.3 percent, respectively, of the voting rights in the IMF, and 5.2 percent and 3 percent, respectively, in the World Bank, and are placed after Germany, France, and Britain, which speaks for itself.

THE WORLD TRADE ORGANIZATION, EUROPE, AND INDIA

Anti-dumping measures against Indian products in European markets and several WTO-plus aspects in the FTA negotiation with the EU leave the Indian public with a negative impression. India had difficulty with the Western agenda in the WTO from the start and blocked demands for liberalization in investment and competition policy, tightening of environmental and labour standards, and reduction of tariffs on industrial goods without reciprocal reduction of farm subsidies. In protecting its interests in services and intellectual property, its positioning in world trade has tended to be adversarial to Europe, especially when it shows itself ready to defend its positions almost alone.

Having registered scant progress since 1995 when the WTO started, or later in 2001 when the Doha Development Round began, 159 countries met at the Ninth Ministerial meeting at Bali at the end of 2013 with a smaller three-point agenda: a trade facilitation agreement (TFA) to boost trade by enhancing transparency, harmonizing and simplifying customs procedures, and improving trade infrastructure; reducing trade distorting subsidies on agriculture; and assistance to least developed countries. Having first accepted a package that accorded a 'peace clause' whereby the 'Green Box' agricultural subsidies, which were allowed up to 10 percent of the 1986–1987 prices provided there were no exports or internal market and no distortion of trade, would not be challenged until 2017, India later held out for a 'single undertaking' and held the TFA hostage to the permanent removal of the cap on agricultural subsidies, or a change from 1986–1987 as base year prices to current market prices, or to index the price to current levels. India's opposition was on the ground that Indian food grain production was subject to the vagaries of the annual monsoon, and it needed some sixty-two million tonnes in storage to provide food security for about 820 million people. India claimed that a temporary amnesty was insufficient, and that the emphasis from the WTO was on pressing ahead with trade facilitation which mainly benefitted big exporters like the United States, the EU, and China, with a lack of interest in resolving the food security aspect. The subsidy issue, New Delhi claimed, had the potential to expose India to a host of challenges: on who was regarded as poor, what should be the level of nutritional support to such people, and what should be the quantum of subsidy. India was impervious to the argument that the TFA would add $1 trillion and twenty-one million jobs to the global economy, and the advanced economies saw India's attitude as a defence of its food security programme, which was costly and full of graft. After an understanding between India and the United States, the deadlock was broken with a decision to rework the formula for food subsidies while addressing the concerns of the developing countries and setting aside any penalties until then. This was the WTO's first global trade agreement in twenty years. The failure of the Doha Round would have led to more regional agreements that are inherently exclusive, since developing economies are not the advanced countries' partners of choice, and the proposed trade groupings would leave countries like India out in the cold.

It may be noted that despite habitual EU-India skirmishes in the WTO, Indian agriculture and pharmaceuticals have been well served under its rules, which are India's ally against western pressure on patents. Europe complains that India has ignored patent rights for some essential drugs when issuing compulsory licenses, which flouts norms, cheats patent owners, and confers a bonus on Indian producers of cheap substitutes. But the WTO permits India the freedom to take a liberal attitude on patent exclusivity and allows government price control and compulsory licensing for drugs deemed critical for national health. India ranks last among twenty-five countries for patent protection, but it is also a victim, since Bollywood and software piracy is rampant.

THE EUROPEAN UNION–INDIA FREE
TRADE AGREEMENT NEGOTIATION

For the EU, a free trade area should stand for free trade and investment, with allied agreements on labour, environment, and human rights standards. The EU sees India as 'an obvious partner for one of the new generation FTAs', but the situation is imbalanced. The EU has 19 percent of Indian exports and 14 percent of imports, while India's share of the EU market accounts for only 2.5 percent of EU's total trade. India was the EU's eighth trading partner in 2011, and it is the third most important trade partner for the EU in Asia after China and Japan. The EU can hardly be underestimated by India—despite its recent woes, it still accounts for nearly 23 percent of world GDP[20].

The Indo-EU FTA is officially termed the bilateral trade and investment agreement (BTIA), and negotiations started in 2007. There is no agreed interpretation of what constitutes the 'substantially all the trade' criterion of the General Agreement on Tariffs and Trade/WTO, but the EU view is that 90 percent of existing trade over ten years, along with the desire to eliminate tariff and quantitative restrictions on 90 percent to 95 percent of tariff lines, would meet the 'substantially all trade' requirement. India has FTAs with several entities and countries, but none is as ambitious in scope as the BTIA with the EU. The agreement is based on presumed political convergences that are value added to economic ties and enhance their potential. Both sides realize that the deeper the integration, the greater the benefit, and the negotiations have covered the broadest possible landscape: trade in goods, sanitary and phyto-sanitary measures and other barriers to trade, trade in services, investment, intellectual property rights, competition policy, customs and trade facilitation, trade defence, government procurement, and sustainable development.

Indo-EU trade was approximately balanced at $107 billion in 2010 and has of late increased by 17 percent annually. European investments in India have tripled to three billion euro from 2003 to 2010, and represents 21 percent of India's total stock of FDI inflow, while Indian FDI to Europe is 30 percent of India's outward stock. Opening the Indian economy will result in more inward investment, technology, and logistical skills from the EU; India could benefit by a putative $9 billion worth of business by this pact; and services could benefit both sides. India maintains substantial tariff and non-tariff barriers, but a major stumbling block is the EU insistence that social issues like child labour, human rights, and climate change be discussed, though India meets the general criteria in EU's Global Europe strategy, including on market potential. India contends that there are other forums for discussion of these issues, which to the EU constitute non-tariff barriers and protectionism. From India's side, there is a demand that the EU cut farm subsidies, because the EU's Common Agricultural Policy mainly benefits big agro-industrial conglomerates, which resort to dumping in developing countries[21]. The EU insists on food safety standards, while India wants not only a package for goods trade including agriculture, but market access in services including cross-border and movement of natural persons.

The process of negotiation between the EU and an emerging Asian economy constitutes an interesting case study. The BTIA has been under negotiation for several years, and many deadlines have come and gone. Both sides know that mere reduction in tariffs will not lead to increased interaction unless non-tariff and regulatory barriers are also eliminated. Therefore, the EU is seeking an agreement going beyond trade liberalization to service sectors like banking and insurance, retail, legal and accountancy services, government procurement, protection of intellectual property, and data exclusivity in drugs that goes beyond trade-related intellectual property rights. The EU wishes to penetrate into several non-trade issues of market access and national treatment in the service and investment sectors, is pushing India on tariff reductions and dispute settlement that go further than the WTO provisions, and wants India to go beyond its domestic commitments on intellectual property rights.

The EU and India are predominantly service economies, which comprise two-thirds of total employment and 50 percent to 70 percent of the respective GDPs. The services sector accounts for more than half of India's GDP, and its importance as an employer has been growing over time, rising from 20 percent of total employment in 1995 to about one-third now. EU-India bilateral trade in services increased from 17 billion euro in 2008 to 19.6 billion euro in 2010. Bilateral services trade accounted for 12 percent of India's global services trade in 2010 but only 2 percent of the EU's extra-EU services trade, since 58 percent of EU trade in services is within EU borders. Despite this, the EU is the largest services exporter in the world with about 25 percent of the total traded. Any EU-India trade agreement that excludes services would exclude the most important sector, but there are significant difficulties to an agreement on services.

India's most restrictive policies are in services trading, with limitations on the operation of foreign banks and a relatively closed insurance sector. Sectors like ICT and telecom are already significantly liberalized, others such as construction, health, banking and insurance, education, retail and courier are moderately liberalized, and legal, accountancy, and postal services are completely closed. The important issues for India in Europe are market access for cross-border services and service professionals, research and development, dental and health-related sectors, and telephone-based services. India wants the ceiling of forty thousand professionals to have no other restrictions like labour market tests and economic necessity tests, and free movement within EU. India is pressing for entry to Europe not only for professionals in information technology but for others like architects, teachers, and chefs; Indian companies to be considered data secure, especially when declared so by the United States; and removal of local presence and residency requirements. Other concerns are the huge minimum capital requirements imposed by the EU, restrictions on legal entity, and the absence of national treatment. India would press for mutual recognition of professional qualifications, avoidance of double taxation on social security benefits of Indian services professionals abroad, and removal of grievances over visa issues. Banking sector licenses granted by any EU member should be acceptable across the EU, as the need to apply for separate licenses in each EU state is among the more cumbersome barriers.

The EU calls on India for removal of equity caps, nationality and residential requirements, fair and equitable treatment on par with Indian companies, clarity in FDI rules, and easing administrative hurdles. The EU wants more banking branches, whereas India prefers subsidiaries to branches and seeks higher investment limits. The EU desires multibrand retailing, abolishing cargo preference for the Indian flag and liberalization of accounting, legal, waste, and sewage disposal services. It wants tariff cuts in autos, wines, spirits, dairy, and a stronger intellectual property rights regime. The EU claims that India threatens intellectual property rights through generic production of branded medicines where a fair balance is not struck between public health and intellectual property concerns, and causes barriers to trade with industrial policies that benefit local industries at the expense of foreign companies, and a preferred market access policy that imposes local production requirements on certain foreign technology firms. The EU seems unlikely to give up its insistence on India complying with environmental standards and labour laws, restrictions on movement of professionals, or intellectual property rights that restrict cheaper generic drugs. Any nation-wide enforcement of human rights, environment, and social standards will always be a problem for India.

For India, benefits are expected to flow from the transfer of technology inherent in greenfield start-ups through new investment, and growth of ancillary industries, removal of regulatory obstacles to trade, and an environment where mutually advantageous private sector contracts and market-led arrangements can flourish. It seeks greater market access for its pharmaceutical exports and opposes EU demands for access to government procurement and liberalization in investment and competition policy which were removed from the Doha Round as not being consonant with development needs, but now are sought by the EU to be introduced through the FTA route. The FTA would not require Indian parliamentary ratification, but there would be political obstacles even from within the government circles. Opening legal services would need parliamentary approval, and there are powerful lobbies opposing this. Harmonizing government procurement could be a problem with the states, with sectors like construction and health being subject to local laws. Freeing agriculture imports would lead to a surge of subsidized EU farm products into India, thereby affecting small and marginal farmers who constitute a strong political constituency. Indian business chambers express concern about the possible impact of the BTIA on manufacturing, in particular consumer durables and automobile spare parts. India is under EU pressure to lower duties on high-value cars and wines and spirits, though Japan and South Korea had made a similar demand for cars that has so far been resisted. Wine and spirits also have strong domestic lobbies.

India contends that intellectual property rights should not curtail production of cheap generic drugs for the domestic market and exports, pointing out that 92 percent of patients on anti-retroviral in low and middle income countries are using Indian drugs. In 2003, Novartis (Switzerland) lost a seven-year battle in the Indian Supreme Court over a patent claim for a cancer drug. India also has invoked 'compulsory licensing' for a patented Bayer (Germany) kidney cancer drug that allowed a generic producer to sell at Rs 8,800 p.m. rather than Rs 280,000. This is regarded by Europe as arm twisting patent holders to grant licenses to Indian generic firms.

Both the EU and India need foreign investment to close the gap in current account. Their relations continue to be hailed as possessing great potential, but the gap between plans and action have widened over the past few years. In 2013, the European Commission's list of twenty top destinations for investment in the next five years did not include India, which disappointed the Indian authorities. The above summary will show that a huge gap still divides the negotiating parties. From the EU's viewpoint, India must be made open to competition, but the EU is unwilling to host more Indian professionals in Europe or permitting services trade through electronic channels, and there is no single set of rules for trade in services across all EU member countries. The BTIA, when concluded, will undoubtedly be the high point, or perhaps the only achievement, in EU-India relations. If there was an agreement, investment from EU could rise by 27 percent, but the Indian boisterous culture of domestic politics will make any final agreement difficult—apart from which, any agreement would require ratification by the European Commission, the European Council and all twenty-eight governments in the EU, which some observers estimate could take about two years[22].

CONCLUSION

Europe still plays a major role in the world economy, but its ability to influence the global political and economic marketplace is steadily waning. Eurocentricity must be replaced by a greater receptivity to cooperation with Asian emerging economies like India. A reappraisal would involve the EU's place in a de-Westernizing world, tension between universal values and regional interpretations of universality, discrepancy between rhetoric and action, and the gulf between a confident internal self-image and the often negative perceptions of the EU from the outside.

The dominance of the West will continue in the areas of technology and human skills, but the engine of new demand growth and spending power will shift to the emerging economies, especially in emerging Asia, with their higher growth rates. Their share in global investment portfolios and FDI will rise sharply. The per capita disparity will however mean there will be extreme price sensitivity in the Asian market. The implications of this development on production, outsourcing, investment, pricing, sales, advertising, and marketing in this century will obviously require research and analysis, and will have a bearing on the future shape of European industry and manufacture, but has so far been neglected.

India in its own interest needs to maximize its connections with Europe. Due to close links from the seventeenth century onwards, India enjoys brand recognition in Europe and holds considerable appeal due to its spirituality, soft power, and economic potential. Europe has no built-in resistance to these. Despite its manifold problems, Europe is a continent of prosperity and an enviable standard of living, and its consumer market is the biggest unified market in the world. This makes it attractive for Indian higher-value goods and services. Europe is a source of technology and expertise in all fields of human enterprise, and a valuable location for Indian investments, which are certain to grow in the future. Europe is a major destination for Indian skilled emigrants, professionals, and students, especially in higher education. Europe is not threatening and does not feel threatened by India. Europe can be clumsy and preachy, but is fundamentally non-intrusive, and can assist in enhancing India's world status. India should not be oversensitive in reacting to European criticism of Indian democratic standards, social structures, and human rights, and should avoid obsession with Europe's relations with Pakistan and China. India seeks a multipolar world, one in which India and Europe should constitute two of the poles. Closer cooperation will help to make this come about. To the extent limited by circumstances, India could even nudge Europe over time to reconsider the merit of instinctively following the US lead in foreign policy.

NOTES

1. Jan Zielonka, 'The EU as an International Actor', *European Foreign Affairs Review* 16 (2011): 281–301.
2. David Marquand, books.google.co.in/books?isbn=14008838053.
3. Joao Cravinho, 'India and the EU: Strategic Partners in a Globalised World', *FPRC Journal*, (2013): 59.
4. Gauri Khandekar, 'The EU and India: A Loveless Arranged Marriage', *FRIDE Policy Brief* 90 (August 2011); Bernd von Muenchow-Pohl, 'India and Europe in a Multipolar World', *Carnegie Paper* (May 2012): 1.
5. C. Sheela Reddy and P. Krishna Mohan Reddy, 'Need for a Look European Union and Look Europe Policy', *FPRC Journal* (2013): 310.
6. Liz Mohn, *Cultures in Globalization* (Gutersloh: Bertelsmann, 2006), 59.
7. Lizza Bomasi, 'Europe and India: Not so Different After All', *FPRC Journal* (2013): 78.
8. I. P. Khosla, *India and the New Europe* (Delhi: Konark, 2004), 39.
9. Stephan Keukeleire and Bas Hooijmaaijers, 'EU-India Relations and Multilateral Governance', *FPRC Journal* (2013): 120.
10. David Malone, *Does the Elephant Dance?* (New Delhi: Oxford University Press, 2011), 243.
11. Bernd von Muenchow-Pohl, 'India and Europe in a Multipolar World', *Carnegie Papers* (2012): 15.
12. R. K. Jain, 'The European Union and the Rise of China and India', in *European Union and Asia*, Reimund Seidelmann and Andreas Vasilache (eds) (Baden-Baden: Nomos, 2009), 277.
13. *Stockholm International Peace Research Institute Yearbook*, 14 April 2014.
14. V. N. Mishra and Rafael Argullol, *From the Ganges to the Mediterranean* (Gurgaon: Shubhi, 2008), 2.
15. www.bbc.co.uk/news/world-asia-india-20637124.
16. Hannelore Roos, "Forging Euro-Indian Ties through Migration," *FPRC Journal* (2013): 353.
17. Ibid, 358.
18. Ibid, 360.
19. World Bank table of GDP 2012.
20. Epp.eurostat.ec.europa.eu, accessed 7 October 2014.
21. The EU with ten million farmers and the United States with three have a farm value to GDP of about $240 billion and $200 billion, respectively. In agricultural subsidy, the EU pays out approximately $107 billion, the United States $156 billion, includ-

ing food stamps, China $166 billion, and India $20 billion (Jacques Berthelot in *The Telegraph*, 28 July 2014).

22. A draft trade agreement needs to be formally approved by the European Commission, agreed to by the European Council, and ratified by the European Parliament. The voting rule in trade matters that fall under EU's full competence is qualified majority. Many elements in a trade agreement do not fall under full EU competence, and member states have in some issues veto rights. Since it is difficult to say exactly where the boundary is between what issues fall under full competence and what do not, the policy is that every country should approve the agreement in a council vote. For votes on a new trade agreement in the council, the present policy is to have all countries voting in favour.

TWO

Europe and South Asia

An Enduring Engagement

Iftekhar Ahmed Chowdhury

Europe's relations with South Asia are undergoing a process of renewals. These have been enduring. They date back a long way, when Alexander the Great in 323 BC knocked at the doors of India and established the Bactrian kingdoms in today's Afghanistan and Khyber-Pukhtunkhwa in Pakistan. Two thousand years later, the Europeans returned as traders, and their flags followed their trade. Lord Clive's victory at Plassey through a combination of dare and deceit over Nawab Sirajuddaula of Bengal began a period of British imperial rule that ended when India (and Pakistan) made their 'tryst with destiny' in Nehru's words in August 1947. It had left a mixed taste in the mouth. However, the close connections continued. Largely because Europe's interactions with India have been dealt with elsewhere in this volume, this chapter will focus on how that continent relates to the other major countries of South Asia: Pakistan, Sri Lanka, Nepal, Bhutan, and Bangladesh—though India and British Bengal will figure when necessary. The Indian subcontinent may be considered a component of emerging Asia; its economic output is expected in the World Bank's estimates of October 2014 to grow by 5.9 percent in 2015 and 6.3 percent in 2016, making it one of the fastest growing regions in the world after East Asia and the Pacific.

The British period witnessed a dichotomization of Bengal[1]. One half joined Pakistan in 1947 and morphed into an independent Bangladesh in 1971. There was a strange sense of mutual abandonment when in 1964 the British joined the European Union, and the subsequent British withdrawal from 'East of Suez' had sentimental and emotional implications for both sides. South Asians, used to British-German rivalry, started to view their newfound linkages with a modicum of puzzlement. International relations had evolved: South Asian nations now had to deal with this new avatar called the European Union (EU). This chapter includes the study of how this phenomenon is developing vis-à-vis the new sovereign segment of the old Bengal, Bangladesh.

NATION-STATES VERSUS UNION

The modern nation-state was the product of the Treaty of Westphalia in Germany in Europe in 1648. It came at the end of the disastrous thirty-year religious war that nearly decimated half of Europe's population. It took two more wars in the twentieth century for man to pause and ponder over the state system and give it a rethink. In Europe, a theory of international relations developed during the inter-war years known as 'functionalism', which saw merit in integration among states on the basis of common interests in limited economic and technical areas and issues. This was more mundane and realistic than the idealism of the philosopher Emmanuel Kant, or even the statesman Woodrow Wilson. 'Functionalism' transformed into 'neo-functionalism' when it was realized that national territories were still important. Mention must be made in this regard of the father of the so-called English School in International Relations, Hedley Bull, who makes this point in his seminal work *The Anarchical Society*. The principal intellectual proponents of 'neo-functionalism' were David Mitrany and Ernst Haas, who saw the integration of individual sectors as furthering the process involving states leading to regionalization. They were the theoretical gurus of the practitioners of European integration such as Jean Monnet, Robert Schuman, Paul Henri-Spaak, and Alcide de Gaspari. Those persons, including myself, who were entrusted with crafting the initial documents of South Asia's regional body, the South Asian Association for Regional Cooperation (SAARC), were also inspired by the 'neo-functionalist' school of thought leaders such as those mentioned herein.

Europe remains a fountainhead of novel ideas, one of them being 'Weltinnenpolitik'. This refers to global domestic politics and is attributed to the German statesman Karl von Weizacker. With the sovereignty of states eroding, he emphasizes the intra-mural politics within nation-states among non-state actors and non-government organizations (NGOs). Are they not better suited to respond to contemporary challenges of poverty, disease, and environment? This might mean today's existing state system is faced with two kinds of challenges: the thrust towards regionalization on the one hand, and on the other, the pull of consolidation of internal communities. This would seem to be a refinement of both the Westphalian concept and the union aspirations of European countries.

The current-day EU can be traced back to the European Coal and Steel Community formed by six countries in 1951 and the European Economic Community (EEC) set up by the Treaty of Rome in 1958. The Maastricht Treaty established the EU in 1993, and finally the Treaty of Lisbon in 2009 gave it its present incredibly complex shape and character. The number of EU members has swollen to twenty-eight with a growing queue of aspirants. It has its own parliament, a cabinet called the Council, a huge bureaucracy called the Commission, and its own foreign service, law court, and central bank. Its total population is over five hundred million, or 7.3 percent of that in the world, and has a gross domestic product of $17.6 trillion, which is over 20 percent of that on the globe. It is a single market; within its Schengen Area there are no passport controls; it enacts common legislation on an increasing list of subjects; and it has a monetary union called the eurozone of nineteen countries, which is currently in some economic crisis, and the sad experience of Greece, Spain, and Italy has resulted in a debate as to whether the EU was structurally dysfunctional to begin with. Europe's problems have ramifications for other regions. For instance, India's economic challenges, such as the decline of its growth rate in 2013 to 5.3 percent, can be traced partly to the recessionary situation in Southern Europe. In today's interconnected world, doubtless when Europe catches a cold, a region as distant as South Asia sneezes.

The EU does not have a common military, but most members are parties to the North Atlantic Treaty Organization (NATO). It has a high representative for foreign policy or foreign minister in Federica Mogherini, but whose influence on global politics has so far been largely unremarkable. That is because while the member-states seek to speak on foreign policy in one voice, they are not always able to. A case in point was the US-led attack on Iraq where the United Kingdom, on the one hand, and France and Germany, on the other, assumed completely different postures. Where they speak with one voice is on trade, which is why only the European Commission speaks for the EU in the World Trade Organization (WTO), but most members retain their ambassadors to that organization who try and protect their individual country's interests in the corridors while maintaining their silence in the chamber. The EU is not just a model for other regions to emulate, but also a school for them to draw lessons from. This also applies to Association for Southeast Asian States (ASEAN) looking to fashion its own union in 2015. The principal lesson is that union for its own sake, the desire arising out of idealism or emotion, without adequately addressing the potential disequilibria, can create more problems than provide solutions. Where the EU believes it is strong rests in its soft power, emanating from, as it claims, its specific European values. These are an amalgam of Europe's rich intellectual and societal history, both revolutionary and evolutionary, and it is through this that it engages with much of the developing world. This phenomenon covers Bangladesh as well. For Bangladesh, this was a reengagement with Europe, taking place at a different time in history, also different in substance and content from the earlier interface between Bengal and Britain in the eighteenth century.

A phenomenon of our contemporary times is the incontestable 'rise' of Asia. This has been marked by the burgeoning political and economic leverage of South Asia, and East and Southeast Asia, the liquidity assets of the Gulf States, the mineral resources of Central Asia, and the intangible power of discrete Asian values. Many Asians might argue that this is actually a 'reemergence', because Asia at one time boasted of a remarkable civilization, or several civilizations, each of which fell into decline as it exhausted itself meeting the myriad challenges it confronted. There are those who do not take this 're-rise' for granted and urge the enthusiasts to be calm. In the case of the two Asian mega-states, the economist Pranab Bardhan makes a point of being circumspect when he entitles one of his books, *China, India Superpowers? Not So Fast!*

The truth remains, however, that Asia is in considerable ferment and in flux. It is changing, often rapidly, and the rest of the world has to work hard to relate to this vast mass of land and humanity[2]. A major problem that Asia faces—and the South Asian subcontinent is no different—is intra-mural irredentist disputes. Europe has had its share of wars, but now, after over three and half centuries of experiencing the Westphalian system, Europe has a union at one level, and at another, clearly demarcated national frontiers. Post-colonial Asia, including South Asia, is still locked in conflicts over borders in both land and sea. This is dangerous as the richer Asian states are acquiring powerful weaponry, both conventional and nuclear. Any war fighting in these parts would have disastrous implications for the region and the world.

Time was when South Asian states would create linkages with external state actors to buttress their strength and reduce the power gap with their preeminent regional adversaries. During the Cold War, for instance, the two major South Asian protagonists linked up with the two contending sides: India with the Soviet Union, and Pakistan with the United States[3]. By the time the EU emerged as a global force to be reckoned with, the Cold War had ended, and the new Europe represented not the hard power of the West with its thermonuclear arsenal, but a 'soft power' of values which they used to engage the South Asian powers. This included trade issues—Europe being a vast market of twenty-eight countries—and Europe used this advantage to influence the framing of global regimes in the WTO where these countries functioned as a single entity through the European Commission. The same principles guided Europe's relations with South Asia.

EUROPE AND SOUTH ASIA

This chapter will focus on how Europe engages with the component states of South Asia other than India, namely Pakistan, Nepal, Bhutan, Bangladesh, and Sri Lanka. All these nations watched with interest as Europe evolved through its 'functionalist' and 'neo-functionalist' stages, the former engendering integration on the basis of common economic interests, and the latter acknowledging the importance of separate national sovereign territories. It was the European experiment that inspired the creation of the SAARC in the 1980s, but the latter's progress has been unremarkable due to its inability to telescope the entirety of the post-Westphalian European experience into three decades.

Europe's relations with Pakistan, Bangladesh, and Sri Lanka can be placed within the overall framework of the EU's development policy, though this is not to say that political elements are ignored. For instance in Pakistan, Europe is interested in eradicating religious extremism as reflected in the actions of the Taliban, and encouraging a constructive Pakistan-Afghanistan relationship, particularly after NATO's withdrawal from Afghanistan as planned following 2014. In Bangladesh, which has tended to be politically volatile and divisive, the EU has emphasized calm and political inclusiveness, and has sought to promote institutions to assist the furtherance of those objectives. In Sri Lanka, the goal has been a peaceful post-conflict society where the aspirations of the Tamils, whose separatist tendencies were brutally suppressed, are able to find a measure of fruition. Yet in all the three countries, the engagement with the EU is mostly through trade and aid.

This flows from the 'European Consensus' adopted by the European Parliament in December 2005. This common vision guides the members of the EU both individually and collectively. It mainly aims at the eradication of poverty in the context of sustainable development, and includes helping development partners in achieving the Millennium Development Goals (MDGs) set by the United Nations for 2015. Other values of the European ethos are also factored in, these being, mainly, respect for human rights and fundamental freedoms, peace, democracy, good governance, gender equality, the rule of law, principles of justice and equity, and commitment to effective multilateralism. A practical aspect of this relationship is the strong support the EU accords to these countries in their electoral processes, including the fielding of a large number of election observers to monitor the polls and assess their credibility. All three countries, Pakistan, Bangladesh, and Sri Lanka, possess a vibrant civil society, reflecting the strong intellectual tradition of these nations. The governments do not possess the wherewithal to reach every part of the populace, and NGOs usually step in to fill the gap. These NGOs have managed to develop a good relationship with Brussels, the EU headquarters, and individual European countries as effective development-cooperation partners[4].

There are formal documents that govern the relationship between the EU and these three countries. That with Sri Lanka flows from the Cooperative Agreement on Partnership and Development that went into effect in 1995. The European emphasis on human rights is reflected in the fact that certain trade preferences were withdrawn, albeit temporarily, in 2010 for Colombo's alleged non-compliance with the UN Human Rights Conventions. With Pakistan, which exports over 20 percent of its total value to Europe, the main guide is a third generation cooperation agreement. For Bangladesh, Europe remains a key partner; the European market takes over 54 percent of its total exports, and as a least developed country, it receives special privileges under the 'everything but arms' scheme. Again a document, the European Cooperative Agreement of 2001, is the frame of reference.

Even if the United States is said to be in 'elegant decline', for South Asia it still remains an important partner, with Europe also strongly participating as its own identity slowly comes into clearer relief. Asia's 're-rise', in which South Asia plays a significant role, leads to the extrapolation that in the decades to follow there will be three main groupings of supra-states in the world: America, Europe, and emerging Asia[5]. This trilateral combine, if relations between them are properly managed, will call the major tunes on the global matrix. But the efforts of each of these groupings to attain the goals of a common identity (except America, which has one already, so I am speaking of only Europe and Asia) will take some time yet, and until then, international relations will largely comprise inter-state relations, as between the countries of Europe and Asia, including those of South Asia.

PAKISTAN

Unsurprisingly, the lead European country in terms of relations with Pakistan remains the United Kingdom. These ties are historical and cover the broad spectrum of political, intellectual, emotional, and economic relations. Until 1956, Pakistan remained a dominion in the British Commonwealth, six years longer than India. Of the 2.2 million Pakistanis who comprise the diaspora in Europe, over one half live in the United Kingdom. Many have been there through generations and have begun to play an important role in different aspects of the host community.

In politics there are many persons of Pakistani origin who sit in both the Houses of Commons and Lords, as well as in the Scottish and European Parliaments. For instance, Sajid Javid and Baroness Syeeda Hussain Warsi from the Conservative Party were respectively culture minister and minister of state in the Foreign Office, and earlier Shahid Malik, of the Labour Party, was a minister for International Development in the Gordon Brown government. In the literary world, Mohsin Hamid, Hanif Kureishi, and Tariq Ali are well-known names, as is Zia Moheyuddin in entertainment. In some ways, they were returning the favours of the nineteenth-century English littérateur Rudyard Kipling, who brought territories now comprising Pakistan to the mainstream of British social and literary consciousness through his fiction such as the great novel *Kim*. In business, Sir Anwar Pervez, founder of the Bestway Group, is the wealthiest Muslim in Britain. Cricket, which provides an abiding link between Pakistan and Britain, has seen many men of Pakistani origin play for England such as Aamer Khan, Usman Afzaal, and Qasim Sheikh. On the unsavoury side, this diaspora has also provided its share of Islamist militants, among them being Abu Bakr Mansha, Hasib Hussain, and Shehzad Tanweer. Originally, the Pakistanis in the rest of Europe were indigent, but over time their general status has improved, and they began to contribute to the welfare of friends and families in Pakistan and to charities, albeit mostly Islamic. They usually learn the language of their host communities and have also begun to take part in the local intellectual life. For instance, Professor Emeritus Ishtiaq Ahmed in Sweden has written extensively on South Asian and global politics.

At one point, Pakistan was a strategic partner of some European countries, such as the United Kingdom, through defence agreements such as the Baghdad Pact, but no longer. The relations are now mostly economic and political. Politically, the European Security Strategy in 2003 identified Pakistan, a country with over a hundred nuclear warheads, as a 'frightening scenario', one in which a terrorist group could acquire weapons of mass destruction. In fact, Pakistan is relevant to all the five key threats outlined in the European Security Strategy: terrorism, proliferation of weapons of mass destruction, regional conflicts, state failure, and organized crime. The stability of Pakistan is important as it continues to be a conduit to Afghanistan for the supplies to European troops from twenty-five out of twenty-eight EU member-states, but this will reduce as the NATO forces withdraw from Afghanistan. The politicians at the EU headquarters in Brussels worry about the possibilities of training of European terrorists in Pakistan, but not overly so, as indigenous terrorists in Europe itself are beginning to occupy their greater attention. On strategic issues, the EU is quite happy to play second fiddle to the United States and concentrate itself on effecting positive transformations in Pakistan through the use of what Joseph Nye has called 'soft power', or the capacity of more gentle suasion through the spread of values. For instance, the third generation agreement ratified in 2004 focuses on democracy and the protection of human rights in Pakistan. There is empathy and understanding in Europe of the key role Pakistan will be required to play in restoring calm in Afghanistan in the future, and that a peaceful and prosperous Pakistan is good for the region and the world. The best way to do this, Brussels has assessed, is for the EU to support Pakistan's economy and buttress its development efforts.

To those ends, the EU remains Pakistan's largest importer and trading partner. The EU imports over 27 percent of Pakistan's exports in goods, with Pakistan receiving more than 15 percent of European sales. The EU policy is to remain constructively engaged with Pakistan at all possible levels. These are mainly three: first, the resumption and upgrading of political dialogue; second, the signing of the third generation cooperation agreement; and third, additional development assistance.

The total assistance provided to Pakistan by EU member states between 2009 and 2013 amounted to 2.4 billion euro, increasing by 50 percent year to year. This support is spread across the European Instrument for Democracy and Human Rights, Food Facility, Instrument for Stability, and loans from the European Investment Bank. There has been considerable humanitarian assistance as well. After the disastrous floods in Pakistan in 2010, the relief provided by the EU amounted to 423 million euro, totalling 30 percent of the total international flood aid. The following year, another 75 million euro was committed for the conflict-affected populations of the province of Khyber Pakhtunkhwa and of the Federally Administered Tribal Areas in Pakistan.

In 2013, the EU granted Pakistan the long-awaited duty-free market access under the Generalized Scheme of Preferences Plus (GSP plus), which became effective as of January 2014. Earlier, Pakistan had undertaken to implement fully its commitments under twenty-seven international conventions on human rights, good governance, labour, and environmental standards. Extremely pleased, Pakistani Finance Minister Ishaq Dar said that the scheme would increase Pakistani exports to Europe by $2 billion a year. Prime Minister Nawaz Sharif also expressed his satisfaction by stating that gaining access to the European markets was the top-most priority of the government as part of its economic development agenda. To complement this initiative, the EU and Pakistan adopted in 2012 a five-year engagement plan that would run into 2017, launching a strategic dialogue that would be expected to cover a wide range of issues from security, including counterterrorism, non-proliferation, and regional cooperation, to human rights, migration, and development cooperation.

Relations between Europe and Pakistan are civilizational, starting with those between Britain and the fringes of the South Asian subcontinent to this day, and in most aspects they are on an even keel. These comprise more than the sum of their parts, for the computation of numbers of trade or aid figures, and sales or purchases cannot fully reflect the complexities of the numerous bonds of varied times that sew these two regions together.

SRI LANKA

Sri Lanka, called Ceylon until 1972, has been part and parcel of the sub-continental ethos for thousands of years. It dates back to the epic *Ramayana*, when it was said to be the Kingdom of Ravana who was alleged to have been the abductor of the saintly Sita, the wife of the god-king Rama (revisionist history now tends to take a more benign view of the Lankan monarch, doubtless coloured somewhat by contemporary religio-ethnic politics). Among the Europeans, the Portuguese were the first to arrive on the Lankan shores, founding Colombo in 1517. The Sinhalese soon moved their capital to the more secure Kandy, whose king in 1638 invited in the Dutch to supplant the Portuguese. The Dutch accomplished this and also founded the Dutch East India Company, mostly manned by their legacy of the mixed race they left behind, the Eurasian *Burghers*. Apprehensive during the French control of the Netherlands during the Napoleonic wars, and in line with a flowering European interest in continental India, the British in 1803 occupied Kandy and snuffed out Lankan independence.

The British introduced tea to Ceylon, imported indentured Tamil workers from India in large numbers, and slowly introduced universal adult suffrage, somewhat to the chagrin of the élites among the Sinhalese, Tamil, and Burgher communities. Eventually, an independence movement followed amid growing Tamil-Sinhala strife, the beginning of what was later to become a deadly ethnic conflict and civil war, and the island became a Dominion in February 1948. The following year, it became fully independent with D. S. Senanayake as prime minister. In 1972, the name of the country was changed to Sri Lanka, a Sinhalese initiative. In this chapter, the country is mentioned as Ceylon during its earlier historical phase and as Sri Lanka when the reference is to more contemporary times.

The Ceylonese have been going to Britain, the colonial mother country, for generations, and about a half million are said to live there now. Overwhelmingly, these migrants are Tamils. Over three million persons from the island live abroad, again mostly Tamils. British legislators in the European Parliament of Sri Lankan origin, such as Nirj Deva, have played an important role in the Sri Lanka–Europe relationship[6]. There have been many visits at high levels between Colombo and European capitals. One European country, Norway, though not a member of the EU, had sought unsuccessfully to contribute through mediation towards ending the Sri Lankan civil war.

Literary and intellectual contacts date back to the British era and continue to this day. The author Leonard Woolf, husband of Virginia Woolf, both of the Bloomsbury Group, lived and wrote as a district officer in Ceylon. In contemporary times, Romesh Gunesekara and Shehan Karunatilaka have made significant contributions to English literature.

Formal relations between Ceylon and the EEC commenced in 1962. Though initially the European Commission covered Sri Lanka from New Delhi, it opened its office in Colombo in September 1995. Earlier, an Agreement on Trade and Economic Cooperation had been signed in 1975, and subsequent economic relations have been governed by a 'third generation agreement'. The Sri Lankan–EU Joint Commission has met a number of times with a view to ensuring proper implementation of agreements and examining ways and means of enhancing cooperation. The Sri Lankan government succeeded in its endeavours to get the secessionist Liberation Tigers of Tamil Eelam listed by the EU in 2006 as a 'terrorist entity', and dialogues with the EU on the fight against terrorism were held in parallel with The Joint Commission meetings. This is not to say the Europeans did not have considerable reservations about the manner in which the Sri Lankan government brought the civil war to a close, alleging the use of excessive force.

Since 1971, Sri Lanka had been a beneficiary of the EEC's GSP scheme offering trade benefits. These benefits were expanded and tariffs reduced to a minimum by the EU in the aftermath of the tsunami in 2005 when Sri Lanka was accorded the GSP-plus status as was the case, later down the line, with Pakistan. But within three years, the EU threatened to terminate this concession if Sri Lanka did not cooperate with the investigations in connection with human rights violations in the civil war. President Mahinda Rajapakse's government firmly refused, and following the adverse recommendations of the investigations, the EU temporarily suspended the GSP-plus facility in August 2010.

These investigations relied on reports by the UN special rapporteurs and representatives, other UN bodies, and by human rights NGOs. These identified significant shortcomings in Sri Lanka's implementation of, specifically, three UN Human Rights Conventions: the International Covenant on Civil and Political Rights, the Convention against Torture, and the Convention on the Rights of the Child. The EU member-states on the UN Human Rights Council voted in favour of strong criticism of Sri Lanka in resolutions in 2013 and 2014. Nevertheless, trade and investments continued to flow both ways, and Sri Lanka to enjoy the earlier 'standard' GSP privileges. In 2013, the total volume was over 3.5 billion euro. Imports from Sri Lanka into the EU amounted to 2.3 billion euro and exports, 1.2 billion euro. Thirty-six percent of Sri Lanka's total exports go to European destinations, more than 50 percent of which comprise textiles and clothing, machinery, rubber-based goods, jewellery, and agricultural products, whereas the imports are mostly machinery. About 40 percent of Sri Lanka's total tourist arrivals are from the United Kingdom, Germany, France, Italy, Netherlands, Sweden, and Belgium.

The bloody civil war, which over a span of nearly two and half decades had cost eighty thousand to a hundred thousand lives, came to an end with the defeat of the Liberation Tigers of Tamil Eelam in May

2009. Western media were very critical of the Sri Lankan army's behaviour, and the British Channel 4 brought out a series of gory episodes, laying the blame squarely on the Sri Lankan authorities. The government of Sri Lanka is making all possible efforts to address Western, in particular, European and Canadian, criticism, not only of the final phases of the war, but of the current Sri Lankan methods of winning the peace.

Sri Lanka appeared to offer a fertile ground for the testing of two important contemporary concepts, both endorsed by the international community at the United Nations. The first is with regard to peace building and implies a series of measures to stabilize a post-conflict society into such equilibrium as to prevent it from sliding back into a situation of chaos. In this respect, much will depend on how the genuine grievances of the Tamil community are addressed. A good way to go about it would be to focus on the 'low-hanging fruits' to start with. There are issues and complaints that could be easily remedied, and 'quick impact projects' that can be easily implemented will be seen by the international, and European, communities as positive gestures. These would be manageable projects that could start with the delivery of welfare to the internally displaced persons. A graduated progression along the 'four Rs' for the affected—relief, rehabilitation, reconstruction, and reconciliation—would help immensely and would assist in the much needed rebuilding of confidence. The setting up of a Truth and Reconciliation Commission, on the lines of the South African model, could be worth examining. A credible enquiry into the events of the final phase of the civil war would have to be undertaken, though Sri Lanka is likely to resist any foreign participation in this.

The second is the concept of the Responsibility to Protect (R2P). Around spring 2009, some Western politicians, including Bernard Kouchner of France, were keen to apply it in the Sri Lankan context, but the Sri Lankans were most resistant, and in any case that phase of urgency is now over. Simply put, R2P means that it is the responsibility of every state to protect its own citizens; if the state in question is unable or unwilling to do so, then the responsibility would devolve on the international community which would discharge it by working through the United Nations. The process would begin with economic support and diplomatic steps, with force to be used only as the last resort. The principle was unanimously adopted at the Summit of World Leaders at the United Nations in New York in 2005, and importantly, it was made applicable to only four situations: genocide, war crimes, ethnic cleansing, and crimes against humanity.

The Sri Lankan government would have none of this and equated any consideration of its applicability to Sri Lanka as an erosion of its sovereignty. It argued that none of the four conditions was to be found in Sri Lanka. However, the point was made that the Sri Lankans could take advantage of any broad economic package that could comprise this 'responsibility to protect', but they preferred not to have anything to do with a concept that might imply that the Sri Lankan authorities were not responsible enough for their own citizens. In any case, any Western, or European, effort to bring any element of R2P into effect in the face of Colombo's resistance would have been negated by China and Russia at the UN Security Council. Nonetheless, Sri Lankans should be wary that it should not be said of them what the Latin historian Tacitus had written centuries ago, that they had made solitude or silence and called it peace. There is an expectation in Europe and in the world that now that the Sri Lankan government has won the war, it must work harder towards winning the peace, or the future will judge this only as an Ozymandian moment that was not seized upon. It is anticipated that all concerned would remain focused on Sri Lanka to see how the victors are able to meet the challenges resulting from the end of the conflict.

The Europeans and others are well aware of Sri Lanka's great potential, both economic and political, to play a positive and constructive role in the region and in the world. In the past, Sri Lankans have helped shape some of the global norms and standards the world lives by today. One is reminded of their effective participation in many international fora, and their contributions on those occasions. This includes the development of the concept of the Indian Ocean as a Zone of Peace. They have had an enormous role in global thinking, progress, and stability. Europe and the world will now await the reengagement of Sri Lanka in sculpting the global future.

NEPAL AND BHUTAN

Nepal's European contacts were, and still are, largely through the United Kingdom. Ties between Britain and Nepal go back a couple of centuries, but it was a conscious policy of Britain 'not to colonize, but to partner and influence', in the words of former British Ambassador to Nepal Andrew Sparkes. It was the Treaty of Sugauli in March 1816 that established a formal relationship between Nepal and Britain as two independent states, confirmed by the 1923 Treaty by which London accepted Nepal as an independent country. Nepal became an important recruiting ground for the British Army of Gurkha troops, who fought valiantly for the British Empire during the two World Wars. The romance of the Himalayas always beckoned European adventuring climbers, including George Mallory, who died in his effort to climb the Everest, as he famously said, 'because it is there!' Today, Britain remains the largest single donor country for Nepal, providing around 150 million pounds sterling annually.

Nepal's formal ties with the EU began in 1975, and the EU-Nepal Cooperation Agreement was signed in 1996. Under its framework, EU-Nepal Joint Commission meetings take place on a biannual basis. The EU uses this forum to discuss with Nepal the existing political situation following the Maoist uprising and Nepal's democratic transition to a republic from a monarchy. The EU's primary focus is on three sectors: first, education, peace, and stability; second, trade facilitation; and third, economic capacity building. Between 2011 and 2013, EU development assistance amounted to 60 million euro. The EU also takes keen interest in such areas as the protection and promotion of human rights, food security, environmental conservation, safe migration, public finance management, and sustainable production and consumption practices. Nepal and the EU cooperate in disaster risk management, as well as adaptation and mitigation on climate change. The Europeans are appreciative of Nepal's role in the United Nations as a major provider of peace-keeping forces.

Bhutan was in a competitive relationship with the British East India Company from as early as the eighteenth century. Apprehensive of British intrusions, the Bhutan ruler *druk desi* signed a peace treaty with the British East India Company in 1774. Bhutan agreed to pay a symbolic tribute of five horses to the British and, more importantly, allowed the latter to harvest timber in Bhutan. However, boundary disputes continued; Bhutan sent an emissary to British Calcutta in 1787 and Britain despatched missions to Thimpu in 1815 and 1838, but those talks were inconclusive. Eventually, the Bhutan leader *Ponlop* of Tongsa, Ugyen Wangchuk, earned British favour by providing various services to secure the Anglo-Tibetan Convention of 1904.

Following the tradition inherited from the days of the British *raj*, Bhutan's foreign relations defer largely to India, and it was the first foreign destination in 2014 of the new Indian Prime Minister Narendra Modi. Nevertheless, Bhutan made an international impact by introducing democratic reforms and suggesting a new index of 'gross national happiness' at the United Nations as a yardstick of progress and development. This concept seeks to balance spiritual and material advancement through sustainable and equitable economic growth and development, preservation and sustainable use of the environment, promotion of cultural heritage, and good governance.

Though the EU does not have any permanent presence in Thimpu, in 2015 the EU and Bhutan will celebrate thirty years of diplomatic relations that began in 1985. The first EU-Bhutan Strategy Paper allocated 15 million euro in assistance with priority accorded to renewable natural resources, especially livestock production and integrated pest management. Support was also given to health and traditional medicine, trade development, and export diversification. The next Strategy Paper (2007–2013) mainly focused on the renewable natural resources sector, and good governance, democratization, and trade facilitation were listed for support. In the financial cycle beginning January 2014, development assistance is planned to be enhanced significantly; the idea would be to buttress Bhutan's own policy of reducing rural poverty by creating income-generating activities in the villages and improving farm-to-market access.

Along with Nepal and Bangladesh, Bhutan is in the UN list of least developed countries, and, therefore, like the two others, a recipient of EU preferential treatment in trade.

BANGLADESH

The historic relations between the old Bengal, of which present-day Bangladesh is a part, date back to the eighteenth century. Following the Battle of Plassey in 1757, the British gradually expanded their sway throughout Bengal and beyond and made Calcutta the capital of the Indian Empire, which remained so until it was moved to Delhi in 1911. The European influence on Bengal was mostly British, though there were minor French and Danish outposts as well. The so-called Bengal Renaissance, the intellectual efflorescence of the cultured Bengali middle-class or *bhadralok*, owed much to British influence. This was markedly so even in the works of the doyen of Bengali literature, Rabindranath Tagore, and Irish strains in many of his musical works are discernible.

With the emergence of East Pakistan in 1947, and thereafter of Bangladesh in 1971, the British influence socially, politically, and economically continued. Bangladeshi diaspora in Britain made substantive contributions to the development of the host culture; writers like Zia Haider and Tahmima Khan are examples. It was the Bangladeshis who rendered *chicken tandoori masala* the most favoured pub fare in England. British politicians of Bangladeshi origin today sit in both the Houses of Parliament and hold several local council mayorships. This is also the case with the Bangladeshi diaspora in Europe, though less prominently so.

The relations between the EEC/EU and Bangladesh are grounded in three major documents that are dated 1973, 1976, and 2001. The last was the most substantial one that included political dialogue. In 2007, the EU drafted its Country Strategy Paper that covered the period until 2013. This identified the following as key challenges confronting Bangladesh: the continued struggle in addressing the structural problems of poverty and to achieve the UN MDGs by the target date of 2015; good governance problems that affect the efficient and effective delivery of basic public services to the poor; and potential economic and political shortfalls following the ending of the WTO textile quota system and the need to diversify the industrial base and to improve the enabling environment for business. It is noteworthy that the document was prepared acknowledging Bangladesh's own response to the challenges contained in its Poverty Reduction Strategy Paper crafted in 2005.

The EU determined that its impact would be maximized and there would be more effective use of resources if development commitments were concentrated in three focal areas: human and social development, good governance and human rights, and economic and trade development; and two non-focal areas: environment and disaster management, and food security and nutrition.

The EU's decision to provide unimpeded market access through the policy of 'everything but arms' has been a great boon for Bangladesh's garment exports. Together with the American, the European market has turned Bangladesh's garment industry into the locomotive of economic growth of that country, helping to poise it on the threshold of being perceived as an emerging Asian economy that takes full advantage of the preferential trading system. The EU is currently the destination of 48 percent of Bangladesh's total exports. As for foreign aid over the next three years, the EU will provide Bangladesh with $413 million for support to health, education, food security, and the rural development sectors. This is part of the plan to assist Bangladesh achieve by 2015 the MDGs set out by the United Nations. While many developed and developing countries are critical of the EU's policy of agricultural subsidy, it ironically renders grain cheaper for a net food importer like Bangladesh. In the setting up of Bangladesh's National Human Rights Commission, European support has been invaluable, as also in the election process in 2008. Having held ministerial office in the government during this period, I would like to underscore the constructive nature of my relationship with the then-EU Commissioner, Austria's Benita Ferrero-Waldner.

THE EUROPEAN CONSENSUS

The EU's development policy, applicable not just to Bangladesh, generally flowed from what has been called 'the European Consensus' that was adopted by the European Parliament in December 2005. For the first time, it provided for a common vision guiding both the member states individually and the EU collectively. The foremost objective of the EU's development policy, it was agreed, would be the eradication of poverty in the context of sustainable development, including the pursuit of the MDGs. Several other elements in line with the standards, norms, and values of the European ethos, as broadly perceived, were to be emphasized. These included respect for human rights, fundamental freedoms, peace, democracy, good governance, gender equality, the rule of law, solidarity and justice, and commitment to effective multilateralism.

The EU was also at pains to demonstrate that its values were consistent with global ones. For instance, the document for Bangladesh stressed the importance of strengthening the social dimension of globalization and in order to do so, it cited in full the relevant article of the 'Outcome Document' of the UN summit of world leaders held in 2005. In it, the member-states committed themselves to 'strongly support fair globalization and resolve to make the goals of full and productive employment and decent work for all, including for women and young people, a central objective of our national and international policies as well as our national development strategies, including poverty reduction strategies, as part of our efforts to win the MDGs'.

Following the Bangladesh elections of January 2014, which gave the ruling Awami League a virtual walkover to power with the main opposition Bangladesh Nationalist Party not participating, political relations between the Dhaka government and Brussels suffered some strains. The Europeans were not pleased with the manner in which the polls were held, and they let it be known both in private and in public. But a working relationship continued, a certain lack of warmth notwithstanding, and Europe and Bangladesh continue to engage each other across a broad range of activities.

A DEVELOPED ASIAN STATE: SINGAPORE

It would be interesting in passing to examine how Europe relates to another type of Asian state, not a developing nation such as those of South Asia, but a developed entity, Singapore. Once again, what comes to the fore would be Singapore's British heritage in terms of the mutual relationship between the island-state and Europe. Stamford Raffles, who worked for the East India Company with its Asian headquarters in Calcutta, the capital of British India, founded Singapore in 1819. He did not belong to any of the three major Singaporean communities: Chinese, Indian, or Malay. Despite, or probably because of, this, he continues to be regarded as the 'founder' of modern Singapore as a useful compromise, and Raffles has become a name associated with anything 'gold standard' in this island-state.

On 31 August 1963, Singapore declared its independence from the United Kingdom, but continued to remain in the mainstream of the British ethos as its leader Lee Kuan Yew shepherded the country from the third to the first world. Contemporary Singapore is highly respected in Europe as a model of efficiency, with former British Foreign Secretary William Hague saying, 'Openness to ideas, enterprise and innovation; cultural soft power and an ability to work cooperatively with other states are among the greatest attributes for success in today's world, and Singapore has these in abundance'.

Commercial contacts between Europe and Singapore are numerous. Over 9,300 EU companies have set themselves up in Singapore, using the city-state as a hub to serve the region. Over thirty thousand British expatriates live and work in Singapore in more than seven hundred companies like Rolls Royce and GlaxoSmithKline, investing billions of pounds. The United Kingdom continues to attract Singaporean students, and over five thousand of them are currently enrolled in British universities. English in Singapore continues to be the *lingua franca* that links the three communities.

Unlike South Asia, where the EU's major economic role is the provider of development assistance, with Singapore it is basically a partner in trade. The negotiations for an EU-Singapore Free Trade Agreement were concluded in 2012. Apart from its impact in improving EU-Singapore trade relations, it has the potential to lay the ground for the EU to engage with the dynamic region of Southeast and East Asia. It also opens the door ultimately to an agreement in the regional framework with the ASEAN group. Singapore is by far the EU's largest trade and investment partner in the region, with trade in goods exceeding 52 billion euro, and trade in services topping 28 billion euro.

SOME PERTINENT CRITICISMS

There are some criticisms to be made of the EU as well—firstly, its firmly held and propagated view that its values are universal. Sometimes this is not an easy sell to partners, particularly in parts of Asia. The latter at times stress their own values that flow from a mixture of Confucianism and other Asian spiritual traits that have underscored hard work, family and company loyalty, and moral high grounds that many also see as the principal determinants behind Asia's recent economic successes. Secondly, the EU has not been able to put its own economic house in order. The eurozone crisis and the problems confronting Greece, Italy, and Spain in particular have brought little credit to the EU. In fact, it has encouraged some 'decoupling' proponents in Asia, who argue that greater safety may lie in emerging Asia restricting its exposure to Europe. Thirdly, despite a sophisticated development cooperation strategy, the EU is seen as a lightweight political player. It has not been successful in projecting itself as a serious diplomatic protagonist on the international scene, the Treaty of Lisbon notwithstanding. Other nation-states, including the country examined at some length here, Bangladesh, still prefer to deal with individual European states such as the United Kingdom, France, Sweden, or Germany. The Brussels-based EU leadership has not yet been able to leave as decisive a footprint on world policy as the leaderships residing in London, Paris, or Berlin.

The EU in its trade and development assistance to South Asia, especially to the least developed countries, has been both generous and welcome, but in its political interventions, it has been less admirable. There is little doubt that despite noble intentions and ideals, the EU has often been maladroit in its dealing with many South Asian countries. It has brought its relations with Sri Lanka to almost a point of rupture by trying to present its views forcefully on post-conflict settlement, driven by its

media and Tamil diaspora voters in member countries. A more persuasive and less belligerent approach would have paid richer dividends,
though it is probable that with the election in January 2015 of a new Sri
Lankan president, Maithripala Sirisena, the degree of mutual animosity
will abate. Its misgivings over the Bangladesh elections of 2014, which
brought it into sharp disagreement with the ruling Awami League
government, did not take into account the fact that the one-sided election
was a result of a boycott by the main opposition party on debatable
grounds, and its dealings with Pakistan, a so-called non-NATO ally in the
war on terror in Afghanistan, causes deep suspicions of double standards
in India, which contends that the EU turns a blind eye to Pakistan's
blatant sponsorship of international terrorism.

CONCLUSION

In the 1930s, Japanese economist Kaname Akamatsu developed a concept
known as the 'Flying Geese Paradigm'. This postulated a model, which
he developed in greater detail later, of international division of labour
based on dynamic comparative advantage. In other words, manufacturing or production would be relocated from more advanced countries to
less advanced ones over time. All countries would progress in the formation of a flock of flying geese, with some leading and others following.
Those following would gather strength and momentum from the wind
generated from the flapping of the wings of the geese in the lead, and at
times shifting places, with lead geese being supplanted by others from
behind moving forward faster. While formulating this paradigm, Akamatsu might have had Japan and the rest of East Asia in mind, but in
modern times China and other parts of emerging Asia would be a relevant scenario. And Europe and South Asia appear to have a relationship
that is not totally dissimilar. Historically, Europe has been leading, and
economically and technologically continues to lead, but South Asia has
been catching up, and in a few instances, might be said to be overtaking.

While Europe–South Asia relations have many features that are enduring and durable, an obvious critique of these connections is that they
cannot be fully and mutually rewarding without the involvement of
America, which is really the elephant in the room, whether seen or un-
seen. Historically, the fact that the United States was not a colonial power
gives it an advantage in terms of an appropriate setting to bilateral relations. After South Asian independence, the United States became, almost
inadvertently, a party to the intra-mural South Asian issues by adopting
Pakistan as a formal ally during the Cold War through defence pacts such
as the South East Asian Treaty Organization and Central Treaty Organization. The American stance shifted in India's favour during the Sino-
Indian war of 1962 and tilted back towards Pakistan during the Bangla-

desh war of 1971. Links with India eventually received a fillip with the 2005 civil nuclear agreement. The American presence in Afghanistan, along with supporting European NATO members, and its war on terror against the Taliban in the 'Af-Pak' (a neologism coined by American bureaucracy to designate Afghanistan and Pakistan as a single area of strategic operation) region again brought the United States to South Asia's doorstep. Today, Washington is apt to view India as a possible counterbalance to China in its 'pivot' to Asia policy, though New Delhi is wary of seeing itself projected in that role. Where South Asia, as a whole, would be willing to cooperate with both Europe and America is to stem the march, both militarily and ideologically, of the new though rapidly advancing danger of the Islamist 'caliphate' created by the so-called Islamic State of Iraq and Syria. Therefore, delinking Europe from America completely in examining Europe–South Asian linkages would not be reasonable.

The EU remains an important entity in the global scene despite the criticisms offered earlier. Slowly, a European identity is emerging. While its engagement with Asia, in particular most countries of South Asia, is still concentrated on development cooperation, as its relations with Pakistan, Sri Lanka, Nepal, Bhutan, and Bangladesh demonstrate, emerging Asia, which is on the rise, is also beginning to acquire certain commonalities, working through its own groupings such as SAARC and ASEAN[7]. Eventually, there will be three main supra-states in the world: America, Europe, and emerging Asia. This trilateral arrangement will become the prime movers in the global matrix. But the struggle of the last two to attain the goals of a common identity will take some more decades yet, and until then international relations will largely comprise conventional inter-state interactions.

NOTES

1. This was the 'Partition of Bengal' of 1905 effected by Lord Curzon, the British governor-general. Ostensibly, it had a two-fold objective, according to the minutes made by Lord Curzon himself: It was the 'reinvigoration of Assam and relief of Bengal', which had become too large and politically sensitive to govern as a single entity. So, Eastern Bengal was hived off from West Bengal and joined to Assam to create a new province, which had a Muslim majority population. In fact, it was the first significant step towards the recognition of the separate identity of the Bengali Muslims, ultimately leading to the creation of (East) Pakistan in 1947 and Bangladesh in 1971. However, the 1905 partition caused convulsive outbursts from the burgeoning political forces of the Calcutta 'bhadralok' or mainly Hindu middle class, and was annulled by the British in 1911.

2. Of late, comparisons have been drawn between the current situation in Asia to that which existed in Europe before the Great War of 1914, with China being seen as a rising and unsatisfied power, as were Germany and Austria in the early twentieth century, pitted against the more mature power of Japan combined with that of the United States, as was the case with Britain and France in Europe at that time. The fear is that apprehensions of perceived power gap may lead to a major conflict, also known

as the Thucydides trap, named after the Greek historian who had explained the Peloponnesian war in these terms: 'When Athens grew strong, there was great fear in Sparta'.

3. Rather than linking up with friends from the newly post-colonial countries, to whom Nehruvian India was giving a modicum of leadership on the matrix of the non-aligned movement, comprising mainly countries of Africa, Asia, and Latin America with a pro-Soviet bias, Pakistan chose to directly join the Western military alliances of the Baghdad Pact and Southeast Asian Treaty Organization. Pakistani Prime Minister H. S. Suhrawardy wryly commented on the newly independent countries, assessing their power in terms of being 'zero plus zero equals zero'.

4. Incidentally, the world's largest NGO, BRAC, and one of the most renowned, Grameen Bank, are located in Bangladesh. NGOs throughout South Asia have been actively contributing to areas of development, including health, education, and poverty alleviation. NGOs are also active in the spheres of human rights, women's empowerment, and security.

5. It is the contention of the author Robert D. Kaplan that the Greater Indian Ocean, stretching eastwards from the Horn of Africa past the Arabian peninsula, the Iranian plateau, and the Indian subcontinent, all the way to the Indonesian archipelago and beyond, may comprise a map as iconic to the twenty-first century as Europe was to the twentieth. He elaborates this thesis in his book *Monsoon: The Indian Ocean and the Future of American Power* (Random House, 2011).

6. Nirj Deva contested for the office of secretary-general of the United Nations, not as a candidate from either the United Kingdom or Sri Lanka, but as a nominee of Fiji, demonstrating the widespread influence of some of the South Asian diaspora members.

7. Contrary to some Western views, Asia's, particularly South Asia's, contribution to the intellectual world is not just spirituality and mysticism. It has the tradition of scepticism and reasoning, sometimes manifest in a more powerful manner. This paves the way for a future Asian and South Asian role in creating a matrix for material development. Nobel Laureate economist Amartya Sen has made strong assertions on these lines in his work *The Argumentative Indian: Writings on Indian History, Culture and Identity* (New York: Farrar, Straus, and Giroux, 2005). One of the results of cross-current interactions with societies such as those of Singapore is buttressing the influence of Confucianism on South Asian work ethics, rendering them more result-oriented.

THREE

Europe and Southeast Asia

The Nature of Contemporary Relations

Evi Fitriani

Relations between Asia and Europe go back more than a millennium, when the two regions were connected through what are called the 'Silk Routes'. Trading networks through land and sea developed between China in the East and Alexandria and Rome in the West between the second century BC and the seventh century AD[1]. Over land, there was the Northern Silk Route that connected Xian in China to Kashgar in Central Asia and on to Europe, or Luoyang in China to Gaza, which was then supplemented by the maritime route over the Mediterranean Sea to Rome[2]. The Maritime Silk Route was believed to start in Guangzhou in China and went through Southeast Asia, the Indian Ocean, the East and West coasts of the Indian Peninsula, and the Arabian Sea, at which point it was bifurcated to the Persian Gulf and to the Red Sea, but they again both ended at Rome[3]. The trading routes from China to Europe were vital for global trade during the later centuries of the first millennium AD until the fifteenth century, and they promoted wealth and civilization along the way. Southeast Asia was a very important commercial hub in this period.

These trade connections were altered by European colonialism after the sixteenth century, which in turn lasted until the middle of the twentieth century, when Europe was ravaged by the Second World War. The European expansionist countries of Portugal, Spain, Netherlands, Britain, and France not only took over the maritime trade routes from the Arabs and Indians but also occupied almost all of Southeast Asia. Monopolizing the commerce of indigenous goods was not sufficient for those European powers, as they also colonized Southeast Asia and practiced economic exploitation either through extractive industries or plantations. The impacts of Asian trade and colonization on European prosperity were obvious; they also stimulated the European shipping industries and an improvement of navigation techniques, besides provoking intense competition among the European powers themselves[4]. However, the adverse impacts of European imperialism on the Southeast Asian countries were more structural, as they created unhealthy dependence on the economic connections with the European countries. According to Narine, '[C]olonialism oriented the colonialized countries, politically and economically, toward their colonial masters rather than each other, a separation that continued for centuries (in some cases) until after the Second World War'[5].

After the Second World War, almost all the Southeast Asian countries gained their independence, though some were as a result of intense struggles, and the trade connections and economic linkages with the 'mother countries' of Europe underwent changes. After recovering from the calamities of the Second World War, Europe kept developing as one of the major global economic centres, while Southeast Asian countries strove to turn their newly won freedoms into economic development and social welfare. Some of these independent Southeast Asian countries contrived to maintain economic ties with the former colonialists while others tried to find other patrons such as the United States and Japan. Currently, the countries in Southeast Asia include Indonesia, Philippines, Thailand, Malaysia, Singapore, Brunei, Vietnam, Cambodia, Myanmar, Laos, and Timor Leste, and the first ten countries are members of the Association of Southeast Asian Nations (ASEAN).

The rise of China since the first decade of this century has not only changed the economic orientation of Southeast Asian countries but has also integrated East Asian economies more deeply, and China's growth serves to generate economic development in Southeast Asia and beyond[6]. The development of the ASEAN Economic Community (AEC) and the establishment of a free trade agreement (FTA) between the China and ASEAN have created an even greater integration among ASEAN economies and stronger relations with China. Recently, while financial crises have diminished the economic status of traditional world economic leaders like the United States and European countries, China and some Asian economies have become a powerful engine for the world's growth.

During the past several years, European countries, either independently or as the collective European Union (EU), have actively sought engagement with Southeast Asian countries, and there have been numerous discussions and studies regarding the roles that the Europeans might play in Asia. Thus, the contemporary relationship between the two regions is of considerable interest as the putative 'Asian century' could be dawning while the European countries are looking for beneficial opportunities in a new approach towards Asia.

This chapter discusses the character of relations between the European and Southeast Asian countries. The question is whether the contemporary European approach to Southeast Asian countries is any indication of a changing structure in their relationship. Does the present economic development in Southeast Asia provide a challenge to the European economic prowess that was created through trade monopoly and colonialism in the past? The purpose will be to find an applicable framework to explain the state of relations between Europe and Southeast Asia. Accordingly, this chapter develops in three sections: the results of European colonialism on Southeast Asia, developments in Southeast Asia, and finding Europe's place in a possible Asian century.

THE LEGACY OF EUROPEAN COLONIALISM ON SOUTHEAST ASIAN COUNTRIES

Except for Thailand, all Southeast Asian countries were colonized by one, two, or more European nations, and this historical setting for Asia-Europe relations created a structural economic pattern that also shaped their post-colonial relationship. On one hand, European colonization helped to incorporate the Southeast Asian countries into the capitalist economic system that was developed from the start by the Europeans, and during the colonial period trade between Europe and Southeast Asia grew robustly. Commercial vessels busily connected the two continents, especially from the maritime nations of the Netherlands, Britain, and France. In addition, European economic activities in those colonized countries brought forward some new developments such as the introduction of new crops and plantation products, and the establishment of unprecedented infrastructure for commerce and the plantation industries. One of the historians of Southeast Asia writes:

> Southeast Asia in the period of less than one hundred years changed from being a region in which export played a relatively minor role and subsistence farming was essentially dominant, to a vital area in the world economy as a whole as its exports met European and American demands that had been fuelled by the changes following the industrial revolution[7].

The text above suggests that the incorporation of Southeast Asian countries into the European trading system established the importance of those Asian nations in the global trading chain, and the commercial links that connected Southeast Asia and Europe that were built up by the colonial powers allowed the former to take part in the latter's economic boom during and after the Industrial Revolution. Concomitantly, these

Asian nations were introduced to European technology, modernity, and notably, Western value and knowledge systems[8].

On the other hand, the position of Southeast Asian countries as supplicant colonial states positioned them as dependent actors in the global economic system. It was the Europeans, and not the Asians, who determined what items were to be exported, to whom, and at what price. It is no wonder that trading centres of exclusively Asian commodities came into being in certain European cities, and these trading centres thoroughly controlled the prices as well as the quantity and quality of the products they wanted to purchase. As the capitalist system was in place, the European colonial rulers mainly focused on products that could earn a high price in the European markets, such as gold and tin. After the nineteenth century, the European colonial powers also introduced new plantation industries that produced highly priced commodities such as sugar, coffee, tobacco, tea, pepper, maize, and palm oil[9], and some of these new plantations were introduced by the use of force. In the colonial history of Indonesia, for example, the Dutch colonialists were known to apply *cultuur-stelsel* or the infamous forced cultivation system in the eighteenth and nineteenth centuries in Java and Maluku, by which farmers were obliged to plant high-value crops at the expense of their staple foods. Despite its important and growing role as suppliers of highly priced commodities for their European colonial masters, the Southeast Asian countries did not enjoy the benefits of welfare as the capital was accumulated only in Europe. It is arguable that the European economic strength was built mainly through trade monopoly in the exploitative colonial economy.

In the post-colonial period, despite their success in obtaining political independence, the Southeast Asian countries were hardly able to establish their economic sovereignty. Countries like Malaysia and Singapore continued their close relations with Britain[10], but Indonesia tried to cut its dependence on the European market and investment through some domestic adjustments. However, the global economic structure after the Second World War remained in the hands of Western countries, including and especially the Europeans. The economic features of this period can best be summarized by four characteristics. First, the Southeast Asian countries remained the source of cheap raw materials and natural resources. Secondly, their dependence on the European market caused great vulnerability on the prices of their export commodities such as oil, tin, pepper, rubber, and coffee—exports which were often the main source of their revenues. Thirdly, Southeast Asian countries continued to remain a favoured investment destination for European capital. Fourthly, the Second World War led to the establishment of the Bretton Woods institutions such as the World Bank, International Monetary Fund, and the General Agreement on Tariffs and Trade, the last of which, in 1995, transformed itself into the World Trade Organization (WTO). These trade and financial institutions reflected the developed countries' domination over the global financial and trading system.

The post-colonial relationship between the Southeast Asian nations and the European countries varied from case to case, but in general the Asian countries enjoyed a special economic relationship with their former colonial overlords, in essence because such ties had been established during the long colonial era. Fundamentally, the same dependent economic relationship continued despite the political sovereignty of the Southeast Asian countries. In addition, perhaps because of the deep socialization of European values, norms, and knowledge systems during the imperial era, consciously or unconsciously, the newly independent Southeast Asian countries tended to treat the European countries as a reference point. This is apparent when they refer to the EU as a basic reference and inspiration for their own regional integration institution, namely the ASEAN. Indeed, some sections of society in the region continue to look towards Europe as an exemplar for lifestyle, fashion, and the development of science and technology. Likewise, the attitudes of the Europeans also did not alter much: there continues the tendency of Europeans to lecture Asians and to be unduly assertive in their interactions with the people of this region, a trend that has been in evidence not only in formal interactions such as in inter-governmental forums, but also in informal encounters between non-governmental circles[11].

RECENT DEVELOPMENTS IN SOUTHEAST ASIA

The contemporary reemergence of China has created a new sense of confidence among the Southeast Asian countries. The dependent position in the world economic structure that they inherited from the colonial period, and which has largely continued in the post-colonial era, is being questioned and brought under scrutiny, while the Southeast Asian economies have notably strengthened as the consequence of the Chinese growth. China has ongoing territorial disputes with four Southeast Asian countries, but despite this, China has become the predominant trading partner for all the countries in Southeast Asia.

The newly independent Southeast Asian countries made efforts to develop their economic relations with other patrons, such as the United States[12] and Japan. Their interactions with the United States were natural because that country had become the world's top economic power after the end of the Second World War, and until the early years of the 1990s, these ties were framed under either a strategic alliance format or a partnership in the context of the Cold War. The United States provided not only a security 'umbrella' but also facilitated economic access to its market, which currently, despite its immense foreign debt, still remains the biggest economy in the world. In addition, from the 1970s to the 1990s,

Southeast Asian nations developed closer economic relations with Japan through the pattern of 'flying geese', in which the Japanese industries and robust economy generated the momentum for strong economic development in Southeast Asia[13]. Accordingly, Japan and the United States became the main economic partners of Southeast Asian countries until the Asian financial crisis intervened at the end of the 1990s.

Nevertheless, the close economic connections between the Southeast Asian countries and the United States and Japan did not necessarily mean that the former had managed to overcome their dependent position in the world economic system. Indeed, these two developed-country patrons were in the same mould generically as the former European imperial countries and part of the Western economic international system, as they are among those economic leaders that benefited from artificially cheap raw materials from Southeast Asia. Together with the European countries, the United States and Japan also dominate international financial and development forums like the aforementioned Bretton Woods institutions and the Asian Development Bank, which were the financial institutions relied upon by Southeast Asian nations for macroeconomic advice, infrastructure financing, and budgetary support. Accordingly, despite having important new economic partners and a more limited economic engagement with the European countries from the 1960s to the 1990s, the Southeast Asian countries' dependent position in the world economic system remained largely unaffected by the new arrangements.

The emergence of China through its impressive economic development now provides an impetus to the development of Southeast Asian economies, and China's rapid growth has encouraged more dynamism in the economic activities in its entire neighbouring region, including Southeast Asia. In effect, China has not only become a regional economic force but also a major global power, and since 2010, China has replaced Japan as the second largest economy in the world[14], surpassed so far only by the United States. Due to the regional dynamic in East Asia and the strategic competition in the Asia Pacific, China perceives the Southeast Asian countries to be important and strategic partners. China is the first ASEAN dialogue partner that signed the Treaty of Amity and Cooperation with the ASEAN countries, and the latter's economic relations have been further strengthened through the China-ASEAN FTA (CAFTA) that was started partially in 2004 and fully in 2010. As a result, China has become the leading trade partner of the Southeast Asian countries since 2009. From 2002 to 2013, trade between ASEAN countries and China grew from $50 billion to $442 billion[15]. In this way, China has not only proved to be an indispensable alternative partner for countries in Southeast Asia; it has become a new economic pole star in the whole region.

The current economic growth in Southeast Asia is not only driven by the Chinese factor but also by the movement towards an ASEAN Economic Community (AEC) that was launched officially in 2003. This initiative to integrate the Southeast Asian countries into a common market was not meant to create an inward-looking fortress but to establish a regional-based production, to strengthen the region's competitiveness, and to participate in the global value chain. The result of this initiative can be seen in the trade figures whereby intra-ASEAN trade and investment have grown apace[16]. Having said that, it still appears that the China factor, even more than the AEC, has added considerable weight in supporting the current revival of the Southeast Asian economies.

The close economic links between China and the Southeast Asian countries are not similar to the relations between the Southeast Asian countries with the European countries, the United States, or Japan. Until recently, China was considered a developing country and, like the Southeast Asian countries, was also a dependent participant in the global economic system. This common position has encouraged China and the Southeast Asian countries to create a synergy to struggle for the interests of the developing countries in the world system and to resolve the exploitative nature of the world capitalist system that they had inherited from the colonial period. Their joint efforts include addressing what is considered to be unfair trade regulations in the WTO, and calling for the assumption of greater responsibility on the part of the Western developed countries to tackle issues such as global warming and the effects of climate change. Certainly, the cooperation existing between China and the Southeast Asian countries is not without its own problems, but the two partners often find that they share the same agenda with regard to what are considered the established and traditional economic powers: the United States, Japan, and the EU.

In most cases, the close ties between China and the ASEAN countries have benefited both the parties. For example, China supported ASEAN when the Southeast Asian countries put forward a proposal to accept Myanmar into the Asia-Europe Meeting in 2004, which had been rejected by the EU countries. As a result, the European countries eventually conceded. In addition, China also played an indispensable role when the ASEAN Plus Three, which consists of ten ASEAN countries with China, Japan, and South Korea, established a multilateral swap agreement under the Chiang Mai Initiative as a response to the International Monetary Fund and Western countries, including the Europeans, during and after the Asian financial crisis. China and ASEAN are also the promoters of the Regional Comprehensive Economic Partnership (RCEP) which in the 2012 East Asia Summit was launched to integrate all ASEAN's existing FTAs into one major scheme. The negotiation of the RCEP was started in 2013 and is presently targeted to conclude by the end of 2015. The RCEP includes the Southeast Asian countries and Japan, China, Korea, India, Australia, and New Zealand. When it materializes, it would account for more than 30 percent of the global gross domestic product and cover about 45 percent of the world's population.

Considering the unrealized potential that has not yet been exploited in their partnership, China and the Southeast Asian countries have agreed to enhance their relationship, including by an objective to achieve $1 trillion worth of trade exchanges by 2020. Recently, China and ASEAN countries have discussed two proposals that were put forward by China's leaders in 2013: an upgraded CAFTA and the twenty-first-century maritime silk route. These two initiatives could unleash the promise of Southeast Asian countries and China that are inhabited by one-third of the world population, and China is predicted to overtake the United States as the world's largest economy in few decades. China has acknowledged that its growth can only be sustained and furthered through closer relations with its neighbouring countries, and especially those to its South; this is the reason why China has placed Southeast Asian countries as a priority in its new neighbourhood policy.

It is necessary to add that the economic performance of the Southeast Asian countries, and the special ties they share with China, have enhanced both their profiles globally. As a result, some global key powers, including the United States and the EU countries, have tried to make approaches to the Asian regional partners, and since the first years of the present decade, the United States has tried to strengthen its position in the East and Southeast Asian regions through its 'pivot' or 'rebalance' policy. This policy is designed to facilitate the United States in reviving its military alliances with its traditional allies in the region, to build naval facilities in Singapore and Western Australia, to place rotating troops in Darwin, to enhance political cooperation with regional countries, and to strengthen its economic presence through a new trade grouping, the Trans-Pacific Partnership. Apparently, the American initiative is not primarily aimed at taking advantage of the economic developments in Southeast Asia; it is mainly directed at the growing China influence and the various flash points in the East and South China seas. At the same time, world attention has recently been directed to East Asia and Southeast Asia because of several circumstances, such as the US-China competitive relations; tensions between China on one hand and Japan, Vietnam, and Philippines on the other; the United States' pivot to East and Southeast Asia; the close relations between China and the regional countries through the CAFTA and RCEP; implicit competition between Trans-Pacific Partnership and RCEP; and the economic performance of the ASEAN community and Southeast Asian countries.

Economic progress in Southeast Asia in the 2000s and 2010s has also attracted the attention of the EU member countries. In 2007, the European Commission launched a policy paper on a *New Partnership for the 21st Century with Asia* that aims to enhance economic relations with India, South Korea, and ASEAN countries. In 2013, the European Commission published the sixth edition of a brochure entitled *EU-ASEAN: Natural Partners* that tried to outline its efforts to enhance ties between the European and the Southeast Asian countries. It is asserted that the EU and ASEAN are natural partners that share a common DNA that the forty-year relationship has nourished. A remarkable turn in ASEAN-EU relations is the EU accession to the ASEAN's Treaty of Amity and Cooperation through an official signing of the document by the then EU High Representative for Foreign Affairs and Security Policy Catherine Ashton in July 2012 in Phnom Penh. The Treaty of Amity and Cooperation includes the ASEAN principles in conducting inter-states relations, one of them being not to interfere in other countries' domestic political affairs, the same principle that had often been subject to criticism by the European countries previously.

In addition, during the past several years, there have been numerous high-level visits from Europe to the Southeast Asian region and various approaches to governments, peoples, and institutions undertaken by the EU establishment. Perhaps not unrelated to the American pivot, EU leaders have on several occasions praised the developments in the region and expressed the European interest to enhance relations with the Southeast Asian countries. One of these visits was by the France's foreign minister, Laurent Fabius, in August 2013. In his speech entitled 'France's policy in Asia' at the ASEAN Secretariat in Jakarta, Fabius said:

> A lot has been said about the US 'pivot' to Asia. I don't know if it's the right word. France, too, has undertaken a 'pivot'. Not to 'blindly follow the crowd' but because France wants to be present where tomorrow's world is built. Asia-Pacific will clearly be central to the 21st century. And also because France is part of the Asia-Oceania space. . . . Our pivot is more diplomatic[17].

Fabius highlighted President Hollande's participation in the Asia-Europe Meeting in Laos and the French prime minister's three visits to five ASEAN countries. He also acknowledged that although ASEAN and its member states were a top priority, France was not still sufficiently active in Southeast Asia. In fact, he was France's first foreign minister to visit Indonesia after a gap of seventeen years. German Chancellor Angela Merkel and British Prime Minister David Cameron have also visited countries in the region in recent years.

In March 2014, the then chief operating officer of the European External Action Service, David O'Sullivan, gave a speech entitled 'EU Priorities in Asia' in which he stated:

> Asia matters to Europe—and will do so even more in the future. We know that recovery at home depends on the ability to harness growth and open new markets, many of which are in Asia. But Asia also matters to Europe in political and security terms[18].

O'Sullivan highlighted the importance of ASEAN countries to the EU and subsequently put forward the EU's intention to play a more active role in Asia and to expand its relationship with ASEAN.

Moreover, European scholars and think tanks have begun to discover rationality in the EU's positive approach to the Southeast Asian countries, and emphasized the importance of Southeast Asian geopolitics as well as its geoeconomic characteristics[19]. There have been many seminars and roundtable discussions that have tried to identify what kind of roles the EU in particular, and Europeans in general, could or should play in Southeast Asia. Nevertheless, the economic aspect still appears to be more prominent and since 2008, the EU has proactively tried to improve its economic relations with ASEAN countries. In the beginning, it set itself an ambitious goal to establish a region-to-region FTA with ASEAN, but in recent years the EU could only negotiate FTAs with a few individual ASEAN countries.

In sum then, the various positive developments in Southeast Asia and the perhaps overblown rhetoric of the Asian century has attracted the European countries to look for incremental economic opportunities, especially because of the deep financial crisis impacting the European Monetary Union. However, on some occasions, the European political leaders and scholars have also expressed a European intention to play a more active role in Asia over and beyond the economic field, and in this connection, one may question if the EU, after considering the methods its main economic competitor has taken up in Asia, also thinks it needs an economic and strategic 'pivot' to Asia. Whether or not a pivot is indeed later undertaken by the EU countries to Southeast Asia, some material may be relevant to show the contemporary level of European engagement in the region.

FINDING EUROPE'S PLACE IN AN ASIAN CENTURY

As indicated previously, in the post-independence period some Southeast Asian countries maintained close relations with their 'mother country', while others attempted to terminate the formal links almost thoroughly. Nevertheless, the economic connections inherited from the colonial period proved enduring and tended to prevail. In terms of ties between regional institutions, the ASEAN and the EU started their relationship in the 1970s but political problems disrupted these inter-regional relations until the middle of the 1990s, and after a series of economic and political setbacks, the ties have revived slowly in this decade[20]. In this section of the chapter, the activities of the European countries in Southeast Asia are observed through the mechanism of the EU, first in the economy, and second, outside the economic field. Despite being afflicted by the ongoing financial crisis, the EU remains an economic power in

Southeast Asia. It is one of the major trading partners, the main source of foreign investment, and the main provider of development assistance for certain regional countries.

With a share of around 10 percent of ASEAN external trade, the EU countries constitute the third largest trading partner for the ASEAN countries, behind China and Japan. For the European countries also, the Southeast Asian countries are the third largest trade partner after China and the United States. The countries from these two regions traded goods and services to the value of $265 billion in 2011[21] but this fell to $238 billion in 2013[22]. The goods that European countries export to Southeast Asia include machinery and transport equipment, chemicals and related products, and miscellaneous manufactured products, as well as food and livestock; the Southeast Asian countries export spare parts like screws, bolts, and tin plates, which do not need sophisticated technology, and primary products like timber, rubber, coffee, tea, and palm oil[23]. Two-way trade between ASEAN and the EU has generally been on a satisfactory rise. The ASEAN countries enjoy a surplus in the trade relationship with the EU countries, but the surplus has decreased lately due to a reduction in exports. In 2013, the surplus shrank to 15.5 billion euro[24] or approximately $20.8 billion.

In addition, the EU countries as a whole are the largest source of foreign direct investment (FDI) into the ASEAN member-states, with an investment amounting to 24 percent of the total foreign investment in ASEAN countries in 2010. The European states take by far the leading position, surpassing all their close economic competitors, namely the United States, Japan, and China. But European FDI in Southeast Asian nations was still below the capital that Southeast Asian countries invested in each other, though collectively the EU countries remain the largest extra-regional investor in ASEAN member-states. Although Europe continues to suffer an acute financial crisis, European investment in Southeast Asian countries still increased significantly from 2009 to 2011. During this period, the European share in the total FDI to ASEAN countries was 17.1 percent[25] and amounted to $43 billion[26], and this level of investment is far above that of other economic giants like China. Most of the European FDI is invested in the manufacturing sector, followed by trade, agriculture, finance, services, and real estate, as shown in figure 3.1.

Thus, collectively, the European countries are key actors in foreign investment in Southeast Asia, and in this connection not least, the Southeast Asian countries cannot but be aware of the economic weight of the EU member-states.

In terms of foreign development assistance, the EU has also taken a leading position. The EU is not only a major development partner for ASEAN countries but also the biggest donor to the ASEAN Secretariat. Among the Southeast Asian countries, EU development assistance has

Evi Fitriani

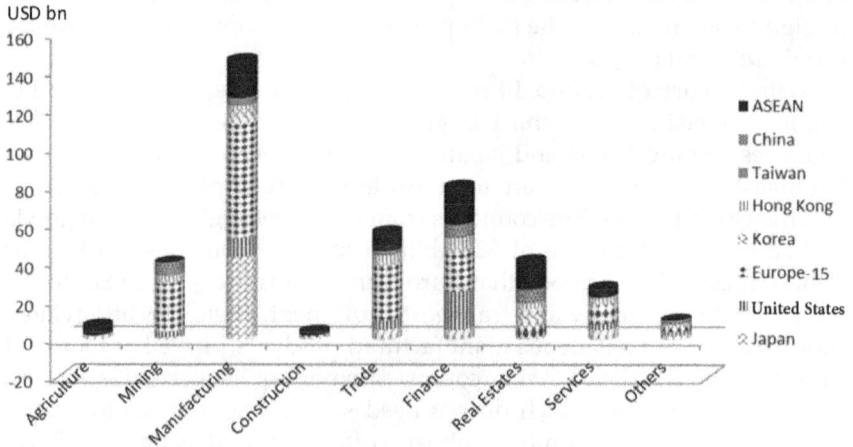

USD bn

Legend: ASEAN, China, Taiwan, Hong Kong, Korea, Europe-15, United States, Japan

Categories: Agriculture, Mining, Manufacturing, Construction, Trade, Finance, Real Estates, Services, Others

Figure 3.1. Total FDI inflows to ASEAN by Country Source, 2000–2011. Source: ASEAN and World Bank 2013.

been allocated to all ASEAN countries except Singapore and Brunei. From 2007 to 2013, the EU granted approximately $2.6 billion to the targeted ASEAN countries, and this development assistance was allocated not only to education, health, poverty reduction, development planning, trade, and investment facilitation, but also to promote good governance and human rights in Thailand, law enforcement in Indonesia, and the peace process in Mindanao in the Philippines[27]. In order to support the efforts of ASEAN regional integration, the EU also provided a grant to the ASEAN Secretariat and other ASEAN programmes. This EU support amounted to around 65.9 million euro for the period 2007 to 2013, and according to one EU source, this amount is likely to increase in the coming period of 2014 to 2020[28]. The EU support to the ASEAN community's programme can be seen in Table 3.1.

However, the Organization of Economic Cooperation and Development data shows that European development assistance to ASEAN countries was actually fluctuating. There is a decreasing trend in the EU's development assistance to the Southeast Asian countries, and this downturn is likely to be the result of the present financial crisis affecting the EU countries. In addition, an evaluation by the European Commission in 2009 found that the multilateral channels of aid disbursement through the individual ASEAN countries and ASEAN Secretariat helped the ASEAN integration process, but there was a lack of suitable coordination on the European side with regard to those channels[29]. The EU countries provide more than half of the world's aid, and the Southeast Asian countries are not the biggest recipient for the European countries. The Europeans are not the largest donors of development assistance to the South-

Table 3.1.   European Union Support to the ASEAN Community 2007–2013

Political-Security Community	Economic Community	Sociocultural Community
Border management	Internal markets	Education
Confidence building	Customs	Biodiversity
International peace and	Standards	Relief and disaster
mediation	Statistics	management
Parliamentarian diplomacy	Trade liberalization	Media
Asymmetric risks	Energy	Climate change
		Science and technology

east Asian countries either. However, Asia as a whole is the second biggest recipient of the EU's Assistance for Trade, surpassed only by the African countries[30].

Being motivated by the developments in East and Southeast Asia, ASEAN's six hundred million–person lucrative market, and by the potential of the ASEAN as the hub into an even bigger market in East Asia, the EU has actively sought an FTA with the Southeast Asian countries. This negotiation was started in 2007 after the signing of the *Nuremberg Declaration on an Enhanced EU-ASEAN Partnership* and the launch of the EU policy named 'New Partnership for the 21st Century with Asia' in May that year, when the EU proposed an EU-ASEAN FTA. After two years' negotiation, the plan for a region-to-region FTA was abandoned. According to the Europeans, the reasons for this change of mood were the profound differences and diversity in the economy and economic policies across the ASEAN member-states[31]. In an EU-ASEAN Forum in 2013, an official of the European Delegation to ASEAN stated that the EU would resume its plan for an EU-ASEAN once the Southeast Asian countries had become more integrated in the AEC. However, the Asians understood that political issues were still an obstacle to inter-regional relations, and because there was a general lack of local enthusiasm for the FTA, this change of the European strategy did not unduly bother the ASEAN countries[32].

Subsequently, the Europeans switched their FTA strategy from ASEAN towards individual countries in Southeast Asia, preferring to establish bilateral FTAs only with the ASEAN countries that were willing to and capable of sharing their ambitions. The first ASEAN country that negotiated an FTA with the EU was Singapore, and this was followed by negotiations with Malaysia, Vietnam, and Thailand. The draft of the EU-Singapore FTA was concluded in 2013, whereas the others are yet in the negotiation process. The largest economy in the region, Indonesia, started negotiations on a Comprehensive Economic and Partnership Agreement in 2012 after a joint economic study involving scholars from both sides, but the negotiations proved problematic and the process has lately re-

mained in a stalemate. It is likely that these negotiations are not a priority
for some ASEAN countries, since they are involved with the AEC while
also negotiating the RCEP, as well as a Chinese proposal for an upgraded
CAFTA. Accordingly, the European presence through the FTA route has
only been evident in a few Southeast Asian countries, and not through a
region-to-region trade agreement.

Moving Beyond the Economy?

By contrast, the European collective presence seems to be more positive in the non-economic fields. To begin with, European trends towards
regional integration have been watched closely by Southeast Asian countries. These are in evidence within the EU itself as a regional institution,
and the movement has become, if not a model, at least an inspiration and
reference point for the steps towards regional integration in Southeast
Asia. Although regional leaders and officials always claimed that AS-
EAN had its own unique model, it cannot be denied that the process of
ASEAN regional integration and institutionalization was adapted to a
considerable extent from those of the EU. A group of ASEAN eminent
persons visited EU institutions in Brussels when it was in the process of
advising on the draft of the ASEAN Charter[33], the discussions on the
ASEAN community began only after the EU countries had signed the
Maastricht Treaty, and in fact the three pillars adopted for the ASEAN
community by the Bali Concord III in 2003 are identical, albeit in a different order, with those clauses of the European treaty that deal with political security, economy, and socioculture. Of course, because of the differences in cooperative culture and diplomacy, ASEAN does not blindly
follow the EU path, and currently at least, a monetary union and a common regional currency are still unthinkable. Nevertheless, the EU as a
regional institution has provided numerous real precedents for those
who are involved in the development of ASEAN institutionalization.

In addition, the European countries' involvement in Southeast Asia is
noteworthy in the areas considered to be post–Cold War issues, that is,
democratization, human rights, and the environment. The European efforts to promote democratization and human rights in Southeast Asia
date back to the 1980s and 1990s, when they were perceived as intruders
into the domestic jurisdiction of the regional countries and consequently
were not appreciated[34]. There has been no reliable analysis as to what
extent any role was played by the Europeans in the current approaches
towards democracy and respect for human rights in ASEAN countries,
but the EU continues to provide support for these fields through its aid
programmes to the regional countries.

Europe is involved in the development of environmental awareness in
Southeast Asia through various EU aid facilities and support for regional
initiatives, and the EU was the main supporter of Indonesia when it

hosted the UN Convention on Climate Change in Bali in 2007. Consistently, the EU countries encourage and facilitate environmentally sound export commodities from the ASEAN member-states, and there are also individual European countries that have made important contributions to Southeast Asian countries in this field. Several years ago, for example, Germany allocated Indonesian debt to a reforestation fund, and presently Norwegian aid provides support to save Indonesia's rainforest through its Reduced Emissions from Deforestation and Forest Degradation Fund.

Importantly, the European countries have actively built and maintained their cultural centres in Southeast Asian countries. These centres include the British Council, Centre Culturelle de France, Goethe Institute, Erasmus House, and the Italian Centre. These centres promote not only the European countries' language and culture, but also facilitate useful people-to-people contacts in order to expand the interactions to a wider group of civil society outside governmental circles, either as individuals or non-governmental organizations. Similarly, political party–based formations from European countries may also make an appearance in Southeast Asian countries but so far only those from Germany exist, which include an institution like the Friedrich Ebert Stiftung that is affiliated to the German Social Democratic Party and has operated in some Southeast Asian countries, namely Indonesia, Singapore, Thailand, and Vietnam, to promote social democratic values. The role of the sociocultural and sociopolitical institutions from Europe in the region so far may not be as prominent as that of European governments and business entities, but their presence is important as they operate at the societal level.

Furthermore, in the past decade, European countries' involvement in Southeast Asia has expanded to new areas such as peace building and disaster response. The EU participation in the successful peace talks and establishment of tranquility in Aceh in Indonesia has always been quoted by the European Commission when talking about the role of the EU in Southeast Asia, and this has become something of a role model, at least in Europe, for the settlement of conflicts between separatist movements and central governments. It was also in Aceh, after the deadly tsunami at the end of 2004, that the EU took part in the efforts to respond to natural disasters in the region. Together with other international and domestic donors, the European countries either individually or collectively through the EU provided assistance to rebuild the cities and civil society in the disaster-affected areas.

Finally, the European countries are also present in Southeast Asia as arms traders. This role is seemingly in contrast with the other activities mentioned previously, but it is a fact that some European countries, namely France, the United Kingdom, Germany, Italy, and the Netherlands, are leading suppliers of deadly weapons to countries around the globe, including those in Southeast Asia. In this case, the trade in armaments is not only a matter of commercial transaction but also involves access to the latest—or next to the latest—technology and strategy of modern warfare. The European role in this sector is important, given the fact that some Southeast Asian countries are, or have been, boycotted by the United States for arms purchases and have become new clients of Russia and China for such weapons.

In comparison with their lopsided relations in the colonial period, the interactions between European and Southeast Asian countries have developed unprecedentedly both in economic as well as non-economic fields. To what extent these relations differ from those in the colonial period will be discussed next.

THE NATURE OF CONTEMPORARY RELATIONS

It is interesting to observe contemporary relations between Asian and European countries not only because this topic is almost absent in the current debate in East and Southeast Asia but also because the countries in the two regions arguably have never been engaged in such novel circumstances previously. On one hand, as stated previously, the Southeast Asian countries, despite certain difficulties and setbacks, are in promising situations due to their potential economic progress, relative political stability, increasing regional cooperation, and their geographical proximity with China. On the other hand, the European countries are suffering from a deep financial crisis with the result that their economic forecasts have been gloomy and their regional integration programs have come under considerable pressure. Indeed, some scholars could assert that the EU is in a period of inexorable decline[35].

This reversed scenario in prospect for emerging Asia and Europe is so plausible that in its 2013 annual conference, the EU Studies Association in Asia Pacific adopted the theme of *EU in the Shadow of Asia? Changing Relationships between the EU and the Asia Pacific*. In the conference's opening ceremony, a European official complained about this theme and asserted that neither Europeans nor Asians were in the shadow of each other. This incident leads to a question as to what extent the current circumstances could change the nature of the structural relations between Asia and Europe that were built up during the European colonial period in Asia. One needs to note several aspects to try to answer this question.

First, in terms of economic relations, although the European countries have been under great stress from their financial crisis and the Asian countries continue to enjoy a good growth rate, the latter are still in a dependent position in the global economic system that was shaped by the former. A previous section of this chapter has shown that the export of cheap raw materials from Asia to Europe still holds good. In the negotiation of the Comprehensive Economic and Partnership Agreement with Indonesia, the EU countries have tried to maintain their imports of cheap raw materials while Indonesia has preferred to export processed products in order to obtain added values for its primary products. In addition, the EU countries have pressed for more 'environmentally sound' products from Indonesia, and these negotiations have been in a stalemate because of the contending interests of the two parties.

Second, the European countries remain a powerful actor that shapes not only the commodity pricing but also the quality and quantity of trade commodities from Southeast Asia that can be accepted in the European markets. The Europeans, indeed, use a significant proportion of their official development assistance, which is intended to be a development assistance fund, to project their trade interests. This attitude suggests that the European countries still strive to maintain the upper hand position in the bilateral trade relationship.

Third, like the colonized countries in the imperial period, the Southeast Asian countries have depended on capital inflows from Europe to construct their manufacturing industries. As the largest source of FDI to the ASEAN regional countries, Europe maintains a strong position to influence these countries' policies on foreign investment. The European proposal for the EU-ASEAN FTA, now in suspense, would also have targeted regulatory frameworks and established standards and conformity assessments that were aimed to create a more conducive environment for European business. Thus, there has been great pressure on the Southeast Asian countries to liberalize their investment policies, while the European investors can exercise their prerogative of choosing in which specific country their FDI would be allocated. With half of the FDI in ASEAN countries directed to Singapore, the capital system in the region has evidently not much changed: The tiny city-state remains the centre of trade and regional economy since the nineteenth century after its establishment by the British colonial government.

Fourth, the proposed FTA that the EU negotiated previously with ASEAN aims for reciprocal and progressive liberalization of substantially all goods and services as well as public procurement and trade facilitation. Those very issues had already rejected by the developing countries in the WTO Doha Round negotiations, but the Europeans kept pushing their agenda in the trade negotiations with the Southeast Asian countries. It comes as no surprise that the EU seemed to abandon its preference for the multilateral approach that it had adopted in 2007 when it had offered a region-to-region FTA to the ASEAN countries. The failure of the interregional FTA shows that there are limits to European influence in the face of strong resistance by the Southeast Asian countries.

Finally, despite their somewhat diminished position in the global economy, the European countries have managed to take the lead position during the FTA negotiations with the Southeast Asian countries. The EU simply changed its FTA strategy from a region-to-region basis to bilateral FTAs once it found that the lack of close integration among the ASEAN economies would bring more harm than benefit to their commercial interests. Therefore, the EU only negotiates FTAs with those few regional countries that can adjust to its requirements and generate more prospects in trade relations. This strategy has been taken up without paying much attention to its impact on the regional countries: the strategy to negotiate bilateral FTAs with only a few countries in ASEAN—in fact, the most advanced ones—is similar to the strategy of the former European colonialists, namely the 'divide and rule' that was so often used in the past to finesse competing European nations in South and Southeast Asia. If and when they materialize, these bilateral FTAs that the EU is negotiating with some ASEAN countries can pose challenges to the ASEAN integration process and the AEC because this could deepen the economic gap among countries in Southeast Asia.

CONCLUSION

Relations between Europe and Southeast Asia are an interesting subject of study because the two had enjoyed a very strong though unequal economic relationship in the colonial past but were in danger of losing these close linkages after the Asian countries obtained their independence. The current global economic trends and developments in Asia could show more robust health in Southeast Asia than in Europe. The European economy of late has been under great stress because of its financial crisis, and the European countries have necessarily sought new opportunities in Southeast Asia. However, the discussion in this chapter suggests that there is yet almost no basic structural change in the postcolonial trading and broader economic relations between the Southeast Asian and European countries.

The FTA is an instrument of strategy used by the Europeans to return to Southeast Asia. Wanting to recapture its previously eminent position in the global economy, the EU has striven to press its objective to become one of the most globally competitive economies. The EU strategy is to provide an overarching framework for trade and regional integration, and as trading nations, the EU member-states make big efforts to dismantle existing trade barriers in Southeast Asia through the proposed FTAs. It is in their interest to promote open trading regimes either through the WTO or through bilateral FTAs with the individual ASEAN member countries.

Apart from the economic and commercial field, Europe is actively present in Southeast Asia in many other areas than the economy, but its role in non-economic sectors needs to be strengthened in order to build a more balanced relationship with the countries of Southeast Asia. There are several measures that can be considered. For instance, in issues relating to democratization, human rights, and the environment, which are actually closely related to values and norms in society, Southeast Asian countries have their own local traditional wisdom, but it seems that there is a gap between that and the concepts that the Europeans are promoting. The role of education and dialogue among stakeholders is critical here to enable Southeast Asians and Europeans to learn from each other and accommodate the other's interests. Other encounters can be fruitfully made through the presence and activities of the European cultural centres in the region. For most common people in Southeast Asia, European countries are still representatives of an enviable culture, technology, and lifestyle. The European countries and the EU can take advantage of this receptive attitude by enhancing the importance and energies of their cultural and intellectual centres as bridges for people-to-people connections. In the end, perhaps, the Europeans need to change their perspectives: Can the Europeans refrain from treating the Southeast Asians as merely a target and opportunity for their economic interests?

NOTES

1. Luce Boulnois, *Silk Road: Monks, Warriors & Merchants* (Geneva: Odyssey Books & Guide, 2012), 30–31, 156–57.

2. Pradumna Rana and W. M. Chia, *The Revival of the Silk Roads (Land Connectivity) in Asia*, RSIS Working Paper (Singapore: RSIS, 2014). See also Boulnois, *Silk Road*, 30–31.

3. Boulnois, *Silk Road*; Leonard Andaya, 'The Search for the "Origins" of Malayu', *Journal of Southeast Asia Studies* 32, no. 3 (2001): 315–30; Milton Osborne, *Southeast Asia—An Introductory History* (Sydney: Allen & Unwin, 2013).

4. Angus Maddison, *Contours of the World Economy, 1-2030 AD* (New York: Oxford University Press, 2007).

5. Shaun Narine, 'State Sovereignty, Political Legitimacy and Regional Institutionalism in the Asia-Pacific', *The Pacific Review* 17, no. 3 (2004): 426.

6. Martin Jacques, *When China Rules the World* (London: Penguin Books, 2012). See also David Shambaugh, *China Goes Global: the Partial Power* (Oxford: Oxford University Press, 2012); Weiwei Zhang, *The China Wave: Rise of a Civilizational State* (Hackensack, NJ: World Century Publishing Corporation, 2011).

7. Osborne, *Southeast Asia*, 111.

8. Beng-Lan Goh, 'Redrawing Centre-Periphery Relations: Theoretical Challenges in the Study of Southeast Asian Modernity', in *Asia in Europe, Europe in Asia*, Srilata Ravi, Mario Rutten, and Beng-Lan Goh (eds.) (Singapore: ISEAS, 2004): 79–101.

9. Maddison, *Contours of the World Economy*, 135; Osborne, *Southeast Asia*. See also J. H. Parry, *Europe and A Wider World* (London: Hutchinson's University Library, 1953).

10. Beng-Lan Goh, 'Redrawing Centre-Periphery Relations'.

11. Evi Fitriani, 'Asian Perceptions about EU in Asia-Europe Meeting (ASEM)', *Asia-Europe Journal* 9 (2011): 43–56.

12. However, the United States is not a new patron for the Philippines. This country was occupied by the United States since the beginning of the twentieth century after defeating Spain.

13. Syamsul Hadi, *Strategi Pembangunan Mahathir and Suharto: Politik Industrialisasi dan Modal jepang di Malaysia and Indonesia* (Jakarta: Pelangi cendekia and Japan Foundation, 2005).

14. www.asean.org as well as the UN Conference on Trade and Development and UNCTADstat.

15. www.asean.org.

16. Ibid.

17. Laurent Fabius, 'France's Policy in Asia', speech transcribed (ASEAN Secretariat, Jakarta, 12 August 2013).

18. Speech of David O'Sullivan, chief operating officer of the European External Action Service, 'EU Priorities in Asia' on 25 March 2014.

19. Sophie Boisseau du Rocher, 'The EU's Strategic Offensive with ASEAN: Some Room Left but No Time', *GRIP Analis Note* (8 January 2014). See also Gauri Khandekar, *Mapping EU-ASEAN Relations* (Brussels: Fride-Agora, 2014); Katharina Meissner, Imke Pente, Nelly Stratieva, Boonwara Sumano, and Kilian Spandler, 'Unlocking the Potential of Interregionalism: Mutual Perceptions and Interests in EU-ASEAN Relations', *The Policy Paper—The Working Group on EU-ASEAN Relations*, the Young Initiative on Foreign Affairs and International Relations think tank. www.euractiv.com/global-europe/practical-way-forward-eu-asean-. Accessed 13 March 2014.

20. Evi Fitriani, 'The Impact of the EU Crisis on EU-ASEAN Relations', *Geopolitics, History, and International Relations* 6, no. 1 (2014): 78–93.

21. EEAS, 'The EU–ASEAN Relationship in Twenty Facts and Figures', October 2013. eeas.europa.eu/asean/docs/key_facts_figures_eu_asean_en.pdf. Accessed 30 June 2014.

22. European Commission, Directorate General for Trade, 'European Union, Trade with ASEAN', 2014.

23. Ibid.

24. Ibid.

25. There are different data provided by different sources. The European Commission's 2013 brochure, *ASEAN-EU: Natural Partners*, has a pie chart showing the European contribution is 21 percent of total FDI to ASEAN countries, whereas in the ASEAN Secretariat website it is written 22 percent (www.asean.org/asean/external-relations/european-union/item/overview-of-asean-eu-dialogue-relations. Accessed 30 June 2014). A campaign paper of the Asia Europe People Power claims that the European share is 24 percent. See Asia Europe People Forum, 'Examining the EU-ASEAN Free Trade Agreement (FTA)'. www.aepf.info/campaigns/eu-asean-fta/33-examining-the-eu-asean-free-trade-agreement-fta. Accessed 18 May 2014.

26. ASEAN Secretariat FDI Statistics in Jayant Menon, 'How to Multilateralize Asian Regionalism,' Opinions, Institute of Southeast Asian Studies Singapore (2013).

27. European Commission, *ASEAN-EU: Natural Partners*, Brochure, sixth edition (Jakarta, January 2013).

28. EEAS, 'The EU–ASEAN Relationship'.

29. European Commission, *Evaluation of the EU Co-operation with ASEAN*, Final Report, vol. 1, 2009. www.oecd.org/derec/ec/47377356.pdf. Accessed 30 June 2014.

30. European Commission, *Europe Aid: Review of Progress of the EU and its Member States* (Brussels, 2011).

31. Maria Garcia, 'From Bottom of the Pyramid to Top Priority: Explaining Asia in the EU's Free Trade Agreement (FTA) Strategy', *Australia New Zealand Journal of European Studies* (ANJES) 4, no. 1 (2012): 42–58.

32. Evi Fitriani, 'EU FTA Strategy and Southeast Asia: Indonesia Perspective', paper presented in the International Conference on *Proactive EU FTA Strategy and EU-Asian Economic Interactions*, Taipei: National Chengchi University, 27 May 2014.

33. Personal interview with a former Indonesia's minister of foreign affairs, Ali Alatas, in April 2008.

34. E. Palmujoki, 'EU-ASEAN Relations: Reconciling Two Different Agendas', *Contemporary Southeast Asia* 19, no. 3 (1997): 269–85.

35. Richard Youngs, *Europe's Decline and Fall: The Struggle against Global Irrelevance* (London: Profile Books, 2010).

FOUR

Thailand's Middle Income Trap and Europe's Assistance

Kriengsak Chareonwongsak

The Asian economy, particularly China, is continuing to experience a high expansion rate, but it is still questioned whether emerging Asia will be able to maintain the growth rate or fall into the middle-income trap (MIT) similar to Latin America and other middle-income countries (MICs) in the past century. The World Bank upgraded Thailand to a member of the upper-middle-income group in 2010. However, the concern as to whether Thailand can pass the MIT still remains, especially due to the post-Asian financial crisis (1997) economic expansion rate that cannot be expected to be sustained at the same level as that prior to the crisis.

Thailand has had a relationship with Europe for centuries, and Europe has played an important role in the Thai economy. Through international trade, investment, human resource development, and technology transfer, this relationship has greatly contributed towards the economic development of Thailand from a poor country to one which is now a middle-income economy. But to develop the country further and overcome the MIT, Thailand needs to restructure the economy to a knowledge-based one, based on high-technology manufacturing. Therefore, the relationship Thailand has with Europe will be beneficial to the economic uplift of Thailand because Europe is an important source of knowledge, technology, and innovation for an emerging economy.

However, the role of Europe in the Thai economy is expected to decrease when compared to its connections with other entities, particularly the emerging economies such as the Association of Southeast Asian Nations (ASEAN) countries and China. This is because of the increase in intra-regional trade and investment, which is a result of the increase in free trade agreements (FTAs) in the region. Furthermore, it is expected that the growth rate of Asian economies will continue to be high, thereby enabling China to become the largest economy in the world. FTA negotiations between Thailand and the European Union (EU) have stopped due to the opposition of interest groups and political problems in Thailand. In this scenario, the development of economic relations between Thailand and Europe has faced challenges and questions whether the two parties can work together to meet the needs of Thailand to overcome the MIT, while at the same time benefitting Europe from its connections with Thailand.

This chapter aims to study whether Thailand will get stuck in the MIT, the factors causing the Thai economy to expand or contract in the past, which obstacles are making it difficult for Thailand to overcome the MIT, and how Europe can contribute to improve the chances of Thailand becoming a high-income country (HIC).

IS THAILAND STUCK IN THE MIDDLE-INCOME TRAP?

The MIT is a phenomenon occurring since the past decade. Many countries in the world have developed from being a low-income country (LIC) to an MIC, but most are not able to progress as an HIC[1]. The process of development from LIC to MIC can be explained by the Lewis-Kuznets framework where the early stage of a country's development involves labour and capital movement from the agricultural sector with low productivity to the industrial sector having higher productivity[2]. But when a country has advanced to become an MIC, wages would be higher and the benefits generated from importing high-technology from overseas and capital accumulation would begin to decrease[3].

The most commonly used indicator for clustering countries is by gross domestic product (GDP) per capita but mutually accepted thresholds do not yet exist. Another indicator is gross national income (GNI) per capita, the Atlas method[4], which is applied by the World Bank in dividing countries in four groups: those falling under the categories of low-income, lower-middle-income, upper-middle-income, and high-income countries. In 2012, a country with GNI per capita between $1,036 and $4,085 was considered a lower-middle-income country. If the income was lower than that, it was regarded as an LIC. Income between $4,086 and $12,615 was classified as upper-middle-income country (UMIC) and if the income was higher than that, it would be an HIC. On the measurement for the MIT, there is no consensus yet. Nevertheless, it is found from review literature that there are at least three methods for measuring the MIT. Conducting an analysis on whether Thailand is stuck in the MIT by applying those three methods furnishes different answers.

Period for Crossing Over the Middle-Income Threshold

Felipe et al[5] states that countries stuck in the MIT had spent a longer time of twenty-eight years in raising the GDP per capita (1990 purchasing power parity dollars) from $2,000 to $7,250 (thresholds of lower middle income), and more than fourteen years in multiplying the GDP per capita from $7,250 to $11,750 (thresholds of upper middle income). If these criteria are considered, Thailand has been an UMIC since 2003. The Thailand Development Research Institute[6] indicates that for Thailand to pass into the upper-middle-income group within fourteen years, its GDP per capita needs to increase by 3.6 percent per annum (p.a.), which seems likely as that is currently a typical growth rate for Thailand. However, assuming that the threshold would always remain constant is not logical, as the threshold would be adjusted up around 2 percent to 3 percent p.a. Moreover, Felipe et al had also set the threshold of HIC at a relatively low rate.

Growth Slowdown

Eichengreen et al[7] defined growth slowdown as situations which are in line with three conditions. (1) Average growth of GDP per capita in the previous period (seven years or more) is greater than or equal to 3.5 percent p.a. (2) Average growth rate of GDP per capita in the present period (seven years or more) is lower than growth in the previous period by 2 percentage points p.a. at the minimum. (3) GDP per capita exceeds $10,000 in 2005 at constant international price. The situation in Thailand is aligned with the first two criteria, that is, the average expansion rate of GDP per capita between 1984 and 1996 was equivalent to 7.37 percent p.a. and has declined to be 3.66 percent p.a. between 1999 and 2010 (see Figure 4.1). But during the slowdown period, GDP per capita was lower than $10,000 in 2005 at the constant international price.

Catching Up with High-Income Countries

This method is to evaluate how much the per capita income of a country is approaching that of a leading country by comparing the ratio of its GDP per capita relative to the United States from the past (1950 to 1960s) to the present[8]. Im and Rosenblatt[9] mentioned that Thailand is required to have its growth of GDP per capita increased by 1.3 and 0.8 percentage points p.a., respectively, to catch up with the incomes of the United States and HICs in the Organisation for Economic Co-operation and Development (OECD) in the next fifty years. In any case, to apply the income level of the United States and the OECD as a threshold for HIC is a high criterion; even countries like South Korea would not be classified as a HIC.

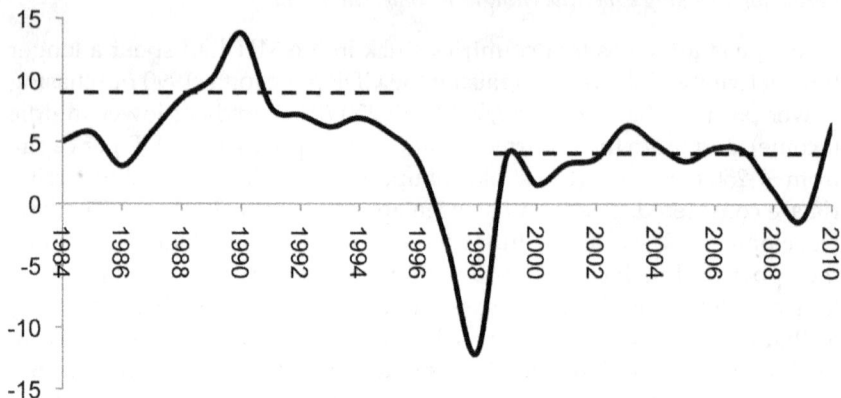

Figure 4.1. Thailand's annual percentage growth of GDP per capita (at 2005 constant prices). Source: Data from Penn World Table.

It cannot be concluded whether Thailand is stuck in the MIT, as there is no consensus on the criteria for measuring the MIT. But from precedents, Thailand runs the risk because the growth rate of per capita income has significantly declined during the past decade as well as falling behind the leading countries. If this is evaluated by thresholds formulated by the World Bank, it would take Thailand a long time to manage to emerge from being an MIC. The Sasin Institute for Global Affairs[10] indicates that if GNI per capita in Thailand grows at the current rate, it will become an HIC in 2036 or take twenty-six years to advance from an UMIC to a HIC (see Figure 4.2).

WHICH FACTORS ARE LEADING TO THAILAND'S ECONOMIC EXPANSION?

This needs a brief synopsis of Thailand's economic development from the past to its present, dividing it into five periods of development, to study the factors leading to economic growth and slowdown, and development policies and outcomes in each period.

1951 to 1958: Military Monopolies

This period was the starting point for Thailand. The GDP had on average increased by 4.4 percent p.a., while the GDP per capita increased by 2 percent p.a. due to the high growth of population. The factor that led to economic growth was the development of capital-intensive industries such as chemicals, cement, and iron and steel, which mostly were public enterprises, resulting in an increase of capital accumulation by 18 percent

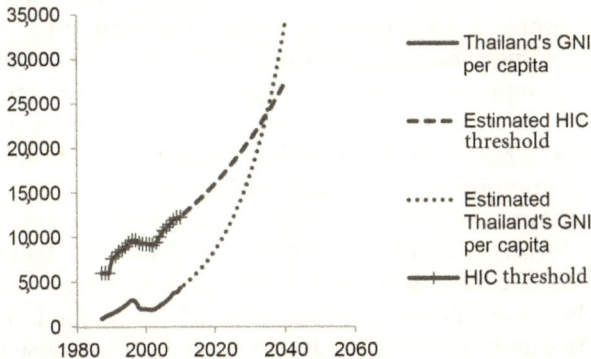

Figure 4.2. Thailand's GNI per capita and HIC threshold (in US$). Source: Adapted from World Bank and SASIN Institute for Global Affairs 2013.

of GDP. But it also led to importing a large amount of capital goods and raw materials, with an increasing import rate of 6.6 percent p.a. Another factor supporting growth was export expansion. A majority of the exported items were primary goods such as rice, rubber, tin, and timber, apart from various agricultural products that were later incorporated. In addition, the government carefully implemented a fiscal policy and efficiently managed taxation. A number of fundamental economic problems were encountered; for example, low capability in agricultural and industrial production as well as services, higher costs of production, low saving rates, lack of specialized people, and the price deflation of major exporting goods[11]. The major businesses were monopolized by public enterprises. The military dictatorship employed an obstructive policy by not allowing Chinese merchants to undertake specified businesses, though the Chinese turned to establishing businesses connected to the military leadership, resulting in business-bureaucrat relationships that have lasted until today.

1959 to 1971: Import Substitution

After Field Marshal Sarit Thanarat seized power, the country was governed by military dictatorship. Economic developments raised the real GDP growth on an average of 7 percent p.a., and the major factors for growth were international standard–based development as mentioned by the World Bank[12]. The government developed the requisite institutions for economic development, and these institutions were the main drivers in formulating the first National Economic Development Plan in 1961. The country required large-scale investment in infrastructure and public facilities such as road and transportation, dams for irrigation and electricity generation, and so on. Although there were innumerable investments, they were implemented with fiscal discipline which stabilized the economy. The government formulated an import substitution policy, which provided incentives for manufacturing activities and protected them from foreign competitors. This policy generated a huge amount of domestic and foreign investments, a reduction in monopoly by public enterprises, and gave rise to an automobile industry in Thailand and other import substitution industries. Additionally, agricultural production expanded due to road and irrigation building, and widening the area under cultivation. However, though the overall production rate had grown, the expansion was due to a surge in factors of production, not a rise in productivity. Moreover, the income gap widened, as people living close to public facilities and factors of production could utilize those facilities in increasing production and incomes more than those living in remote locations lacking factors of production.

1972 to 1986: External Shock

Economic expansion grew on average at 6.2 percent p.a. and in some years even reached 9 percent to 10 percent, while per capita income increased by 3.3 percent p.a., which was slightly lower than the target. The major factor for economic expansion was international trade, which went up from 34 percent of GDP in 1971 to 51 percent in 1980. The growth rate of exports was high at 14 percent p.a., but most of the exported goods were still primary products. The expansion of exports was partly a result of price increases of food and raw materials in the global market and partly the development of export industries. Imports also rose to 11.5 percent p.a.[13]

The major obstacles for economic expansion in the 1970s were both internal and external. The oil shock of the early 1970s, depreciation of the American dollar, global inflation, the issue of the country's political stability, and threats from communism all had roles to play, and raised the inflation rate to 12 percent p.a. Domestic investment stagnated and fixed capital accumulation increased by 5.2 percent p.a. as compared to 9.5 percent in the 1960s. Unemployment became serious in industries and services. From the late 1970s until 1986, Thailand's real GDP growth was lower than 5 percent p.a., resulting from the second oil shock in 1979, the developing world's debt crisis, high global interest rates, and an oversupply problem leading to lower commodity prices. Government spending was magnified to satisfy demand for resolving the slowdown, resulting in fiscal imbalance, which led to an intense public debt problem in the early 1980s. In 1981, the government was pressed by the International Monetary Fund (IMF) to devalue the Thai baht and to implement austerity measures and fiscal discipline. With austerity, Thailand's economic expansion was on average 4.4 percent p.a., which was primarily the outcome of expansion in domestic demand. The economy became more stable with the reduction of inflation to 2.9 percent p.a. due to slowdown in global inflation and oil prices, and the price of agricultural goods and raw materials dropped.

1987 to 1996: Japanese Flying Geese

Thailand's economy on average expanded at 9.1 percent p.a. and in 1988 to 1990 exceeded 10 percent p.a., which corresponded with what the World Bank called the 'East Asia Miracle'[14]. Although the poverty percentage went down from 32.6 percent in 1988 to 11.4 percent in 1996, income distribution worsened. The Thai economy changed in many aspects: The GDP share of the agricultural sector decreased from 19 percent to 9 percent, whereas the industrial sector increased from 24 percent to 41 percent. Exports advanced from 36 percent of GDP to 47 percent through exporting more industrial than agricultural goods. The major factor for high economic growth was massive foreign direct investment (FDI), which escalated rapidly from $351.9 million in 1987 to around $2,335 million in 1996. The influx of investment was the outcome of the Plaza Accord in 1985 that devalued the dollar; the Thai baht pegged to the dollar depreciated, which led to the movement of the production base of Japanese companies into Thailand. Thai baht depreciation enhanced the competiveness of Thai exports. Another factor was financial liberalization with the establishment of the Bangkok International Banking Facility, which provided an opportunity to financial institutions for easier borrowing from abroad since the interest rates in other countries were lower than in Thailand.

In 1996, the Thai economy again slowed due to diminishing exports and investments. Thailand had a higher current account deficit than 8 percent, and short-term external debt was higher than 25 percent of GDP and 114.2 percent and 99.7 percent of international reserves in 1995 and 1996, respectively. With financial institutions approving large loans for investment and speculation in real estate, a bubble began to form. Lack of good governance in the financial institutions led to lending to politicians at levels higher than collateralized assets. The Bank of Thailand failed to manage the exchange rate policy and to tackle speculation of Thai baht value until international reserves became exhausted. These problems were a cause of the Asian financial crisis, which occurred in 1997. Economic growth increased factors of production, both capital and labour, but the development of productivity was ignored (see Table 4.1) and competitiveness went down.

1997 to Present: Trade Dependency

In 1997, the government decided to float the Thai baht, which was devalued from 25 baht to 54 baht to the dollar and needed support from

Table 4.1. Thailand's Gross Domestic Product Component between 1980 and 2012 (Percent of Gross Domestic Product)

GDP Component	1980	1990	1995	2000	2005	2010	2011	2012
Private consumption	66.42	56.51	54.19	54.61	55.05	51.73	52.33	52.41
Government consumption	11.70	8.75	7.86	9.32	9.00	10.00	10.09	10.19
Private investment	20.43	32.84	32.92	12.61	17.60	15.77	16.87	18.16
Public investment	9.06	5.81	8.90	7.48	5.95	5.16	4.70	4.81
Change in inventory	0.71	1.05	1.45	0.86	2.00	0.81	0.16	0.93
Exports	21.35	36.09	46.9	65.48	66.66	69.46	75.92	73.42
Imports	29.66	41.05	52.23	50.37	56.27	52.94	60.09	59.93

Sources: Data adapted from Office of the National Economic and Social Development Board, "All Tables QGDP," *Quarterly Gross Domestic Product*, 18 August 2014, www.nesdb.go.th/Portals/0/eco_datas/account/qgdp/data2_14/AlltableQ2_2014.xls; and Office of the National Economic and Social Development Board, "GDP 1996 (1951–1996)," *National Income*, www.nesdb.go.th/Portals/0/eco_datas/account/ni/ni1997_2004/gdp51-96p.xls.

the IMF. Many financial institutions had a large amount of non-performing assets leading to liquidity problems. Depositors flocked to withdraw their money from the bank and creditors in other countries revoked. The government had to guarantee all loans and to capitalize the financial institutions. When fifty-six financial institutions went bankrupt, it triggered a rise in public debt from 14.9 percent of GDP in 1996 to 57.2 percent in 2001. The growth rate became −1.4 percent and −10.5 percent, respectively, in 1997–1998 due to lower domestic consumption and private investment. But the devalued Thai baht expanded exports, turned the current account balance to surplus again, and made the economy expand in the following year.

From that crisis until now, the average economic expansion rate has settled at 4.1 percent p.a. and GDP per capita on average at 3.47 percent p.a., which is lower than before the crisis. The major factor in growth was higher international trade. Whereas private investment used to be the major driving factor, the economy receded from 32.92 percent of GDP in 1995 to 15.77 percent of GDP in 2010 (Table 4.1), the ratio of public debt was down to 43 percent in 2007, and international reserves were up to 240 percent of external debt. The expansion rate of Thailand's GDP increasingly fluctuated; this was from various situations such as 9/11 in 2001, the tsunami in 2004, the subprime mortgage crisis in 2008, and the 2011 Thailand floods (Figure 4.3).

Thailand's development has characteristics corresponding with the definition of getting stuck in the MIT. The economy is approaching a

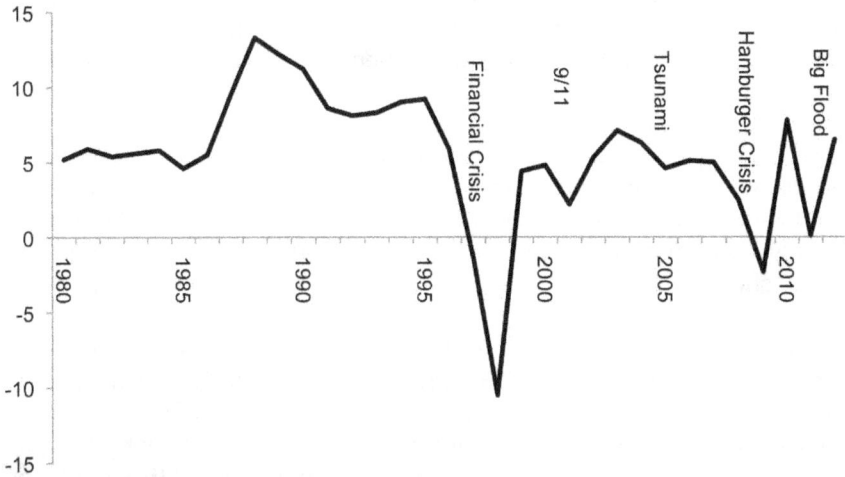

Figure 4.3.   Thailand's GDP annual percentage growth rate in 1980–2012.
Source: Chareonwongsak 2014.

stage of higher labour wage, and the returns granted by importing technology and capital accumulation are declining, causing the country to lose competitiveness. To develop the economy to a higher growth, the country will need new factors, strategies, and knowledge.

OBSTACLES IN BECOMING A HIGH-INCOME ECONOMY

Thailand is required to address various domestic factors. This section will discuss the factors that are obstacles for Thailand advancing towards becoming an HIC.

Delayed Economic Restructuring

The economy has been restructured from an agricultural economy to a labour-intensive industrial economy and has been developed to become more high-tech. Thailand's share of primary products decreased from 14.88 percent to 10.21 percent of total exports during 1997 to 2007; the share of labour-intensive and resource-based products dropped from 27.32 percent to 22.08 percent, whereas its share of high-technology products increased from 52.20 percent to 62.87 percent. The structural change is the movement from low-productivity to higher-productivity manufacturing sectors.

Most high-technology manufacturers in Thailand are contractors for brand owners or original equipment manufacturers (OEMs), which is the lowest-value-added activity in the value chain and similar to the example of electricity and electronic equipment, which Thailand had exported at a value of 24 percent of total exports in 2011. This industry is essentially a foreign investment and OEMs that depend on technology, product design, and purchase orders from overseas. Most of the manufacturers in the electricity and electronic equipment industry are downstream industries with high import content. The study by Tran[15] found that the international competitiveness index[16] of low skill-intensive products of Thailand was likely to continue to go down since the late 1990s, and the index of high skill-intensive goods had gone up, but has not risen after the crisis, showing that the industrial sector of Thailand lacks competitiveness.

Another issue is the delay in the economy entering the service sector. Since the economic crisis in 1997, restructuring of the Thai economy has become static, as the service sector has a constant share of approximately 50 percent of GDP and the agricultural sector of 9 to 10 percent (see Table 4.2), which is similar to the economic structure of global MICs while the structure of an HIC will have a large service sector on average at 66 percent of GDP and an agricultural sector on average at 2 percent of GDP. The National Economic Social Development Board has forecast that the agricultural sector will have a declining share at 6.5 percent of GDP in 2027, the service sector will have a constant share at approximately 50 percent, and the industrial sector will have an even greater share[17].

The major factor causing a delay in economic restructuring is the service sector, which currently comprises businesses with lower labour productivity than the industrial sector, which can be observed from the share of the service sector in GDP and employment at 50.2 percent and 46.6 percent in 2012, respectively, whereas the industrial sector had shares at 41.1 percent and 14.1 percent. For high value-added service business, restriction of competition still prevails as Thailand, MICs in ASEAN, and China all have service trade restrictions[18].

Higher prices of agricultural products and the implementation of agricultural subsidy caused a delay in moving labour from the agricultural sector. The government did not clearly define its direction and the private business sector focuses only on ad hoc issues, thus being unable to become an investment leader. The employment of illegal migrant labour

Table 4.2.   Thailand's Economic Structure between 1975 and 2012 (Percent of Gross Domestic Product)

	1975	1985	1995	2005	2008	2009	2010	2011	2012
Agriculture	24.78	19.08	9.02	9.01	8.68	8.83	9.16	8.30	8.63
Industry	21.57	24.32	41.16	41.43	41.83	42.31	40.84	42.96	41.14
Service	53.64	56.60	49.82	49.56	49.49	48.87	50.00	48.74	50.23

with low wages is another reason why businesses do not adapt themselves for higher productivity.

A Shortage of Quality Labour

Thailand is likely to be short of labour as the demographic structure is becoming an aging society faster than neighbouring countries in ASEAN due to the success of birth control. Age dependency ratio will be at 17 percent of the population in 2020, increased from 13 percent in 2010, while the labour force between ages fifteen and sixty-four will have a declining share at 68.5 percent of the population in 2030 compared to 71.5 percent in 2010[19]. The 'window of opportunity' for Thailand is closing as its advantage from cheap labour wage would no longer continue. The labour force aged between twenty-five and sixty-five consists of 66.2 percent with primary school education or lower; whereas in the developed countries most of the labour force has a high school education. At the same time, there is in Thailand a shortage of middle-level labour force and labour that has obtained vocational education, whereas 91 percent of those with a high school education and vocational certificate study further in institutes of higher education. The major factor causing a shortage of middle-level labour force is the huge gap of wage levels between labour with vocational education and those with a bachelor's degree. Among those holding a bachelor's degree, 70 percent have studied social sciences and 30 percent studied science and technology. Most of the graduates in the science and technology field do not work in the field they graduated from; only 23 percent work in their graduated field. The shortage of high-skilled people in the science and technology field is not in line with the requirements for developing the economy to an HIC. The shortage of labour in quantity is a problem and its quality is an issue, resulting from the insufficient quality of the education system. The Asian Development Bank[20] indicated that the main reason that Thailand may get stuck in the MIT is the shortage of high-quality human capital, particularly in the service sector, which is mostly a low value-added service. The quality issue in Thailand's educational system is seen from the Programme for International Student Assessment scores of Thai students, which are lower than those of neighbouring countries and developed countries. This inferiority in quality of Thai education causes the contribution of education to GDP growth of Thailand to be only 0.08 percentage points to 0.10 percentage points, which is relatively low when compared to G7 countries with a value of 0.12 percentage points to 0.5 percentage points.

Research and Development are Not Prioritized

The main obstacle keeping Thailand from progressing to an HIC is its inability to develop its own technology. Thailand has very few investments in research and development (R&D) as compared to an HIC, which can be observed from its R&D expenditure at only 0.2 percent to 0.3 percent of GDP, whereas an HIC has an R&D expenditure of more than 1 percent of GDP. The private sector in Thailand does not conduct much research; most of this research is done by the public sector with no collaboration with the private sector, and many research results cannot be further developed or commercially utilized. This problem can be confirmed from the number of patents granted each year: only 46 patents in 2010, which was lower than other countries such as Japan (44,814 patents), South Korea (11,671 patents), Taiwan (8,238 patents), China (2,657 patents), Singapore (603 patents), and Malaysia (429 patents). The reason why Thailand has a small focus on R&D is because the government gives no weight in this area as the return cannot be grasped in the short term — it prefers to back other areas that can build political popularity. The supporting factors for R&D are not adequate: There is a lack of infrastructure to support investment and incubation for R&D and the product design industry, and a powerless intellectual property protection institution. But the most important aspect is the shortage of researchers; the ratio of researchers is only 3.3 persons per 10,000 as opposed to 8 per 10,000 in Malaysia and 64 researchers per 10,000 in Singapore.

Inequality of Income

Thailand's economic development had generated additional per capita income and the number of poor has declined from 34.1 million people in 1988 to 8.8 million people in 2011, but the income distribution did not improve; the income of 20 percent of the poorest population has approximately a share of 4.6 percent of the national income, whereas the income of 20 percent of the richest population has approximately 54 percent of the national income. In an absolute sense, the average income of these two groups greatly differs: In 2011, the income differential had reached 11.75 times[21]. Many of the reasons for inequality in Thai society come from the concentration of development; this is observed from the annual high government expenditure allocated to Bangkok, the capital city, in which the difference in quality of public services (education, public health, and public utilities) between the metropolitan area and the rural areas is obvious, as well as the difference of economic opportunity between people living in the metropolitan area and rural area. Another reason is that Thailand still has a large informal economy at 62.66 percent of the labour force in 2012, which has not changed throughout the past years. Most of the 'informal-economy' sectors are not efficient and lack standards in producing goods and providing services as well as knowledge and capital in boosting productivity. Informal workers are not granted protection by labour laws or by the social security system, which causes low income and problems of unemployment, insufficient income, and insecurity. Inequality is an obstacle for economic growth, whereas resolving the problem of inequality supports economic growth because it will raise the income of most people, widen the domestic market, help the government collect more revenues, and strengthen political stability[22].

Governance Problem

Governance problems in Thailand appear in many forms. One of them is corruption, which is seriously problematic. Corruption in Thailand is severe; it is said that a corporation wishing to acquire a government project is required to bribe politicians; some bidders might need to pay 50 percent of the project value. The Transparency International Corruption Perception Index placed Thailand at 102 in 2013, from being positioned at 88 in 2012. Corruption and conflict of interest problems are enormous obstacles for progressing to an HIC as these cause the national revenues to be not fully or purposefully spent by politicians and civil servants who exert authority in defining policy for their personal rather than the national benefit.

HOW EUROPE CAN CONTRIBUTE TO IMPROVING THE CHANCES OF THAILAND BECOMING A HIGH-INCOME COUNTRY

Thailand is quite likely to get stuck in the MIT, and it has many internal problems that are obstacles for its upgrade to an HIC. The economy cannot grow as it did before the 1997 Asian financial crisis by conventional factors or approaches; moving beyond the MIT will require new methods. This section will deal with the role of Europe in assisting Thailand to progress beyond the MIT by considering its role in the past as well as the channels or opportunities that European countries and Thailand could jointly collaborate in for mutual benefit.

Promoting Trade

Historically, Thailand, formerly called the Kingdom of Siam, was pressured by the British Empire to liberalize its foreign trade with 'colonial power' countries from Europe, especially in signing the Bowring Treaty with the United Kingdom in 1855. This was because of high tariff rates for Western merchandise imported to Siam, coupled with a prohibition on foreigners exporting rice. The Treaty cancelled the trade monopoly of Siam's state, lowered the tariff rates, and gave permission to the British to trade with Thai people. Consequently, there was a change of domestic production from a subsistence economy to a market economy with the United Kingdom being Siam's major export market comprising

70 percent to 80 percent of Thailand's export value. After the Bowring Treaty was signed, Siam had to sign free trade treaties with other European colonial countries in order to mitigate Britain's trade monopoly and to balance British power in Siam. Before World War II, the majority of trade transactions were with European countries, and Thailand then began to transact more business with Japan. After World War II ended, more commerce took place with the United States and Japan, and from the first to the current National Social and Economic Development Plan, Thailand was predominantly dependent on exporting to the United States, Europe, and Japan. Trade between Thailand and Europe was characterized as intra-industry trade and the majority of Thai goods exported to the EU were automatic data processing machines, motor vehicles for transportation, and air conditioning equipment, whereas goods imported by Thailand from the EU consisted of electronic integrated circuits.

The share of exports from Thailand to Europe in terms of Thailand's total export value has constantly declined, whereas Thailand's share of exports to emerging markets has increased. In 2013, the ASEAN was ranked as the first export market for Thailand, China was second and the United States, EU, and Japan came third to fifth, respectively (Figure 4.4). The factor that changed the structure of Thailand's export market is regionalization; namely, the European Community, the North Atlantic Free Trade Area, and the ASEAN Free Trade Area, which expanded intra-regional trade and minimized the dependency on the markets outside the region. The next factor is the trade barrier; in particular the market access restrictions of the EU for agricultural imports from foreign countries outside the EU in order to protect domestic agriculture; for instance, defining the most-favoured nation tariff rate range between 18 percent and 28 percent for agricultural and fisheries goods, and employing the tariff rate quota measures for agricultural goods, sanitary and phytosanitary measures, and technical barriers to trade measures.

The discontinuation of free trade negotiations between Thailand and the EU is another factor causing trade between Thailand and Europe to have declining shares in Thailand's total trade. In the meantime, Thailand concluded agreements with various countries such as ASEAN, Japan, China, and Australia, which led to expanding trade with countries that have an FTA. As a result, Thailand will tend to be more dependent on the export market in Asia in the future. The EU has concluded FTAs with many countries, and most of the countries that made bilateral agreements are developing countries. In addition, the EU started a negotiation process for an FTA with Singapore, Malaysia, and Vietnam that are important trading partners and competitors of Thailand's. Hence, the delay in negotiations between Thailand and the EU is a factor that diminishes Thailand's competiveness in the EU market.

Although free trade negotiations between Thailand and EU are advocated, they are likely to be dormant because presently Thailand does not

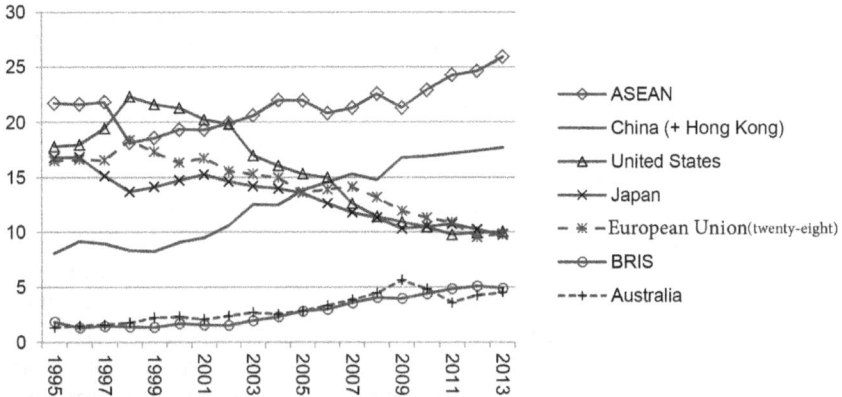

Note: BRIS refers to Brazil, Russia, India, South Africa

Figure 4.4. Thailand's export market structure (% of total export value). Note: BRIS refers to Brazil, Russia, India, South Africa. Source: Bank of Thailand.

have an elected government. This has prompted the EU to suspend negotiations until the situation normalizes. Furthermore, such negotiations between Thailand and the EU, as well as with the United States, are closely watched by non-government organizations and civil groups who disagree with several issues in the Agreement on Trade-Related Intellectual Property Rights, such as the protection of drug patents and patents on plants and animals. Thailand and the EU should nevertheless speed up negotiations on an FTA to promote expansion of trade. If, considering the structure of imported and exported goods of both parties, it is found that they are complementary, then trade liberalization is an opportunity for trade creation, which means more trade expansion and also results in more growth in investment. An FTA negotiation between Thailand and the EU does not need to liberalize every item of goods and services in the comprehensive list, but it could proceed by starting with liberalizing the items from which both parties could mutually benefit, before moving to further trade liberalization in the next phase. Thailand and the EU should also negotiate on coordination and exchanging information about trade-related measures such as sanitary and phytosanitary and technical barriers to trade measures, and collaborate to provide support for Thai entrepreneurs to gain knowledge on such trade measures and regulations. Any increase in trade liberalization will be a chance for Thailand to enhance its competiveness in the EU market as well as for the EU to maintain and expand its trade to emerging Asian economies within this region, since Thailand has a high potential of becoming a trade and transportation hub.

Developing the Service Sector

Scholars and technocrats in Thailand realize the importance of re-structuring the economy as a service economy by developing this sector for higher productivity. The service sector needs to be liberalized, and liberalization of the sector would develop high-level knowledge and technology, reduce inefficiency, and reduce the existing monopoly in this area. The EU has an interest in investing in Thailand's service sector, which was noticeable from investments made in banking during the Asian financial crisis, when Thailand needed to deregulate foreign ownership in banking businesses due to the liquidity problems of its financial institutions. In the negotiations on a free trade area with Thailand, the EU demanded the liberalization of trade, services, and investments in the service sector where areas of interest to the EU consist of telecommunications, parcel and postal service, financial services, and international transportation services. These services are knowledge and technology intensive, in which the EU has a comparative advantage. Trade and investment liberalization in the service sector under a Thai-EU FTA would be an opportunity for Thailand to be a more attractive investment destination, leading to higher FDI, more knowledge and technology transfer, and more competitiveness.

Nonetheless, the liberalization issue in the services field causes resistance within Thailand because those are areas where Thailand lacks both competitiveness and an institution for governing and protecting adverse impacts from investment. Accordingly, Thailand and the EU could join hands in developing the capacity of the service sector for preparing its readiness towards liberalization. The EU could play a role in technical support for more efficient business development and higher standards in the service sector, in developing people to gain higher knowledge and expertise, and in developing the regulations as well as institutions for governance in order to create free competition and a standards-based service quality.

Tourism in Thailand is another service sector in which European countries are keen to invest, as a large number of European tourists visit the kingdom yearly, accounting for 30 percent of the foreign tourists. There are still some restrictions on foreign investments in tourism, coupled with ineffective law enforcement. There are attempts to find gaps in the law such as having local Thais as nominees to invest in properties in tourist attraction areas and registering tour companies by using Thai guides in name but not in practice. Foreign tourists generate income for local people but can cause many problems, like destruction of the environment of sightseeing sites, drugs and crime, prostitution, raising property and land prices, and so on. These adverse effects of tourism have naturally led to objections from the Thais. It is suggested that Thailand and the EU should coordinate action to solve these problems. EU support will enable Thailand to develop sustainable tourism, which will also protect the rights and welfare of tourists from Europe.

Research and Development Collaboration

The EU comprises the major group of investors in Thailand. The value of FDI from the then European Economic Community has continuously accelerated from $0.9 million in 1970 to $1,460.8 million in 2010. After the Plaza Accord, more investments from Japan and the newly industrialized countries flowed into Thailand, causing a decrease in the share of FDI from the EU approximately at the average rate of 10 percent of the net inward flow of FDI. The industries invested in by the EU consist of chemicals, paper, electronics, and electrical appliances, and investments from Europe and other developed countries are an important factor in changing the industry structure from a labour-intensive to a high-technology industry. However, Thailand's industrial structure is still OEMs, relying upon technology and design from foreign countries.

The Thai economy is facing two aspects of competition: the first is competition from neighbouring countries with lower wages and the second is competition from countries with a higher development level. The economy needs to be restructured to become a high value-added production sector through upgrading the domestic manufacturing corporations from OEMs to one which is an original design manufacturer and original brand manufacturer. Thailand needs to focus more on R&D by increasing R&D expenditure in its private sector. To build a pool of R&D individuals, scholarships should be granted to study in the fields required for developing the country's strategic industries. Importing researchers from foreign countries should be encouraged as well as investment promotion in R&D activities and developing infrastructure that will support R&D activities and the incubation of technology business.

Companies in the EU are inclined to move more R&D activities to developing countries since those countries play increasingly important roles in R&D and innovation. When only R&D expenditure in Asia is considered, its shares are up to 39 percent of world R&D expenditure[23], resulting in many new innovation sources in Asia. Asia is also an external R&D location or target, where foreign companies are coming to invest in R&D. The reason that leading global corporations outsource R&D to Asia is that the cost of design and research in Asia is cheaper than in the West; in the future, Asia will have a large pool of scientists and engineers. Due to compatible trends for R&D demand between Thailand and the EU, Thailand has an opportunity for cooperation with the EU in R&D; for instance, encouraging companies in the EU to invest in R&D and design in Thailand, matching the business sector of Thailand and universities within the EU for joint research, and exchanging researchers in R&D.

Human Capital Development

Europe has significantly contributed to human capital development in Thailand. In the past, Thailand was shaped to be modern and to escape from the threat of colonialism by relying on knowledge and people who graduated from Europe; the country was reformed based on Western approaches in education, public health, transportation, and state administration, as well as a political regime transformation in 1932. In developing the country since 1961, the neo-economic development approach, which was initiated by the United States and Europe to be implemented through international organizations like the World Bank and the IMF, was pursued.

Many high-level personnel in Thailand graduated and received training from the West, and this can be noted from the high number of students and government officers, under supervision of the Office of the Civil Service Commission, who studied and received training from the EU and will rise from 31 percent in 2001 to 46 percent in 2014. In the meantime, those who studied and got training in the United States were ranked as number two with about 30 percent share (Figure 4.5).

Thailand still has a shortage of qualified labour, which reflects the problem at every level of the educational system in Thailand. The entire Thai education system has to be reformed to upgrade its quality. Qualified teachers need to be trained, and teachers who are more qualified should have their compensation restructured to attract talents to become teachers. The school should be transformed as a bilingual and eventually trilingual school to develop its quality and instruct learners to become global citizens[24]. The universities have to collaborate with the business sector or groups of industry in education arrangements, training, and

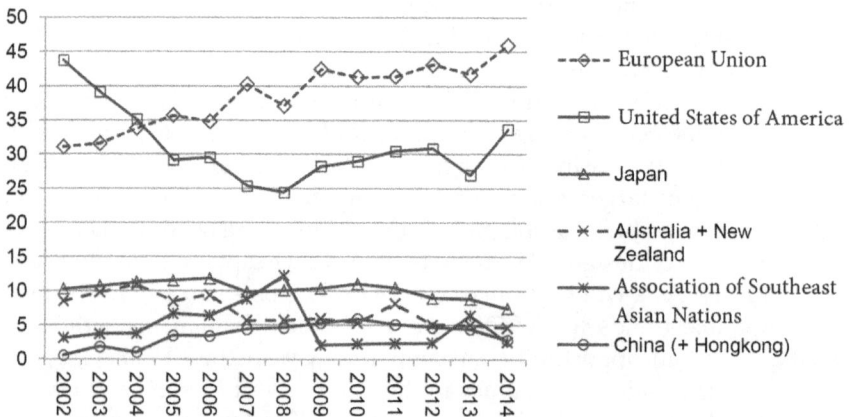

Figure 4.5.   Study Abroad Statistics (in percentages year wise). Source: Office of the Civil Service Commission (OCSC).

R&D to gain ability in producing personnel and research that meet the industry's requirements. Each university may need to self-adjust to attain subject matter expertise to respond to the requirements of some industries, whereas some universities may be developed to gain higher quality in various fields to become world class institutions.

Thailand could cooperate with the EU in educational development. Thailand and the EU could join hands to grant scholarships, both Thai government scholarships and EU educational institution scholarships, for Thai people for strategic scholarships aligned with the country's needs, but not haphazardly as at present. Thailand could also collaborate with the EU in developing the quality of vocational training as well as foreign language teaching, especially in English, and such cooperation could consist of knowledge transfer, curriculum co-development, teacher and student exchange, and providing Thai students an opportunity to take up internships at leading corporations in the EU.

Promoting Good Governance

An important aspect of creating good governance in Thai society is resolving the corruption problem and conflict of interest in the political and civil service systems. People must be instilled with an awareness of citizenship and should be more cooperative in performing political activities and expressing their opinion on national development. Political parties have to be peoples' parties rather than being controlled by big financiers or domineering political actors. The inspection system must be effectively developed and opened up for the people to have an opportunity to get involved in investigating politicians and civil servants. The information related to spending national revenue has to be disclosed and permission must be given for inspection by the people. The EU currently takes part in developing Thailand's democracy through the operations of the government sector and private organizations. The EU could also be involved in resolving the governance problems in Thailand, especially the corruption found in the government's procurement policies, by finalizing an agreement on government procurement for exchanging information and regulations on inter-governmental procurement and developing a transparent process of governmental procurement as well as an anti-corruption mechanism in the international procurement process.

Arrangements as those described above may appear difficult to implement soon because Thailand is being ruled by a government that was not the outcome of any election. The EU and some individual EU member-states have expressed their disagreement with the seizure of power by the military and called upon Thailand to return quickly to the democratic process that constitutes greater legitimacy. In addition, some EU countries have announced that they will officially suspend their assistance and cooperation with Thailand. However, the rule by the military government could be of a short duration. The ruling National Council for Peace and Order (NCPO) has announced a road map that provides that the army will return power to the people and elections will be held within one and a half years. For this military government to stay in position longer than that provided by the road map may prove difficult because there will otherwise be a great deal of opposition from many people who want such elections to take place. If we reflect on the durations of the takeovers of the military governments in 1992 and 2006, we can note that their governing periods were not of very long duration.

The West's attitude in the present circumstances is in opposition to the Thai military coup, but China and ASEAN member countries still continue to cooperate with the Thai government despite the fact that the ruling regime has not come about as a result of elections. The Asian attitude towards the present Thai government reflects existing international competition to have some influence on the reform process of the NCPO, and participate in the implementation of state investment projects, as the NCPO has planned to invest $8 billion in infrastructure, which is a sum equal to the Thai annual budget. Therefore, cooperation between Thailand and Europe is not likely to halt entirely, though at the present time it might appear less formal and be conducted through non-governmental agencies.

CONCLUSION

The Thai economy seems to be growing at a satisfying level, but evaluating it through quantitative indicators, and considering the factors impacting its historical expansion, signals that it faces a risk of getting stuck in the MIT. Problems and internal weaknesses continue to beset the country and are obstacles for developing the economy to be competitive. As a result, the progress of the country beyond the MIT is seen to be a challenging task; a task which requires new factors to be made use of in order to drive economic development and expansion. The factors that are considered to be of critical importance in making this possible are technology, knowledge, and innovation, which are what will help the economy of Thailand become one based on knowledge.

The development of a strong and mutually constructive economic relationship between Thailand and Europe as a whole, and the EU in particular, is believed to present a good opportunity for Thailand, as it would allow the country to become an HIC with Europe having a major role to play in terms of being a trade partner, investor, and source of knowledge and high technology for Thailand.

However, in the present era, Thailand has a tendency primarily to expand its economic and trade relationships with nearby Asian and other emerging markets. The United States has increased its interest towards

ASEAN. At the same time, the traditional relationship between Thailand and Europe seems to have slowed down due to stalled trade talks on an FTA and the military coup in Thailand as well as to economic and financial problems in the eurozone and the EU itself. Thailand and the EU need to give more importance to the quality of their relationship and focus more in the future on cooperation to develop human capital, R&D, and economic structures; to raise the standards of entrepreneurs, for the development of economic and political institutions; and to close the development gap between Thailand and the EU. These new aspects need to be implemented side by side with the traditional focus on the quantitative relationship, such as the expansion of trade and investment opportunities.

NOTES

1. World Bank, 'China 2030: Building a Modern, Harmonious, and Creative High-Income Society' (Washington, DC: World Bank, 2013).

2. Gianluca Grimalda and Macro Vivarelli, 'Is Inequality the Price to Pay for Higher Growth in Middle Income Countries?' *Journal of Evolutionary Economics* 20 (2010): 265–306.

3. Pierre-Richard Agénor, Otaviano Canuto and Michael Jelenic, 'Avoiding Middle-Income Growth Traps', *Economic Premise* 98 (2012): 1–7.

4. GNI per capita has been proved to correlate to other non-financial quality-of-life indicators such as life expectancy at birth, mortality rates of children, and enrollment rates in school. But limitations of GNI per capita are non-inclusion of income from informal sector and income distribution. The Atlas method is an adjustment for the difference between the rate of inflation in the country and international inflation.

5. Jesus Felipe, Arnelyn Abdon, and Utsav Kumar, 'Tracking the Middle-Income Trap: What is it, Who is in it, and Why', Levy Economics Institute of Bard College, Working Paper no 175 (2012), www.levyinstitute.org/pubs/wp_715.pdf, accessed 5 August 2014.

6. Thailand Development Research Institute, *Raingarn Chabub Somboon Krongkarn Nayobai Satarana Pue Yok Radub Thai Hai Pon Kubduc Raidai Parnklang* (Final Report on Public Policy for Uplifting Thailand Beyond the Middle-Income Trap Project) (Bangkok: Thailand Development Research Institute, 2013).

7. Barry Eichengreen, Donghyun Park, and Kwanho Shin, 'Growth Slowdowns Redux: New Evidence on the Middle-Income Trap', *National Bureau of Economic Research*, Working Paper 18,673 (2013), www.nber.org/papers/w18673, accessed 5 August 2014.

8. World Bank, 'China 2030'.

9. Fernando Gabriel Im and David Rosenblatt, 'Middle-Income Traps: A Conceptual and Empirical Survey', World Bank, Policy Research Working Paper 6,594 (2013), documents.worldbank.org/curated/en/2013/09/18220959/middle-income-traps-conceptual-empirical-survey, accessed 5 August 2014.

10. Sasin Institute for Global Affairs, *Raingarn Chabub Somboon Krongkarn Boriharn Karnpleanplang Krasoung Karnklung* (Final Report on Change Management of Ministry of Finance Project) (Bangkok: Ministry of Finance, 2013).

11. National Economic Social Development Board, *Pan Pattana Settakij Lae Sungkom Hangchat Chabub Tee 1 Raya Tee 2 Por. Sor.2507-2509* (Economic and Social Development Plan, vol. 1, Phase 2-2507-2509 BE.) (Bangkok: National Economic Social Development Board, 1964).

12. International Bank for Reconstruction and Development, *A Public Development Program for Thailand* (Baltimore, MD: John Hopkins University Press, 1959).

13. National Economic Social Development Board, *Sarouppon Karnpattana Prated Nai Choung Pan Pattana Chabub Tee 3 (2515–2519 BE.)* [Summary of the Development in the period of the Third National Economic and Social Development Plan (1972–1976)] (Bangkok: Office of National Economic and Social Development Board, 1977).

14. Lawrence MacDonald et al (eds.), *Main Report, The East Asian Miracle: Economic Growth and Public Policy. A World Bank Policy Research Report*, vol. 1 (Washington, DC: World Bank Group, 1993).

15. Van Tho Tran, 'The Middle-Income Trap: Issues for Members of the Association of Southeast Asian Nations', ADBI Working Paper 421 (Asian Development Bank Institute, 2013), www.adbi.org/working-paper/2013/05/16/5667.middle.income.trap.issues.asean/, accessed 5 August 2014.

16. International competitiveness index is defined as $(X - M) / (X + M)$, where X is export value of a product in a year and M is import value of such product in the same year

17. Arkom Termpittayapaisit, 'Karn Prubkroongsrang Settakij Hai Peungping Toneng Lae Kangkun Dai Nai Sungkom Lok' (Economic restructuring for Self-Sufficiency and Competitiveness), paper presented at the 2008 National Economic Social Development Board Annual Meeting *Vision Thailand 2037* (National Economic Social Development Board, 15 August 2008), www.nesdb.go.th/portals/0/news/annual_meet/51/g1/presentation%20group%201_%E0%B8%A3%E0%B8%A8%E0%B8%8AE0%B8%AD%E0%B8%B2%E0%B8%84%E0%B8%A1.pdf, accessed 15 August 2014.

18. Ingo Borchert, Batshur Gootiiz, and Aaditya Mattoo, 'Policy Barriers to International Trade in Services: Evidence from a New Database', *World Bank Economic Review* 28, no. 1 (2014): 162–88.

19. National Economic Social Development Board, *Karn Karn Pramarnkarn Kong Prachakorn Kong Prated Thai (Radub Parnklang) Pee 2543–2573* (Estimation on population of Thailand (medium level) between 2000 and 2030) (Bangkok: National Economic Social Development Board, 2007).

20. Asian Development Bank, *Asian Development Outlook 2012 Update: Services and Asia's Future Growth* (Manila: Asian Development Bank, 2012).

21. Korbsak Putrakul, 'Kunnapap Kong Karn Chareon Terbto Chak Miti Kong Karn Krachai Raidai: Punha Lae Tangoog' (Quality of Growth, Income Distribution Dimension: Problem and Solution), paper presented at the 2013 Bank of Thailand Symposium (Bank of Thailand, 19 September 2013), www.bot.or.th/Thai/EconomicConditions/ResearchPublication/symposium/2556/Paper4.pdf, accessed 15 August 2014.

22. Pasuk Phongpaichit and Pornthep Benyaapikul, *Political Economy Dimension of a Middle Income Trap: Challenge and Opportunity for Policy Reform. Thailand* (Bangkok: The Asian Foundation, 2013).

23. Reinhilde Veugelers, 'The World Innovation Landscape: Asia Rising?' Bruegel Policy Contribution 2013/02 (Bruegel, 2013), www.bruegel.org/publications/publication-detail/publication/766-the-world-innovation-landscape-asia-rising/, accessed 15 September 2013.

24. Kriengsak Chareonwongsak, 'Naewnom Tourloke Pai Nai Tis Rongrean 2 Lae 3 Pasa' (Global Trend: Shift to Bilingual and Trilingual School), *Karn Suksa Upgrade (Education Upgrade)* 89 (2008).

FIVE

Korea and Asia-Europe Relations

Jin Park

Asia and Europe perceive each other as increasingly important partners for global peace and prosperity in the twenty-first century. Despite the geographical distance across the Eurasian continent, the two regions have been interacting with each other on multiple dimensions, including the economic, political, security-related, and sociocultural areas. And there is no shortage of documents and reports in which the European Union (EU) as well as individual EU member states acknowledge the increasing importance of East Asia as an emerging market and as a partner for cooperation[1]. The European Council states that 'East Asia is a region of especially dynamic change in which the EU and its member-states have substantial interests'[2]. The development of the Asia-Europe Meeting (ASEM), an inter-regional consultative process, is a natural testament to that shared awareness of strategic imperative; through nine biennial summit conferences so far, the ASEM has been expanding the scope of communication and cooperation between Asian and European countries[3].

South Korea, which hosted the third ASEM summit in March 2000, has been an active participant in the ASEM process, playing its part as a key coordinator between advanced and developing countries. In 2013, President Park Geun-hye visited Brussels to meet the EU leaders and discuss future Korea-EU partnership for promoting democracy, free market economy, and human rights as well as peace and security around the globe. South Korea is thus fully committed to pursuing further this multifaceted partnership with Europe.

Above all, in economic cooperation, while the eurozone crisis may have somewhat impaired the dynamism of trade and investment between Asia and Europe, the recent signs of recovery in Europe certainly offer a promising prospect for the Asian economy. South Korea has already signed a free trade agreement (FTA) with the EU initiated in October 2009, and also with the United States. That South Korea is so far the only Asian country to do so clearly demonstrates its proactive approach to inter-regional cooperation and creates a certain level of pressure on other nations in their relations with Europe and in their trade policy direction.

The subsequent increase of bilateral trade and investment between South Korea and the EU is expected to continue, although the former is currently running a trade deficit with the latter. There is no question that the European market, once the recovery is well in place, will provide a major stimulus to the growth potential of the expanding Asian economy, including South Korea.

In the political realm, South Korea, as a pioneering democracy in East Asia, has been closely engaged with the EU in pursuing various political dialogues with European nations within the context of the Framework Agreement, first signed in 1996 and updated in 2010. Korea's High-Level Political Dialogue with the EU, along with bilateral strategic dialogues with EU member states such as Britain and France, represent multichannel efforts to establish a constructive habit of engagement. Within Asia, on the other hand, there currently is no collective regional security institution like the North Atlantic Treaty Organization in Europe, with the exception of the Association of Southeast Asian Nations (ASEAN) where member-states work through a consensual institutional arrangement. The resolution of regional conflicts in Asia, including territorial disputes, therefore, is basically left to the individual nations. In addition, the Asian security structure has been inseparably linked to the United States through the network of bilateral alliances; yet the region and this US-centric security network now face a much more complicated security dynamic as the rising China seeks to expand its power and influence. Being one of closest allies of the United States, Korea's position on regional cooperation and Asia-Europe cooperation should present a distinctive perspective, especially when compared to those of other Asian nations.

Amidst this fluid and unpredictable security landscape, the military role of Europe in Asian security has been relatively limited, but Europe can still play a significant role in the maintenance of peace and security in Asia through such fora as the UN Security Council, the International Atomic Energy Agency, and the ASEAN Regional Forum (ARF). Asia and Europe also need to upgrade their joint efforts to cope with international terrorism, transnational crime, and challenges to human security. On the Korean peninsula, the EU has been making a substantial contribution to the peace and security of the divided nation by supporting the denuclearization of North Korea and denouncing Pyongyang's nuclear tests and missile launches. The EU, together with South Korea, can also encourage North Korea to open up gradually and reform itself. At the same time, South Korea and the EU have been closely cooperating with each other to promote human rights in North Korea.

Asia and Europe should continue to cooperate in the sociocultural field to deepen and widen their bilateral partnership for a better future. The economic advancement, expansion of the middle class, and political democratization seen in many Asian countries will inevitably bring the two regions closer together. Asia and Europe are mutually complementary partners in social development and cross-continental cultural fertilization. The revolution of digital communications and public transportation will exponentially increase the inter-regional human exchanges and idea sharing between Asia and Europe. Moreover, the dynamic Korean cultural wave or *Hallyu* (the Korean wave), such as popular music, television drama, food, and fashion, is attracting many Europeans, especially young people, who look more towards Asia. Asia and Europe, therefore, will continue to move towards sociocultural convergence while maintaining their own distinct identities.

ECONOMIC PARTNERSHIP

While the sheer size of the two regions alone presents an imperative need for closer relations, Asia and Europe each have their own set of strong motivations to engage in active cooperation with one another. Europe, with its advanced yet aging economies, needs to find new space and new markets to invest its capital and technology. Asia, with its rapidly developing economies and enormous growth potential still remaining, offers a perfect opportunity for Europe. On the other hand, Asia needs Europe's technology and investment to manufacture products, which in turn will be consumed in the integrated market across Europe. Accordingly, economic exchange and integration is now of mutual interest to both Europe and Asia, unlike the exploitive relations of the colonial past.

The continued growth of Europe-Asia trade despite the global and regional economic downturn is therefore a natural manifestation of the need for such cooperation. 'Mainland China (including Hong Kong and Macau), Taiwan, Japan, Korea and ASEAN account for around 21 percent of global gross domestic product (GDP) and for some 28 percent of the EU's global trade in goods and services in 2010 and these proportions continue to rise'[4]. This is already significantly greater than the EU's trans-Atlantic trade, which stands at around 23 percent. Such growing importance of Asia to Europe has been widely acknowledged: 'The continuing increase in our economic interconnectedness reflects the fact that growth in Asia has continued to surpass expectations, even in times of global recession'[5].

Among the burgeoning trade and investment relations between Europe and emerging Asia, Korea's relationship with the EU stands out for its dynamism and accelerated pace. Korea is the first Asian country to sign both a Framework Agreement and an FTA with the EU, representing full and eager commitment on both sides to enhancing cooperation. And the figures speak for themselves. By 2013, the EU had become Korea's second largest trading partner. Korea took a somewhat smaller proportion of the EU's global trade as the latter's ninth largest trading partner, but the absolute volume of trade between the two is by no means insignificant, standing at well over $100 billion in 2013: Korea's export to the EU came in at $48.9 billion, and import from EU at $56.2 billion.

Facilitating such remarkable trade relations, of course, is the Korea-EU FTA, now in its third year, which has been praised for its mutually beneficial comprehensiveness[6]. Unfortunately, the first few years of the Korea-EU FTA were marred by global and regional challenges as the eurozone crisis took its toll on the EU's domestic market and elsewhere. In particular, Korea's shipbuilding industry was badly hit as its European clients suffered; the industry's export to Europe, which accounts for a significant portion of Korea's total exports to the EU, fell sharply both in price and quantity: from 9.75 percent in 2011 to 6.91 percent in 2012.

However, during the general downturn, the Korea-EU FTA proved itself to be of formidable assistance across numerous industries. Those Korean export items that had benefited from the Korea-EU FTA saw a significantly smaller margin of fall (–1.5 percent) compared to those that were not covered by the FTA (–12.2 percent). In other words, the challenge of unfavourable market conditions in fact turned out to be a timely chance for demonstrating the efficacy of the FTA as the Korea-EU FTA did much to guard Korea-EU trade from the damaging impact of the eurozone crisis and global recession. It is to be particularly noted that, despite the general fall in trade in recent years, small and medium enterprises (SMEs) trading between Korea and the EU saw a 1.7 percent increase in their trade thanks to the Korea-EU FTA. The trade in items that were covered under the FTA rose by 7.9 percent. Many Korean businesses opened trade connections with the EU because the FTA now offered profitable channels of business while many existing trades, such as trunks, handbags, plastic sheets, and films, rocketed in quantity[7].

Meanwhile, the EU's export to Korea has actually increased sharply as the FTA eliminated or significantly reduced tariffs on high-quality consumer goods from the EU. Most notably, Europe's share of the Korean automobile market has almost trebled compared to the pre-FTA level; European cars, already widely popular in Korea, are now available at more affordable prices. After further reductions in tariff came into effect in July 2014, this share is expected to rise even higher. In contrast, the export of Korean automobiles has not seen a significant increase as many Korean automobile manufacturers operate factories within the EU to supply the European market. Also, due to the continued instability in the Middle East and sanctions on Iran, Korea has turned to the EU as a part of its strategy to diversify its energy supply. Aided by the FTA, the import of European crude oil has risen sharply, making it the second largest import item from the EU to Korea. The effect of the FTA is clearly evident here again as the EU's export of those items not covered by the FTA, such as equipment for manufacturing semiconductors, actually fell in volume (–7.1 percent) while the EU export of FTA items, on the other hand, rose sharply, to +14.1 percent.

Over the past three years, the Korea-EU FTA has managed to eliminate tariffs on over 95 percent of imports from the EU and over 99 percent of exports from Korea. Yet reducing tariffs and opening markets in services, government procurement, and intellectual property are only a part of the FTA effect. The Korea-EU FTA is expected to have far-reaching implications that go well beyond the economic benefits of reducing prices and making available greater choice for consumers; it will deepen and broaden exchanges in all areas of life from education and culture to innovation and welfare[8].

In line with growing trade, Korea-EU investment relations have also continued to expand. The EU is now the biggest investor in Korea as a single economic bloc, accounting for no less than 43 percent of foreign investment in Korea, which stands at an average of $3 billion per year. A large proportion of the EU's investment in Korea is concentrated in service industries, especially in finance, insurance, and banking—industries which, in turn, have the potential to promote further increase in trade and investment in other sectors. Also, as four West European nations (Netherlands, the United Kingdom, Germany, and France) take up over 80 percent of the EU's total investment in Korea, there is still much potential for expansion by encouraging other European nations to increase their investments. Korea's investment in Europe, mostly in manufacturing, stands at around $3 billion in recent years, but this is a significantly reduced amount following the aftermath of the recent eurozone crisis.

The next challenge for Korea-EU economic relations, then, is to achieve that scale and scope of cooperation that will guard trade and investment from occasional and cyclical glitches. Given the relatively small size of the Korean market when compared to that of the EU, the asymmetrical interdependence also limits the opportunity for greater cooperation.

This is why it is important to make concerted efforts to establish a broader framework of cooperation between Northeast Asia and the EU at a bloc-to-bloc level: Korea-EU trade and cooperation can be promoted much more effectively through that regional framework.

REGIONAL INTEGRATION FOR STRONGER
ASIA-EUROPE COOPERATION

Of course, for there to be any meaningful attempts to pursue Northeast Asia-Europe cooperation, Northeast Asia must first achieve its own regional integration. Korea, China, and Japan should be able to share substantial common objectives among themselves and establish an efficient mechanism for trilateral coordination before they can engage themselves with Europe as a Northeast Asia bloc.

Economic integration in Northeast Asia, in turn, should begin with firm and coordinated domestic housekeeping in each country. The three Northeast Asian nations are currently at very different stages of economic and social development with distinct models of growth. Of course, wide disparity in the mere size of the three economies alone makes it only natural that they are so different. And that diversity may well be what makes economic cooperation in Northeast Asia attractive as the three nations deploy their respective strengths. However, meaningful and mutually beneficial cooperation between such widely different economies will only be possible when there is a level playing field for fair competition and cooperation. The three Northeast Asian nations must achieve major reform in their own domestic market regulations, tax system, industrial practices, and labour practices to make themselves more compatible with one another. Without consistent rules and open systems, regional integration will mean rather little[9].

The race to seize the initiative in Northeast Asian trilateral cooperation, therefore, somewhat ironically, comes down to which of the three countries will be the first to achieve the necessary domestic reforms and still have sufficient political drive left to engage others in discussion. In China, President Xi Jinping has been pursuing a vigorous programme of reform, especially against corruption at all levels and in all spheres of China's one-party-led society. While Xi appears to have been relatively successful in pushing through unprecedentedly high-profile cases of corruption charges, it will take more time before his drive to rationalize China's economic and political system delivers its full impact across China. Until then, it is likely that China will continue to struggle to offer any constructive leadership in the region.

The Japanese Prime Minister Shinzo Abe, meanwhile, has yet to shoot the 'third arrow' of his 'Abenomics' in earnest. While the highly risky bet on monetary easing seems to have paid off in the short term, time is running out for the Abe government to capitalize on that window of opportunity through a dramatically weakened yen and its boost to Japan's industries, by following through with substantial structural reforms. The favourable result of the 2014 Japanese House of Councillors election vindicated Abe's bold policy at large, but there will be a limit to maintaining popular support with the nationalistic policy that Abe and his conservative political partners have so far projected. According to a recent opinion poll, more people in Japan are concerned about the changed interpretation of the Peace Constitution and the introduction of the collective self-defence than those who support the ideas.

In Korea, President Park Geun-hye is also driving forward a campaign for a creative economy and deregulation. Taking a zealous stance against bureaucratic regulations, President Park chaired an eight-hour televised meeting of government ministers, business leaders, and academics in order to address the issue. Originally, the main thrust of the government reform policy was centring on the theme of economic democratization, but the gravity of the policy direction has now shifted to economic recovery and growth. Now well into the second year of her five-year term in office, time is at a premium for President Park; the aftermath of the tragic sinking of Ferry Sewol and difficulties with key government appointments may constrain the new ambitious political agenda for national renovation. Meanwhile, after the June 2014 cabinet reshuffle, Park's second economic team will focus on the deregulatory measures to revitalize the sluggish Korean economy. In the medium-to-longer term, however, Korea's strategy for trilateral cooperation in Northeast Asia may offer a useful framework through which regional integration could be initiated. Korea is currently working on an FTA with China on one hand, having on the other hand expressed an interest in joining the Trans-Pacific Partnership, of which Japan is a key member as well as the United States. Whereas negotiating a straightforward trilateral FTA among Korea, China, and Japan remains a colossal task, if Korea manages to sign those trade engagements on each side, it may be able to act as an intermediary in shaping favourable conditions for a trilateral arrangement. In particular, much progress has been made in negotiations for a Korea-China FTA; especially for China, which seeks to expand its influence in all spheres of Northeast Asia, a major trade agreement with Korea will have an added layer of strategic significance.

In order to fully leverage such dynamic potential of regional integration in Northeast Asia, strengthening economic cooperation between Korea and Europe is an indispensable strategic ambition for both sides, and there are real, solid grounds for optimism. Following President Park's summit with British Prime Minister David Cameron in 2013, the two leaders announced their joint pledge to double trade and foreign direct investment stocks between Korea and the United Kingdom by 2020. This is certainly an ambitious goal, but not an unrealistic vision as the importance of Eurasian commerce and exchange can only continue to grow. Epitomizing that irreversible trend of closing the distance between Europe and Asia is the grand vision for a Eurasian Railway, advocated by President Park during her visit to Central Asia in 2014. By connecting the southernmost end of the Korean peninsula to the Trans-Siberian Railway and all the way westward to London, Europe and Asia will truly become one continent through a new Silk Road Express. Of course, the challenge of connecting Europe and Korea hinges on one of the most stubborn obstacles in modern history: North Korea and Korean reunification. Until the Trans-Korean railway can run through the North Korean territory and connect to the Trans-Siberian network, South Korea will remain a geopolitical island. So, we turn to our next question: How could South Korea and the EU work together to bring about peace and stability on the Korean peninsula and in Northeast Asia?

POLITICAL COOPERATION

Growing economic interdependence is one thing, but translating it into political cooperation is quite another. Unlike commerce, which is largely driven by private profit incentives, political engagement between nations is often about sharing costs and responsibilities. This requires sustained political will projected at appropriate geopolitical opportunities[10]. Strategic partnership between Korea and the EU, then, is an extraordinary achievement given the considerable geographic distance between them[11]. In the absence of immediate geopolitical overlap, sustained political cooperation could be interpreted and appreciated as a product of a conscious effort on both sides. It is also a telling sign that both powers aspire to global influence and responsibility.

The recent update on the 1996 EU-Korea Framework Agreement seems to reflect such an awareness of the strategic importance of bilateral cooperation. The new Framework Agreement, which was signed in 2010 and has officially come into force as of June 2014 after ratification by EU member states, was built on the 1996 Framework Agreement, which was primarily focused on economic cooperation, as well as on the Joint Declaration on Political Dialogue. It significantly extends the scope of bilateral cooperation to include a whole range of political and security issues. In addition to further strengthening economic cooperation, it provides a legal and systematic foundation for bilateral, regional, as well as multilateral cooperation on issues as diverse as democracy, human rights, international security, weapons of mass destruction, non-proliferation, international crime, terrorism, judicial cooperation, and immigration.

Such an extensive agenda for cooperation has since been faithfully acted upon with continued high-level exchanges and cooperation. Since 2011, the Korea-EU High-Level Political Dialogue has been held between Korea's vice foreign minister and the European External Action Service deputy secretary general. Since her inauguration in early 2013, President Park has already made visits to the United Kingdom, France, Belgium, the EU headquarters, the Netherlands, Germany, and Switzerland. In the United Kingdom, she agreed to elevate the bilateral strategic dialogue to the foreign ministerial level and to pursue further cooperation on cybersecurity and international development. In France, her twenty-minute address in French at Mouvement des Entreprises de France did much to win the hearts of the French business community (she had stayed in Grenoble for a brief period during her twenties as a French-learning student). President Park's 2013 visit to Belgium resulted in a joint declaration to commemorate the fiftieth anniversary of diplomatic relations between Korea and the EU; this joint declaration reaffirmed their commitment to bilateral and multilateral cooperation, in particular reaffirming the EU's support of the Park administration's North Korea policy.

Of course, it takes more than general amicability for bilateral cooperation to become a truly strategic partnership. What is required to take the Korea-EU relations to the next level is identifying common challenges as well as substantive frameworks that will engage both parties in tackling those challenges. Here, we turn to take a closer look at security cooperation between Korea and the EU, first in the Northeast Asian context and then on the pressing issue of North Korea. Given the importance of a stable and prosperous Asia to Europe's own growth, these questions pose a real and urgent challenge to Korea-EU cooperation.

PEACE AND COOPERATION IN NORTHEAST ASIA

The security landscape of Asia is often expressed as the 'Asian Paradox', where ever-growing economic interdependence between Asian nations coexists with worsening tension in the absence of an established multilateral mechanism for security cooperation. Such a discrepancy between dynamic economic interaction and strained political relations is perhaps most acutely manifested in Northeast Asia, creating uncertainty and instability. From territorial confrontation in the South and East China seas to unresolved historical disputes, the region finds itself fraught with sensitive issues[12].

As for Korea, the territorial dispute with Japan over Dokdo continues to cast a long shadow over the prospect of friendly cooperation with Japan. While Korea's dispute with Japan is perhaps less overtly confrontational than other territorial disputes found elsewhere in East Asia, the territorial issue is unavoidably tangled with unresolved historical disputes, leaving all of them far more complicated. Indeed, the last couple of years have marked one of the most difficult times in Korea-Japan relations as President Park continues to engage with her Japanese counterpart Prime Minister Shinzo Abe, demanding that Japan takes genuine and unmistakable action to demonstrate its sincerity about repentance and reconciliation. Meanwhile, Prime Minister Abe and his conservative allies have done much to complicate the situation: Abe's 2013 visit to the Yasukuni Shrine, where Japanese war criminals are commemorated, attracted critical response from Korea and China and even from the United

States. The Japanese government's insistence on reviewing the 1993 Kono statement, which acknowledged the Japanese Imperial Army's involvement in the operation of 'comfort women' facilities, is interpreted in Korea and China as Japan's de facto denial of its past wrongdoings, and Japan's stockpile of weapons-grade plutonium, reportedly capable of producing thousands of nuclear weapons annually, is a potential source of concern.

Indeed, Prime Minister Abe has introduced an ambitious programme of defence and security policies designed to reinstate Japan as a major security player in the region. From the more direct military initiatives such as increasing military expenditure and proactive participation in overseas UN missions to his campaign to 'normalize' Japan through a new interpretation of its post-war pacifist constitution and claims to collective self-defence rights, his security policy has caused much consternation in neighbouring countries.

What further complicates the situation is the ambiguous stance of the United States in Northeast Asia. Traditionally a significant presence in Northeast Asian security affairs with its forces stationed in Korea as well as in Japan, the United States has recently been struggling between the financial reality of sequestration at home and its stated vision of rebalancing to the Asia-Pacific under the 'Pivot to Asia' strategy. American support for the Abe government's desire to play a greater security role at Japan's own political and budgetary expense is therefore understandable, yet it has caused many in Korea to question the committed role of the United States in the region. What is more, Japan's rearmament policy has caused China to take a more confrontational stance in Northeast Asia. For instance, China's unilateral announcement of its new Air Defence Identification Zone in the East China Sea was widely seen as China's bold counteracting gesture against Japan as well as the United States; the newly announced Air Defence Identification Zone covers most islands over which China is in dispute with Japan and Korea.

Meanwhile, China has been making continuous efforts to improve relations with South Korea. In addition to a series of affable gestures and summit meetings, President Xi Jinping made diplomatic history by visiting Seoul in July 2014 before visiting Pyongyang—the first time a Chinese leader had done so since the normalization of South Korea–China bilateral relations in 1992. While South Korea is rather cautious about its rapprochement with China as it maintains a delicate balancing act between the traditional foundation of the South Korea–United States Alliance and the immediate gravity of a newly rising neighbour, the growing strategic importance of China to Korea is already a reality. However, other than a largely notional proposal for a 'new type of great power relations with the [United States]', China has yet to offer a clear model for its leadership in the region.

In the midst of such complexities in Northeast Asia, the Park Geun-hye administration in Seoul has announced a series of policy initiatives to address security challenges in the region[13]. In particular, Park's Northeast Asia Peace and Cooperation Initiative proposes a Korean role as a middle power to lead the 'Seoul Process'—a Northeast Asian application, especially around the Korean peninsula, of the Helsinki process in Europe. The idea is to begin with 'softer' issues such as climate change, energy cooperation, disaster relief, cybersecurity, and humanitarian assistance where it may be easier to attain consensus and cooperation. Then, through repeated exercises in building a habit of trust and cooperation, the region may proceed to tackle more difficult issues in traditional security, territorial claims, and historical reconciliation. Ultimately, Park's Peace and Cooperation Initiative is indeed an ambitious call for a grand reconciliation among the three Northeast Asian nations. President Park's vision needs a detailed programme of substantial and realistic initiatives that South Korea can act upon. Especially in the absence of an immediately actionable opportunity in the current security climate, the Park government is trying to explore ways to launch the process of building trust. The Northeast Asian Initiative is to provide a regional setting for a comprehensive and collaborative solution to the North Korean issue, which might help create a favourable environment for inter-Korean dialogue and trust-building.

Where in this picture, then, will the EU fit? There can be little doubt that common policy objectives and consensus among the European states clearly acknowledge the need for the EU's positive engagement in Northeast Asian affairs. The question, then, is exactly how such interests and concerns can be materialized into a substantive role. Here, it is possible to consider a couple of policy directions for the EU. First, the EU may maintain a limited presence and engagement in Northeast Asia, primarily supporting the American policy objectives in the region. While this approach may sound somewhat passive and reactive, given the geographical and political distance, it may nonetheless present a realistic option. Indeed, this seems to be the default option for the EU: 'The [United States'] security commitments to Japan, the Republic of Korea and Taiwan as well as certain ASEAN countries, and the associated presence of US forces in the region, give the [United States] a distinct perspective on the region's security challenges, and makes the [United States] an important contributor to regional stability. It is important that the EU remains sensitive to this'[14].

On the other hand, it may be quite possible and desirable to find a distinctive role for the EU in Northeast Asia. Of course, such proactive initiatives will have to overcome several barriers. For instance, China's response to a new player in the regional game will have to be managed strategically. Also, there has to be a consistent and committed political leadership within the EU in order to generate consensus among its member-states; while most European states share a common interest in Asia as an important market, there remains divergent views as to just how far the EU can and should be engaged in Asia's political and military affairs. The key here will be to identify and articulate the EU's strategic interests in Asia with persuasive clarity[15].

There are a number of ways in which the EU may pursue a more direct and effective engagement with Northeast Asia. First, cooperation may be sought in areas where challenges are less geographically defined, and those areas may be much broader than commonly contemplated, because various threats to security and stability are rapidly becoming transnational in nature. While traditional state-to-state conflicts have hardly declined across the globe, peoples and nations around the world face more diverse and dynamic threats, which transcend national borders: acts of terrorism by non-state groups, international crime, climate change, and so on. One particularly potent example is cyberterrorism, which takes places in virtual space where there simply are no geographic boundaries; an increasing number of cyberattacks on governments, private firms, and some of the most critical infrastructure are being organized and executed by international groups. Here, Korea may join its information technology strengths with European expertise in facilitating international collaboration to lead Northeast Asia and the rest of the world in combating cyberterrorism. The Seoul Conference on Cyberspace in 2013 presented a central platform for such cooperation, as did the inaugural Korea-EU Cyber-Policy Consultation held in Brussels in May 2014. Cooperation in anti-piracy operations may also be another area where the EU could strategically engage with the common interest of Northeast Asian nations, namely the freedom and safety of navigation. Korea is already working with the EU in its operations to fight piracy in the Somali waters in Northeast Africa.

Second, the EU may venture to play a more active role in the existing regional dialogues such as the ARF. Without a formal multilateral platform for political and military cooperation, ARF remains one of few channels through which Asian nations can discuss security issues and attempt to find diplomatic solutions. Here, the EU could perform a valuable role as a facilitator and mediator by sharing its experience of conflict resolution and regional integration, and the EU may do so not as an outsider but as an interested party since, among many other issues, guarding the freedom of navigation in the East and South China seas is as important to the EU as it is to Asian nations.

Of course, working through a multilateral mechanism in Asia will require flexible thinking, and drawing direct comparisons between the historical case of European integration and the prospect of multilateral cooperation in Asia can be misleading. Yet Europe's experience of multilateral consultation and negotiation can offer some valuable guidance to coordinating the diverse and divergent interests of Asian nations.

Finally, to facilitate a more focused and expeditious cooperation, an EU+3 forum (Korea, China, and Japan) could be established. With the EU accounting for 18.7 percent of world GDP as of 2013—a sharp fall from over 25 percent in 2010—and the three Northeast Asian nations generating 23 percent, the two groupings alone represent more than one-third of world GDP[16]. Creating a bloc-to-bloc forum for the EU and Northeast Asia will thus open a more pointed framework for Euro-Asian multilateral dialogue based on growing common interests. Here again, the forum could begin with trust-building exercises in areas where cooperation can be achieved without getting into old disputes. The Trilateral Cooperation Secretariat in Seoul between South Korea, China, and Japan has already established a prototype mechanism for regional cooperation in Northeast Asia, and it could serve as a pioneering body for the Northeast Asian community in partnership with the EU.

FUTURE OF THE KOREAN PENINSULA

At the very heart of the Asian paradox in Northeast Asia lies the conundrum of the Korean peninsula with its six-decade-old partition between the two Koreas. With some of the world's most powerful military forces all located within close distance from Seoul (American military forces in Korea and Japan; China, Russia, South Korea, North Korea, and Japan), the Korean peninsula remains one of the last unresolved legacies of the Cold War.

The security situation on the Korean peninsula has not made any meaningful progress over the last five years. Since the sinking of the South Korean naval vessel Cheonan by a North Korean torpedo attack in 2010 and North Korea's shelling of the South Korean Yeonpyeong-do Island later that year, it has been virtually impossible to make any meaningful progress in inter-Korean relations. The suspension of the Six-Party Talks for the denuclearization of North Korea offers an illustration of the current stalemate; the 2012 Leap Day agreement between the United States and North Korea, in which the United States promised substantial food aid in return for North Korea's moratorium on missile test and uranium enrichment verified by an International Atomic Energy Agency inspection, broke down only a few weeks later when North Korea announced and executed the launch of its so-called satellite rocket. With successive administrations in Seoul having difficulty in dealing with Pyongyang and the Obama administration unable to commit any real initiative due to its financial constraints and troubles elsewhere on the globe, the situation on the Korean peninsula still waits for a fresh breakthrough.

Meanwhile, the North Korean leader Kim Jong-un appears to have consolidated his power base, at least among North Korea's élite leadership. It is not easy to ascertain exactly what motivated the ruthless execution of his uncle-in-law Jang Sung-taek and the purge of many other power élites, but the politics of fear combined with xenophobic propaganda continues to be the order of the day in Pyongyang. What remains unchanged is North Korea's nuclear ambition; in fact, the North Korean regime has taken advantage of the last several years of political standoff to advance its nuclear and missile capability. While most intelligence assessments consider North Korea to be a de facto nuclear power, North Korea is fully leveraging its threats of nuclear tests and missile launches to sustain internal tension and a sense of crisis on the Korean peninsula. Kim Jong-un's stated goal of the 'parallel pursuit' of a nuclear programme and economic development may well be an impossible mission and against all common sense, but as long as China continues to supply substantial food and energy to North Korea, it is quite possible that the Pyongyang regime will sustain itself for the time being.

Indeed, China has long been a patron of the Kim dynasty, blocking effective international action at the United Nations and acquiescing in a series of provocations and non-compliance by North Korea. The new leadership in Beijing is reported to be in the process of recalibrating its North Korean policy, although the Chinese attitude towards Pyongyang remains, at best, ambivalent. Given that China is the only power that can exercise a decisive leverage on the North Korean regime to induce a real change in its behaviour, the key to solving the Korean peninsula dilemma is very much in the hands of the Chinese leadership. While there appears to be some grounds for optimism as President Xi, during his 2014 visit to Seoul, expressly proclaimed China's intention not to tolerate a nuclear North Korea, the international community must work together to encourage China to take a more active role in bringing North Korea to the negotiation table.

What is important is that China finds its own strategic interest in creating a peaceful Korean peninsula—and ultimately a unified Korean peninsula. Here, an interesting insight may be gained by China's contingency plan for North Korea's collapse, reported in the Japanese media this year[17]. According to that document, China, bordering North Korea along two rivers, which can and are frequently crossed on foot by traders and defectors from North Korea, fears a massive inflow of displaced civilian refugees in the event of North Korea's collapse. This concern is aggravated by the fact that China's Northeastern province, which borders North Korea, is already populated by a Korean-Chinese ethnic minority. Addressing such concerns about the destabilizing impact of a radical change in the status quo, along with the control of nuclear facilities in North Korea, may well provide an opportunity to engage key regional players in an earnest discussion about the post-unification arrangements for the Korean peninsula.

In Seoul, President Park's trust-building process on the Korean Peninsula has yet to yield any major breakthrough in inter-Korean relations. While the resumption of operations at Kaesong Industrial Complex has almost returned it to its normal state, the reunion of separated families in February 2014 has been followed by little, if any, progress in trust-building; instead, the Korean peninsula has been on constant alert during 2014 as North Korea maintained its threat of nuclear/missile tests[18]. In order to engage North Korea in a trust-building exercise, President Park delivered a speech during her visit to Germany, which was christened the 'Dresden Declaration', the choice of location in the former East German city was no doubt a symbolic nod to German reconciliation. The speech conveyed several proposals to North Korea, including regular family reunions, humanitarian assistance through the United Nations, and the establishment of an 'Inter-Korean Exchange and Cooperation Office'[19]. What remains to be seen is how the Park government will engage North Korea on those initiatives without compromising a principled stance.

The EU has long been acutely aware of the relevance of the Korean question to its own strategic interests: 'Problems such as . . . the Korean Peninsula impact on European interests directly and indirectly . . . nuclear activities in North Korea . . . are all of concern to Europe'[20]. Such awareness has historically led to the EU's continued engagement in multilateral efforts to resolve the North Korean problem. In 1997, the European Commission joined the Korean Energy Development Organization, which was established to replace North Korea's graphite-moderated reactor and reprocessing plant at the Yongbyon site with light-water reactors. The EU's contribution to denuclearization investment amounts to one hundred million euro since 1995, with some member-states such as Austria, Germany, and France also making their own individual contributions[21]. Europe has been consistently supportive of South Korea in inter-Korean relations, as documented in the Seoul Declaration for Peace on the Korean Peninsula, adopted at the 2000 ASEM summit in Seoul. The EU has also made a significant contribution to humanitarian assistance in North Korea. The EU's Humanitarian Aid and Civil Protection department has provided some 124 million euro worth of aid through over 130 projects between 1995 and 2008. The EU's Humanitarian Aid and Civil Protection department closed its office in Pyongyang in 2008.

Yet there is much more that the EU can do to be engaged in the affairs of the Korean peninsula to mutual interest. The EU, and Germany in particular, could offer valuable experience and advice as Korea prepares for peaceful unification. Although many in Korea look to the German experience of unification with aspirations for a similar process on the Korean peninsula, one must be mindful of the dissimilarities between the two cases; most notably, the two Koreas fought wars against each other whereas the two Germanys did not, and the former Soviet Union bloc's power behind East Germany was itself falling apart, whereas China,

North Korea's main economic sponsor and political ally, continues to be
steadfastly behind the North. Still, there are some lessons for Korea to be
learned from German unification. The importance of continued exchange
and dialogue between the two sides needs to be mentioned. After six
decades of ideologically driven disassociation, Korea could benefit greatly from studying how West Germans maintained their interaction with
their East German counterparts. And the German case also tells us that an
important part of the preparation for reunification is to make people on
both sides of the border opt for unification. Particularly with the people
of North Korea, the value of sustained and effective projection of information can hardly be overemphasized; they must know about, and
strongly desire, the better quality of life in a unified Korea under a liberal
democracy. Again, while consistent political efforts are required to improve relations and gradually to shape conditions for unification, as was
the case with the West German Ostpolitik, the actual moment of unification could take us by surprise. When the Berlin Wall crumbled on 9
November 1989, German Federal Chancellor Helmut Kohl was out of the
country on an official visit to Poland. The German experience of managing the sudden collapse of East Germany calls for South Korea's preparations for unexpected internal change in North Korea.

As Korea better prepares its plan for a contingency situation in North
Korea, the EU's strategic role might be carefully revisited. Historically,
the absence of European military presence on the Korean peninsula has
limited the scope of the EU's engagement in the Korean peninsula's security affairs to a largely perfunctory participation in the UN Command
in Korea (UNC), created by UN Security Council Resolution 84 adopted
on 7 July 1950. Indeed, one may legitimately question just how much of
an influence the EU can realistically exercise in Northeast Asia without
any real commitment of force projection. However, as the importance of
contingency planning grows in Korea with the prospective transfer of
wartime operational control over Korean forces, in addition to the existing preparations against an all-out aggression by North Korea, the EU's
potential contribution to peace-keeping and peace-building operations
may merit serious rethinking, especially in line with the UNC's role in
military or military-led operations north of the Military Demarcation
Line[22]. For instance, if it is deemed that the deployment of United States
forces north of the Military Demarcation Line would cause unnecessary
hostility from the North Koreans as well as China, the deployment of UN
peace-keeping forces could offer an effective alternative. Also, European
participation in the effective management of humanitarian crises on the
Korean peninsula in case of contingency and mass refugee breakouts
would be important. Currently, Denmark, France, the United Kingdom,
and Norway, along with Australia, Canada, and New Zealand, continue
to participate in the UNC, but a significant shift in Korea's strategic planning could well see greater engagement from Europe, be it through the

UNC or any alternative mechanism. Of course, bilateral and multilateral military cooperation, from force training and exercises to disaster response and defence industries, will be an important basis on which strategic flexibility can be contemplated. The British Royal Navy destroyer HMS *Daring*'s visit to Busan in December 2013 was one such example. In addition to a joint exercise with Korea, a British military delegation signed a memorandum of understanding on the operation of Lynx helicopters.

Most importantly, the EU could make its most significant contribution to peace on the Korean peninsula by serving as a mediator between North Korea and the rest of the regional actors. For example, Sweden, the only Western country with diplomatic representation in Pyongyang until 2001 (now seven EU member states, including the United Kingdom and Germany, have embassies in Pyongyang), acts as a protecting power for Australia, Canada, and the United States. That North Korean and Japanese delegations chose Stockholm as a location for their meeting in May 2014 hints at the possibility of the EU offering more than a neutral space for negotiation with North Korea. Of course, the EU could not remain wholly neutral in its mediating capacity: During her meeting with the Korean foreign minister in May 2014, Catherine Ashton, the then High Representative for foreign affairs and security policy for the EU, reaffirmed the EU's support for South Korea's North Korea policy. And since 2007, the EU has faithfully transposed UN Security Council sanctions on North Korea into EU law. The EU Council's regulations also echo UN Security Council resolutions concerning North Korea.

Nonetheless, the EU can offer a more accessible channel of communication through which North Korea could, should it so wish, reach out to the international community and make real and significant improvements in the human rights of its people[23]. Itself a regional community built up on a custom of constant cooperation and negotiation, the EU's greatest contribution will be in building a framework of rules and norms that is less ideologically nuanced and thus more mutually acceptable. The prospect of the EU joining the Six Party Talks as a mediator is somewhat questionable (as is the prospect of success in the resumed Six Party Talks itself), but there should be a number of alternative platforms through which the EU could facilitate multilateral engagement with North Korea[24].

EXCHANGE OF TECHNOLOGIES AND CULTURES

The best way to share prosperity is to build it together. Finding and developing future sources of growth, be it in science and technology or culture and education, is an essential foundation for any sustainable, future-oriented partnership. Korea-EU cooperation in promoting free and productive exchanges of ideas and cultures will be of immense benefit not just to the two parties but also to the rest of the world.

Korea, a pioneer in cutting-edge technology, has firmly established itself as an Asian research and development (R&D) powerhouse. President Park's 'creative economy' policy is a timely call to transform the very nature of Korea's industrial base from manufacturing excellence to creative innovation. Sandwiched between the innovation leaders in the West and rapidly growing and advancing competitors from the developing world, Korea urgently needs to take the next leap forward. The European intellectual tradition of foundational science and cultural creativity makes the EU an ideal partner for Korea's innovative transformation. For instance, whereas Samsung and LG have come up with some of the most popular and technically advanced mobile phones, Korea has yet to win a single Nobel Prize in the sciences. The EU, having produced almost half of all Nobel Prize laureates, can marry its solid research foundations with Korea's strength in applications.

Korea's R&D cooperation with Europe has so far been mostly bilateral. This is the case with the Korea-France Industrial Cooperation Commission for Joint R&D in information and communications technology and software development, or the Korea-Germany Industrial Technology Cooperation Forum, during which the outcome of a Korea-Germany joint fund programme for SME R&D was shared and the Korean Ministry of Trade, Industry and Energy, and Germany's Federal Ministry for Economic Affairs and Energy signed a memorandum to promote joint R&D programmes.

While these bilateral initiatives have done much to promote joint research and exchange, a more systematic and strategic framework that brings together a multitude of partners will further enhance Korea-EU cooperation in R&D[25]. For instance, Korea has been a part of the joint development of the Galileo global satellite navigation system since 2006. In addition to the obvious technological benefit that Korea's advanced information technology can bring to the project, it is potentially politically significant that Korea has joined in the development of the EU's alternative to the US-controlled global positioning system or China's Beidou[26]. During President Park's visit to Belgium and the EU in 2013, the energy technology R&D common fund was launched; combining Korea's technology with the EU's research foundation will bring about significant progress in the development of solar battery, fuel cells, secondary battery, smart grid, and so on. President Park's visit also saw the opening of a Korea-EU Research & Innovation Centre, which will serve as a hub for collating R&D information and facilitating R&D cooperation.

Since Korea joined the Eureka initiative in 2009 as an associate member, the annual Korea Eureka Day has attracted hundreds of firms and research institutes to be matched with prospective R&D partners. In particular, the greater number of SME participants, thanks to the Eurostars

Programme, demonstrates the importance of dedicated funding and support for research-performing SMEs.

Most recently, South Korea and the EU adopted a joint declaration to pursue R&D projects in 5G network technology, quite literally the next generation of mobile communication. This is an interesting joint venture as Europe, once a market leader with a global system for mobile communications standards, has recently struggled to keep up with the latest trends in mobile technology. Korea's mobile carriers as well as mobile phone manufacturers will commit huge investments, forecast to be $1.57 billion over the next seven years, to combine their efforts with the EU to consolidate their edge over rapidly advancing competitors such as China.

Finally, cultural initiatives and academic exchanges between Korea and the EU represent the intellectual dimension of a shared future. In Korea, a number of European cultural centres such as the British Council, Goethe Institute, and Alliance Française have for many decades continued to provide the Korean public with access to various arts, culture, and European trends. The influence of European culture and ideas on Korean society, from the very early days of Christian missionaries to the lineup for modern rock music festivals in Korea, has been most profound.

Recent years, then, have seen the rise of Korea as a new Asian cultural magnet across almost every genre, ranging from cinema and pop music to fine art and design. Dubbed *Hallyu* (the Korean Wave), the export of Korean cultural products has already swamped the Asian market and is now heading towards the European market. Korean entertainment giants like SM and YG have already made several tours of Europe with their artists, while Korean actors and directors are now regularly invited to prominent European film festivals. Korean cultural centres in London, Paris, Berlin, Warsaw, Madrid, and Budapest are actively promoting Korean culture to learn how best to target the European audience. What makes the European reception especially important for those working to promote Korean culture is that Europe provides an established and globally respected arena for cultural and intellectual exchange. The introduction of Korean literature and fine arts to the European institutions, therefore, is seen as an essential pathway for the global spread of the Korean culture. Academically, Korean studies are rapidly being established as a regional studies discipline in its own right at an increasing number of universities across Europe, an important step in building a lasting foundation for future cooperation between Korea and Europe.

CONCLUSION

Korea remains the only country to have signed all three major agreements in the political, economic, and security realms with the EU—the FTA, the Framework Agreement, and the Crisis Management Participation Framework Agreement. Currently, Korea and the EU are operating no fewer than thirty active channels of cooperation covering a wide range of topics from politics, security, and economy to innovation, education, culture, and peoples' exchanges. Now the shared mission for Korea and EU is to further broaden the scope of such solid cooperative relations to address new challenges and threats to common prosperity, such as cyber-security, human rights, climate change, and food security. And that partnership should be a truly global one in its agenda and impact.

In particular, as leading democracies, Korea and the EU must jointly take a more proactive role in spreading the ideals of democracy and human rights around the world. According to The Economist Intelligence Unit's 2012 Democracy Index, South Korea was ranked twentieth among twenty-five full democracies, a remarkable achievement for a country that was totally devastated in an all-out war only six decades ago, and remained under authoritarian politics until the mid-1980s. Korea's remarkable growth as a liberal democracy, of course, has been greatly informed and inspired by the vision of the European democratic tradition with its active civil society and mature political institutions. While Korea has much room for improvement and Europe is not without its own problems, the strength of their common ideals and values obliges them to work together to support and foster the spirit of liberal democracy across the globe.

The immediate task at hand will be North Korea. Korean unification should no longer be seen as an issue of geopolitical conflicts, but rather as an important task for a universal campaign to advance democratic values and basic human rights.

Of course, there has to be more than good will and moral obligation to the EU's engagement in Northeast Asia and the Korean peninsula; real strategic interests must form the basis of the EU's conscious choice to take on a substantive role in the region. Here, what motivates the mutually beneficial partnership between Korea and the EU should be a forward-looking awareness of the enormous potential for growth and prosperity that Korean national unification will bring. It is in this sense that the claim to a 'natural partnership' should be hearkened to—as the joint declaration in commemoration of the fiftieth anniversary of diplomatic relations between the EU and the Republic of Korea puts it—'we are natural partners who share common values and principles and the experience of rising from the ruins of war'.

NOTES

1. Foreign and Commonwealth Office, *The UK and China: A Framework for Engagement* (January 2009); Michito Tsuruoka, 'Defining Europe's Strategic Interests in Asia', *Studia Diplomatica* 64, no. 3 (2011): 95–107; HM Government, *Securing Britain in an Age of Uncertainty: The Strategic Defence and Security Review* (2010); La Documentation

Française, *Defense et securite nationale: le livre blanc* (White Paper on Defense and National Security, foreword) (2008): 33–34, 46, 47.

2. Council of the European Union, *Guidelines on the EU's Foreign and Security Policy in East Asia* (June 2012).

3. Sung-Hoon Park and Heungchong Kim, 'Asia Strategy of the European Union and Asia-EU Economic Relations: Basic Concepts and New Developments', revised version of paper presented at the international conference on 'The EU-Asia Relations: Building Multilateralism?' Hong Kong Baptist University, 20–21 May 2005.

4. Council of the European Union, *Guidelines on the EU's Foreign and Security Policy in East Asia* (June 2012).

5. Ibid.

6. S. Park and S. Yoon, 'EU Perceptions through the FTA Lens: Main Results of Interviews Among the Korean "Elites"', *Asia Europe Journal* 8, no. 2 (2010): 177–91.

7. Ministry of Trade, Industry & Energy, *Press Release: 2nd Anniversary of Korea-EU FTA* (Seoul: MTIEP, 21 June 2013).

8. Axel Marx et al, 'EU–Korea Relations in a Changing World Project: Main Results and Recommendations', *Asia Europe Journal* (December 2013).

9. Patrick Messerlin, 'North East Asia Peace and Cooperation Initiative: A European Perspective', paper presented at the international conference on Korea-EU Cooperation for Peace and Regional Development in Northeast Asia hosted by HUFS-HRI EU Centre, 24 April 2014.

10. Lee Whee Yoe, 'Can the EU be a Serious Security Actor in Asia?' *Asia Europe Journal* 11, no. 4 (2013): 465–67.

11. Robert Kelly, 'Korea–European Union Relations: Beyond the FTA?' *International Relations of the Asia-Pacific* 12 (2012): 101–32.

12. François Godement, *Divided Asia: The Implications for Europe*, Policy Brief, European Council on Foreign Relations.

13. President Park Geun-hye's address before a joint session of the USA Senate and the House of Representatives, 8 May 2013.

14. Council of the European Union, *Guidelines on the EU's Foreign and Security Policy in East Asia* (June 2012).

15. Mathieu Duchâtel, 'The EU's Security Role in Northeast Asia', paper presented at the international conference on Korea-EU Cooperation for Peace and Regional Development in Northeast Asia hosted by HUFS-HRI EU Centre, 24 April 2014.

16. European Union, *The EU in the World 2013* (2012).

17. J. Ryall, 'China Plans for North Korean Regime Collapse Leaked', *The Telegraph*, www.telegraph.co.uk/news/worldnews/asia/northkorea/10808719/China-plans-for-North-Korean-regime-collapse-leaked.html.

18. 38 North, 'North Korea's Punggye-ri Nuclear Test Site: April 29 Update', 38 North, 38north.org/2014/04/punggye043014/.

19. President Park Geun-hye's address at Dresden University, 28 March 2014.

20. European Council, *A Secure Europe in a Better World: European Security Strategy* (12 December 2003).

21. François Godement, *France's 'Pivot' to Asia*, Policy Brief, European Council on Foreign Relations.

22. Since the Korean War, wartime operational control (OPCON) of Korean forces has been held by the ROK-US Combined Forces Command, led by a USA general. There has been an ongoing discussion on returning wartime OPCON to Korean forces and its timing. Currently President Park's government is in negotiation with the United States to seek another postponement of wartime OPCON transfer, at present scheduled for December 2015 according to an agreement between former President Lee and President Obama.

23. M. Lee, 'A Step as Normative Power: The EU's Human Rights Policy Towards North Korea', *Asia Europe Journal* 1, no. 1 (2012): 41–56.

24. Axel Berkofsky, 'The European Union in North Korea: Player or Only Payer?' Policy Brief no. 123 (Instituto per gli studi di politica internazionale: March 2009).

25. Second EU-KOREA Cooperation Roadmap in Science, Technology and Innovation (2011–2013).

26. Nicola Casarini, 'EU-Korea Cooperation in Northeast Asia Peace and Security', paper presented at the international conference on Korea-EU Strategic Partnership and the Trust-Building Process on the Korean Peninsula hosted by HUFS-HRI EU Centre, 25 April 2013.

SIX

Britain, Europe, and Emerging Asia

A Tale of Opportunity and Frustration

James Mayall

Britain should be in a strong position to help fashion a new and more coherent European policy towards emerging Asia. It is still the world's sixth largest economy and, with Germany and France, one of the big three within the European Union (EU). Although it can no longer aspire to be a global power militarily, its permanent membership of the Security Council provides it with a measure of global diplomatic reach. More immediately, its close historical links with many of the most important Asian powers, its membership of the Commonwealth with its headquarters in London, and its traditional outward-looking policy based on the country's long established dependence on international trade should give the British government a comparative advantage in guiding the EU in its engagement with Asia to the advantage of Britain and its Asian partners, and indeed of both continents. This is certainly the objective of the coalition government that held office between 2010 and 2015, and it is difficult to imagine any future government that would not share it. Whether they will be able to exploit these advantages remains to be seen: It is difficult to be confident on the matter for many reasons, some of which will be explored in this chapter.

After the 2010 general election, the new Prime Minister David Cameron made it clear that he believed that Britain should look to emerging Asia, increasingly the dynamic hub of the global economy, if it was to export its way out of trouble. He criss-crossed Asia, with multiple visits to India and China and stopovers in several other regional capitals, in an effort to push British exports and secure inward investment. There have been some large-scale if seldom spectacular deals, but overall the results were decidedly underwhelming. To take an example at random: Belgium trades more with India than Britain[1]. Building one of the 'most defining relationships' of the twenty-first century, as the prime minister proposed, was clearly going to be an uphill task. Indeed, not only did all this diplomatic activity take place in a geopolitical environment that made assessing its likely outcome hazardous, but the problem was compounded by a deep rooted uncertainty about the nature of Britain's political identity, let alone its national strategy. Nor was there any sign that it was likely to be resolved soon.

How, for example, do Britain's relations with its European partners, and the EU, influence its attitude towards, and relations with, Asian countries? This is a particularly challenging question at the present time, partly because Europe itself is in turmoil as a result of the prolonged financial crisis, which has dominated its politics and stunted its economic growth since 2008, but also because Britain's place in the EU once again threatened to become a toxic issue in British domestic politics, despite the coalition government's efforts to consign it to the shadows. To be fair, these days euro-scepticism is by no means a British monopoly. As the performance of populist parties of both the right and left in many EU member-states in the elections for the European Parliament in 2014 clearly demonstrated, being against the EU is something of a growth industry in contemporary Europe[2]. In Britain, the huge gains made by the UK Independence Party reflected the fact that in the country at large anti-immigrant sentiment is running at an all-time high. For the mainstream parties, this is an unsavoury reality but one which none of them can afford to ignore. It means that notwithstanding the economic case for prioritizing foreign policy in general and the country's relations with emerging Asia in particular, the focus of political attention and debate is even more inward-looking than usual.

When one adds to the mix the referendum on Scottish independence that was held in September 2014, and which might have begun the process of dismembering the United Kingdom into its constituent parts, it is not at all clear that in the immediate future any British government will have a secure domestic platform from which to launch a confident strategy of building an economic and diplomatic partnership with the emerging Asian powers. In any event, predictions that this was an unlikely outcome[3] proved correct, although not before the polls had declared that the result was too close to call, causing predictable if short-term panic on the stock and foreign exchange markets. The final vote was 55 percent to 45 percent in favour of the Union, sufficiently close to ensure that all the major parties agreed that there would need to be substantial further devolution of power, not merely to Scotland but to other parts of the United Kingdom as well. Since the parties, while agreed on the principle of constitutional reform, were divided on its nature and timing, the political class seemed destined for a prolonged period of introspection.

In normal circumstances, one might reasonably expect the historical depth of its engagement with many parts of Asia to cast Britain in a natural leadership (or at least interpretive) role among its European partners. Faced with such multiple uncertainties of its own, however, the British government will find it difficult to exploit this comparative advantage in framing a coherent European policy towards emerging Asia. Nonetheless, Britain's long entanglement with Asia—and particularly with China and India, the two potential world powers in the region— make it difficult to envisage a strengthened relationship between the EU and emerging Asia, which bypasses Britain. In India—and to a lesser degree in China also—the government tends to view its relations with Europe through a British lens. This chapter will accordingly attempt to unravel the complexities of Britain's relations with both Europe and Asia. It will do so by examining them under four heads: the legacy of the past in shaping British policy towards Europe and Asia, respectively; postcolonial assets, including the positive aspects of Commonwealth immigration into the UK; the problems, but also the opportunities, for the country's relations with emerging Asia that stem from its relationship with the United States; and the place of values, on which, in their attempt to establish soft power foundations for British foreign policy, recent British governments have placed considerable emphasis in the country's relations with the leading Asian powers.

THE LEGACY OF THE PAST

The past casts a long shadow over British relations with both Europe and Asia. Britain's traditional European policy—to prevent the emergence of a dominant continental power and to avoid entangling or permanent alliances—was largely dictated by the desire to retain a free hand to pursue global (at that time imperial) interests. After World War II, both major political parties found it difficult to come to terms with the new political reality and Britain's much reduced international stature.

The Sources of British Euro-scepticism

On neither side of the political divide was Europe yet seen as Britain's natural, or at least inevitable, political destination[4]. On the left, the Labour Party contained strong elements that were almost equally suspicious of the United States, believed to be ideologically committed in opposition to the interests of working people, and of the emerging institutional ideas about European economic integration. When the Treaty of Rome was finally signed in 1957, many believed the European Economic

Community (EEC) to be a capitalist cartel and wanted to have nothing to do with it. On the right, the Conservative Party was divided between business interests that were more interested in the 'special relationship' with the United States and the traditional rural base of the party, which largely consisted of empire loyalists. Many of them shared the distaste of the left for both the United States and Europe. Both groups clung tenaciously to two unrealistic beliefs: that the Commonwealth, the successor organization to the empire, would secure Britain's continued right to a seat at the top table of world powers, and that it could provide the economic framework for Britain's post-war recovery and future prosperity.

Harold Macmillan, who had succeeded Anthony Eden as prime minister after the fiasco of the Suez Crisis in 1956, was personally convinced that Britain's political as well as its economic destiny lay in Europe. He grasped, earlier than most members of his party, that the age of empire was over and that the Commonwealth, whatever its therapeutic merits in easing the trauma of Britain's descent from power, and to an extent in allowing the country to transform its remaining colonial liabilities into post-colonial diplomatic assets, could no longer define British foreign and strategic policy in the way the empire had done. Backed by a growing number of British businessmen who now favoured British entry into the EEC, Macmillan tried to paper over the historic fault line in his own party by selling the idea of British membership of the EEC as a quick fix to Britain's economic sickness with minimal political implications for British sovereignty or the country's place in the world. President de Gaulle of France twice vetoed Britain's application to join, but when Edward Heath finally negotiated the terms of entry in 1973, it was this formula that was used to quiet the continuing but latent opposition within the party.

Thus was British euro-scepticism born, with bipartisan support albeit with quite separate left and right wing political origins. It has persisted, although over time the anti-EEC/EU baton changed hands between the parties. The pro-Europeans in the Conservative Party took Britain into the EEC once the French veto had been lifted at the end of the 1960s. Labour opposition was strong enough to force Harold Wilson to conduct a referendum on membership in the mid-1970s and also to undertake a token renegotiation in order to maintain the country's membership. Mrs Thatcher's fall from office had both internal and external sources: domestically, her ideological commitment to the introduction of the community charge, popularly known as the poll tax, was seen by her colleagues as an electoral disaster, but externally her fall was also a consequence of her growing opposition to further European integration. Initially, the Labour Party had opposed Mrs Thatcher's economic policies by advocating protectionist methods that would have breached both its international and European obligations under the General Agreement on Tariffs and Trade and its treaty of accession to the EEC. By the mid-1990s, however, the

Labour Party finally realized that the costs of withdrawal would be prohibitive and rebranded itself as the party of Europe.

The love affair did not last. This was partly because President George W. Bush's foreign policy was opposed by France and Germany but supported by Britain, with the result that Prime Minister Tony Blair was undermined in his strategic vision of bridge-building across the Atlantic between the EU and the United States. But it was also because continued divisions within the party kept Britain out of the euro, a decision which, in the wake of the euro crisis, seemed to many across the political spectrum to have been justified. Theoretically, it should also have freed up the government to pursue energetically its relations with emerging Asia. To an extent it no doubt did, but there was also a downside to Britain maintaining its arms-length relationship with its European partners in monetary as well as strategic affairs. The original intention had been that Britain would join the euro once its economy had converged with that of its partners and once 'five economic tests' had been passed. Opinions differ about whether these conditions had been met, but in 2007 Gordon Brown, then Chancellor of the Exchequer, ruled out Britain joining for the foreseeable future, a position that has been endorsed by subsequent governments and public opinion. Whatever its economic justification, British absence from the key decision-making process on the central issue of European financial policy was arguably at the price of reduced British influence over European foreign policy more generally.

Britain and Asia: Imperial Liabilities

The shadow cast over Britain's relations with Asia is a result of its imperial past and Cold War alignments. It has a mix of negative and positive implications for the future development of the relationship. Broadly speaking, the problem for the British government has been how to turn what by the end of World War II had come to be seen as imperial liabilities into post-imperial assets.

On the negative side, there are still anti-imperial reflexes and sensitivities that can be easily aroused and lead to misunderstandings and sometimes frigidity in Britain's relations with the countries it once ruled. Relations with Malaysia under Prime Minister Mahatir, who was often openly critical of what he regarded as the arrogant behaviour of the British government, and more generally of British and Western business interests, is one such example[5]. British relations with China are complicated by what the Chinese see as the British role in the two centuries of humiliation, which their foreign policy is now intent on reversing. When the British Prime Minister met the Dalai Lama in 2012, the Chinese made no secret of their displeasure, and a planned prime ministerial visit to China was put on hold until, once public tempers had been allowed to cool, the new leader, Xi Jinping, invited Prime Minister Cameron to visit Beijing at the end of 2013[6].

The past also complicates Britain's relations with the Indian subcontinent. As the author of partition, or at least as the responsible power at the time, British governments have always sought to pursue an even-handed policy towards the two (later three) successor states to the British Raj[7]. Inevitably, this has pleased neither India nor Pakistan, particularly when British diplomacy has tried to persuade both countries to resolve their bilateral wrangling over Kashmir in particular, and to recognize a common strategic threat as identified by Britain and its Western allies, primarily the United States. The result of such efforts at the time of the 1962 Sino-Indian war was to marginalize British (and Western) diplomacy when India and Pakistan went to war with each other three years later, and it was left to the Soviet Union to broker the peace. After the terrorist attacks against the United States in September 2001, Blair postponed the Commonwealth Heads of Government Conference in Brisbane and flew instead to New Delhi and Islamabad in a futile effort to orchestrate a common South Asian approach to the American overthrow of the Taliban government in Afghanistan and its international aftermath. India in particular was understandably irritated, since it was itself the victim of terrorist attacks originating in Pakistan and, it believed, sanctioned by the Pakistani government. At a time when the West was buying Pakistani support with both weapons and money, India was unlikely to make any concessions over Kashmir despite its shared interest with the West (but not unambiguously with Pakistan) in the overthrow of the Taliban.

Commonwealth Immigration

There is another aspect of Britain's historic relationship with the subcontinent, which is a source of both strength and weakness in the country's relations with the governments of the successor states. The empire has fought back in the post-imperial age in the form of the large number of British citizens—nearly 5 percent at the 2011 census—who are of South Asian origin within the British population[8]. Over the long term, there can be little doubt that Britain—a mongrel country if ever there was one, which has been built up by a constant trickle of immigrants from many parts of the world over the centuries—has been greatly strengthened, culturally and economically, by this recent infusion from South Asia. These positive consequences will be discussed in the next section of this chapter. For the moment, it is worth considering the short-term diplomatic and political problems that can arise, and indeed have arisen, in the recent past.

In a sense, the core problem is a general one that arises whenever one country contains a sizeable minority, whose actual loyalties, regardless of their legal status, are divided: the exercise of freedom of speech and association guaranteed by the constitution and the granting of citizenship in one country may nonetheless be seen as an unwarranted interference in the domestic affairs of another. A vivid example was provided in the aftermath of the assassination of Indian Prime Minister Indira Gandhi in 1984. The anti-Sikh riots to which the assassination led were followed by expressions of outrage and solidarity by the Sikh diaspora across the world. A BBC programme in which one British Sikh declared that he personally intended to sleep on the floor until the day the Sikhs were avenged, caused great offence in India. The British response that the BBC operates under a charter that guarantees its editorial independence may have been true, but was unlikely to be regarded as adequate by the Government of India. Nor was it.

The most recent example of the problems that arise from the intermingling of British and South Asian politics is the result of the radicalization of young British Muslims in Britain and Europe to fight on the side of Al Qaida and similar organizations in Afghanistan, and since 2011, in Syria and Iraq. This phenomenon is not directly related to emerging Asia, since in recent years Pakistan, which is the country of origin for the parents or grandparents of most of these young people, has been more often described as a failed or potentially failed state than as an emerging economic power. Nonetheless, its fallout, not only for the security of the British state as defined by its government but also for British relations with both India and Europe, is severe.

Insofar as the British state is concerned, successive governments have struggled to find an effective strategy to prevent the alienation and radicalization of a significant minority of the Asian youth, particularly in the northern cities of the United Kingdom, which have the highest concentration of South Asian Muslims. Anti-immigrant sentiment, which in Britain as elsewhere, is most prominent when unemployment is high, has many other causes as well as the rise of Islamic extremism, but the persistence of the problem clearly feeds the rise of ultra-nationalist groups and therefore makes it much more difficult for the government to ignore public opinion on the issue. As already noted, the Conservative Party, the senior partner in the 2010–2015 coalition, felt acutely vulnerable on this score, because although it could ignore the proliferating fringe groups with virulently anti-Muslim views, it was aware that its support could leach away to UK Independence Party if it did not itself make a show of vigorously tackling the problem[9].

The impact on India is an indirect consequence of the British government's dilemma and its failure to resolve it. The government certainly regarded India as a major Asian power in the emerging post–Cold War order, and indeed would have liked to consolidate its historic relationship into what Prime Minister Cameron called 'a special partnership'. His government was constrained by the domestic political context, by its liberal ideology, which holds across all serious political parties and is built on the principle of non-discrimination, and no doubt by the fact that public opinion was broadly against immigrants from wherever they come, and finds it difficult to distinguish between different groups in general, let alone from South Asia. The result has been a tightening of the immigration regime across the board. In an effort to check the flow of illegal immigrants into the country—many of them from Pakistan—new visa restrictions have been imposed, making it much more difficult than previously for Indian students, among others, to study in Britain. The consequences not only for prospective Indian students but also for British universities, which have lobbied vigorously in their own interest against the new restrictions, are ominous.

There was some evidence that their arguments registered with the government. During his visit to India in 2013, David Cameron tried to reassure prospective Indian students by insisting that there was no cap on bona fide students coming to Britain. It is too early to say whether his intervention in the debate will reverse the trend, but the damage already done to one of the strongest links between British and Indian society suggests that it is unlikely. The number of Indian students studying in Britain fell by nearly a quarter between 2011 and 2012 to fewer than thirty thousand, a more dramatic fall than for Pakistan, which suffered a 13.4 percent reduction. From a British point of view, there was consolation in the fact that the fall in the numbers of South Asian students was compensated for by a rise of five thousand students coming from other parts of emerging Asia, mainly China, Singapore, and Indonesia, but the figures do illustrate some of the negative cultural and economic implications of Britain's entanglement with South Asia's security problems[10]. Unlike its neighbour, India has not exported its instability to the rest of the world, but it cannot avoid getting caught in the cross-fire.

Britain's problems with immigration also sour its relations with Brussels. In 2012, the British press revived an earlier EU estimate that there were over eight hundred thousand illegal immigrants in the United Kingdom, amounting to one in four of all those in the EU[11]. Such estimates are notoriously unreliable, but whatever the accurate figure, it was large enough to have adverse effects on the country's relations with the rest of Europe, much of which was also struggling to contain the uncontrolled movement of people. These illegal immigrants also no doubt make it more difficult for the government to influence European policy on Asian relations and also complicate travel arrangements between Asian countries, Britain, and the rest of the EU. Britain is not a member of the Schengen Agreement, which has effectively created a borderless union among its continental members. This does not create any problem for the British themselves, who as EU citizens can travel freely once they cross into another member country, but it does mean that business and other visitors from Asia have to obtain separate visas for the United Kingdom and the Schengen area, making it even more difficult for them to grasp the idea of a united Europe than it is for the Europeans themselves.

These difficulties are compounded by the way the Europeans for their part engage with Asia. Although the EU has a Common Security and Foreign Policy, its own European External Action Service, which provides overseas diplomatic representation, and a High Representative (currently Federica Mogherini) who speaks for the Union on agreed foreign policy issues, individual countries—particularly the big three, Britain, France, and Germany—jealously guard their sovereignty over bilateral relations with individual countries. The EU presides over broad policy positions that have been agreed upon by the Council of Ministers such as the Union's position in multilateral trade negotiations, but where European countries are engaged in competition among themselves for markets and to secure inward investment, they act on their own behalf and in their own interest. One consequence of this division of labour is that the EU is likely to be viewed in Asia as the representative of the second tier of smaller member-states, whose interests are currently less well developed, and where the European External Action Service can provide them with both intelligence and services that they could not afford to obtain for themselves. This is a useful function, although when it comes to crafting a new Europe-wide policy towards emerging Asia, it smacks of the tail wagging the dog.

POST-COLONIAL ASSETS

Despite all these complexities, Britain has not been wholly unsuccessful in translating its imperial liabilities into post-colonial assets. Assuming Britain's Europe problem can be resolved, or more probably contained, some of these may even be useful in forging a more constructive relationship with the leading Asian powers in the second decade of the twenty-first century. The cost in terms of both blood and treasure resulting from the country's involvement in expeditionary warfare and humanitarian peace-keeping missions since the end of the Cold War would have exacted a heavy toll in the best of times, but while successive governments have been struggling to recover from the worst economic recession since the 1930s, it has made them acutely aware of the need to husband their resources. Defence budgets, along with all other public expenditures, have been cut to the bone and attention has increasingly turned to mobilizing, to use the fashionable phrase, the country's 'soft power' assets as a means of maintaining British influence overseas.

The trouble with 'soft power', as Christopher Hill and Sarah Beadle have correctly pointed out in a recent study written for the British Academy[12], is that it is least effective when a deliberate attempt is made to employ it as an instrument of foreign policy. Conversely, it works best when it forms part of the operating environment, which attracts attention and respect because it can be taken for granted without making any direct appeal to particular national interests. In this respect, the English language is probably the main conduit for British, and paradoxically even European, influence and interests in Asia. Emerging Asia is not of course part of the English-speaking world, and for China, Indonesia, and South Korea, English is neither the language of government nor of secondary and higher education. But in those countries that were once ruled from London (India, Bangladesh, Sri Lanka, Malaysia, Singapore, and Hong Kong), English has remained the leading language of administration, business, and education, easing at least the most formidable obstacles of incomprehension across cultural boundaries. The fact that the United States is an English-speaking country has ensured that English has established itself as the leading world language and ensured that even where the official language is different, a significant proportion of the political and professional class will have a reasonable level of competence in that language. By the same token, as the membership of the EU has steadily expanded, the rule that each national language will be an official language of the Union has become increasingly symbolic, and English has established itself as the de facto working language within the EU and in its relations with the outside world. Thus, by a historical accident, Britain finds itself in an advantageous position as an interlocutor in both Europe and Asia.

The Commonwealth could not realistically hope to survive as the major framework for British foreign policy once the period of decolonization had passed. Nor was it likely to assume pride of place among their international associations for any but the smallest island member-states. On the other hand, with a membership drawn from all five continents, it does represent a valuable resource of well-established intergovernmental and non-governmental networks[13]. In principle, and again for contingent rather than instrumental reasons, the Commonwealth, with its secretariat in London, seems well designed to act as a facilitator for deepening the relationship not only between Britain and Commonwealth Asia but between Europe and Asia more generally.

The inter se doctrine[14], under which Britain and the Commonwealth dominions had assumed an identity of interests, has long since withered on the vine, but the constitutional inheritance still ensures a level of familiarity with governmental systems in Commonwealth Asia, while the organization of the public and armed services and the judiciary makes for ease of access and regular interchange between élites in both directions. In practice, for reasons to be examined in the final section of this chapter, the British do not always use their membership of the Commonwealth in ways that allow them to optimize this potential. But in some cases—the Royal College of Defence Studies is a prime example—the forging of a common leadership culture that is both culturally sensitive and effective does work and reaches well beyond the Commonwealth, although it shares its imperial origins: the Royal College of Defence Studies annual courses bring together senior officers and public servants from around fifty countries, including most members of the EU and all the emerging Asian countries, whether members of the Commonwealth or not.

Despite the difficulties already discussed, there is no doubt that the major resource on which the British can base their Asian diplomacy is to be found in civil society, and the mingling of both high and low cultures that is constantly taking place between the Asian diasporas in the United Kingdom and, to a lesser extent, in many other European countries. There are now very few even small towns in the British Isles that do not boast of a Chinese and an Indian restaurant, and many have more than one of each. And British research universities and institutes are deeply engaged with their counterparts across emerging Asia, particularly in the natural and life sciences.

Economically, there is already an increasingly two-way flow of trade and investment. Cobra beer, amongst India's premier brands, was first developed for the British market by Lord Karan Bilimoria, the first person of Parsi origin to sit in the House of Lords. Britain has retained its position as one of the leading foreign investors in India since the Indian economy was modestly opened up at the beginning of the 1990s, while India has become increasingly prominent as a source of investment into the United Kingdom. The Tata Group of companies in particular has established an enviable and highly respected position amongst foreign investors, initially following their takeover of British Steel and more recently in the British automobile industry[15]. A similar story could be told with regard to China. No frisson in the country's political relations with Europe is allowed to threaten its pursuit of economic markets in Europe, and the Chinese have become increasingly active in using their capital surpluses to acquire assets abroad. During the visits of the British and Chinese prime ministers in 2013 and 2014, the Chinese were said to have earmarked more than $50 billion for investment in British infrastructural projects alone, and the British government was eagerly seeking Chinese finance to relaunch the British nuclear industry[16].

BRITAIN, THE UNITED STATES, AND EMERGING ASIA

A major obstacle to the creation of a more coherent European policy towards emerging Asia lies in the continuation of the European ban on the sale of arms to China. This is partly because of differences over the interpretation of the ban within Europe itself, partly because of potential disputes within Asia, and partly because it is an issue that directly impinges on both Europe's and Asia's relations with the United States.

The EU imposed a ban on arms sales to China following the suppression of the Tiananmen Square protests in 1989, but Britain and France in particular have interpreted the ban narrowly to allow them to sign profitable 'dual use' contracts for the export of goods with possible military application[17]. Although most Asian states would in normal circumstances tend to regard politically motivated trade embargoes as unwarranted interference in the internal affairs of a sovereign state, there is considerable apprehension, not merely in India but among many of the smaller littoral states in the South China Sea, about the scale and scope of China's military modernization and expansion. It is by no means certain that whatever their theoretical attachments to the sovereignty principle, they will necessarily favour any change in European policy that might adversely impact on their own security.

Other things being equal, emerging Asia would probably like to see a stronger relationship with Europe as a partial balance to the influence of the United States. For the time being, however, neither the EU nor Asian governments are likely to challenge America's stated policy of repivoting towards Asia, particularly as US policy faces much the same dilemma with regard to China as their own.

The dilemma of how to maintain an economic relationship, which has become increasingly important to both the global and regional economies without making political concessions that involve surrendering legitimate territorial and other interests, has no obvious or predictable resolution. Except in one respect, there is little to separate American policy from that of the EU, including Britain, and indeed most of emerging Asia. The one historical difference that separates Britain and probably the majority of emerging Asian economies on the one side and the United States and particularly 'new' Europe within the EU on the other concerns the reluctance of the former to use economic warfare, or even the imposition of sanctions, as an instrument of foreign policy. Britain's opposition to sanctions is rooted in the country's dependence on overseas markets for both raw materials and food, and goes back to the repeal of the Corn Laws in 1848. Its consequence, even during the Cold War, was to make British governments resistant to allowing ideological or political differences to stand in the way of international trade. Britain recognized the Peoples' Republic of China long before the United States and consistently resisted American attempts to include a wide range of civilian items on the strategic embargo list on the grounds that they could have a dual use. The belief that commerce and politics should be separated as far as possible has been maintained, although these days, of course, the British are not alone in economically wooing the Chinese. Whether Britain will risk alienating the United States by backing the lifting of the EU arms embargo on sales to China—they have already insisted on a liberal interpretation of the ban—and whether, if it did, Britain would have sufficient weight in Brussels to effect the change is perhaps doubtful on both counts. At any rate, it remains to be seen.

THE AMBIGUOUS IMPLICATIONS OF TRANS-ATLANTIC RELATIONS FOR EMERGING ASIA

In all other respects, Britain seems more likely to continue to side with the United States even when arguably its Asian partners would prefer to see Britain taking the lead in forging an alternative European policy towards the region. In this context, it is worth considering the implications of Britain's traditionally Atlanticist orientation in foreign policy for its relations with the leading Asian powers. On both sides of the ledger, Britain's relations with Washington introduce a measure of ambiguity into the analysis.

As already noted, the widespread use of the English language, and in the countries that were once ruled from London the legal, military, and administrative institutions that it helped to create, makes for an ease of access, and possibly even acts as a source of soft power for the British government. The ambiguity derives from the basic fact that the United States is also an English-speaking country and commands far greater economic, technological, and cultural resources than the United Kingdom. Britain may have a comparative advantage in this respect over its European partners, but in those areas where Britain is in competition rather than in alliance with the United States, it inevitably comes off as second best. To take just one example: Many British institutions of higher education are world-class and attract increasing numbers of Asian students, but even before the introduction of the new visa restrictions, not nearly as many as does the United States.

In the security field, there are similar ambiguities. It is possible that if the United States' rebalance to Asia really takes hold, this might at some point force the British to reconsider their Atlanticist security orientation in favour of a serious development of a European defence capability. Were this to happen, it might provide the basis for the development of a more genuinely independent European policy towards emerging Asia, in which Britain's historic links with several Asian countries would be an important asset. But this seemed a remote possibility even before Russia's reabsorption of Crimea and the ongoing crisis in Eastern Ukraine breathed new life into the North Atlantic Treaty Organization, and it has now retreated even further into the realm of speculation.

RELATIONS WITH CHINA

The British military, and even more so its intelligence establishment, remain very close to their American counterparts, and although the debate about whistle-blowing following Edward Snowden's leaked revelations has divided opinion in both countries, the official British and American positions are much more closely aligned with each other than with the rest of the EU[18]. The British (and indeed most European governments also) currently share both the American enthusiasm for strengthening economic relations with Asia, and particularly China, and American concerns about China's territorial claims and its apparent willingness to engage in cyberespionage, in which it has invested hugely, in an effort to catch up with the West.

On the former issue, it is difficult to avoid the conclusion that the EU, with or without British involvement, can do relatively little to influence the outcome of any of the disputes in the South China Sea or in Northeast Asia between China and Japan. Britain and France retain some capacity for expeditionary warfare, but it is much reduced and could not support a prolonged deployment into the region, even in support of the United States. The United States, or so it is said, has also been unenthusiastic about any European involvement in Asian security, no doubt because of fears that the emerging Asian powers might be tempted to play the two Western power blocs off against one another.

At least in the immediate future, this is not a serious proposition. Since their withdrawal from East of Suez in 1967, the British have ultimately relied on the US Navy to keep the seas open in much the same way as the Americans relied on the Royal Navy in the nineteenth century. Keeping Southeast Asian sea routes open, however, does remain a key British and European interest, and one they share with the United States, Japan, India, and the Association of Southeast Asian Nations (ASEAN). An EU-ASEAN seminar on maritime security, which was organized in Jakarta by the Indonesians in 2013 (it was attended by Chinese, Japanese, and Indian participants as well as from the ASEAN and EU countries) identified a whole range of issues, including safety of navigation, illegal fishing, piracy, and armed robbery at sea on which there was scope for increased EU-Asian cooperation, although, reading between the lines of the communiqué, it seems clear that China had insisted on a bilateral approach to dispute settlement against the wishes of some of the other participants[19].

The EU, including Britain and France, like its Asian partners and China, but unfortunately not the United States on whom it must rely, is a party to the UN Convention on the Law of the Sea. It is arguable, therefore, that the most useful role that the United Kingdom and France can play as permanent members of the Security Council, not merely at the United Nations but in multilateral fora more generally, is to insist that China respects the framework of international law that has defined international society since the middle of the seventeenth century and which, after 1945, was used to underpin the new multilateral order. After Deng Xiaoping opted for active engagement with the liberal world economy,

China has benefited greatly from its participation, and it seems reasonable to suppose therefore that other states should insist that Beijing plays by the same rules as other countries.

Not much work appears to have been done specifically on EU-Asian relations on cybersecurity, certainly when compared with the growing attention that US-China cyberrelations have received in both policy and academic circles, culminating in 2014 with the American indictment of five Chinese generals on charges of cyberespionage against US corporations. But it is clear that no government can afford to ignore the issue if only because of the central strategic role of the Internet and mobile telephony in the development of the global economy. Britain, for its part, has identified cyberthreats as a tier 1 threat under its 2010 National Strategy, and on this issue is fully engaged with the EU, which in 2013 announced its own Cyber Strategy[20]. Not surprisingly, this document laid the most emphasis on using cyberspace in addition to its territorial diplomatic resources to project the EU's core values of transparency, open government, liberal trade, and respect for fundamental freedoms worldwide. But it also makes reference to cybersecurity and its commitment to assisting other countries in capacity building to build a more secure cyber-environment.

EUROPEAN AND ASIAN ATTITUDES TO INTERNATIONAL SOCIETY

The diplomatic confusion on how to conduct international relations in cyberspace represents a strategic challenge for all states since it is by no means clear that these can be accommodated within the existing multilateral order without significant reform. The global economy is so dependent on information technology that one might expect such reform to be a fruitful area in which to refresh the relationship between Europe and North America on the one side and emerging Asia on the other. Yet, the two events referred to above illustrate the difficulties that are likely to be encountered on both sides.

The Chinese generals may or may not be guilty as charged, but their very public indictment tells us more about inter-agency rivalry within the US government and the lack of a coherent strategic approach to the management of cyberspace than about how the issue is likely to evolve in the future. No one doubts that the United States, like most countries that have any capacity in this area, uses information technology to gather information about other societies on issues that those governments would prefer to remain hidden. Since they are unlikely to stop these activities themselves, foghorn diplomacy in particular cases seems inherently unlikely to bring the matter under control: Indeed it is more likely to trigger retaliatory action. The question is whether international society can regulate the Internet in ways that protect legitimate sovereignty interests without unduly damaging the global economy.

The EU's pronouncement that its cyberstrategy will be used as a conduit for the projection of its values worldwide may sound innocuous, anodyne even, in the West but runs the danger of being regarded as patronizing in Asia. The fact that the EU is a hybrid political form, more than a simple trading bloc but less than a state, already creates problems for emerging Asian countries which, in order to do business in Europe, must navigate between the Europe-wide regulatory order and the refusal of the states, acting under the principle of subsidiarity, to surrender more to Brussels than they must. Being in addition lectured at by the Europeans on how they should conduct themselves at home as well as abroad is often resented, particularly in countries where the political system is itself based on the same 'enlightenment values' as in Europe, and several of which countries have greater weight within the international order than many EU member-states. The fact that the EU has its origins in the search for a permanent alternative to military competition between nation-states—it is this that leads some Europeans to refer to it as a civilian power—makes it difficult for EU spokespeople to avoid a normative language, which can often appear to outsiders as merely patronizing and moralistic. Greater familiarity with the political culture of much of emerging Asia should ideally sensitize Britain to this danger. Unfortunately, for better or worse, there is no essential difference between Britain and the rest of the EU in terms of the public presentation of foreign policy: Pronouncements from Whitehall place just as much emphasis on the importance of good governance, transparency, and human rights as those from Brussels.

THE REFORM OF THE MULTILATERAL ORDER

The control of cyberspace is only one of a series of contemporary international problems—climate change is another obvious example—that are truly global in the sense that they can only be resolved within the multilateral order. The broader question for the topic of this book is whether a new kind of partnership between Europe and emerging Asia, based on shared interests and mutual engagement and respect, could break the gridlock and make an important contribution to their resolution.

A good start would be for the EU, including Britain, to lobby vigorously on behalf of emerging Asia in seeking reform of the multilateral order to make it more equitable in its representation and management. This is easier said than done. Some adjustment of the voting rights within the Bretton Woods institutions in favour of Asian and other non-Western countries was hurriedly agreed upon at the time of the 2008 financial crash, but this was the price that had to be paid for Chinese and Saudi support in the rescue operation and fell a long way short of surrendering, or even sharing, strategic control of the key international financial institutions. Yet, if these institutions are to retain their prestige and 'gate-keeping role' within international society, already under challenge from a raft of new regional organizations, at some point the central importance of Asian economies for the growth and stability of the global order will have to be recognized politically as well as economically.

Much the same could be said of the political and security arrangements of international society. European support for Indian and Japanese membership of the Security Council has already been given in principle, but this is an easy concession for the Europeans to make since the real obstacles to Security Council reform lie in Asia and not in Europe. If Britain and France were to lead the way by agreeing to merge their permanent seats so that there would be one EU seat, its occupancy perhaps to rotate along with the EU presidency, it would certainly signal European support for a more rational sharing of power, but at least for the foreseeable future this seems extremely unlikely to happen.

The UN Charter, the nearest thing that international society has to a constitution, was essentially a Western document drawn up in the wake of World War II. Its insistence on sovereignty, non-interference in the domestic affairs of other states and territorial integrity, was however enthusiastically endorsed by countries in other parts of the world, including Asia. These states, particularly among those we are considering, Bangladesh, China, and India, have also been enthusiastic contributors to UN peace-keeping operations[21], not originally included in the Charter but always interpreted as falling under Chapter VI, but they have been much less enthusiastic about supporting the concept of a more intrusive international system whether in the fields of human rights, humanitarian intervention, or by endorsing the principle of Responsibility to Protect (R2P).

Since the end of the Cold War, the Western powers and their supporters have tried to qualify the traditional but still predominantly Western principles of Westphalian international society by redesigning the international order along democratic lines. It has not been a resounding success and is only tepidly supported, if at all, in emerging Asia, including in India, the world's largest democracy. As early as 1993, the UN World Conference on Human Rights, which was held in Vienna, witnessed a strong stand by the governments of China, India, and Singapore on the importance of not allowing the Western agenda of individual human rights protection to trump more traditional Asian values, which, or so it was claimed, place more value on the community and on pairing rights with responsibilities.

In 2005, the Canadian-inspired principle of R2P was eventually passed unanimously, but India in particular was very reluctant and finally persuaded to go along in order to preserve the solidarity of the G-77[22].

Similarly, UN Security Council Resolution 1973, which invoked R2P and gave authority to the North Atlantic Treaty Organization to come to the aid of besieged civilians in Libya, only avoided a veto because of the support of the Arab League. When the Western powers interpreted their mandate as legitimizing regime change, they lost the support of emerging Asia and many other states. Prediction in international affairs is seldom prudent, but clearly support for R2P will be difficult to regain.

WESTERN AND EASTERN VALUES

Beyond the particular problems that have divided Europe and Asia, there is the deeper issue of the place of values, and their nature, in international relations. Great powers habitually try to imprint the international order with their own image. One does not have to endorse the view that power is irrevocably shifting from West to East to acknowledge that a more equal balance between the major powers is emerging. In this new diplomatic landscape, there is no obvious reason to believe that China and India will behave any differently from other Great Powers in the past. But although China has invested heavily in its attempt to project its own version of Confucian soft power, it has not made many friends as opposed to business partners.

It is difficult to know, therefore, what qualitative difference India, China, and the other emerging Asian powers will make to the organization of international society and the conduct of international relations. Will it be the traditional game of realpolitik, but with additional players, or a new game altogether? Clearly the evolution of international society will require a more serious debate between different value systems and traditions than has so far taken place. It should begin without delay and it is to be hoped that Europe, including Britain, will play a full and constructive part in it. Whether Britain will be able to occupy pole position in energizing this debate will largely depend on the events referred to at the beginning of this chapter but beyond its scope.

CONCLUSION

Britain, in or out of Europe, and Asia need one another: Britain needs Asia as a market and increasingly as a source of inward investment and skilled manpower in sectors where there is a shortage; Asia needs Britain for the same reasons and because in the process of their own development, Asian countries can gain from access to British institutions of higher education and technological and scientific achievements. Both Britain and emerging Asia have strong common interests in a stable, open, and equitable international order, based on international law, mutual tolerance and respect, and freedom of movement for people, goods, and ideas.

Britain's historic engagement with much of the region should ideally create many opportunities for refashioning the relationship to the advantage of both sides. These objectives would be far better pursued with Britain wholeheartedly within the EU than outside it, partly because of the continued economies of scale that EU membership provides, and partly because by playing a leading part in shaping European policies towards Asian countries, Britain will gain influence for itself by helping Asians in their efforts to understand the EU and navigate what is not only a major economic market and economic powerhouse, but a political system, albeit without a conventional political centre.

In this chapter, it has been argued that these opportunities are matched by a number of frustrating constraints, some historically derived, others stemming from difficult but hopefully transient features of contemporary British politics. The EU, Britain very much included, sees itself as the latest avatar of western civilisation. The assumptions of Western hegemony are so deeply rooted that they are mostly taken for granted, but if Britain and Europe are to remain relevant in a rapidly de-Westernizing world, there is an urgent need to rethink and reform the international order to make it more genuinely multipolar. Since, for historical reasons, as Krishnan Srinivasan points out in his chapter on India and Europe, India at any rate tends to see the EU through a British lens, it is important that Britain overcomes the built-in frustrations that have so often becalmed its relations within Europe and towards Asia, and takes a lead in this process.

NOTES

1. In 2011–2012, Britain's share of India's export and import market stood at 1.57 percent, placing it twenty-first among India's trading partners. Its share fell to 1.41 percent in 2012–2013. In the same two years, Belgium's share was 2.14 percent and 2.6 percent, respectively. *Guardian Data Blog*, 13 February 2013.

2. For immediate reactions to the results, see 'Eurosceptic "Earthquake" Rocks EU Elections', *BBC News, Europe*, 26 May 2014.

3. See Daniel N. F. Bell, 'Predicting the Outcome', Economic Social and Research Council paper, published online for the Economic Social and Research Council (May 2014).

4. For background on Britain and Europe, see Andrew Geddes, *The European Union and British Politics* (London: Palgrave Macmillan, 2004).

5. See Shakila Yacob and Nicholas J White, 'The Unfinished Business of Malaysian Decolonisation: The Origins of the Guthrie Dawn Raid', *Modern Asian Studies* (Cambridge University Press, 2010): 18–26.

6. Robert Winnett and Malcolm Moore, 'Political Deep Freeze between Britain and China Finally Over', *Daily Telegraph*, 25 June 2013, www.telegraph.co.uk/news/worldnews/asia/china/10142457/Political-deep-freeze-between-Britain-and-China-fin ally-over-following-Dalai-Lama-row.html, accessed 8 January 2015.

7. In the vast literature on the Indian subcontinent since 1947, it is surprising how little has been written about British policy. For useful background on British policy towards the two successor states of the Raj, see Peter Lyon, *Conflict between India and Pakistan : An Encyclopedia* (Santa Barbara, CA: ABC-Clio, 2008).

8. Guardian Datablog, www.theguardian.com/news/datablog/2012/dec/11/census-2011-religion-race-education, accessed 9 July 2014.

9. Andrew Osborn, 'Cameron's Conservative Party Drops Hostile Tone to UKIP after Vote Losses', *Reuters,* 24 May 2014, ukreuters.com/article/2014/5/UK-EU-elections, accessed 9 July 2014.

10. 'Number of Students Coming to UK from Outside Europe Falls', 24 January 2014, www.ft/cms/s/o/b56069bo-7edf-11e3-a2a, accessed 9 July 2014.

11. *Daily Express,* 18 December 2012.

12. Christopher Hill and Sarah Beadle, *The Art of Attraction, Soft Power and the UK's Role in the World* (London: British Academy, 2014), 45–46.

13. James Mayall (ed.), *The Contemporary Commonwealth: An Assessment 1996–2009* (Abingdon, England: Routledge, 2010), Introduction and chapters 6 and 11.

14. J. E. S. Fawcett, *The Inter se doctrine of Commonwealth Relations* (London: Athlone Press for the Institute of Commonwealth Studies, 1958).

15. In 2008, Tata acquired Jaguar Land Rover after it had been turned down for a government bailout and has turned it into a highly profitable and expanding business.

16. A memorandum of understanding clearing the way for Chinese investment in the British nuclear industry was signed by Chancellor of the Exchequer George Osborne during a visit to the Taishan nuclear site in Southern China in October 2013. *World Nuclear News,* 17 October 2013.

17. Since the imposition of the arms embargo in 1989, among other items the British have sold radar equipment that can be used in maritime surveillance and the French have sold AS-365N helicopters. Stockholm International Peace Research Institute, 'EU Arms Embargo', updated 20 November 2012, www.sipri.org/databases/embargoes/eu_, accessed 11 July 2014.

18. In June 2013, Snowden, an American computer professional working under contract for the National Security Agency, leaked thousands of confidential documents that revealed numerous global surveillance programmes. He first travelled to Hong Kong and was in 2014 living in Russia. However, his action was controversial everywhere, including in the United States, where some regard him as a traitor and others as a patriot defending fundamental civil liberties. For more general background on Anglo-American intelligence cooperation, see John Dumbrell, *A Special Relationship: Anglo-American Relations in the Cold War and After* (London: Macmillan, 2001), 173–95.

19. EU-ASEAN–Jakarta Seminar on Maritime Security, EU-Asia Centre, 27 November 2013, www.eu-asiacentre.eu/news_details.php?-news, accessed 11 July 2014.

20. European Commission, Joint Communication to the European Parliament, The Council, The European Economic and Social Committee and the Committee of the Regions, 'Cybersecurity Strategy of the European Union: An Open, Safe and Secure Cyberspace', *JOIN,* Brussels, 2 July 2013.

21. In 2013, in the UN list of the 116 countries contributing to peace-keeping operations, Bangladesh came first with 8,316, India third with 7,847, and China fifteenth with 1,846.

22. For India's attitude to the principle of R2P, see Kadira Pathiyagoda, *India's Approach to Humanitarian Intervention and the Responsibility to Protect*, Oxford Institute for Ethics, Law and Armed Conflict, Working Paper, November 2013.

SEVEN

Whither Asia-Europe Trade Relations and Political Cooperation?

Fredrik Erixon

Trade and investment between countries in emerging Asia and Europe have expanded rapidly in the past twenty years. The acceleration has been the factor of economic modernization and reforms in Asia and, more recently, growing affluence in the region, spurring exports from Europe. For many Asian countries, exports to Europe have been helped by the globalization or fragmentation of supply chains in multinational firms, intermediated by rapidly growing investments by European firms in Asian countries. Trade and investment have largely grown bottom-up and not as a consequence of top-down policy arrangements. The institutional framework for the expansion in cross-border commerce has been the basic agreements of the World Trade Organization (WTO) and not special bilateral trade-policy arrangements.

In this chapter, I will argue that this era, bringing significant economic gains through trade to both Asia and Europe, has now ended. Trade and investment between emerging Asia and Europe will most likely continue to expand, but at moderate levels, far below the growth rates experienced in the past decades. The growth rate of emerging Asia-Europe trade has already declined. Like global trade in general, it contracted sharply in 2008 and 2009 during the West's financial crisis. Trade recovered in the subsequent two years, returning for most countries to pre-crisis levels, but in the past three years, however, trade between the European Union (EU) and most parts of emerging Asia has been flat. Sluggish demand in Europe is one explanation. Even if European growth picks up, it will take a long while before Europe has grown out of its crisis and pared down on the debts accumulated in the past decade of financial excesses and crisis. Absent any strong performance of other vehicles of growth, European demand will remain muted for quite some time.

Emerging Asia is slowing down, too. Some countries in Asia are clearly showing signs of approaching a middle-income trap. Other countries are still struggling with basic economic reforms and economic modernization. Structural economic imbalances in a country like China are worryingly large, suggesting that it will experience accelerated growth moderation, let alone larger financial problems, in the next decade. Even under more sanguine scenarios for growth in Asia, this new so-called Asian century is not likely to return Asia-Europe trade and investment growth back to past levels. The texture of Asia's past integration in the world economy has been dependent on the liquid markets in the developed world, especially in the West. The final consumer of goods produced in Asia was typically someone in Europe or the United States, but this has begun to change and is likely to change even faster in future. Geographical proximity is likely to become stronger in Asia's trade patterns and, in a way, the profile of Asian trade will come to resemble the strong intra-regional trade patterns in Europe and North America. Consequently, demand for imports may grow at moderately high levels, but it will be served by producers in other Asian countries.

Slowing commercial integration has consequences for non-commercial cooperation. Political relations between the EU and Asian countries are predominantly about commercial policy. Despite talks about deeper and more strategic partnerships, it is difficult to find evidence that issues other than commercial policy lend weight to these relations. Nor is there a natural match between the two regions if their broader political directions are considered. This chapter therefore argues that the capacity of the EU and Asian governments to deepen their cooperation will be a reflection of the developments in bilateral trade and investment. And the big question for the commercial-policy relationship between the EU and Asian countries is if there is a sufficient desire to shape the new era with policies enabling trade and investment growth to orbit into a higher trajectory. This chapter argues that there should be such a desire, but that it has yet to make an appearance.

MERCANTILISM—THE GLUE OF EUROPEAN UNION–ASIA POLICY RELATIONS

The policy relationship between the EU and emerging Asian governments is by and large about commercial affairs. Only a few member-states of the EU have relations with Asian governments outside the field of commercial policy that can be characterized as something more than cordial and aspirational. EU institutions, mainly the Commission and the

Parliament, have also strived to move policy cooperation into areas such as the environment, energy, and research. China and the EU, for instance, have more than twenty sector or issue-specific committees and working groups under the auspices of the High-Level Trade and Economic Dialogue and the Strategic Partnership, most of which are not directly related to trade or economic matters. Despite such ambitions, a great deal of the policy cooperation outside the trade and commerce fields lacks structure, substance, and direction.

Is it a good time now for the EU and Asian governments to change the character of the relationship to make it more strategic? Or to put it differently: Are Asia and Europe willing to rekindle their relationship, to fuse it with energy other than buoyant mercantilism and tangential political squabbles, the two defining characters of Asia-Europe relations over the past twenty years? The answer is not obvious. While diplomats on both sides miss no opportunity to talk up the importance of emerging Asia-Europe relations, neither side seems to have any clear idea about what they actually want to do with each other.

Europe, weakened by the crisis in the eurozone and its long-term relative decline, is struggling to find a role in the new Asian century. It mixes free-trade optimism and grand aspirations with introvert protectionism and political grandstanding. It confesses continued affinity with multilateralism and thrives on a political narrative that deepened political integration in Europe would maintain Europe's role as a global leader next to the United States. Yet none of these discourses sit easily with Europe's sombre economic realities.

Global leadership requires economic strength. Europe remains the largest economy in the world, but its apparent economic problems over the past years have undermined its capacity for leadership. Europe's idea of multilateralism is still influenced by the post-war atmosphere of international economic cooperation and the factors that shaped the key international organizations and institutions. Many of these institutions were essentially about serving European needs and ensuring peace on the European continent. They helped Europe to break away from its political traditions of war and militarism, but they created for the Europeans an introspective culture towards broader international cooperation. For all the incremental good purposes and consequences of international cooperation, Europe was supposed to be the main beneficiary. The character of these institutions has changed over time, but Europe struggles to dispense fully with the perception that they are mirror images of what happens on the so-called old continent.

Multilateralism or other forms of international cooperation are not compatible with the idea that global institutions should aspire to reproduce an image of Europe in other parts of the world, and emerging Asia has challenged this idea of multilateralism. The bigger Asian economies no longer feel any need to express even token respect for Europe's global political ambitions when they believe it is not in their interest. Previously, there were governments in Asia, and other parts of the world, that were willing to go along with European views because they wanted to please donor countries, or because they did not have an opposing or rival view. That situation has now changed.

Nevertheless, the Asian governments, on the other hand, have not made up their mind as to how Europe fits into their various global, regional, or economic strategies, other than as a destination for their exports. Few Asian governments have an idea about what role they see for themselves in global cooperation. None of the large economies in emerging Asia has a positive view of where it wants to take global economic policy. Those nations take part in initiatives that partially compete with existing institutions for global cooperation, such as the New Development Bank (also known as the BRICS [Brazil, Russia, India, China, South Africa] Bank), but these enterprises are scattered and tentative, often constrained by rival interests among the group of emerging or emerged countries that stand behind them. Equally, these emerging nations offer little guidance to those who ask: You may not like the current leadership and institutions of the world economy, but what specific alternatives do you envisage and are willing to work towards?

Europe has no real influence on Asia's political direction. It is neither an inspiration nor an irritation. It is not much different the other way around either, and Asia or individual Asian governments do not command much influence in Europe. Their general trajectories of positioning in the world system are also different. Many Asian governments are climbing the ladder of global economic status while Europe is descending. Inevitably, such diverging trends result in frictions, and in the past decades, there have been several reasons for Asian and European governments to clash with each other in areas like trade policy, climate change, and Middle Eastern conflicts. Because their differences diverge on broader principles of cooperation rather than its execution, it is not obvious at present that there are gains for both sides to be made from an attempt to charge the relationship with new cooperative ambitions going much beyond the current arrangements.

Yet the status quo is not a good option either. Mercantilism, or the desire to export ever more goods and services, is no longer the glue that can keep relations together and help to create an overall cooperative environment. Take the examples of China and India, the two biggest economies in Asia. Trade between China and Europe is no longer growing at the high levels witnessed over the past decades. While China's annual growth in exports to Europe used to be in the region of 15 percent to 20 percent, it fell last year and did not grow much at all during the previous year, according to statistics from Eurostat. Trade between India and Europe followed a similar pattern: It was flat between 2011 and 2012, and shrank somewhat last year. Trade between the EU and India has not been nearly as large as trade between China and the EU, but India had a strong trade boost in the years after 2008 that also included its trade with EU. That spurt has now ended.

Weak economic growth in Europe is of course a major factor behind the slow growth of trade in the past years. But even if Europe's ailing economy is recovering, no one expects medium-term growth levels to be much higher because the continent is weighed down by a high debt burden that will continue to mute demand and consumption for several years. There is a structural dimension to the trade slowdown, too, that should worry leaders in both the Asian and European capitals. Both European and Asian economies have problems of substantial overcapacity in several industrial sectors. Several economies are in the process of adjusting to a world economy that is not going to grow as fast in the next fifteen years as it did in the past fifteen. That adjustment will have an impact on the trans-continental trade relationship.

Moreover, there are obvious signs that a good part of the structural potential for trade growth between Asia and Europe has been exhausted. Trade will continue to follow cyclical trends, but the fast growth of bilateral trade in the past twenty years has had less to do with cyclical trends and more to do with the fact that Asian countries had opened up their economies and that Europe stood to benefit quite substantially from both the new integration with, and competition from, Asia. But the windfall of Asia's real entry into the world economy, which has happened over the past twenty years, can no longer carry trade growth alone. Absent new reforms that open up trade and investment, it is difficult to see how trade between Asia and Europe can generate any surprise on the positive side. Stalling trade growth is a problem for both sides, especially if trade is really what has powered political cooperation between Asia and Europe in recent times. Many political or diplomatic problems shrink in the presence of fast trade growth, but they generally tend to expand disproportionally when trade no longer grows, let alone when it contracts.

The decline in trade also presents a more direct economic problem. In contrast to the United States, economic growth in both Asia and Europe is generally more dependent on trade than on innovation. While American growth historically has been a factor of the 'perennial gale of creative destruction', to use economist Joseph Schumpeter's way of portraying a country whose economic model is based on innovation, the growth in Europe, China, and South and Southeast Asia has to a larger extent followed the model of Adam Smith. In both emerging Asia and Europe, the economy has grown through specialization and the exploitation of comparative advantages.

A 'Smithian' model of economic growth is sensitive to the overall conditions for trade and trade-induced structural economic change, and it depends on a continuing process of reforms that raises the potential for trade. Yet neither Asia nor Europe has excelled in delivering such reforms in recent years. China's economic attention has been focused on stimulating investments and monetary liquidity, and its crisis management programme ushered in more government control of the economy. India's economic reform programme has largely stalled, and emerging economies in Southeast Asia have moved from buoyancy to complacency. In Europe, harsh fiscal realities have pushed it to cut expenditures and raise taxes. Some economies have engaged in structural economic reforms to raise the growth potential, but in general, too little has actually been done in terms of major economic reforms to boost productivity and competition.

PROFILING EMERGING ASIA–EUROPEAN UNION TRADE RELATIONS

Let us take a closer look at recent developments in trade between Asia and Europe, and put them in a larger context of structural factors behind trade. Trade growth between emerging Asia and Europe has been one of the important trends in global trade in the past decade or two. The EU is the largest trading entity, or trading bloc, in the world, and large shifts in its trading pattern will have an impact on global trade aggregates. In the past two decades, one of the strongest shifts in Europe's trade profile has been the growing trade with emerging Asia and, in relative terms, the declining role of the United States. Figures 7.1 and 7.2 reveal this trend[1].

Both charts take stock of EU external trade and do not include trade between the countries in the EU. Generally, the shift in Europe's trade pattern has been far stronger on the import side than on the export side. While Europe's exports to Asia have largely followed the general pattern of EU exports, imports from Asia have grown significantly above Europe's general import trend. On the trend between 1995 and 2013, Asia would soon be three times bigger than the United States in terms of share of EU imports.

However, the importance of Asia-EU trade does not look that significant if the role of Europe in Asia's trade profile is considered. While Asia has become more important for the EU, both as a source of imports and as a destination for exports, Asia in general has experienced an opposite pattern: Europe, like the United States, has lowered its share of Asia's import and is at considerable risk of significantly reducing its importance for Asia's trade. In other words, the trade of Asian countries with the rest of the world has grown faster than their direct trade with the EU. Figure 7.3 shows the share of the EU and the United States in Asian imports. In 1995, approximately 15 percent of Asian imports were sourced from the EU, but by 2013, that had declined to about 11 percent.

A similar trend can be found in exports from Asia. The EU and the United States have lowered their share of Asia's total exports while a

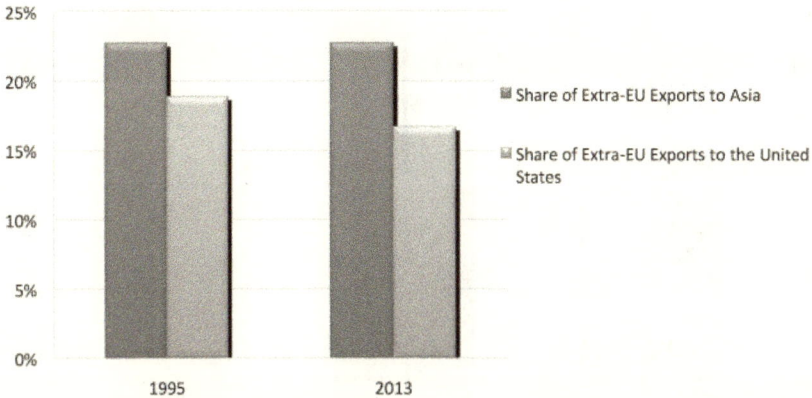

Figure 7.1. Share of Extra-European Union exports to Asia and the United States*. Source: UN COMTRADE 2014. Classification: SITC Rev. 3; own calculations. Comment: Unless otherwise stated, this and other tables are based on the following data definitions: EU is data for EU27; Asia is data for (in order of country acronym in data catalogues) Bangladesh, Brunei, Bhutan, China, East Timor, Fiji, Hong Kong-China, Indonesia, India, Japan, Cambodia, Korea Rep., Laos, Sri Lanka, Macao, Micronesia, Myanmar, Malaysia, Nepal, the Philippines, Palau, Papua New Guinea, Korea Dem. Rep., Singapore, Thailand, Taiwan-China, and Vietnam.
*Extra-European Union trade is external trade for the European Union as a bloc and does not include trade between member-states in the European Union.

greater share of Asian exports is destined for another Asian country. This is shown in Figure 7.4. In other words, the export profile of Asia is growing more dependent on countries in the same region, while markets farther away are shrinking in importance.

It is important to keep in mind that trade data shows the immediate source and destination of trade. A significant part of this trade, however, is import destined for export, especially trade in intermediate goods (such as trade in parts and components for computer and electronic goods). Studies using other forms of data sources have shown that a country like China has a significant share of processing trade in its overall trade profile. For two decades, up to around 2010, the share of China's exports that can be classified as processing exports was as high as 50 percent[2]. In other words, a significant part of China's imports from other Asian countries was processed for exports from China, often to a non-Asian country. The role of processing trade has declined, however, and a greater share of existing processing trade in Asia now goes to another Asian country.

Europe's trade with Asia is not evenly dispersed between Asian countries. It is highly concentrated in a few countries and one country in particular represents a very high share of Europe's total trade with Asia, namely China. Figure 7.5 shows the volumes of trade between the EU

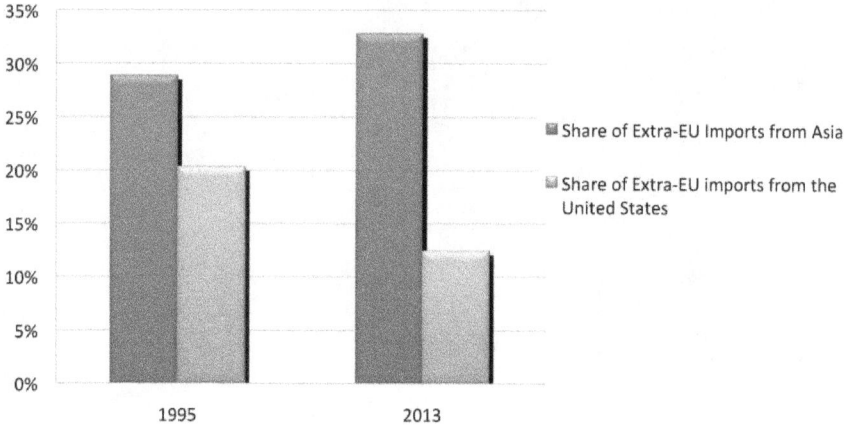

Figure 7.2.   Share of Extra-European Union imports from Asia and the United States*. Source: UN COMTRADE 2014. Classification: SITC Rev. 3; own calcula-tions.
*Extra-European Union trade is external trade for the European Union as a bloc and does not include trade between member-states in the European Union.

and China, Japan, Korea, India, and Indonesia, respectively. The EU's trade with China is not only bigger than the combined trade between the EU and Japan, Korea, India, and Indonesia, it exceeds the total trade between the EU and all other Asian countries covered in the figures above. The EU runs a trade deficit with all the countries in Figure 7.5 except for India. Europe's total trade deficit with China, which includes a trade surplus in services, peaked in 2011 at about 152 billion euro.

It is particularly difficult to exaggerate the shift in Europe's trade profile in the past decades and its growing integration with Asia. This is a trade relationship that has generated economic benefits to Europe as well as Asia. Scale and specialization benefits have been particularly strong. Through its expanding trade with Asia, Europe has managed to secure a greater degree of specialization in both its trade and its general produc-tion. The more a country in Europe has been exposed to trade with Asia, the faster has the process of specialization evolved[3].

However, Asia-EU trade has not been free from friction. Nor has there been universal political support for fast trade integration between Europe and Asia, and especially between the EU and China. Yet the economic gains have outweighed the political opposition and trade frictions, such as disputes around dumping or subsidization of exports, and these irri-tants have not changed the general direction of the trade.

It is unlikely that this era of fast and remarkably peaceful trade growth will continue for another decade. There is already clear evidence that the trade performance in the past years are harbingers of a structural change in the trade relations between the EU and Asia, and herald a far

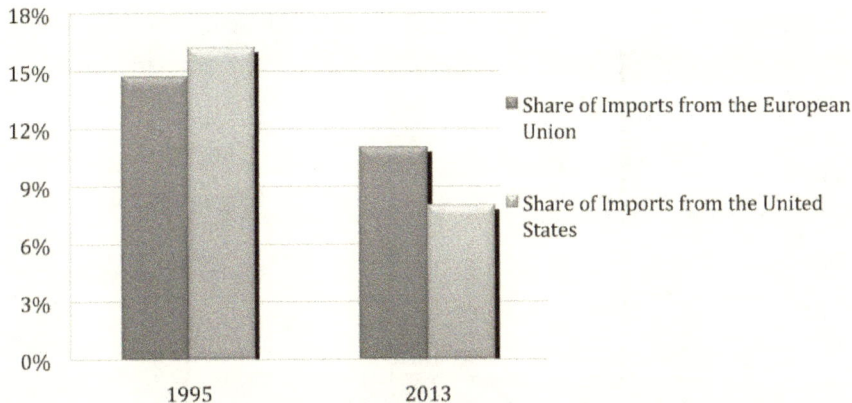

Figure 7.3. **Share of the European Union and the United States in Asia's imports. Source: UN COMTRADE 2014. Classification: SITC Rev. 3; own calculations.**

more politically complicated commercial relationship for the future. It was already mentioned in the previous section that the past two years have witnessed a change in the direction of trade growth between the EU and China and India, respectively. The same is true for general trade between the emerging Asian nations and the EU.

As Figure 7.6 shows, there has been a marked shift in trade growth in the past two years. Between 2002 and 2008, total trade between Asia and the EU almost grew by a factor of 3. The financial crisis in 2008 and 2009 led to a drop in trade of approximately 20 percent, a development that largely followed the effect of the crisis and the credit freeze on global trade. But trade recovered in the subsequent year and by 2011 trade had almost returned to its pre-crisis trend. In the last two years, however, total trade has contracted, and in raw volume terms, the contraction is bigger than the contraction during the financial crisis. And it is not just a contraction in Asian exports to the EU; EU exports to Asia have fallen, too.

FACTORS SLOWING DOWN ASIA–EUROPEAN UNION TRADE GROWTH

There are four reasons why the EU and Asian governments should prepare for a trade relationship in the next decade that is closer to the developments in the past two years than to the trend up to 2011.

First, demand in Europe is likely to grow very slowly for the next decade. Europe's economic growth remains sluggish, and even if the recovery is stronger in the middle part of this decade than currently, no

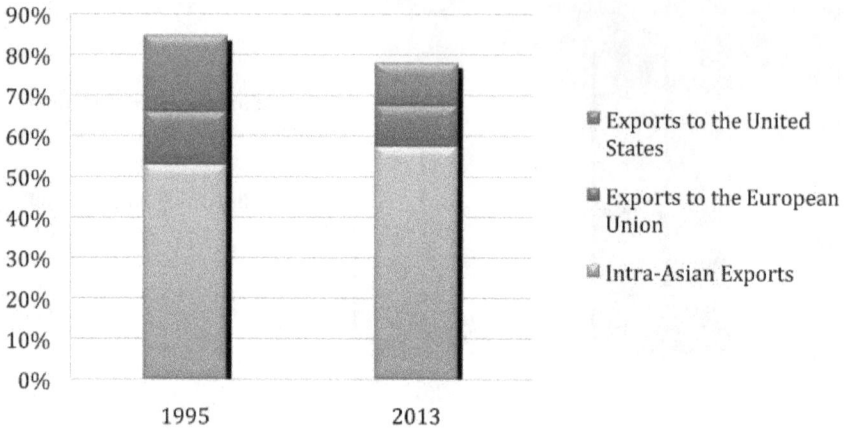

Figure 7.4.   Destination of Asia's exports (%). Source: UN COMTRADE 2014. Classification: SITC Rev. 3; own calculations.

one is expecting growth in Europe to be high for the rest of this decade. This is partly a consequence of the remaining structural problems in the eurozone and the design of the European Monetary Union. Yet the crisis owes as much to the ineffective manner of addressing the problem when it occurred. More than six years after the start of the financial crisis in September 2008, far too many banks in Europe remain weak and have not fully recovered, and Europe's crisis responses have reorganized the problems in the banking system rather than resolving them. Many governments in Europe are still in the process of consolidating their fiscal positions by cutting expenditures and raising taxes, and at some point, they will also have to begin to reduce their debt burdens. Continued austerity, followed by improving debt ratios through fiscal surpluses, may or may not be a good medicine for the ailing European economy, but it will undoubtedly have an effect on demand, and when demand is not growing, nor will imports grow.

Second, economic growth in emerging Asia is also slowing down, and the recent growth deceleration in China, the most important country in Asia as far as Asia-EU trade is concerned, is not just temporary but part of a long-term goal on the part of that government's authorities to rebalance the economy. Europe's export to China has been increasing in many different product categories, but it has been particularly strong in machinery, investment goods, and infrastructure. As China is trying to move away from an investment-led model of growth, the slowdown in investment will have a clear effect on Europe's exports to China.

Third, a significant part in the trade expansion between Asia and Europe over the past two decades involved the globalization of supply chains and value chains by multinational firms. On the back of increasing

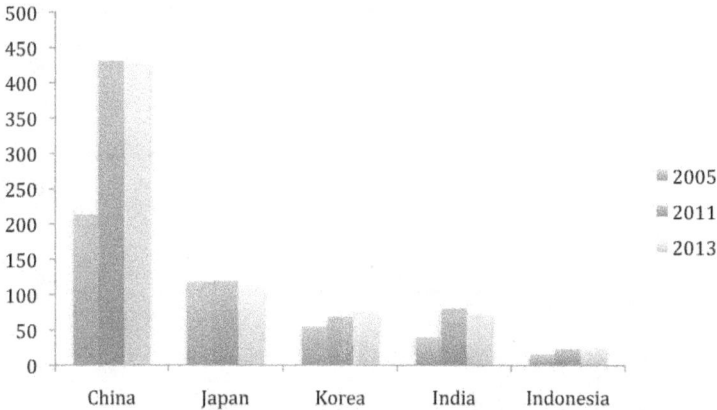

Figure 7.5. Total trade between the European Union and selected Asian countries (bn. EUR). Source: Eurostat; own calculations.

investments in Asian countries, European firms offshored different components of their supplies. While there is still some potential for greater fragmentation of production, it is unlikely that such a dynamic will drive trade in the future as it did in the past. A good part of the potential for supply chain trade has already been exhausted by past and recent offshoring to Asia. European firms may continue to move their sourcing of supply to a new Asian country in the future, but if they do, it is more likely that the move will be from one Asian country to another rather than from Europe to Asia.

In sectors where there is a good economic rationale for fragmenting the supply chain, such as in sectors that produce parts and components with low transaction costs, they have to a large extent already made changes in their supply chain. There remains a good potential for globalizing the value chain and for using the comparative or absolute advantages of certain countries or regions for fragmenting production higher up in the value-added chain. Yet such fragmentation is far more sensitive to political and policy conditions for trade and investment, and while it is driving growth, it is not driving trade to the same extent as the fragmentation of supply chains. It is clearly a process that has been going on for some time, but value-chain fragmentation tends to be stronger between countries that are similar, and offer equivalence in the institutional milieu.

Fourth, the growth in intra-regionalism in Asia's trade is likely to increase in the future as these economies become more affluent, sophisticated, and less dependent on western markets for the final sale of goods and services produced in Asia. In a way, the continental patterns of trade in Asia will mirror the patterns of trade in Europe. While countries in the

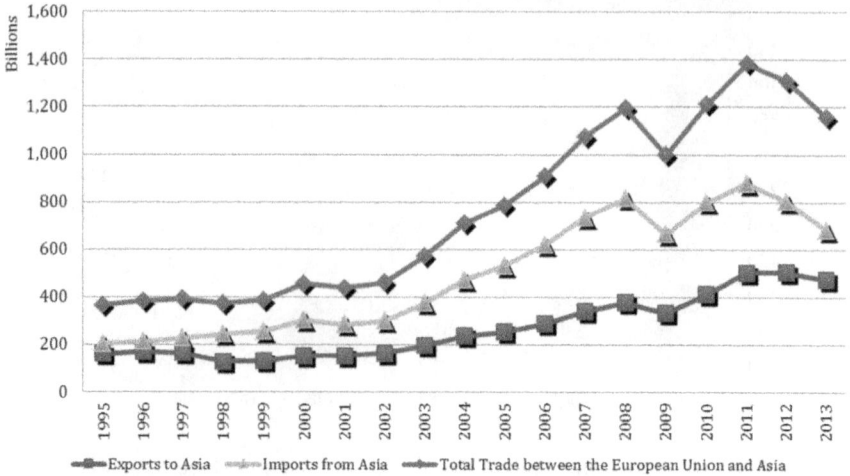

Figure 7.6.   Trade between Asia and the European Union (bn. EUR). Source: UN COMTRADE 2014. Classification: SITC Rev. 3; own calculations.

EU have expanded their external trade—their trade with non-EU countries—the intra-regional pattern of trade remains very strong. For many EU countries, trade with other EU countries grows faster than their trade with non-EU countries, despite the sharp relative economic decline of Europe. Like Europe, Asia is a geographic area with many countries in relatively close proximity. The more Asian economies have modernized and moved away from commodities or cheap labour as the prime integrative element with the global economy, the greater are the forces moving Asian economies closer to each other. Consequently, the role of proximity for Asia's trade performance is likely to grow even if factor endowments between Asian countries are becoming more similar.

These four factors are economic and do not take into account the political conditions for trade. Can better conditions in trade policy counter these economic trends, and help Asia-EU trade to orbit into a higher trajectory closer to the levels of trade growth up to 2011? We will turn to the politics of trade in the next section.

ASIA–EUROPEAN UNION TRADE POLICY: MUCH ACTIVITY, BUT LITTLE ACHIEVEMENT

The policy conditions for trade between the EU and Asian countries are defined by the agreements of the WTO and unilateral trade liberalization going beyond WTO obligations. There is only one bilateral free trade agreement (FTA) on the books so far: between the EU and the Republic of Korea. With a stalled momentum of unilateral trade liberalization in both the EU and Asia, it remains safe to say that improvements in the conditions for Asia-EU trade will in the foreseeable future be dependent on the success of ongoing bilateral trade negotiations. The WTO is not in itself a vehicle for significant improvements. While there may be new plurilateral agreements signed in Geneva on services and an update of the accord on trade in information technology goods, many Asian governments are not part of these talks. Nor is it likely that the WTO's Doha Round, with or without a Bali agreement, will revive in the foreseeable future.

However, greater orientation towards growth markets, especially in Asia, has been a central plank of EU trade policy since 2006. Until then, the EU had put a moratorium on its bilateral or preferential trade policy in order to give political momentum to the trade negotiations in the WTO. That moratorium was stronger in symbolism than in real effect on trade policy, and it was not a clean break with the policy tradition in the EU. As a leading actor in preferential trade arrangements, the policy of the EU towards bilateral trading arrangements was until 2006 directed towards its immediate neighbourhood and countries that cherished the aim of joining the EU. One of the key steps of several countries in the former Eastern bloc that acceded to the EU in the 2000s had been to sign a FTA with the EU, aligning trade policy arrangements with the Common Commercial Policy of the EU.

The new strategy from 2006 named 'Global Europe' was significant because the EU then joined the bandwagon of FTAs in the rest of the world. It declared an intention to sign bilateral or regional trade agreements with countries in Asia where the EU expected fast growth but still encountered higher-than-average trade barriers. These agreements were part of a strategy to increase European growth and welfare, and not to prepare other countries for political integration with Europe. Some considered it a strategy of putting greater political pressure on the WTO negotiations: If Europe signalled an interest to take its trade policy business elsewhere, other countries would reduce their resistance against the key components of the expected Doha Round agreement. True or not, this was in any case never the result of Europe's strategy.

The Global Europe strategy remains valid. It has changed in recent years, primarily by the launch of trade negotiations between the EU and the United States. Similarly, the launch of bilateral trade negotiations with Japan also signifies a significant shift. The economic crisis and low growth prospects are the main reason for this shift, and there is now a greater urgency in securing trade deals with the biggest markets in the world. Another reason for the shift in the strategy is that Global Europe had not been delivering many benefits, and that some of the initial initiatives had failed. The EU initiated negotiations with the Association of Southeast Asian Nations (ASEAN) about forming a region-to-region trade agreement, but that agreement faltered because there were too many differences between ASEAN countries as far as their willingness to sign an ambitious trade agreement with the EU was concerned. Nor did the EU find a way to address the awkward political situation of imposing sanctions against Myanmar, an ASEAN country, and refusing to include it in the imagined ASEAN-EU agreement, while promoting the deal as a way to progress the ASEAN aspirations to create its own single market.

What has been the fate of other trade initiatives taken with Asian countries?

European Union–Republic of Korea

One of the first countries that agreed to begin free trade negotiations with the EU was Korea. Korea was already a good way into its negotiations with the United States about a similar agreement, and shared the aim of negotiating a high-standard trade agreement that would significantly reduce trade barriers, including non-tariff barriers, which tend to be higher in Asian economies than in Europe.

This trade negotiation was completed successfully and the agreement entered into force in the middle of 2011. It remains a newly minted trade agreement, and it is far too early to evaluate its effects on trade and growth. There are, however, some trends in the trade data. Between 2011 and 2013, EU exports to Korea have increased, despite the overall decline in EU exports to Asia in the same period. The cumulative increase in goods exports to Korea during this period has been almost 20 percent, which is significant, and cannot be explained by cyclical factors alone. And export of services has increased by a little more than 10 percent. More granular trade data also show that the expansion in exports has been faster in product categories that were fully liberalized as a consequence of the trade agreement.

This agreement, however, has not yielded an increase in Korea's exports to Europe. Korea's export of goods to the EU between 2011 and 2013 has followed the general trend of Asian exports to the EU: The EU imports less from Korea today than before the agreement came into effect. However, the decline in Korea's exports to Europe has not been as sharp as for Asia as a whole, suggesting that the EU-Korea FTA has at least had a moderating effect on the declining trend.

The EU-Korea trade agreement has been hailed by authorities on both sides as a 'new generation trade agreement', going beyond tariffs and taking the first steps in reducing non-tariff barriers and restrictions on trade in services. It has been presented as a benchmark for the EU's other trade negotiations with Asian countries. In other words, the EU has the ambition of signing with other countries in the region trade agreements that have a similar scope and depth as the EU-Korea FTA.

European Union–Singapore

The EU and Singapore have recently finished their negotiations, starting in 2010, about an FTA. The agreement was initialled in the autumn of 2013, but it has not yet entered into force because the EU has not yet ratified it[4]. Given Singapore's free trade policy, it was not a big hurdle to eliminate tariffs in this agreement, and the agreement will also provide for some reductions in technical barriers to trade and in restrictions to trade in services. Generally, the substance of the agreement follows the standards set by the EU-Korea agreement. The effect of this agreement, however, will be low for the EU. It is expected only marginally to increase EU exports to Singapore and lead, over a ten-year period, to about 550 million euro in increased gross domestic product (GDP). Singapore, however, will enjoy greater benefits: Its GDP is expected to increase by almost 1 percent as a consequence of the agreement[5].

European Union–India

The EU and India launched bilateral negotiations for an FTA in June 2007. Seven years later, these negotiations remain far distant from a conclusion. While negotiators have met regularly for negotiation rounds up to 2013, much of the energy in these talks was lost several years ago. Supporters of an EU-India FTA are investing a lot of hope that the new Indian government will have a stronger interest in concluding the FTA than the previous government, but that remains to be seen. While there have been political obstacles to liberalization, the two parties also remain a good distance from each other in determining how far liberalization should be ushered in by this trade agreement. In other words, the two sides have still not agreed on exactly what the negotiations need to be about.

European Union–Malaysia

The EU and Malaysia have been negotiating an FTA since the autumn of 2010. The negotiations have proceeded in fits and starts, and both parties agree that they are far apart from each other in terms of intentions for liberalization. As a fast-growing economy in Southeast Asia, Malaysia has invested far greater energy for its membership in the Trans-Pacific Partnership (TPP) negotiations than in its trade talks with the EU. Both the EU and Malaysia argue that, while important, the agreement is not likely to have a considerable impact on trade or GDP. Absent substantial potential gains from an agreement, the talks lost direction fairly soon after they started.

European Union–Japan

Trade between the EU and Japan is significant, as they are both major trading entities in the world. Japan's export to the EU has declined significantly in the past years, while the export from Europe has increased. Japan had run a trade surplus with the EU for a long time, but that surplus has now practically disappeared. The EU-Japan FTA is a big event in global trade policy, and it was launched, in 2013, around the time of Japan's entry into the TPP negotiations. While Japan has been hesitant to negotiate trade agreements with Europe or the United States because it has some politically sensitive interests to defend, it believes that trade agreements with the West have to become an important part of its future general strategy to address the rise of China and the implications for Japan's economy and security.

It is far from obvious that the trade negotiations between the EU and Japan will finish successfully. The problems are not only about defensive Japanese interests; the EU has equally strong defensive interests, and several key governments in Europe, including the German government, have acted as if they would prefer these negotiations to slide into obscurity. In contrast to some other EU trade negotiations with Asian countries, a high-standard trade agreement would be consequential for EU imports. Moreover, as the distance between the two in terms of GDP is not as large as in several other FTA negotiations, a trade agreement would have to be based on greater equivalence in liberalization than what the EU should normally accept as a part of any trade agreement. While the logic of most other trade negotiations is that the EU should liberalize far less than other countries because it can deliver benefits to the negotiation partner by the sheer size of its economy, any trade agreement with Japan would imply reductions in trade barriers that have a protective value for selective industries.

A safe assumption is that the TPP negotiations will finish before the EU and Japan have concluded their FTA. Japan has signalled that it places a higher value on getting an agreement that includes the United States, and its calculation is based on perceived geostrategic consequences of the agreement rather than its direct economic costs and benefits. Furthermore, a guiding view for Japan is that the TPP agreement would put far greater pressure on the EU to conclude an agreement with Japan. According to estimates, the TPP agreement would have significant trade diverting effects on Europe's exports to Japan—and it would thus be in Europe's interest to avoid the disadvantages from the TPP by also getting an agreement with Japan[6].

European Union–China

One conspicuous absentee in Europe's strategy to break into Asian growth markets is China. The EU and China are currently negotiating a new EU-China bilateral investment treaty (BIT), substituting some BITs now existing between China and some EU member-states. They have also been engaged in a high-level trade and economic dialogue since 2008, a dialogue forum that started on the assumption, at least on the European side, that some trade policy issues could also be negotiated. At an EU-China summit in early 2013, the two sides concluded that a deep and comprehensive FTA could be considered at an unspecified date in the future, though trade negotiators on both sides appear convinced that this date is not likely to occur anytime soon. The new BIT is likely to have components that resemble a trade agreement rather than an investment treaty, but the objective for market access liberalization in the BIT is far distant from the standards of liberalization that the EU demands in an FTA.

It is not surprising that there is no prospective trade agreement planned or envisaged by the EU with China. The EU is not interested in signing trade agreements that do not follow high standards of market-access liberalization, and China is not yet in a position to commit itself to a much higher degree of trade openness in sectors that now remain fairly closed to trade or foreign business. Even if China would reform, however, there would be resistance from many member-states in the EU to negotiate such an agreement. The trade ties between the two entities are already subject to considerable friction, and the EU maintains a defensive posture in some areas. EU institutions have tried to take some measures that would have a clearly negative impact on China's integration with the EU, such as closing access to public procurement and establishing a new mechanism to screen foreign direct investment for alleged security implications. Europe's trade defence policy is today highly focused on China, and the reality is that China represents such a dominant part of all existing trade defence actions by the EU that it would be more accurate to call it a China-specific policy.

Even if China and the EU are not in the process of negotiating a trade agreement with each other, they expend a good deal of trade diplomacy effort to contain frictions and political flare-ups related to trade. The strategy is only partly successful: The two sides have prevented larger trade wars, but it has not delivered any positive result in trade policy. Both sides agree that trade between each other is 'too big to fail', but they still do not have any ambition, let alone a strategy, for taking the trade relationship to a higher level.

STRUCTURAL OBSTACLES TO EUROPEAN
UNION–ASIA TRADE AGREEMENTS

While there is much superficial activity in EU-Asia trade talks, few of the launched negotiations have many achievements to show for themselves, and while some of the initiatives might yield results in the future, they will not do so quickly. Furthermore, they will have to find ways to address profound obstacles, some political, others economic. To better understand what is keeping several Asia-Europe trade negotiations far from success, this section is organized on the basis of the classical triptych of international political economy: ideas, institutions, and interests.

Ideas

Ideas matter, even for something as ostentatiously technical as trade policy. Essentially, trade liberalization is constructed on the belief in open markets and an open world economy. This belief is supported by dispassionate analysis and proven experience, but trade policy, multilateral, bilateral, and unilateral, performs against a backdrop of broad economic liberalism. It is essentially a process that implies more markets and less government. One may agree or disagree with the foundational idea of trade liberalization, but one cannot expect trade negotiations to work smoothly if the prevailing climate of ideas is biased against further economic liberalization, which is simply not an environment that can facilitate more opening of markets.

The climate of ideas today is different compared to the period of broad trade liberalization in the 1980s and the 1990s, and has shifted in the direction of a less favourable attitude towards open trade. Rightly or wrongly, the crisis following 2008 has reinforced a distrust of the free market economy and greater support for government intervention in markets. The new mainstream view largely accepts the reality of the market economy and globalization, but rejects the notion of comprehensive liberalization. The spurt of new regulation the world has witnessed in the post-crisis era has no doubt blazed the trail for even more market divergence. The new compact holds that trade liberalization cannot take place any longer without attendant regulations to even out the conditions for competition, and it is biased in favour of new forms of trade policy that often regulate trade more than they open markets.

There is nothing wrong in challenging the ideological pillars of trade liberalization, but trade negotiations cannot be expected to yield much result in a climate biased against the idea of more markets and less government. Arguably, this fundamental lies at the heart of current trade negotiations in most parts of the world, and Asia-EU trade negotiations are no exception. While there is an undercurrent in many Asian countries in favour of economic liberalism, these economies tend to have government interventions in trade and in product markets that prohibit trade more than similar regulations do in Europe. However, there is a strong shift in ideas in Europe's attitudes to trade liberalization as well, and mercantilism has become much stronger as a consequence of the crisis. Governments in Europe are keen to get better conditions for their exports, but they are more defensive about opening up their own markets. They are increasingly considering trade agreements as a way to boost exports rather than as a forum for political and reciprocal bargains between countries about their openness to trade.

This sentiment is particularly strong in Europe's attitude towards trade agreements with Asian countries: They are instruments for the EU to collect greater export benefits and not to transact reciprocal bargains. While it is true that trade openness in the EU is greater than in most Asian countries, no trade agreement today can be based on a very uneven bargain for policy reforms.

Institutions

Modern trade policy is not only about liberalizing barriers to trade. Equally important is the process of building institutions for commerce or making existing institutions more compatible across borders. While tariffs were the central component of trade negotiations in the past, modern trade policy has many other preoccupations. They are, to name a few, about standards for intellectual property rights, trade distortion or discrimination in competition or anti-trust policies, rules for state aid to industry or for state-owned enterprises, political preferences in government procurement processes, and diverging standards to determine the safety of a product.

In the trade negotiations that have stalled between the EU and Asian governments, the reasons behind the negotiators' problems are far more about institutions and regulations than they are about tariffs. The EU and India, for example, have sparred on the issue of automobile tariff protection, but the bigger problems have been in areas such as intellectual property rights, local retail regulations, prudential banking regulation, and the movement of people. The talks about an agreement between the EU and Malaysia were held up over procurement rules for telecom infrastructure. A politically charged issue for the EU-Japan trade negotiation has been whether private train operators in Japan should be covered by a government procurement code.

Changes in such institutional practices tend to have a larger impact on trade than reductions in classic border protection. But the structure of policy in these areas is also much more difficult to address, especially if, as in the case of trade negotiations between the EU and emerging Asian countries, there are differences in political cultures, economic development, and the way existing institutional practices affect production and employment. Institutions tend to be more difficult to change than tariffs or measures of direct border protection. There is not always, perhaps not even often, a position that is obviously better than other positions, and some efforts to reduce diverging institutional practices may close opportunities for trade rather than open them. Other solutions may yield benefits in bilateral relations, but make trade agreements with other countries less feasible.

It has proved difficult to construct new institutions or institutional practices through bilateral trade policy. When it has worked, it has often involved a developing country with clear institutional deficiencies that would stand to benefit substantially by a trade agreement with an affluent market. Few current trade negotiations, however, fit that profile, and the potential benefits from a bilateral trade agreement are usually far too small to motivate countries to change their institutions. While there is an interest on the part of some countries to reduce more banal regulatory differences, negotiations have often stumbled upon the absence of trust between countries, or trust in the quality of government of the other entity.

Interests

Modern trade policy rests on the idea of an all-inclusive grand bargain between countries. In crude and very simplistic terms, trade policy in the past was hinged on the idea that countries of developing status would get better access to rich-country markets for agricultural and semi-industrial products while developed countries would get better access to other rich-country markets *and* to developing-country markets for services and advanced industrial and consumer goods. This view can often be found in the way that governments approach trade negotiations. It sometimes looks good on paper or in the abstract: The economic logic of trade is that the bigger the economic differences are between the contracting parties, the greater the benefits. In reality, however, this strategy is not working.

The essential problem revolves around the change of trade policy from an effectively *inter*-sectoral to a *multi*sectoral activity, and how political perceptions about adjustments to new trade liberalization do not fit with the modern reality of multisectoral trade and value chains that increasingly combine goods and services[7].

Until a decade ago or so, trade negotiations were effectively about negotiating trade in manufactures, and other sectors were exempted. This was the golden era of reciprocity — the overall philosophy of trade policy as a give-and-get haggling between countries, leading to broadly equal results. Reciprocity was a formula for success, mainly because those with an active stake in trade negotiations (countries that would be asked to take on new real liberalization) were of similar level of development and industrial structure, and because the agenda was limited to one particular sector, such as manufacture. Negotiations then were largely inter-sectoral and focused on tariffs and simple border measures, all of which are fairly easy to measure, compare, and (technically) to bargain over. Industrial production is also a comparatively easy sector to liberalize as the economics of manufactures essentially rests on economies of scale.

But reciprocity has not been a successful formula in the multisectoral structure that characterizes modern trade policy. The problem is partly technical: It is difficult to design agreements with known effects in areas like services. Moreover, it is equally difficult to estimate the impact on trade, or the distributional effects, when non-tariff barriers are considered an important element for a trade agreement. Yet a bigger problem in modern trade policy is to find the political compact for reciprocity. It is essentially about factor mobility and the effects of trade on the factors of production, primarily labour.

In the past, factor mobility was largely an issue of inter-sectoral mobility. If a textile worker in, say, the EU, became unemployed because of increased trade, he or she could get a new job in another manufacturing sector. This adjustment process was fairly smooth and in the heyday of industrial growth it did not matter much that many countries employed labour-market policies that prevented mobility. Industrial jobs were typically in plentiful supply and the unemployed worker could get a new job without a substantial period of re-education. On-the-job training usually sufficed.

Today's multisectoral structure is different. Industrial production is no longer primarily an activity by developed countries in the Western hemisphere. The type of transfer envisaged in the grand-bargain structure of trade will require a movement of labour *between* sectors, and this is true also for consequential trade agreements between the EU and Asian countries. In stylized and crude terms, a farmer in France, unemployed because of new competition, has to find a new job in a growing and advanced service sector that has benefited from an Asia-EU agreement. However, even less extreme examples of factor mobility are difficult to mediate, and the problems have been exacerbated by policies that have restricted labour-market flexibility, preventing mobility and locking people into specific sectors.

This is a European problem, drawing the attention of politicians in the EU and Europe's key political capitals. The problem can also be nuanced. Trade is only one element that is changing labour markets; technological change and changed consumer preferences are the more important factors behind structural labour market changes. Moreover, the adjustment process is seldom immediate or direct. Companies usually have the capacity to manage new competition by changing their product supply and assortment, at least for a while, without reducing labour and invested capital. Obviously, the overall economic benefits of a trade agreement are reflections of how much a new agreement forces new competition upon an economy: no pain, no gain.

Political concerns about trade-induced labour substitution have affected trade policy in several ways. In Europe, there are stronger fears that while trade agreements may deliver net economic benefits, it is not possible to accommodate the adverse labour-market consequences arising from them. The problem may or may not be real, but it affects the way that the EU can build a coalition of interests that favour trade deals. Such coalitions are increasingly important, especially as the European Parliament now has greater power in trade policy than ever before. One way to address such fears has been for Europe to insist on various components in trade agreements that by and large restrict trade. For instance, it is a key issue in EU trade negotiations with emerging Asian countries that the EU should yield its standards for labour and environmental protection that are intended to close the opportunity for other countries to benefit from not having a similar standard as the EU. Most Asian countries, however, continue to resist calls by the EU to build in non-trade standards in trade agreements that will have consequences for trade.

The problem of finding a reciprocal structure of trade is also manifest in other ways in the Asia-Europe trade agreements: The costs and benefits of any trade agreements with emerging Asia are not evenly shared between EU member-states. There are big differences between countries in Europe as to how far they have integrated with the Asian economies. Some economies like Germany have taken great advantage of Asian growth, while other economies, like Greece or Italy, consider trade liberalization with Asian countries to be a matter of increased competition rather than increased export opportunities. In the past years, countries that are less integrated with Asian economies have been suffering from bigger economic problems than in other parts of Europe, and these economic problems have provoked resistance to new trade agreements when they have come up for ratification in the EU. For instance, the trade agreement between the EU and Korea was delayed because Italy feared competition from Korean producers of medium-sized cars at a time when the Italian car industry was going through a slump. Yet many of the crisis economies in Europe have not been in a position to block the process of launching new trade negotiations with other countries because they have commanded less authority when they have been asking for exemptions or special favours in Europe's crisis policies. If, or when, some of the current trade negotiations between emerging Asian countries and the EU are subject to ratification, it is likely that such resistance will become stronger and more visible.

CONCLUSION

Trade policy, or commercial policy more broadly defined, is at the centre of cooperation between the EU and the emerging Asian economies. Both sides have made efforts to build deeper policy relations beyond matters of commerce. Several Asian countries, for instance, have signed (or are currently negotiating) partnership agreements with the EU that involve areas such as climate change or human rights. However, none of these agreements or negotiations comes close to energizing policy cooperation as much as the bilateral trade agreements signed, or currently under negotiation, between Asian countries and the EU. Several European countries talk about greater ambitions for deepening their non-commercial integration with Asian countries. This is true for countries with a colonial past in Asia, such as the United Kingdom, as well as for countries with a tradition of non-colonial international cooperation, such as Germany and Sweden. But these goals either stem from a desire to prosper on the back of Asian growth or lack an essential ingredient for successful partnership, namely, a convergence of interest. It is difficult to find one example of non-commercial policy collaboration with an Asian country that is consequential for the way European countries have designed their policy, or that has forced them to change their policy.

While real people-to-people or business-to-business integration has been growing from the bottom-up, there are, however, not many existing policy frameworks between the EU and Asia that have had significant impacts on commercial integration. For most of the time, and especially over the past two decades, the absence of such agreements has not mattered much. Trade and investment between Asia and the EU have grown very fast and made the two continents important for their respective economic performances.

This period of the Goldilocks principle is about to end, if it has not ended already. Trade will grow much slower in the future than in the past, and the existing levels of commercial integration may in some instances be reduced. Absent strong trade growth, existing and future frictions in trade and other fields are likely to become more pronounced, and they can no longer be hidden behind the perception that greater trade and more economic development will eventually make these tensions fade away. And when the economic pie remains constant, political and economic interests will place stronger pressures on political leaders and officials to ensure that they get their share, or at least that they should have a larger share at the expense of someone else.

The EU and several governments in Asia are engaged in negotiations to liberalize trade bilaterally and to establish better rules and disciplines for institutional practices. As shown by the EU-Korea FTA, such agreements do have a favourable impact on trade, but they are difficult to negotiate and transact. The more the economic logic of a trade agreement is based on changing institutional practices, the more difficult it is to conclude such negotiations successfully.

Current bilateral trade negotiations between Asia and Europe have also been influenced by a large number of strategic and geopolitical factors. Emerging Asia and Europe are moving along different trajectories. While the United States also suffers from relative economic decline, its share of the world economy is not going to be reduced as much as that of Europe. The economic centre of gravity in the world is moving from the Atlantic to the Pacific—it is moving away from Europe, but not away from America. Rightly or wrongly, the United States can maintain a strong strategic relevance through its global military power, and that position tends to make it a more attractive trade partner for many countries.

Europe's relative economic decline is not catastrophic. Nor is Asia's economic rise inevitable. These will both be a factor of political choices. A more competitive European economy will make it more attractive in Asia, and the Asian economies that show a willingness to transact economic reforms will find a Europe that is more than willing to conclude reciprocally beneficial trade agreements. These political choices, however, are not matters of trade or commercial policy negotiations alone, but they will rather reflect domestic politics. Until that moment occurs, trade and economic integration between Asia and the EU will be slower, selective, and more susceptible to political squabbles. Cooperative efforts will remain mostly about commercial affairs, but they will essentially lack direction and purpose.

NOTES

1. Unless otherwise stated, this and other figures are based on the following data definitions: EU is data for EU27; Asia is data for (in order of country acronym in data catalogues) Bangladesh, Brunei, Bhutan, China, East Timor, Fiji, Hong Kong-China, Indonesia, India, Japan, Cambodia, Korea Rep., Laos, Sri Lanka, Macao, Micronesia, Myanmar, Malaysia, Nepal, the Philippines, Palau, Papua New Guinea, Korea Dem. Rep., Singapore, Thailand, Taiwan-China, and Vietnam.

2. For an authoritative analysis of processing trade in China's trade, see Miaojie Yu and Wei Tian, 'China's Processing Trade: A Firm-level Analysis', in *Rebalancing and Sustaining Growth in China*, Huw McKay and Ligang Song (Canberra: Australian National University Press, 2012).

3. Bianka Dettmer, Fredrik Erixon, Andreas Freytag, and Pierre-Olivier Tremblay, 'The Dynamics of Structural Change', *Chinese Economy* 44, no. 4: 42–74.

4. The ratification of this FTA has not been delayed because of significant opposition from member-states or the European Parliament. The agreement is likely to be approved by all EU institutions once the European Parliament has returned to a normal working schedule.

5. European Commission, *The Economic Impact of the EU-Singapore Free Trade Agreement*, Brussels, European Commission, Directorate General for Trade (September 2013).

6. Kenichi Kawasaki, 'The Relative Significance of EPAs in Asia-Pacific', *RIETI Discussion Paper Series* 14-E-009 (January 2014).

7. For a longer discussion about this shift in trade policy, see Paul Collier, 'Why the WTO is Deadlocked: And What Can Be Done About It', *World Economy* 29, no. 10 (2006): 1423–49.

EIGHT

European Union–China Trade Relations

The Past, Present, and Future

Zhang Xiaotong

China's trade relations with Europe can be traced back to ancient Roman times two thousand years ago, when the two great ancient civilizations of Rome and China were linked up by the famous Silk Road. There are so many told and untold stories concerning this trade route. I start this chapter by simply paraphrasing the opening of *The Romance of the Three Kingdoms*, a classic Chinese historical novel written in the fourteenth century, which enriched the Chinese view of history:

> The rolling Yangtze River flows eastward, heroes come and go. They may be right or wrong, win or lose, they are but fleeting shades. Green mountains are always there just as the sun sets every day . . . it is a great happiness to drink with you, and there are many stories to be told at our cheerful chats, be they old or new.

There are indeed enough stories in European Union (EU)-China trade relations to enrich a lengthy conversation. It goes back to the historic visit by Christopher Soames, former vice president of the European Commission in charge of external relations, to Beijing in May 1975, where he met Chinese Premier Zhou Enlai. As early as the end of 1971, Zhou had personally spoken in favour of the European Economic Community (EEC), when remarking to an Italian journalist, 'as a first step towards an independent Europe, the Common Market was a good thing'. In May 1972, he also mentioned to a French journalist the possibility of establishing a Chinese diplomatic mission to the Community:

> Since the establishment of the [EEC], there has been a steadily growing tendency towards unity among the West European countries. Withstanding external pressure and interference, they have made continuous efforts to safeguard their sovereignty and independence. This is a positive development in the international situation. We would like to see better relations developing between the EEC and the Third World countries. It is our belief that so long as all countries that are subjected to superpower aggression, interference and control stand united, they will certainly frustrate the schemes of the superpowers to seek hegemony.

Zhou received Soames in the Beijing Hospital, where Zhou was under medical treatment for advanced cancer, just eight months before his death. At that meeting, they agreed in principle to establish diplomatic relations between the People's Republic of China and the EEC, and to start negotiations towards a trade agreement, later to be known as the 1978 EEC-China Trade Agreement. The European Parliament gave overwhelming support for the establishment of relations.

This chapter intends to examine the logic underpinning the evolution of the EU-China trade relationship since the establishment of diplomatic relations between the People's Republic of China and the EEC in 1975. Three key variables are identified for understanding that historical logic, including the *'strategic foundation'* of relationship, *'reciprocity'*, and *'institutions'*. Based on these three key variables, an historical overview is offered of the evolution of the EU-China trade relationship. The history is divided into three periods: between 1975 and 1988, it is the start-up period for the EU-China trade relationship; between 1993 and 2004, the trade relationship was developing at full speed; and from 2005 until now is the period of mutual readjustment and adaptations for a new global context and the bilateral relationship between Europe and China.

The term 'strategic foundation' refers to the pattern and configuration of world politics and economics, as well as decision-makers' perceptions thereof. It provides a systemic environment for bilateral relationship. There is a Chinese equivalent, *shi* (势), which is used to denote the overall configuration of the world order, and it is believed in China that a good foreign policy derives from a sound understanding of *shi*[1]. 'Reciprocity' implies examining whether the trade relationship is mutually beneficial and reciprocal. A trade deficit is usually seen as a feature of the lack of reciprocity. The term 'institutions' refers to all the formal documents such as agreements, treaties, policy papers, and dialogues established between the EU and China, in particular in the economic and trade areas. These three variables are the actual determinants for the direction, soundness, and process of the EU-China trade relationship.

HISTORICAL OVERVIEW OF EUROPEAN UNION–CHINA TRADE RELATIONSHIP

Phase 1 (1975 to 1988): Starting Up

For more than ten years since the establishment of diplomatic relations between the EEC and the People's Republic of China in 1975, both Chinese and European leaders managed the relationship with a strategic vision. That laid a solid strategic foundation for the development of a bilateral trade relationship. From 1946, immediately after World War II, to 1974, just before China established diplomatic relations with the EEC, the former Chinese leader Chairman Mao Zedong put forward, and on several occasions improved, his strategic thoughts on the 'Middle Zone' and the 'Three Worlds' theories[2]. Europe was seen as the second 'Middle Zone' after the developing countries[3], and Europe was understood by the Chinese side as an important force that desperately wanted to get out of the close control of the United States. In the 1970s, when China and the United States achieved a détente: The Soviet Union became a key threat for both Europe and China, given the fact that Western Europe was in alliance with the United States. In February 1979, when former Chinese leader Deng Xiaoping met with Roy Jenkins, the then President of the European Commission, Deng proposed working together with Europe against the threat of the Soviet Union. Deng put it in a vivid way, 'when the bear bites, you held the bear's forepaw. When it kicks, we hold its after-paw'[4]. When European countries tried to remove themselves from the control of the United States and fought against the threat of the Soviet Union, China was undoubtedly the key country Europe could rely on. Moreover, the European countries encountered economic recession in the first half of the 1970s, while the Chinese market was big, was rich in raw materials, and enjoyed rapid growth. This lucrative market had long attracted American and Japanese businesses, who had already taken a big share of the Chinese market. Without responding to this challenge, European countries would risk losing the whole Chinese market, and therefore felt a strong urge to develop proper relations with China.

Guided by the 'Middle Zone' and the 'Three Worlds' theories, China sent out several diplomatic signals in the 1960s and the early 1970s, recognizing and promising support for European integration. The Chinese government also took the initiative in inviting Christopher Soames, the then vice president of the European Commission in charge of external relations, to visit China. Soames finally made his trip to China in May 1975, starting the icebreaking trip for the China-EEC relationship. After Soames made it clear that the EEC would not establish any official ties with Taiwan, he was warmly received. Premier Zhou Enlai, who was already hospitalized due to cancer, met Soames in a Beijing hospital, agreeing to establish diplomatic relations with the EEC, to sending an ambassador to Brussels, and to signing a bilateral trade agreement[5]. In the 1980s, even after the China–Soviet Union relationship and the Soviet-European relationship entered into a period of détente, the China-Europe relationship kept up a good momentum of further development.

Economic reciprocity was another basic foundation for the China-EEC relationship in the early years, indispensible for the establishment of the diplomatic relationship and the further development of their trade relationship. The negotiation for an EEC-China Trade Agreement started in 1975, and the agreement took effect in 1978. According to that agreement, both parties agreed to promote and strengthen bilateral trade, granting the products of the other party preferential considerations in market access, and the European Communities (EC) agreed to grant China the most-favoured nation status[6]. With the China-EEC Textiles Agreement taking effect in 1980, the EEC agreed to double the quota of Chinese textile exports to Europe from twenty thousand tonnes to forty thousand tonnes. Starting from 1980, China was granted the Generalized System of Preferences by the EEC, and the 1985 China-EEC Trade and Economic Cooperation Agreement broadened the trade relationship from just trade links to other areas of economic cooperation. In summary, this period witnessed reciprocity and mutual benefit in the EEC-China trade relationship, and the bilateral trade value increased from $2.4 billion in 1975 to $12.87 billion in 1988. European exports to China witnessed rapid growth and enjoyed a long-term surplus position, and European investments in China also increased. China also expanded its exports to Europe and received some urgently needed capital, technology, and managerial expertise from Europe, which was important for China's economic growth.

This period was also a very important period for institutional innovation in the EEC-China economic and trade relationship, and the Trade Agreement and the Textiles Agreement, as well as their updates, provided a predictable legal framework. The 1978 Trade Agreement established a joint commission of trade and economic cooperation between China and the EEC, which provided a platform for annual consultations. Today, the level of the joint commission has been raised from the director general level to full ministerial level, and it has played a pivotal role in managing bilateral trade.

Phase 2 (1993 to 2004): A Golden Era

The 1989 Tiananmen Square events plunged the EEC-China relationship towards a freezing point, which negatively impacted on the trade relationship. In the immediate aftermath of the Tiananmen events, the leaders of the twelve European member-states reacted strongly, imposing the EC's economic sanctions, including suspending high-level contacts, cooperation projects, and other economic exchanges, which formed part of European economic diplomacy in the form of negative incentives. The EEC-China relationship had entered into a very difficult period.

However, the evidence does not support an explicit causal relationship between the EEC's economic sanctions and a change of course of action by the Chinese government. Neither did we witness any improvement of China's human rights situation as expected by the Western world during the period of 1989 to 1991 as a result of the sanctions imposed by the EC, the United States, and other Western powers. It was generally recognized that Beijing did not bow to international pressure after the Tiananmen incident and abided by its own rhythm and pace of domestic economic and political reforms. For example, Beijing did not allow the admission of independent observers to the trials or to visit the judicial process. Nor did the Chinese accept the human rights standards advocated by the Western world, and even a constructive dialogue on China's human rights record was not gaining any traction. The European Commission later admitted the ineffectiveness of its tough declarations and the imposition of sanctions in its 1995 Communication on China, 'There is a danger that relying solely on frequent and strident declarations will dilute the message or lead to knee-jerk reactions from the Chinese government'[7].

The EEC's linkage strategy did not hold good for long, and most of the sanctions were lifted by the end of 1991. Roughly in 1992, the EC and its member-states started to readjust their China policies. First, they de-linked the improvement of China's human rights situation with the amelioration of their relations with China. Secondly, they de-linked the position of the economic relationship with human rights. They believed that their China policy should not hold the aim of pushing for the collapse of China's communist regime, since that was not possible. Instead, they came to the conclusion that China should be transformed and encouraged gradually to integrate itself into the international society through economic and trade cooperation and other means of engagement[8]. After 1993, the EU and its member-states started to think about their long-term strategy towards Asia and in particular towards China, and these new moves ushered in a golden era for the EU-China trade relationship.

Although the strategic content of the China-EU relationship went through some changes, the strategic foundation was still solid. The guiding principle for China's diplomacy evolved from the 'Middle Zone' and the 'Three Worlds' theories to constructing a multipolar world and promoting democratization of international relations[9]. In parallel, as European integration entered into a fast-track in the 1990s, the EU was becoming an increasingly significant factor in world politics and started to play an important role in international affairs[10]. China regarded Europe as a very important force for promoting multipolarity. As Chris Patten, the former EU commissioner for external relations, ironically commented in his book, *Not Quite the Diplomat,*

> continuing European integration—the launch of the single currency, the broadening of the single market, enlargement—fitted into China's world view, in which there are several poles of influence not simply one hegemony: not a very surprising idea if you represent over a fifth of humanity. I sometimes felt when I met Chinese visitors that they seemed to believe more strongly in Europe's world role than we did ourselves[11].

Moreover, what the EU advocated as effective multilateralism clearly rejected the unilateralism so often practiced by the United States, and on many occasions, what China promoted as multipolarity matched well with what Europe promoted as multilateralism. The 2003 Iraqi war imposed a big scar on the trans-Atlantic relationship and divided Europe, when some big European member-states, namely France, Germany, and Italy, made common cause with China against the American unilateral invasion of Iraq. That like-mindedness proved later to be a solid strategic foundation for the China-EU relationship, including the trade relationship. During this period, China-EU ties developed in major strides from 'constructive partnership' to 'comprehensive partnership' and finally to a 'comprehensive strategic partnership', so declared by the policymakers on both sides, thereby achieving the so-called hop, skip, and jump in the EU-China relationship.

The main theme for the EU-China trade relationship during this period was China's efforts to resume its status in the General Agreement on Tariffs and Trade (GATT) and later to join the newly established World Trade Organization (WTO). The EC was among the first negotiating parties with which China engaged[12]. China's former Vice Premier and Minister for Trade Li Lanqing disclosed in his book how the Chinese trade negotiators viewed the EC when in 1987 China started to pursue negotiations with the EC for the resumption of its GATT membership.

> The European Communities are a powerful trading group, holding a very important position in the GATT second only to the United States. China has an excellent relationship with the European Communities. Politically, the EC welcomes and supports China's request for resuming its GATT membership, but when negotiating the terms of China's resumption of GATT membership, the EC took an uncompromising approach and seized on every economic interest. Therefore, as we see the EC as one of our major negotiating interlocutors, we need to lobby hard and enhance mutual understanding. On the one hand, we should elaborate upon our position and views on resumption of GATT membership, state China's policies of opening-up and economic reform, and show our sincerity and determination to participate in the multi-

lateral trading system. On the other hand, we should listen to the EC's feedback on China's request and have a good understanding of the specific requests from the European Communities.

In the EU-China WTO accession talks, the EU seemed intent on playing the long game, starting early but ending late. Former Commissioner for Trade Pascal Lamy took a hard line, pressing for further market access concessions after the United States and China had already signed a market access deal in November 1999. Lamy managed to conclude the talks in May 2000. He was demanding, but he was very well aware that allowing China to join the WTO was not only a necessity for the EU's commercial interests, but also an inevitable historical trend as China was re-emerging onto the world stage and committed to becoming part of the existing multilateral trading system. In his book, Lamy revealed an interesting conversation between himself and Chinese President Jiang Zemin on the strategic basis of the EU-China relationship after the bilateral market access talks were finally concluded.

> Jiang: Our relationship has existed for thousands of years and should intensify in both commerce and education. The world is so small and I'm happy that China and the EU have reached this agreement.
>
> Lamy: Perhaps because China and Europe are situated at the extremities of the same continent, our relationship has the particularity of sharing a long history. Our concept of a world organized on a basis open to all, multilateral as we said, rather than bilateral and exclusive, reunites us. This is the vision that inspired the construction of Europe.
>
> Lamy: I've noticed that we have reached this agreement just in time for the [twenty-fifth] anniversary of the celebration of the establishment of diplomatic relations between China and Europe. This is perhaps the reason which has led your minister, my friend Shi Guangsheng, to accelerate the movement . . . don't we both wish for multipolar balance in the world?
>
> Jiang: Your remarks invite me to make an additional remark. Yes, China and Europe wish for a multipolar rather than unipolar world—just as in physics one cannot obtain a balanced situation without the meeting of several forces[13].

China eventually joined the WTO at the end of 2001. During that historical process, reciprocity was fully reflected in the China-EU trade relationship. Bilateral trade value increased sharply from 30.9 billion euro in 1993 to 175.7 billion euro in 2004[14], namely by 469 percent. It is fair to say that this period witnessed the largest scale so far of mutual markets opening up between Europe and China.

Other features of this period in the EU-China relationship were the institutional innovations. Both China and the EU published soft policy papers in respect of each other. Together with the binding trade agreements signed in the 1970s and 1980s, these soft policy papers provided an institutional environment for the development of the China-EU relationship. From 1995 to 2003, the EU published four policy papers all told on China, and China responded in 2003 with its first EU policy paper. These policy papers helped the EU to coordinate issues among its member-states on China policy and to speak with one European voice. During this period, these non-binding policy papers played an important role in internal coordination and external publicity, and contributed to stabilize the bilateral economic relationship. History has amply proved that the EU, as a normative power, had gained more benefits from China through soft means than through hard means, which the EC had tried to do during and after the 1989 Tiananmen Square incident.

Phase 3 (2005 to the Present): Mutual Adaptations

The underlying strategic foundation during this period has not undergone any substantial changes. In particular, in regional and international affairs, we have seen increased coordination between China and the EU. But as Song Zhe, the then Chinese ambassador to the EU said, the European perceptions of China lagged behind the world changes and actual development in China, and therefore needed to make further efforts in adapting to and catching up with the changing realities[15]. In 2005, the EU's integration plans encountered setbacks in passing the European Constitutional Treaty, which occupied most of the EU's energies and forced it to accord priority to internal affairs. Moreover, with the end of the Iraq war and a new generation of European leaders coming into office, Europe made great efforts in rebuild its trans-Atlantic relationship. These new developments seemed to decrease the EU's strategic reliance on China. Unfortunately, French President Sarkozy met the Dalai Lama in 2008 when France was taking over the EU presidency. This transgressed the red line of China's interest and caused a serious blow to the EU-China relationship, leading to China postponing the 2008 EU-China Summit. After the Lisbon Treaty was passed in December 2009, the EU gained new competencies in the foreign policy area by establishing the positions of an EU president and an EU 'foreign minister', and the European External Action Service in order to strengthen the EU foreign policy outreach and coordination among member-states. But just when Europe gradually recovered from its integration problems, the EU encountered first the global financial crisis and later the European debt crisis, and compared with the two previous historical periods, China and Europe both now needed to work doubly hard in convincing the other side that the strategic foundation of their relationship had not been seriously weakened. To make matters worse, the second pillar of the China-EU relationship, which is in economic and trade cooperation, encountered new problems, the essence being that the reciprocal nature of the trade relationship had started to be called in question.

The 2005 textiles crisis was seen as a turning point for the EU-China trade relationship. As a cabinet member of the then Trade Commissioner Peter Mandelson summarized it, '[in the textile case], it was the first time that the EU witnessed China's genuine commercial power and massive build-up of its exporting capabilities, and directly experienced the tensions among European consumers, producers, importers and retailers'[16]. The year 2006 was to mark a watershed for China-EU trade relations. Five years since China's accession to the WTO, China had largely fulfilled its WTO commitments, and the sweeping mutual market openings between China and Europe came to a halt. Globally, one witnessed the slowdown of liberalization, the so-called reform fatigue in China and an increased opposition to the 'Washington Consensus'. All these events made China and the EU face unprecedented pressures in carrying through their respective liberal trade policies. Although Peter Mandelson suggested some new ideas and policy recommendations, including reforming the EU trade defence instruments, and put forward the first EU trade policy towards China, the implementation of Mandelson's trade policy encountered great obstacles.

The trade tensions came to a high point in mid-2007, when French President Sarkozy strongly criticized Peter Mandelson's China policy as being 'too naïve' and demanded 'the end of naivety' and reciprocity[17]. In October 2007, in a private letter (later leaked) to European Commission President Barroso, Mandelson said, 'To some extent the Chinese juggernaut is out of control', and that the European Union was 'sitting on a policy time bomb . . . I believe that there is greater scope for discussion and collaboration with the United States'[18]. The 2007 EU-China Summit witnessed great tensions that were unprecedented in the bilateral relationship. These were mainly focused on alleged Chinese currency manipulation, trading balances, and other issues, but the real causes behind the suddenly increasing tensions included the inability of the EU to adapt to globalization and the failure of the European constitutional treaty, which all led to the needless politicization of the EU-China economic and trade relationship. In short, China was made the scapegoat for the economic setbacks facing the EU. On the other hand, the resolution of China's economic concerns, such as being recognized as a market economy in anti-dumping investigations, had not been much advanced. After 2008, although the China-EU trade relationship had recovered somewhat, there emerged a new set of troubles. In 2010, without recognizing China's market economy status, the EU started an anti-subsidy investigation into China's wireless modems[19], and in 2011 the EU started to impose anti-subsidy duties on Chinese coated paper. Almost at the same time, China began to impose anti-subsidy duties on EU potato starch. Although the Chinese government clearly denied that this was a retaliatory action, some foreign media still regarded it as such. Among all the trade remedy cases, the most dramatic one was the solar panel affair, which was a symbolic case of economic diplomacy characterized with the use of political influence as a blunt instrument for economics.

In 2012, the European Commission launched anti-dumping and anti-subsidy investigations on Chinese exports of solar panels, involving over $20 billion, constituting the highest value trade dispute between China and the EU. The Chinese government, represented by its Premier Li Keqiang, launched a series of high-profile media campaigns and high-level political consultations in order to exercise some political influence vis-à-vis his European counterparts. Li met German Chancellor Angela Merkel, seeking German support for an amicable solution, and phoned the president of the European Commission, stating that 'nobody wins in the trade war . . . if the European side insists on punitive measures, China will surely take retaliatory measures'[20]. The outcome of these démarches was that the preliminary anti-dumping duty rate was reduced from 47.6 percent to 11.8 percent. On 2 December 2013, the Council backed the Commission's proposals to impose definitive anti-dumping and anti-subsidy measures on imports of solar panels from China, and in parallel, the Commission confirmed its decision to accept the undertaking with Chinese solar panel exporters applied since the beginning of August 2013. Those Chinese exporters that participated in the undertaking and that met the conditions of the undertaking could be exempted from anti-dumping duties, which was 47.7 percent on an average[21]. The solar panel case became a litmus test, which shows that China had skilfully used its economic diplomacy built upon its increasing strength and confidence.

During this period, the reciprocal nature of the EU-China trade relationship had come into question. The bilateral relationship moved slowly and both parties entered into a difficult period of mutual adaptation to a new bilateral and global context.

Although the EU-China bilateral trade relationship encountered difficulties, the institutional arrangements had witnessed encouraging signs of new developments, which helped create an enabling environment for the trade relationship. This fully demonstrated that institutional arrangements could be an important variable for the evolution of the China-EU trade relationship. In 2007, after lengthy preparations, both sides agreed to launch the negotiations for a partnership and cooperation agreement as well as negotiations for updating the 1985 China-EEC Trade and Economic Cooperation Agreement, and the tenth EU-China Summit decided to establish a vice-premier level economic and trade dialogue called high-level economic dialogue (HED). Between 2008 and 2013, China and the EU successfully held four sessions of the HED. From a broad strategic viewpoint, both sides discussed in detail a wide range of issues such as economics, finance, trade, and investments, and reached a consensus in many areas, in particular at a time when concerted efforts were desperately needed in mitigating the negative implications of the global finan-

cial crisis and the need for advancing European and even global economic recovery.

The HED is a new type of strategic economic dialogue and an institutional innovation, and it was created for several reasons. On the one
hand, the EU-China economic and trade cooperation had reached an unprecedented width and depth and therefore both parties looked for a new
mechanism to provide strategic and forward-looking guidance and planning for the bilateral trade relationship. On the other hand, China and the
United States had launched in 2006, one year earlier than the establishment of the China-EU HED, a strategic economic dialogue, which was
seemingly a success and therefore invited curiosity and rivalry from the
European side, which wanted to establish a European version of the strategic economic dialogue. To some satisfaction, the HED has provided a
stable and healthy institutional framework for the EU-China economic
relationship.

HOW TO IMPROVE EUROPEAN UNION–CHINA
TRADE RELATIONSHIP

We need to adopt a long-term historical view of the EU-China economic
and trade relationship. If we view the 1975 to 1988 period as an upward
spiral of the European-Chinese relationship, the period of 1989 to 1992
was a downward trend, followed by a new upward trajectory for the
1993 to 2004 period. However, such a buoyant period ended in 2005 and
the relationship again moved downward. It is unclear when the downward development will strike the bottom and pick up again. But it is
obvious that for the relationship to rejuvenate, the preconditions would
be that Europe successfully overcomes its debt crisis, and both China and
Europe make far-reaching reforms of their respective economic and social systems. Apart from fulfilling these preconditions, the key is to improve three variables.

First, how should we improve the strategic foundation of the China-
EU trade relationship? Some European scholars have doubts about the
nature of the strategic partnership in the China-EU relationship. Eberhard Sandschneider, director of the Research Institute of the German
Society for Foreign Policy, felt 'Most so-called "strategic partnerships"
are not "strategic" in a strict sense of the word. In a more narrow definition strategic partnerships should be based on a mutual perspective on
basic values, interests and actions to be taken in specific situations.' According to such definitions, he pointed out, 'China is too big and the EU
too multifaceted to simply declare a "strategic partnership" and paint the
world in black and white'[22]. Some other European scholars believe that
Europe should work together with other partners in balancing China's
influence. They suggest Europe needs to coordinate its own policy more

effectively and to cooperate with other countries to increase its presently limited leverage over China[23]. But ironically, when these European scholars advocate balancing China's influence based on the trans-Atlantic relations, some American intellectual élites represented by Fred Bergsten of the Peterson Institute put forward and promoted the idea of a 'G2', a concept that is sometimes called 'Chimerica', about growing cooperation between the two dominating countries in world affairs. That surprised and disappointed many European scholars and policymakers who thought it distanced Europe from international leadership or feared a 'G2' to be incompatible with the spirit of multilateralism and international norms. In order to reassure his European counterparts, Chinese Premier Wen Jiabao made it clear at the eleventh China-EU Summit on 20 May 2009 that 'the G2 idea was baseless and wrong'. Wen went on, 'It was impossible for one or two big countries or groups of countries to solve all the global issues. Multipolarity and multilateralism are the right trends and what people's hearts belong to'. That being said, some Chinese scholars still place a question mark on the strategic nature of the China-EU relationship, believing that after the debt crisis, Europe is in a crisis with a reduced strength and the China–United States 'G2' should represent the future.

Which observation is correct about the strategic nature of the EU-China relationship: whether the EU-China relations were not of a strategic nature, or whether the strategic foundation of EU-China relationship was still valid? My view is that the strategic nature of EU-China relationship still remains valid, and is even solid, but both sides need to make greater efforts in reinforcing it in light of today's global context. This is mainly because the EU-China relationship has gone far beyond a pure bilateral relationship to being one with global implications. The agenda of the EU-China relationship is now covering a much wider range, including energy, environment, climate, and even development assistance, given that both China and the EU are key players in these areas. For example, the EU-China Partnership on Climate Change has received fresh attention and is a platform for collaboration over clean energy sources. Moreover, the European Union and its member-states are the world's biggest donor of official development assistance. As China has expanded its own development assistance, and moved to increase its role as donor, there is a stronger urgency in China-EU talks over donor coordination. In Asia, the EU's influence is still rising through signing and negotiating more free trade agreements. Even if China is not negotiating a bilateral trade agreement with Europe, both sides acknowledge that China's big role in intra-regional trade in Asia requires attention in bilateral strategies vis-à-vis Asia. As America is now pivoting towards Asia, China would have more interest in working together with the EU, rather than less. In the economic and trade spheres, multipolarity is becoming a reality. As the world's biggest economy and trading power, the EU is an important pole. Equally, the EU's reliance on China is on the rise, in particular after Europe suffered from its debt crisis. Europe has and will have an increasing demand for China's capital and market. Although the EU feels it necessary to coordinate with China in macroeconomic and financial policies, it is accurate to say that Europe feels an instinctive urge to coordinate more with its trans-Atlantic partner, both being established powers, in response to China's rise. According to an established theoretical framework for this triangular relationship, the optimal scenario for China in its relationship with the United States and Europe is to have good relationships with both the United States and the EU and prevent any trans-Atlantic alliance against China. It is equally important for China to strengthen its relationship with other BRICS (Brazil, Russia, India, China, South Africa) countries and change its disadvantageous positioning in the United States–EU–China triangular relationship[24]. Historical experience has taught us that economic and trade cooperation is the cornerstone of the overall EU-China relationship and will play a very important role as a stabilizer and as ballast. Apart from that, China and Europe need to strengthen their strategic consensus, in particular in the areas of common values and world outlook. Both China and the EU desire a world order based on peace, prosperity, respect for self-determination, and national sovereignty. They also believe there has to be a better stewardship for generational issues like environmental degradation.

Secondly, how should we view and improve the principle of reciprocity in the EU-China economic and trade relationship? In recent years, more and more European policymakers and scholars have started to believe that the EU-China economic and trade relationship is not reciprocal, and some of them even argue in favour of using negative reciprocal action to press China to make concessions. As mentioned earlier, from mid-2007 French President Sarkozy called for trade reciprocity and greater protectionism. The then EU Trade Commissioner Peter Mandelson rebuffed Sarkozy's claim. Mandelson said he would defend European companies from unfair competition, but 'the response to a fortress Europe is a fortress [United States] or a fortress China and India. We need reciprocal openness, not reciprocal barriers'[25]. Despite Mandelson's rebuff to the idea of negative reciprocity, the new EU Trade Commissioner Karel de Gucht pushed forward a legislative proposal with a prominent instrumentality of negative reciprocity. This proposal provides that if the other governments close down their government procurement markets, the European governments can reciprocally shut down their own[26]. With some dubious justifications for upholding fair trade, that particular EU legislative proposal is a typical expression of negative reciprocity, which is, at the end of the day, at odds with the principle of free trade. It seems that in Europe today free trade proponents are fewer and fewer, while the advocates of managed trade or fair trade are much more numerous.

There are three principles that might be helpful in handling the reciprocity issue in the EU-China trade relationship. The first is to take a panoramic view of the overall economic relationship, not just trade, but also other issues ranging from investment and financial cooperation to energy, climate change, urbanization, education, and tourism cooperation. The summit and HED mechanisms in particular are established for exactly such a grand bargain. The second is that both China and Europe need to take a historical view, not just over the current difficulties, but also about the future opportunities. Thirdly, both sides need to look at the trade relationship from a long-term viewpoint that turns the EU-China trade relationship from a problem-focused relationship to a new relationship of strategic cooperation. Robert Keohane, a leading American political scientist, distinguished two types of reciprocity[27]. The first is 'specific reciprocity', such as in the case of reduction of customs duties. If Country A reduces a certain percentage and number of tariffs lines, Country B reduces similar amounts. The characteristic of this kind of reciprocity is simultaneity in trade-off. The second type of reciprocity, called 'diffuse reciprocity', is not seeking any immediate return or trade-off. Instead, it seeks the overall balance of benefits over the long term. That type of reciprocity could be developed into a norm of international cooperation. This kind of reciprocity is sustainable and has spillover effects for other issue areas. In my opinion, diffuse reciprocity is of a more strategic nature than the specific reciprocity currently prevalent in the politics among nations. The level of trade cooperation between China and Europe is not a one-off arrangement. In the future, the two sides need to develop an increased level of bilateral economic integration aimed for the long term and have even greater cooperation in the economic, financial, fiscal, and trade areas. If one day the China-EU economic relationship reaches the level of the trans-Atlantic one, the basic foundation of the EU-China relationship would be even stronger.

Finally, a reflection about the institutional arrangements of the EU-China trade relationship. Agreements, legal documents, policy papers, and the various levels of dialogue mechanisms all constitute the institutional foundation for the trade relationship. Given that European integration is still evolving and the China-EU relationship often encounters new issues and problems, the institutional environment for the EU-China trade relationship is far from being consolidated. In particular, after the Lisbon Treaty and in response to the euro debt crisis, we are seeing an increased need for making full use of the existing institutional structures. The overall trend for European integration is that member-states concede more sovereignty at the EU level, albeit with some reluctance. As a result, the member-states and the EU are experiencing a greater number of disputes about sovereignty and competencies. As the EU level gains more and more competencies, China needs to give more weight to developing a sound institutional environment for a bilateral trade relationship. The

HED needs to benefit from past experiences and to further increase efficiencies. For example, more participation by businesses, interest groups, think tanks, and scholars could be considered as part of the HED preparations and for strategic planning. China needs to adapt to the EU member-state dual-level structures and tackle the appropriate problems, which rightly fall into the area of EU competences. There are, however, some often positive developments in institution-building. At the sixteenth EU-China Summit held in Beijing on 21 November 2013, both sides jointly adopted the EU-China 2020 Strategic Agenda for Cooperation, which provides strategic guidance to their relationship. Moreover, during the visit by Chinese President Xi Jinping to Brussels in March 2014, China issued its second EU policy paper after the first one issued in 2003, and after the EU had issued six China policy papers.

CONCLUSION

History records that the strategic foundation, reciprocity, and institutions have been the three key variables for the EU-China trade relationship: they can either facilitate or obstruct the development of the bilateral relationship. When all the three variables are inclined to be positive, the bilateral trade relationship enjoys a good momentum, such as during the periods of 1975 to 1988 and of 1993 to 2004. Otherwise, the trade relationship is negatively affected. These variables should be able to support and complement each other, in particular for the post-2005 period. Although the EU-China strategic foundation has been eroded and full reciprocity is still largely unrealized, some solid and often self-innovating institutions such as the summit meetings, the HED, and many other ministerial and below-ministerial dialogues somehow managed to consolidate the strategic foundation and help facilitate economic reciprocity, thereby playing a key role in preventing the EU-China relationship from deviating from the pursuit of the right track.

But more fundamentally for the EU-China trade relationship, the key lies in China's domestic reform process and its ambition to achieve major country ('大国', Chinese characters, roughly equivalent of 'great power') status. The Chinese side has launched an ambitious reform program, which was elaborated upon at the third plenum session of the eighteenth Congress of the Communist Party. But it is still far from a mission accomplished, and there are increased resistances from vested interests against a profound reform of the system. It is equally challenging for China to realize its ambition to become a great power against the background of the US Asian 'pivot' and worrying island disputes between China and its Eastern and Southeast Asian neighbours. Given those fundamental factors, the EU's tilt towards the United States through the Transatlantic Trade and Investment Partnership and its assertive trade remedies vis-à-vis China would certainly be of no help to promote mutually beneficial future EU-China trade relations.

NOTES

1. Zhu Liqun, 'China's Foreign Policy Debates', *European Union Institute for Security Studies Chaillot Papers* (September 2010): 11.

2. Li Jie, 'The Multi-polarization Trend of the World and Mao Zedong's Three World Theory', (*Shi Jie Duo Ji Hua Qu Shi Yu Mao Ze Dong De San Ge Shi Jie Hua Fen Li Lun*), in *Revisiting China's Diplomatic Thoughts* (*Zhong Guo Wai Jiao Xin Lun*), Liu Shan and Xue Jundu (Beijing: World Knowledge Press [Shi Jie Zhi Shi Chu Ban She], 1997).

3. Chinese Ministry of Foreign Affairs and the Central Committee of the Communist Party of China Literature Review Office, *The Selected Works of Mao Zedong's Diplomacy* (Mao Ze Dong Wai Jiao Wen Xuan) (Beijing: Zhong Yang Wen Xian Press, n.d.), 487–86.

4. E. Reuter, 'A New Agenda', in *China-EU: A Common Future*, S. Crossick and E. Reuter (eds.) (Singapore: World Scientific 2007), xi–xiii.

5. H. Kapur, *China and the EEC: the New Connection*, (Boston: Martinus Nijhoff Publisher, 1986), 31.

6. Kapur, *China and the EEC*, 47

7. Communication of the European Commission, *A Long-Term Policy for China-Europe Relations*, COM 279/final (1995).

8. Q. Yuanlun, 'The EU's Long-Term China Policy and the Sino-EU Economic and Trade Relationship', 8 *World Econ.* 4 (1999) (Chinese periodical).

9. Jiang Zemin, *Report to the 16th National Congress of the Communist Party of China*, 8 November 2002, news.xinhuanet.com/ziliao/2002-11/17/content_693542.htm, accessed 23 October 2014.

10. The Ministry of Foreign Affairs of the People's Republic of China, *Policy File of China to EU*, October 2003, news.sohu.com/59/17/news214371759.shtml, accessed 23 October 2014.

11. C. Patten, *Not Quite the Diplomat: Home Truths about World Affairs* (London: Penguin Books, 2005): 273.

12. Li Lanqing, *Break—the Days of Door's Opening* (Tu Wei-Guo Men Chu Kai De Ri Zi) (Central Literature Press [Zhong Yang Wen Xian Chu Ban She], 2008), 332–35.

13. Pascal Lamy, *L'Europe en Premier Ligne* (Seuil, 2003).

14. Eurostat External and Intra-EU Trade: Statistical Yearbook, Data 1958–2008.

15. Song Zhe, year-end interview of Xin Hua News Agency 'Reference News', Ministry of Foreign Affairs website, 26 December 2008.

16. Interview with Per Haugaard, a cabinet member of Commissioner Mandelson, Brussels, 22 July 2009.

17. N. Sarkozy, Speech at the international aerospace show, le Bourget, 23 June 2007, see www.ambafrance-uk.org/President-Sarkozy-s-speech-at-Le.html.

18. 'EU Trade Chief Calls for Aggressive Action against China', *New York Times*, 17 October 2007, www.nytimes.com/2007/10/17/business/worldbusiness/17iht-trade.4.7932574.html.

19. In addition to anti-subsidy, the EU also launched anti-dumping and safeguards investigation against Chinese exports to Europe's wireless data card. On 25 January 2011, the European Commission terminated the safeguards investigation of this case and on 3 March 2011, the European Commission terminated the anti-dumping and anti-subsidy investigation of this case, too.

20. S. Castle, 'EU Trade Chief Calls for Aggressive Action Against China', *The New York Times*, 17 October 2007, www.chinaelc.cn/ch_jxzl/2013081280666.html, accessed 12 August 2013.

21. European Commission, *EU Imposes Definitive Measures on Chinese Solar Panels, Confirms Undertaking with Chinese Solar Panel Exporter*, COM IP/13/1190 (2013).

22. Eberhard Sandschneider, 'The Strategic Significance of China Partnership (Speaking Points)', *Foreign Affairs Journal*, The Chinese People's Institute of Foreign Affairs, Special Issue (November 2009): 81.

23. Francois Godement, 'A Global China Policy', *European Council on Foreign Relations*, (June 2010): 1, www.ecfr.eu/content/entry/a_global_china_policy.

24. Chen Zhimin, 'China and the United States and Europe: The Cooperation and Competition of the New Trilateral Relations', *World Economics and Politics*, no. 1 (2010); Zhang Xiaotong, 'The Thinking about the Tripartite Game Among China and America and Europe in Economic and Trade Fields', *European Issues Reference*, no. 19 (2010): 1–4.

25. 'Mandelson to Attack France over Free Market', *Financial Times*, 30 June 2007, www.ft.com/cms/s/0/d7204ac8-26a5-11dc-8e18-000b5df10621.html.

26. European Commission, *Trade, Growth and World Affairs—Trade Policy as a Core Element of the EU's 2020 Strategy*, (2010), 6.

27. R. Keohane, 'Reciprocity in International Relations', *International Organization* 40, no. 1 (Winter 1986): 1–27.

NINE

Why China–European Union Relations Are Not So Strategic

Ten Hypotheses

Wang Yiwei

The China–European Union (EU) Comprehensive Strategic Partnership was constructed in 2003, twenty-eight years after the establishment of diplomatic ties between China and the European Communities (EC).

There are many debates on the strategic quality of the relationship thereafter. The key questions to be framed are: Why are China-EU relations not so strategic, and how can the relationship in the future be made truly strategic? In keeping with the Chinese government's good intentions, the optimistic argument cautiously affirms that the strategic partnership is really a work in progress but not yet a reality [1].

How real at present then is the China-EU 'strategic partnership'? Europeans will complain that although China is one of the EU's ten so-called strategic partners [2], in effect the relationship is more competitive than cooperative. And as for the Chinese, the EU is just one of more than sixty strategic partners it already has, and it usually complains that the EU's policy towards China is based squarely on commercial rather than any strategic considerations.

On both sides, these complaints come from misperceptions about the real nature of a strategic partnership. China sees it as meaning a long-term, comprehensive, and stable relationship beyond everyday domestic and international issues. For Europe, on the other hand, the emphasis is on market access and on China's attitude to global governance issues.

Only in the China-EU 2020 Strategic Agenda for Cooperation document, that was released on the tenth anniversary of the establishment of the China-EU Comprehensive Strategic Partnership, does the strategic nature of China-EU relations appear to be less debatable, because it is the first time that peace and security, instead of economic cooperation, have been placed as the first priority in the China-EU strategic agenda for cooperation. The agenda says:

> The two sides will fully implement the Strategic Agenda for Cooperation through their annual Summit, which provides strategic guidance to the relationship; through the three pillars directly underpinning the Summit (the annual High Level Strategic Dialogue, the annual High Level Economic and Trade Dialogue, and the bi-annual High Level People-to-People Dialogue); through their regular meetings of counterparts and through their broad range of sectoral dialogues[3].

How will the two parties bridge the gap between words and deeds? In other words, how do they intend to implement the strategic agenda?

DIFFERENT PERCEPTIONS OF STRATEGIC PARTNERSHIP

The erstwhile Chinese Premier Wen Jiabao gave the following definition of the China-EU Comprehensive Strategic Partnership in his meeting with former President of the European Commission and Former Prime Minister of Italy Romano Prodi on 25 November 2008:

> 'Comprehensive' means the promotion of political trust and mutually beneficial cooperation, and 'strategic' requires that both sides make concerted efforts in a far-sighted way to ensure the lasting, stable and healthy development of China-EU relations.

But the truth is that China-EU relations have witnessed zigzags in reality, not following Wen's expectation. There are more than a few Chinese complaints that the market economy status and the arms embargo issues have dominated and made a mockery of the China-EU Comprehensive Strategic Partnership during Wen's own charge of European affairs between 2003 and 2012. And with the United States' proposed 'pivot' back to Asia, few Chinese expect the EU's return to Asia to counterbalance the United States. And this is viewed with concern.

These differing perceptions tend to ignore the fact that there are numerous layers to any strategic partnership. Because China is the world's biggest developing country and the EU is the largest group of developed countries, both have been shaping their intended partnership from different standpoints rather than on the basis of common expectations. In other words, the China-EU strategic partnership is far from being a traditional one, and it is aggravated by such unresolved issues as the arms embargo, the non-award to China of market economy status, and the EU's anti-dumping and countervailing duties cases that are targeted against China.

In Chinese eyes, their country's engagement with the EU has three significant values. First, the EU helps to resist the world's 'Americanization', not just in economic development but also in the US way of life and even in its way of thinking. Without the EU and its achievements, the United States would find it even easier to dominate the international community. And secondly, not only does the EU counterbalance Americanization, but it also helps the world to deal with uncertainty. Europe contributes to world peace and prosperity through its peace-keeping missions, its use of diplomatic means for dispute settlement, peace-building, and non-traditional security mechanisms. And thirdly, as the world's largest aid donor, the EU exports peace and development, while the United States exports wars.

The EU has done much to maintain stability and peace now that Europe is no longer a cauldron of wars. It has also had a '28 × 3' effect on its own neighbours—Russia, the countries around the Mediterranean, Central Asia, the Caucasus region, and even Turkey may not now be interested in joining the EU, but to a greater or lesser degree they remain very much part of the broader European culture. The EU is the only successful achievement after Charles the Great's unification of Europe and the extension of European civilization in the globalization era. Turkey and Russia claim their European identity as the representatives of the Second and Third Roman Empire, respectively, which triggers the clashes relating to the legitimacy of European civilizations, as being indicated in Turkey's joining the EU and the Ukraine crisis.

There are other reasons, too, why China correctly values its European connection:

- The EU is China's largest trading partner and a major resource for technology transfers. Its technical, financial, and market strengths do much to support China's own reforms and modernization. The EU model has respected China's values and helped to sustain its wealth creation efforts. The EU has backed China's nation-building project and its expansion of domestic economic demand.
- The EU's history has been an inspiration for China's foreign policies. Europe's emphasis on peaceful development has been an example for China's goal of building a harmonious world by its peaceful rise; that is, of peace, by peace, and for peace. China's rise is undertaken in a peaceful environment, just as European integration is undertaken in a peaceful way, aiming at win-win cooperation and for world peace, just like the EU's contribution for regional and international peace, and assistance for development.
- China's twelfth five-year plan has certain similarities with the EU's 'Europe 2020' strategy for sustainable, smart, and inclusive growth.

Thus, the second China-Europe High-Level Parties Forum in 2011 made the theme of 'New Opportunity and Prospect of China-Europe Cooperation' by comparing China's twelfth plan with the EU's 'Europe 2020' strategy.

Having narrated this, it seems only proper to add that Europe's perceptions of China seem inherently contradictory, because the EU has no clear or coherent strategy for engaging with China. Some EU countries — Germany for instance — benefit more than others from China's economic rise. And those who do not tend to feel challenged by the economic competition increasingly coming from China. However, the German view of China is paradoxically generally more negative than those of most of the other European states, particularly concerning the Chinese military rise[4].

TEN HYPOTHESES ON NOT BEING SO STRATEGIC

There should be more fundamental reasons to explain this phenomenon beyond the perceptions and misperceptions. Why are China-EU relations not yet so strategic? There are ten hypotheses offered in the following for the reasons.

1. The asymmetry of the relationship. Ninety percent of China-EU relations are in the nature of economic and trade relations, and trade is essentially a transaction issue between producers and consumers. Basically, it is business as usual, and China-EU political ties have been used as the tool to manage economic and trade cooperation and to eliminate frictions between the two trading entities.
2. The asymmetry of the systemic arrangements. As a strange international animal with many heads, the EU compromises its individual member-states' China policies, without enough matching strategic capability, which obliges China to focus on strategic relations with big three: the United Kingdom, France, and Germany. Britain and France are permanent members of UN Security Council, a factor that obstructs the EU from strategic cooperation with China, particularly within the UN framework. In negotiating with others, the EU institutions usually play the bad cop while member-states play the good cop. Such a phenomenon has left China disappointed and frustrated time and again. Besides, the EU is the result of multilateral negotiation among member-states, without enough top-down design, which prevents China having pre-strategic bilateral cooperation with the EU on subjects like a Eurasian free trade zone. Multilateral projects inhibit strategic choices.

3. The asymmetry of diplomacy. The EU is strong in multilateralism but weak in bilateralism, while China is the complete opposite. The decline of global multilateralism reduces the EU's strategic ability and directly affects China-EU strategic relations. In recent years, the EU has turned to free trade agreements, especially the trans-Atlantic FTA with the openly declared objective of preventing China setting the standards for global trade, and indirectly declaring the demise of the Doha Round of the World Trade Organization negotiations. This has damaged the EU's reputation in China greatly. The EU is not a single state but a union with twenty-eight member-states, and when negotiating with China, what it wants are the maximum demands of all twenty-eight member-states, whereas what it can give up are the various combinations of concessions of all member-states. China always feels it is unfair negotiating with the EU, which prohibits it from having strategic cooperation with the EU. It is easy for twenty-eight member-states to reach consensus over soft issues, such as cultural exchanges, but not hard issues, particularly in the strategic fields.

4. The asymmetry of identities. The real reason for China-EU disharmony in global governance is the clash of identities. China is trying to keep a balance among four identities: (1) developing country, (2) emerging power, (3) Eastern civilization, and (4) socialist state. The EU also holds four identities in the eyes of the Chinese: (1) the biggest developed bloc, (2) post-modern model, (3) Western civilization, and (4) European capitalism. This entails four paradigms for China-EU relations: relations between the biggest developing country and the biggest developed bloc, between an emerging power and post-modern model, between Eastern and Western civilizations, and between socialism and capitalism [5].

5. The asymmetry of society. The EU stresses the power and participation of civil society and populism prevails, whereas China stresses the power of the nation and nationalism prevails. The stronger and very aggressive role of the European Parliament is more of a hindrance and less of a help in the development and implementation of strategies if the members of the European Parliament do not update their mentality about China. For instance, in October 2008, Chinese jailed dissident Hu Jia was awarded the Sakharov Prize for Freedom of Thought by the European Parliament. The Europeans focus on individual rights and consider the dissident as representing the independent civil society, while the Chinese focus more on collective rights of the Chinese as the whole. Such asymmetry prohibits the strategic coherence between China and the EU.

6. The asymmetry of the development stage. China is at the modernization stage and is benefiting more from globalization as the late-

comer, whereas the EU has entered a post-modern period, not only benefiting from globalization, but also suffering from the risks and challenges of globalization, which make China and the EU less cooperative and collaborative strategically in global governance. For instance, in climate change negotiation, China highlights the principle of the 'common but differentiated responsibility' of a developing country under the Kyoto Protocol, while the EU, as the biggest bloc of the developed countries, denies China's identity and claims.

7. The asymmetry of development trends. The EU countries, other than Germany, are almost all in decline (although the United Kingdom and France might not recognize that or be reconciled to it), which results in a conservative, defensive Europe being wholly preoccupied with the commercial considerations of gains and losses. Even more seriously, many Europeans still think that the EU holds more sticks than carrots to force China into measures of unwelcome reciprocity. When Chinese President Xi Jinping put forward the concept of the 'Chinese dream', while the European dream was initiated by American scholar Jeremy Rifkin, it reveals again that Chinese are more confident about the future. The EU missed the opportunity to invite China to join the Galileo System due to concern about Chinese catching up with the EU in high technology. The multipolar attempt to balance the United States' global positioning system failed, and this encouraged China to build its own Beidou Global Navigation Satellite System.

8. The asymmetry of strategic independence. EU security policy is subject to the North Atlantic Treaty Organization, a values-based diplomacy and coordination with the United States. It has less strategic independence than China. China's financial dependence on the United States, and the EU's security dependence on the United States, makes it easy for the United States to intervene and impair China-EU strategic cooperation. The Ukraine crisis and the eurozone crisis tells China that the EU's security and financial power are either dependent on the United States or not able to balance the American dollar at all. So, when the United States pivots back to Asia, no Chinese person expects to invite the EU to balance the United States. At the same time, the Chinese worry about the Transatlantic Trade and Investment Partnership along with the Trans-Pacific Partnership to isolate China in forging a high standard of globalization.

9. The asymmetry of mentality. The EU is a regional organization more intent on avoiding war and not repeating historical strategic mistakes than on achieving peace and development, which makes it difficult for the EU to seek strategic goals with China. The EU holds attitude and mentality as a normative power, making it diffi-

cult to keep a balance between strategy and values. For instance, the EU abandoned its human rights dialogue with China without achieving many concrete results. EU member-states' relations with China wittiness a zigzag on the issue of meetings with the Dalai Lama by their leaders. China had to cancel the summit with the EU in 2008 when French President Nicolas Sarkozy during his EU presidency met the Dalai Lama. Strategy needs to trade, and the EU will never be prepared to make trade-offs against its cherished universal values such as the rule of law. Many Chinese prefer pragmatism, viewing the EU from the perspective of a nation-state. However, the EU holds a post-modern concept of China. The unique characteristics of European politics and democracy in the EU prevent closer strategic understandings.

10. The asymmetry of words and deeds. The EU recognizes China's strategic value but lacks the initiative for any coherent strategic actions. It deals with China on a case-by-case, and issue-by-issue, basis. China in turn recognizes the strategic value of the EU, but its subconscious hesitations and guardedness have prevented any consistent engagement. The strategic player needs to balance the short-term pains and long-term gains, and converge internal diversities. However, different national conditions make China and the EU promote a multipolar world more in words than in deeds.

HOW TO MAKE THE RELATIONSHIP MORE STRATEGIC

Forging a real Sino-EU strategic partnership will not come about easily[6]. China represents both a strategic competitor and an opportunity for the EU, while Europe's sovereign debt crisis is both a challenge and an opportunity for China. The Chinese initiative of building the twenty-first century Maritime Silk Road and the Silk Road Economic Belt will connect China and Europe once again through the Eurasian continent, making China-European relations more strategic in shaping globalization through a new regionalization. Given that the European élites worry that 'the Union and its member-states could slide into marginalization, becoming an increasingly irrelevant western peninsula of the Asian continent'[7], this initiative is a great opportunity for Europe to change its strategic role in the new globalization. Besides, the two Silk Roads change the situation of the two continents without overlapping geopolitical confrontation or cooperation between China and the EU. Hence, in general, China-EU relations have entered the possibility of real strategic cooperation.

In practice, there are a number of measures that could do much to improve China-EU strategic relations.

- Their trade relationship could be made more strategic. Trade can be seen at three levels, namely, free trade, fair trade, and strategic trade. China and the EU must show solidarity on free trade, be restrained on fair trade, and be more active on strategic trade. For example, selling China's rare earths to Europe rather than to Japan would constitute a strategic trade policy measure. And both sides should also upgrade China-EU trade relations to include financial cooperation.

- China and the EU have over the past years become each other's biggest, or second biggest, trading partners, but investment levels between the two do not match the levels of their trade. A China-EU FTA, combined with a mutual investment treaty, would greatly improve the strategic quality of the China-EU partnership. A mutual currency exchange agreement between the renminbi and the euro would also have a promising effect on trade and investment. For example, China signed a $358 billion currency swap agreement with the European Central Bank in October 2013.

- Reform of the international financial system is extremely important. Apart from the American dollar, the euro is the next most important foreign reserve currency, while the renminbi is in the process of becoming internationalized and thus is a possible candidate for becoming accepted as the third largest reserve currency. The EU and China both should have a growing interest in reforming the international monetary system in a balanced, sustainable, secure, and inclusive direction.

- The main obstacle to closer China-EU ties is that the EU is internally diverse but attempts externally to appear united. It is up to China to encourage levels of consistency within and outside Europe, and to facilitate Europe's efforts to gain respect around the world. At the same time, it is for the EU to promote the appreciation and acceptability of China into the world community and to win general recognition of its world status.

However, the EU and Chinese governments apparently do undertake considerable efforts to make the relationship more strategic. For instance, negotiations have commenced for an EU-China Bilateral Investment Agreement, the first investment agreement that the European Commission has ever initiated on behalf of its twenty-eight member-states. This initiative might lead the way to the possibility of negotiating a China-EU FTA in due course of time. Chinese and European new Silk Roads initiatives can combine with each other and jointly shape a Eurasian version of globalization. The Silk Road is not only a Eurasian trade route, but also a link between European and Asian civilizations. The Silk Road Economic Belt inherits the ancient trade and civilization channel in this age of globalization, and initiates globalization on the land to hedge against the risks of maritime globalization, ushers in civilization communication to realize Eurasian peace and prosperity, and opens up a new sustainable civilization. The mission of the Silk Road Economic Belt lies in the integration of development, security, and governance; the revival, transformation, and innovation of Chinese, Muslim, and Christian civilizations, and the economic integration of Europe and Asia.

As important actors in a multipolar world, China and the EU should commit themselves to enhancing dialogue and coordination at bilateral, regional, and global levels in order to meet regional and global challenges together, and work to make the international order and system more just and equitable[8]. Particularly, China could welcome the EU to join the East Asia Summit and other existing platforms in Asia, such as the Conference on Interaction and Confidence-Building Measures in Asia or a possible new one such as a Maritime Cooperation Organization. In return, Europe could accept China as the leader of Asia, politically and economically, though this would cause misgivings among other major nations in Asia, and also accept that China can affect Europe's future much more than Europe can affect China's. Europe is tied to the United States' strategic policies in the Asia-Pacific, which makes it a less than credible independent partner for China.

Other major efforts have been taking place between the two entities, as follows.

Deepening High-Level Exchanges and Political Dialogue

Compared with the other ten strategic partners, EU-China has the most frequent, wide, and fruitful dialogue. Eleven of the total of sixty-five mechanisms are related to political issues, which are even more than the EU–United States dialogue. China will step up high-level exchanges and political dialogues with both EU institutions and member-states, and further improve the structure of all-dimensional, multitiered, and wide-ranging China-EU dialogues and cooperation. Both sides should give full play to the role of the China-EU Summit in providing political guidance to the China-EU relationship, and make use of the China-EU high-level strategic dialogue for communication, coordination, and oversight over China-EU relations and major international and regional issues of mutual interest.

Strengthening Coordination and Cooperation in International Affairs

Both the EU and China should make maximum efforts to :

- Strengthen consultation on international affairs, work jointly for political solutions to international and regional tensions and crisis situations, and uphold peace and stability.
- Commit themselves jointly to upholding the authority of the United Nations, safeguarding the gains of victory in World War II and

the post-war international order, supporting the United Nations in playing its leading role in upholding world peace, promoting common development, and advancing international cooperation.

- Support reforms of the United Nations and uphold international equity and justice, and step up exchanges in UN peace-keeping activities and promote cooperation in this field between the two sides through training of personnel and sharing of experiences.
- Deepen exchanges and cooperation in the framework of the Asia-Europe Meeting; promote equality, mutual trust, and practical cooperation between Asia and Europe; and enhance the role and influence of the Asia-Europe Meeting in upholding world peace and regional stability, promoting world economic recovery and sustainable development, and working for solutions to global issues.
- Step up macroeconomic policy coordination within the G-20, and commit to working together for a bigger role of the G-20 in international economic and financial affairs as the premier forum for international economic cooperation; and encourage the G-20 to build closer partnerships, commit to reforms of the international monetary and financial systems, promote trade and investment liberalization and facilitation, oppose protectionism, and maintain and develop an open world economy. As the second China's policy paper on the EU indicates:

> China and the EU, the world's most representative emerging economy and the group of developed countries, respectively, are two major forces for world peace as they share important strategic consensus on building a multipolar world. The combined economic aggregate of China and the EU accounts for one-third of the world economy, making them two major markets for common development. Being an important representative of the oriental culture and the cradle of Western culture and with a combined population accounting for a quarter of the world's total, China and the EU stand as two major civilizations advancing human progress[9].

Under the new guidelines, China and the EU should endeavour to achieve the following four partnerships, which will distinguish their relationship from any other strategic partners of either party:

1. China-EU partnership for peace: China stands ready to work with the EU to bring the two major world centres closer and to pursue peaceful development in a multipolar world, with respect and accommodation of each other's core interests and major concerns, to make the international order and international system more just and equitable, to advocate democracy in international relations,

and to create a peaceful, stable, equitable, and orderly development environment for all countries.

2. China-EU partnership for growth: China stands ready to work with the EU to bring the two major markets closer; to build a China-EU community of interests; to strengthen the bonds of common interests between the two sides at the global strategic, regional, and bilateral levels; to carry out win-win cooperation at higher levels; and to contribute more to the building of an open world economy.

3. China-EU partnership for reform: China stands ready to work with the EU to better align China's comprehensive deepening of reform with the EU's reform process and readjustment, to draw upon each other's reform experience, share reform dividends, jointly improve the ability of reform and governance, and actively to participate in the formulation and reform of the standards and norms of global governance.

4. China-EU partnership for civilization: China stands ready to work with the EU to bring the two major civilizations in the East and West closer together and to set an example of two different civilizations seeking harmony without uniformity, promoting diversity, and learning from each other with the objective of enjoying common prosperity[10].

In the future, the above four aspects should extend to a China-EU partnership for peace and security; a China-EU partnership for growth and development, including sustainable, balanced, and inclusive development; a China-EU partnership for reform and governance, including inter-regional and global governance; and a China-EU partnership for civilization and culture.

CONCLUSION

The China-EU Comprehensive Strategic Partnership currently represents more of the Chinese desire to provide substance to the relationship than the ambitions of the Europeans. The EU highlights the need for partnership, whereas China highlights the need for clearly understood strategies and mutual comprehension. Partnership with China is important for the EU's domestic, regional, and global governance aspirations, while the EU is still only a yet unachieved hope in regard to hedging against the risks of US hegemony. The United States is indeed the most important external force that makes the China-EU Comprehensive Strategic Partnership less than strategic, or not strategic at all in the American mind, given the EU's security, economic, and ideological dependence on American leadership with its overall goal of hegemony over the West. The arms embargo issue and the current Ukraine crisis reveal this only too clearly.

The key to analysing the China-EU Comprehensive Strategic Partnership is that neither is it 'partnership' nor 'strategic' nor 'comprehensive', since the EU cannot be regarded as a comprehensive international player in the world system. The European integration process is more evident in trade than in security issues. For instance, even though Chinese-German trade accounts for as much as one-third of China-EU trade, Germany is just part of the overall strategic partnership between the EU and China, because Germany is not a permanent member of UN Security Council. Only when the strategic powers are transferred from member-states to Brussels can the EU be regarded as a full strategic player, and then that can turn the China-EU Comprehensive Strategic Partnership from being merely a work in progress into a reality.

However, both sides must continue to make great efforts to discover the new meanings of the expressions 'comprehensive' and 'strategic' in promoting China-EU relations. From a partnership between two major forces, two major markets, and two major civilizations, China-EU relations have been moving towards the direction of being a strategic partnership for peace and security, for growth and development, for reform and governance, for civilization and culture. With the major Chinese initiatives of the Silk Road Economic Belt and the twenty-first century Maritime Silk Road in order to build mutual connectivity in policy, trade, transportation, currency, and people-to-people relations, they can only add an impetus to promoting Eurasian integration, China-EU relations should turn into not just a real Comprehensive Strategic Partnership, but for furnishing guidelines for a new type of Comprehensive Strategic Partnership altogether.

Non-Strategic Partners			
Sl.no.	Name of Country	Date of Diplomatic Ties	Notes
1	Austria	28 May 1971	
2	Cyprus	14 December 1971	
3	Estonia	11 September 1991	
4	Finland	20 October 1950	
5	Latvia	12 September 1991	
6	Hungary	6 October 1949	
7	Ireland	22 June 1979	
8	Lithuania	14 September 1991	
9	Luxemburg	16 November 1972	
10	Malta	31 January 1972	
11	Slovakia	6 October 1949	
12	Slovenia	12 May 1992	
13	Sweden	9 May 1950	Strategic partnership in sustainable development.

Bilateral Relations within Framework of China-EU Comprehensive Strategic Partnership			
Sl.no.	Name of Country	Date of Diplomatic Ties	Notes
1	Czech Republic	6 October 1949	Development of good relations within framework of China-EU Comprehensive Strategic Partnership as stated in *Joint Statement Between the Government of the People's Republic of China and the Government of the Czech Republic* of 8 December 2005.

Strategic Partners			
Sl.no.	Name of Country	Date of Diplomatic Ties	Notes
1	Poland 7 October 1949		Strategic Partnership established by *Joint Statement of the People's Republic of China and the Republic of Poland* on 20 December 2011.

All-round Partnership on various Specific Issues			
Sl.no.	Name of Country	Date of Diplomatic Ties	Notes
1	Belgium	25 October 1971	All-Around Friendly Cooperative Partnership by joint declaration on 31 March 2014.
2	Germany	11 October 1972	*Joint Communiqué of the People's Republic of China and Federal Republic of Germany on Comprehensive Promotion of Strategic Partnership* on 18. July, 2010. All-Around Strategic Partnership by joint declaration on 28 March 2014.

Table 9.1. Current Relations of EU Member-States With China.

Comprehensive Strategic Partnership			
Sl.no.	Name of Country	Date of Diplomatic Ties	Notes
1	Denmark	5 November 1950	Comprehensive Strategic Partnership by joint declaration on 25 October 2008.
2	France	27 January 1964	Joint declaration for strengthening comprehensive strategic partnership on 4 November 2010; Comprehensive Strategic Partnership formally established by another declaration on 26 March 2014.
3	Greece	5 June 1972	Comprehensive Strategic Partnership established on 19 January 2006 by joint declaration, enhanced by another declaration on 21 June 2014.
4	Italy	6 November 1970	Stable, Friendly, Long-Term, and Enduring Comprehensive Strategic Partnership by joint communiqué on 9 May 2004.
5	Portugal	8 February 1979	Comprehensive Strategic Partnership by joint declaration on 9 December 2005.
6	Spain	9 March 1973	Comprehensive Strategic Partnership by joint declaration on 15 November 2005.
7	United Kingdom	13 March 1972	Comprehensive Strategic Partnership by joint declaration on 10 May 2004.

Miscellaneous			
Sl.no.	Name of Country	Date of Diplomatic Ties	Notes
1	Bulgaria	4 October 1949	Comprehensive Friendly Cooperative Partnership by joint communiqué on 13 January 2014.
2	Croatia	13 May 1992	Comprehensive Cooperative Partnership by joint declaration on 26 May 2005.
3	Romania	5 October 1949	Comprehensive Friendly Cooperative Partnership by joint declaration on 14 June 2004.
4	Netherlands	18 May 1972	Comprehensive Mutual-Beneficial Partnership by joint declaration on 16 May 2007, as a strategic step in bilateral relations.

Table 9.1. (cont.).

NOTES

1. Xinning Song, 'EU-China Relationship in Transition: Challenges and Opportunities', in *Europe and China: Strategic Partners or Rivals*, Roland Vogt (ed.) (Hong Kong: Hong Kong University Press, 2012), 36.

2. The European Union has established ten strategic partnerships with the United States (1995), Canada (1996), Japan (2001), China (2003), Russia (2003), India (2004), Brazil (2007), South Africa (2007), Mexico (2010), and South Korea (2010). See: strategicpartnerships.eu, accessed 12 October 2014.

3. China-EU 2020 Strategic Agenda for Cooperation released at sixteenth China-EU Summit, 23 November 2013, www.fmprc.gov.cn/mfa_eng/wjdt_665385/2649_665393/t1101804.shtml, accessed 12 October 2014.

4. According to 2014 data, 64 percent of Germans view China negatively. www.pewglobal.org/2014/07/14/chapter-2-chinas-image/, accessed 10 January 2015.

5. Yiwei Wang, 'China and the EU in Global Governance: Seeking Harmony in Identities', in *China, the EU and Global Governance*, Jan Wouters, Tanguy de Wilde, and Pierre Defraigne (eds.) (Cheltenham: Edward Elgar Publishing Limited, 2012), 50–60.

6. Gustaaf Geeraerts, 'EU-China Relations', in *The Palgrave Handbook of EU-Asia Relations*, Thomas Christiansen, Emil Kirchner, and Philomena Murray (eds.) (Hampshire: Palgrave 2012), 502.

7. *Project Europe 2030—Challenges and Opportunities*, May 2010, www.consilium.europa.eu/uedocs/cms_data/librairie/PDF/QC3210249ENC.pdf.

8. China-EU 2020 Strategic Agenda for Cooperation released at the sixteenth China-EU Summit, 23 November 2013.

9. www.china.org.cn/chinese/2014-04/02/content_31981279.htm.

10. China's Policy Paper on the EU, 'Deepen the China-EU Comprehensive Strategic Partnership for Mutual Benefit and Win-win Cooperation', April 2014, www.fmprc.gov.cn/mfa_eng/wjdt_665385/wjzcs/t1143406.shtml, accessed 12 October 2014.

TEN

Central Europe, the European Union, and Emerging Asia

Agnieszka Kuszewska

The vast majority of political and economic analysts who focus their re-search on the dynamics of contemporary international relations empha-size the growing importance of Asian states as key players in global affairs. The worldwide impact of Asia's role in shaping the structure of the political and economic international system in the twenty-first centu-ry is unquestionable. Asia is widely perceived as the core driver of the world's economy and its role in political and security-related challenges has sharply increased and cannot be neglected in any contemporary re-gion-to-region analysis. A report published by the Center for a New American Security confirms that 'the rapid growth of Asian markets has created what will likely be the global centre of power in the twenty-first century. Thirty years of population growth, industrialization and eco-nomic development have laid the foundations for a long-term shift in world power away from the Northern Atlantic powers to Asia'[1].

The rise of the emerging Asian powers and their legitimate aspirations to play a greater role in the global world order remain a major political, strategic, and institutional challenge for the European Union (EU). The EU has been rapidly developing its external relations, and over the past three decades it has made efforts to strengthen its multifaceted relations with Asia, one of its key objectives being to establish and develop strate-gic partnerships as a framework for extended cooperation. This paper reviews the progress of the EU's relations with two major Asian coun-tries, China and India, with special reference to political dialogue and security cooperation. At first glance, the differences between these three actors seem common: Apart from geographical distance, they are shaped by distinctive historical experiences and cultural determinants, have their own varied political and socioeconomic systems, and different geopolitical environments. Moreover, the EU is not yet a state, but a unique international actor consisting of politically and economically diverse sovereign member-states. This has a direct impact on how the EU is perceived by its external partners and results in misunderstandings concerning the overlapping prerogatives of European institutions and member-states' governments in determining foreign and security policy goals.

On the other hand, there are some meaningful similarities between the three parties. First, all of them are influential regional actors occupying a vast territory: the EU 4.3 million square kilometres, China 9.5 million, and India 3.2 million[2]. Secondly, they are the most populated regions in the world: China and India, the world's most populated countries, accounting for 37 percent of the world population, with EU's twenty-eight countries inhabited by over 507 million people, constituting over 7 percent of global population[3]. Thirdly, all three regional actors have particular characteristic features, including ethnic, cultural, and religious diversity[4] that contribute to their internal richness on one hand, but pose some security-related challenges on the other. The exchange of experiences and knowledge in these fields could be a mutually beneficial contribution to a more inventive discourse within the framework of the EU-China and EU-India strategic partnerships. Last but not least, they all share similar strategic goals designed to enhance their position in global trade and economy, to emerge as political actors with growing status and presence in world affairs, and to legitimize their responsibilities for global security. Analysing and differentiating the foreign policies and security strategies of the EU, China, and India, especially in the context of developed entities (EU) and developing states (China and India), can thus be a contribution to the ongoing debate on today's world order evolution and the aspirations of emerging powers in global governance.

China and India were identified as critical EU partners in the 2003 European Security Strategy. The Regional Strategy Paper 2007–2013 worked out by the European Commission[5] pointed out that at the political level Asia was marked by the emergence of China and India, multiplicity of systems of governance, and a variety of security-related challenges, but economic factors remained the key determinants for developing EU-Asia relations. The World Economic Outlook database of the International Monetary Fund enumerated China, India, and Japan as three of the world's countries with the most economical potential, and both China and India have registered relatively high growth rates in recent years. The forecast for China is that growth will remain at about 7 percent in 2014–2015, only a slight decline from 2012–2013. For India, real gross domestic product growth is projected to strengthen to 5.4 percent in 2014 and 6.4 percent in 2015, assuming that government policy aimed at reviving investment growth succeeded and exports will be increased. Economic growth in the euro area is optimistically projected to reach 1.2 percent in 2014 and 1.5 percent in 2015, and in the whole EU, including non-eurozone states, it is supposed to reach 1.8 percent in 2015[6]. These economic forecasts suggest that mutually reinforcing economic and political relations with both Asian countries must remain an important part of EU's external strategy in the near future, though the EU's relations with the other big Asian economies like Indonesia, South Korea, and some members of the Association of Southeast Asian Nations (ASEAN) will also be of considerable importance.

Any analysis of region-to-region relations with reference to EU's strategic interests in contemporary world affairs requires a scrutiny of its ability to perform globally in an efficient manner. This task is challenging, as the EU is not a military hard power, and it is perceived as a normative civilian power that makes a contribution to the development of peaceful relations and focuses on exporting certain values, such as the rule of law, democratic culture, parliamentary democracy, human rights, and social market economy. This chapter explores these capabilities in the specific context of region-to-region relations by examining mutual attitudes and perceptions, and by conducting a broad analysis of the evolving nature of strategic partnerships in EU external policy. The study examines the current dynamics and future prospects for the EU's political and security strategy specifically towards the two emerging nations of Asia based on an assumption that international security is a multidimensional phenomenon that includes many non-military challenges, such as economic, environmental, and security issues.

The chapter approaches the topic in three key parts. The first part analyses the origins and evolution of the EU's global strategy and the meaning and role of strategic partnerships in developing relations with non-Western nations. The idea and capabilities of international 'actorness' of the EU and the notion of 'strategic partnership' in EU, Chinese, and Indian foreign policies are discussed with the conclusion that the ability of the EU to replicate its Europe-centred experiences and system of governance to other regions appears to be utopian. The minimal contribution of the 'new' EU members from post-communist Central and East Europe to the development of EU global strategy is an important aspect of the problem discussed in this part of the chapter, put under scrutiny with special reference to Poland as the leading representative of post-communist states. It was the leader of democratic changes in Central Europe, which started in the 1980s with the 'Solidarność' movement and then the 'Round Table' talks and free democratic elections. Its population of thirty-eight million, political leadership, and biggest economy of post–Soviet bloc states with relatively stable growth make it a useful point of reference as far as Central European engagement in EU's Asia strategy is concerned. Poland is a country that has emerged as an economic success story whose policies several countries try to emulate, has become an important leader country in the EU, and is yet again beginning to discover the world outside Europe after twenty years of looking only towards its West. The second part looks at the EU's political strategy towards China as well as recent institutional developments and their impact on strengthening cooperation between these two actors. It is focused on the problem of political differences and 'fragile issues' which are an obstacle in expanding bilateral relations. The EU-China human rights attitudes are briefly examined. Growing EU interest in strengthening relations with India has been observed since the 1990s. The third part provides an analysis of the current challenges and future prospects of EU-India and EU-China relations, while examples of mechanisms aimed at deepening dialogue and partnership relations, and the importance of intellectual, knowledge-based exchanges and cooperation between EU-China and EU-India are noted. The conclusion discusses the prospects for further development of cooperation and offers some recommendations for arriving at a mutually reinforcing partnership between Europe and emerging Asia.

THE EVOLUTION OF THE EUROPEAN UNION'S ASIA STRATEGY

The EU, China, and India take an active part in the transformation of the new world order, with emphasis on promoting a multipolar conception that challenges the dominant role of the United States in world affairs. These three regional actors have made significant efforts to strengthen their status in shaping this new order. The political strategy of Europe towards Asia has its own dynamic and specificity determined by many global and regional factors, and there is some kind of duality in the perception of China and India in Europe. On one hand, they are recognized as emerging Asian powers aspiring to increase their impact on international affairs, while on the other they are considered as still developing countries undergoing economic transitions. This concerns especially China, which is identified as a potential world power and a leader of the developing world at the same time. An enhanced understanding of the specificity of Europe-Asia relations requires to be preceded by a brief analysis of their recent evolution. The Cold War global rivalry heightened the American and Soviet Union's strategic and economic profiles in Asia, and the European withdrawal in the post-colonial era was accompanied by a certain temporary weakening of its commercial influences. Global divisions and bipolar superpower US-Soviet rivalry were among the major factors hindering prospects for developing ties between the European Community, China, and India. Until the 1993 Maastricht Treaty, the European Economic Community as such had scant contacts with the nations of what was to become emerging Asia, and such contacts were essentially bilateral in nature between individual nations.

The turning point in the EU-Asia policy took place in the early 1990s when the changed geopolitical situation enabled Europe to promote its political and economic involvement in Asia. It is worth taking a closer look at the changes that occurred in the international landscape after the fall of the Iron Curtain and how they determined Europe-Asia relations. In the Western world, the collapse of European communism was triumphantly announced as the victory of Western liberal democracy and capitalism, and for many analysts it seemed apparent that democracy would prevail globally as the only correct system and that the free market would pave the way to enhanced inter-regional and intra-regional cooperation. In Europe, the collapse of the repressive, authoritarian communist state was followed by a wave of optimism and belief in quick democratic transitions in post-communist societies, which subsequently joined the European 'family' within the Western European institutional and functional framework. These regional reshuffles prompted the European governments in the 1990s to develop large-scale plans for strengthening intra-European cooperation, and raised hopes for political integration on an unprecedented scale with enhanced participation in multipolar global governance, while the European example of integration and democratization was supposed to serve as a structural precedent and inspiration to other regions as well. Institutional reforms were gradually introduced along with increasing focus on inter-regionalism as an agreed mechanism for managing political and economic ties. The EU upgraded its political identity and emerged as a significant actor at the global level in 1993 when the Treaty of Maastricht entered into force. Its political structure was based on three pillars, one of them being the Common Foreign and Security Policy comprising key components such as democracy, human rights, and foreign development assistance. Europe's external strategy was based on developing active engagement with global power shifts and the evolution of decision-making processes that were becoming more polycentric.

At the same time as the Asian rise became apparent, the EU acknowledged that higher priority in its foreign strategy should be given to emerging Asia as part of upgrading region-to-region alliances. The first bilateral summit with an Asian country was organized in cooperation with Japan in 1991, and subsequently, progressive institutionalization of the Europe-Asia dialogue was introduced. In 1993, the European Commission issued a white paper titled *Growth, Competitiveness, Employment—the Challenges and Ways Forward into the 21st Century*. This document stated that the traditional definition of security (primacy of military security, defence against military threats, and use of force) should be broadened to include non-military aspects of security, such as the economic or environmental sectors[7]. In 1994, the European Commission, taking into consideration the increase of Asia's importance, adopted a document *Towards a New Asia Strategy*, which laid a foundation for enhanced region-to-region relations, and determined the following key objectives, which formed the basis for future cooperation:

- Strengthen the EU's economic, political, and security-related presence in Asia;
- Enhance trade and investment flows;
- Engage in efforts aimed at reduction of poverty and sustainable development in Asia;
- Promote democracy, good governance, respect for rule of law, and human rights;
- Strengthen partnerships with major Asian countries; and
- Spread mutual interregional awareness[8].

At that time, this strategy was focused on the Southeast Asian 'tiger economies' and Japan; references to China and India were still rare. In fact, subsequent papers issued by the Commission pointed out that the consequences of Chinese growth adversely affected the EU's economic security, and an appropriate strategy towards an emerging China should be thoroughly considered. However, European political leaders and business communities steadily started to understand that cooperation with China and India afforded potential opportunities for further development and should be considered a crucial long-term objective.

It was at this time that the 'strategic partnership' mechanism of enhanced political cooperation was introduced as a part of this reevaluation of the EU's external policy. It is difficult to offer any conclusive definition of a strategic partnership because there is no binding one. It could be understood as a political declaration of intent or even as an 'honorary degree' conferred by the EU on particular countries[9] with the special aim to upgrade multifaceted relations between EU and one particular partner. The introduction of the strategic partnership into foreign relations strategy was a major turning point in the evolution and understanding of the European identity, which had to be adapted in accordance with the fin de siècle and its new geopolitical challenges. At the same time, economic and political developments, first in China and then in India, which started to emerge as strong regional political and economic powers, provided new opportunities for expanding all-around cooperation.

THE EUROPEAN UNION: A RISING
POWER IN WORLD AFFAIRS?

At the turn of the century, the EU started to attach greater significance to the fact that global developments increasingly affected its own internal dynamics and had to be considered in its policymaking process. Since then, the EU has been rapidly expanding its relations with non-Western nations and regional international organizations. Importantly, a multidimensional perception of security was adopted by the EU as a framework for enhancing its political influence and strengthening relations in the globalized world, and these efforts have contributed to the rise of the EU as a major power in world affairs. The Treaty of Lisbon, which came into force in December 2009, gave the EU a single legal personality and established new institutions such as a president of the European Council and a high representative for foreign affairs and security policy. The aim was to strengthen the EU's ability to act as a single entity and enhance its international presence by making it more unitary and coherent, but since then the EU's abilities to act effectively in the multiple fields of global foreign affairs have come under critical scrutiny. There are doubts concerning the president and high representative's leverage over the European decision-making process, concluding that they are unable to fulfill their duties effectively because of the dominant role exercised by the leaders of the three biggest EU economies. It seems that the boundaries of competences between the EU's appointed leadership and member-states' governments have not yet been clearly enough defined and regulated. These contradictory internal diversities remain inseparable elements in the process of implementing the EU's strategic partnerships.

Clarifying the EU's global 'actorness' and estimating its effectiveness to speak with one voice in its relations with Asia or other regions is a difficult task, which does not provide any final answers. On one hand, it can be assessed positively: The EU as a non-military political actor has actively contributed to the promotion of good governance, democracy, human rights, and free market economy, and its soft power policy serves as an indispensable political tool to enhance the leverage of European political philosophy, thereby promoting the democratic culture of free and open dialogue. The basic assumption of this policy is that democratic freedoms are essential for economic growth and development, and they generate the frameworks for substantive transformation. On the other hand, however, when discussing the EU's ability to affect the world's political and economic situation, we have to consider not only the policies pursued by the EU's high representative within its institutional framework but also the varied strategies of the EU's most influential triangle of the United Kingdom, France, and Germany. It is reasonable to conclude that at least to a certain extent, the EU's external activities reflect the interests of its most powerful member-states. This dichotomy within the EU makes China, India, and other emerging countries of Asia more than a little confused about which Europe to deal with in conducting any substantial dialogue: the big three powers, or the EU's foreign policy representatives.

The EU members vary greatly in terms of their economic development, and the regional economic powers like the three above-mentioned countries dominate the other European countries and have greater capabilities to enter into and strengthen bilateral relations globally. These major exporting countries and global service providers are interested in strengthening their own broad-ranging cooperation with non-Western big economies like China, South Korea, Indonesia, and India[10]. This aspect has made a heavy contribution to the fact that China and India's strategic relations with Europe have focused to a great extent on these influential states, and a significant part of their trade and defence agreements are negotiated bilaterally. This dualism has become an interesting and characteristic feature of the relations between the EU and major Asian power centres, and it is unlikely to change in the near future. Germany, the United Kingdom, and France are among the world's ten biggest exporters of weapons, and India and China are the two largest importers. Consequently, this has a direct impact on the security strategy of these Asian countries and forms the basis for bilateral understandings with arms suppliers. China is one of the main recipients of French arms exports, accounting for 13 percent of the supplier's total export, and India is the third major client of British arms exporters, representing 11 percent of the United Kingdom's total exports[11]. It is natural that strategic ties between China and India and these European countries will be prioritized over the rest of the EU member-states.

The introduction of a common European global policy is also problematic due to internal economic problems within the Union reinforced by the recent eurozone crisis and austerity measures introduced by various governments. This has reinforced the euro-sceptic attitude among the European public, which was manifest by the victories of euro-sceptic nationalists in the last elections to the European Parliament. Considering these factors, it might be justified to conclude that the EU is unlikely to become any supra-national state in the foreseeable future and its capabilities to exert influence in global affairs are significantly limited, although it has successfully managed to introduce some mechanisms of external strategy. Shaping a common global policy and introducing appropriate mechanisms for it have become *conditio sine qua non* for establishing the position of Europe as an important actor in contemporary multipolar relations, and consequently the EU continues to make efforts to emerge more visibly as single political union with one common foreign and security policy.

The main element of the EU's foreign strategy is based on pacific ideals. Selling weapons on one hand and spreading the idea of pacifism seem to be mutually exclusive, but economic gains and security issues have always gone together as a top priority for European global strategy. At the same time, the EU aspires to disseminate certain normative, fundamental values into the international system, and in this sense, it is justified to perceive the EU as a normative power, contributing to raise global awareness of certain values such as democracy, equal participation, and human rights. On their part, China and India adhere to the principles enumerated by both states in 1954 as part of the Five Principles of Peaceful Coexistence. Two of them may be noted with reference to their relationship with Europe: First, mutual respect for sovereignty and territorial integrity, and secondly, non-interference in each other's internal affairs. Taking into consideration the sensitivity over internal problems that both countries face—the Tibet issue and ethnic violence in Xinjiang for China; Kashmir-related challenges for India—both states strongly reject any foreign involvement in dealing with these problems, and categorically do not wish to be given lessons by the EU concerning their resolution.

Currently, therefore, EU-Asia relations proceed on both bilateral and multilateral tracks. Europe has developed a security dialogue with individual states such as China, India, Japan, and South Korea, and established relations with two regional organizations: ASEAN and South Asian Association for Regional Cooperation (SAARC). Moreover, the EU has entered into some inter-regional mechanisms with the purpose of regulating and coordinating its cooperation with Asia. One of the most important is the overarching framework of the Asia-Europe Meeting (ASEM), a forum set up at the initiative of Singapore on behalf of ASEAN; the first summit was called in 1996 as a loosely structured meeting to exchange ideas on a wide range of topics. Initially an inter-governmental political initiative, ASEM now engages civil society institutions as well, and comprises three pillars on which cooperation is developed: political, economic, and social/cultural/educational.

CENTRAL EUROPE'S LACK OF ENGAGEMENT AND ITS CONSEQUENCES

More than a decade has passed since the EU was enlarged by adding the former communist states from Central Europe in 2004, and this enlargement changed the identity of the EU more than all its previous enlargements. Ten member-states from Central/Eastern Europe (Cyprus, the Czech Republic, Estonia, Hungary, Latvia, Lithuania, Malta, Poland, Slovakia, and Slovenia) added 20 percent to the population of EU, but only 4.8 percent to its total gross domestic product[12]. In 2007, two more former Soviet bloc nations, Bulgaria and Romania, joined the EU as new members, taking the number to twenty-seven and deepening its internal political and cultural diversity. Croatia from the former Yugoslavia joined the EU as the twenty-eighth member in 2013. In order to be granted EU membership, all these states had to undergo political, economic, and social transformations, but they were still economically backward in comparison to the 'old' EU member-states. Ten years after 2004, the contribution of Central European member-states to Europe's engagement with Asian rising powers is worth examination.

The post–Cold War era provided an opportunity for the Central European states, drawing upon their Soviet era ties, to initiate a new model of cooperation with China, India, and other Asian nations and add value and innovation to the EU's Asia policy. This could and should have been done after the process of democratic transformation was fulfilled. But the post-communist EU members from Central Europe did not manage to add any significant quality or contribution to the development of EU-China and EU-India relations in this century because their attention was only directed Westwards towards West European countries and especially the United States. In the 1990s, after decades of the Soviet regime, Russia was strongly resented and nobody wanted to learn Russian, although it had been compulsory until the late 1980s. German, English, or French were now the second languages of choice, and the Western way of life was considered the ideal. This is more or less still the case today. One and a half decades later, when Russian was to some extent popular again, there were no teachers and hardly any expertise on Russia with an unbiased attitude. Trade between India and Poland declined precipitously after the Council for Mutual Economic Assistance's collapse, with India's share of Poland's overall trade falling 70 percent in 1997 from what it had been in 1987. The same was the case with the other Visegrad countries; Hungary's total trade with India fell by 80 percent and Czechoslovakia's (later Czech Republic and Slovakia) by 40 percent over the same decade. If this was one instance of the abandonment of the advantages of past decades in connection with India, other Asian emerging countries fared even worse in the attentions of the 'new' Europe.

Poland's Example

Being then part of the Soviet sphere of influence, Central European states like Poland had to pursue their foreign policy in accordance with Soviet external policy. In South Asia, Pakistan entered into military alliances with Western powers, which inclined India towards advancing its political and strategic relations with the Soviet Union. With Moscow's approval, cordial diplomatic, cultural, political, and economic relations were established between Poland and India and confirmed by the exchange of numerous high-level visits. Piotr Jaroszewicz was the first Polish prime minister who visited India in 1958, while Jawaharlal Nehru and Indira Gandhi both paid visits to Poland as prime ministers. Military and technological cooperation was significantly upgraded. Indian Air Force officers used to travel to the Polish city Radom for training, and the Shipping Corporation of India bought ships from Poland until the 1980s. Poland initially also had warm relations with China, though the Sino-Soviet rift led to a long freeze in ties between communist Eastern Europe and communist China. After the collapse of the Iron Curtain, Poland and other Central European countries gave the highest priority to their domestic economic and political transformation to liberal democracy, followed by their integration with Western European institutional structures. These watershed geopolitical changes in Central and Eastern Europe coincided with the major economic reforms launched in China by Deng Xiaoping.

Even today, there are hardly any Polish or, generally speaking, Central European specialized publications, reports, or literature available that cover contemporary Asian issues. These European nations are focused on regional or even local issues directly influencing their security, such as relations with Russia in terms of energy security and the idea of an Eastern Partnership, which aims at strengthening their relations with East European countries such as Belarus, Georgia, Armenia, Azerbaijan, Moldova, and most importantly, Ukraine. The last Indian prime minister who visited Poland, the biggest and most important Central Europe country, was Morarji Desai in 1979, which speaks volumes of the little significance India attaches to its relations with this part of Europe. Given the developments in Ukraine and Russian revisionism, which has become a looming threat to Europe, and the Chinese and Indian views that are not aligned with the West in this connection, it is highly unlikely that the Central European states will perceive their involvement in enhancing the EU-Asia security strategy to be any high priority.

This gap in prioritization in Central Europe needs to be filled, however. Some initiatives, which should not be overestimated, have already been undertaken by a few academics and non-government organizations (NGOs). Some Polish examples will suffice. In December 2011, the Warsaw-based think tank Poland-Asia Research Centre organized a seminar 'The Rise of Asia—Perspective from Eastern Europe' in the European Parliament, a unique opportunity to exchange views and ideas on the EU's Asia strategy. The bureaucrats in Brussels were taken aback that anyone from the central part of Europe could be interested in Asia, which says much about the lack of engagement of Central European governments in Asian issues in the EU. The Central European governments give little support in organizing such events, and the Asia experts from this part of Europe seem to have become invisible in the EU. As far as the Polish Foreign Ministry is concerned, the people who work there usually have only some basic knowledge about Asia and only engage in speculations that hardly translate into concrete actions. Polish mainstream media rarely cover the Asian issues and if they do, it is 'yellow' journalism rather than in-depth or relevant analysis. When Prime Minister Donald Tusk paid an official state visit to India in 2010, the Indian press, perhaps showing more optimism than realism, gave wide coverage to this event but there was hardly any mention of his visit in the Polish press. These are signs of missed opportunities and the necessity to improve the East-

West intra-European exchange of knowledge and ideas about emerging Asia. Warsaw-based think tanks could serve as useful source of analytical multilayered knowledge on Asia in Poland, with special reference to China and India.

The year 2014 marked the sixtieth anniversary of India-Poland diplomatic relations. Many diplomatic, political, and economic events were organized both in India and Poland to commemorate this anniversary, and one of them is worth mentioning. In May 2014, the University of Warsaw organized an international conference 'India in International Relations—Polish and European Experience'. At this gathering, the results of my research were presented in a paper titled 'Hard Power, Soft Power or Terra Incognita? The Perception of India among Young Poles Aged 17-25'. This showed that 83 percent of them confirmed they were not taught about India at school and 15 percent answered 'just a little'. It was revealed that they draw their knowledge on India only from the popular media and associated India with Bollywood, cultural diversity, good cuisine, female infanticide, and discrimination against women, which are the topics mostly touched upon by the Polish mainstream media. A total of 28 percent identified India as a cultural power and 20 percent as an economic power, but 78 percent could not identify a single Indian company. It is worth emphasizing, however, that 88 percent of the respondents agreed that the EU should strengthen cooperation with India, which is a good prospect for the future and proves that people are progressively aware that Asia means not only China in terms of power status aspirations.

The people in Poland are rarely interested in Asian affairs, and when it comes to any substantial discussion, their knowledge about Asia and other parts of the developing world outside Europe is superficial and sometimes based on prejudices. This situation would be replicated in all Central and East European countries. Multilateralism has to be taken into serious account in the education process with the aim to foster some renewed Central European commitment to EU-Asia policy. Importantly, this concerns not only China and India, but also other emerging Asian nations such as South Korea and Indonesia, and Central/Eastern Europe should attach more significance to the role they could play in shaping EU policy. Its minimal contribution to the EU's Asia policy has to be upgraded, although this might be a long, drawn out process. Without such engagement, the EU-Asia region-to-region strategy will continue to be totally imbalanced in favour of the West European EU member- states and consequently will not reflect the entirety of the EU. Importantly, it also conveys the impression of EU disunity to the Asian emerging countries.

EUROPE-CHINA ON THE WAY TO COMPREHENSIVE PARTNERSHIP

Over the past decades, China has experienced impressive transformation, which started in the late 1970s when political and economic reforms were launched. It resulted in staggering economic developments, and China successfully entered the global economy, capturing a large part of the world's trade and investment flows[13]. China has strengthened its involvement in international affairs in different dimensions: political, economic, social, security, and military. It is active in world diplomacy, hosting summits with foreign partners like African leaders and international organizations such as the Asia-Pacific Economic Cooperation. An EU-China trade and cooperation agreement was signed in 1985, and cooperation frameworks were designed to assist China's development and were focused primarily on economic assistance and trade.

In the early 1990s after China introduced significant reforms, the European Community rightly assumed that better relations with China might open the vast Chinese market for European goods and services, and as a result China was by 1994 one of the EU's largest trading partners. The evolution of the EU-China relationship paved the way to the formulation of an EU-China enhanced partnership aimed at strengthening cooperation in security matters and global economy issues, which was set out in a 2006 document titled *EU-China: Closer Partners, Growing Responsibilities*, and in 2007 the outlines for further cooperation were delineated and comprehensive dialogue within a partnership and cooperation agreement replaced the agreement of 1985. The Chinese government released its first China's EU policy paper in 2003, pointing out that the two actors shared a common goal of developing a global system based on a more balanced and effective mutually beneficial multilateralism, and recognized the status aspirations of the EU by agreeing that it was a major force in the world that would increase its regional and global influence.

Wen Jiabao, the then Chinese prime minister, pointed out in 2004 that comprehensive partnership had to be multilevel, wide-ranging, and based on win-win results. Today, the EU-China continuous dialogue is one of the most wide-ranging that the EU holds with any Asian country, and the term 'strategic' signifies the importance attached to upgrading this cooperation. The economy, comprising bilateral trade issues and European investment in China, dominates bilateral EU-China relations, although steadily other matters have been added to the agenda[14] and interaction between experts in various fields takes place annually during the EU-China summits. The talks cover all the most important challenges of contemporary international affairs: nuclear energy, environmental and social problems, education, trade, security, people-to-people contacts, and so on. Members of the European Parliament also regularly meet their counterparts from the ruling Chinese Communist Party.

SOME CHALLENGES IN EUROPEAN
UNION–CHINA RELATIONS

Unprecedented economic growth has not introduced significant changes in the Chinese one-party political system, and one of the major problems in EU-China relations is the perception of violations of human rights. The 1989 Tiananmen protests, which were forcibly suppressed by the Chinese authorities and were followed by a massacre of unarmed civilians, temporarily froze Europe-China relations, and took place at the same time as the outbreak of democracy when Central/Eastern Europe was unchaining itself from totalitarian Soviet occupation. The critics of enhanced political and strategic partnership with China pointed out that its autocratic regime hindered prospects for cooperation, and even after the gradual upturn in Europe-China ties, some scholars, politicians, and human rights activists accused the EU of pursuing double standards and turning a blind eye to the Chinese suppressing freedom of expression and religious freedoms, banning access to the Internet, and other human rights abuses. Different perceptions of the necessity for human rights protection are undoubtedly important obstacles for an expanding cooperation between the two entities.

Europe-China relations will definitely be influenced by the manner in which the new Chinese leadership wields its power. Since taking over as communist party leader and president in 2012, President Xi Jinping has consolidated power into his own hands, and major decisions announced in 2013 during the party plenum introduced the most significant changes since Deng Xiaoping's wave of reforms was launched in the 1980s. The new leader has launched an anti-corruption campaign to improve his image and weaken the influence of his political opponents, and analysts of the Chinese political scene observe that the country experiences some form of neo-authoritarianism with Xi Jinping playing the main role. Taking into account the geopolitical determinants, hard power strategy will continue to determine Beijing's political attitudes in the foreseeable future.

China's leadership has two major challenges to tackle: economic and security-related issues. The first is aimed at overseeing the necessary reform of China's economy, which has to be transformed into a more mature, consumer-driven model if China wants to avoid the risk of economic downturn and improve its prospects for stable and sustained economic growth. The second is connected with China's internal and external problems, the internal being conflict-prone unrest in two regions populated by ethnic and religious minorities, which question the Chinese rule, Tibet and Xinjiang, and the external being the potential flashpoints with neighbours in the East and South China seas. For China, any form of interference in its internal affairs is unacceptable, and human rights issues in Tibet have been a major contention in its relations with Europe. In Beijing's point of view, Tibet-related issues have to be 'properly handled' by its foreign partners. A Chinese Ministry of Foreign Affairs statement corroborates this attitude and dispels doubts concerning any external interference into 'fragile' issues:

> The Chinese side appreciates the position of the EU and its member states of recognizing Tibet as part of China's territory. The EU side should properly handle Tibet-related issues based on the principle of respecting China's sovereignty, independence and territorial integrity and non-interference in China's internal affairs, not allow leaders of the Dalai group to visit the EU or its member states under any capacity or pretext to engage in separatist activities, not arrange any form of contact with officials of the EU or its member-states, and not provide any facilitation or support for anti-China separatist activities for Tibet independence[15].

The ongoing power restructuring in China may turn out to be another step backwards from democracy and freedom. During the transition period when new reforms are to be introduced, the leadership will remain determined to suppress any organized dissent and may reject any external pressure on human rights. This will have an impact on future EU-China relations, making Beijing more assertive in building its external strategy. But the economic challenges, when tackled successfully, may contribute to alleviating human rights divergences between EU and China. The future transition to a knowledge-based economy and growing people-to-people contacts may serve as an important factor in raising awareness of human rights issues in China and consequently could add a new dimension to the EU-China dialogue. All these aspects have to be taken into consideration by both Europe and China to develop mutually beneficial relations. Stanley Crossick and Etienne Reuter point out that,

> On the one hand, Europe should not listen to Europeans who assume Europe has all the answers for China as though it was somehow cloning Dolly the sheep, because it does not; on the other hand, China should not listen to those Chinese conservatives who believe that China is so different that it can only learn from within[16].

Another geopolitical aspect of China-EU cooperation is based on Beijing's attitude of assuming that relations with Europe are free from strategic rivalry, which is not the case where Sino-American relations are concerned. Unlike the EU, Washington has great geostrategic interests in East Asia. The upgrading of EU-China relations is perceived in Beijing as part of an anti-containment policy with reference to American global domination and to promote its campaign aimed at establishing a multi-

polar world. In order to avoid future disillusionment and mutual credibility deficit, EU human rights policy has to be flexible and should be
conducted with reference to the pace of current Chinese reforms and all
the changes that China has been going through. Otherwise, given China's
adamant stance on the question, this policy may turn anachronistic, imbalanced, and failure-prone, and undermine the efforts aimed at developing region-to-region relations.

THE EUROPEAN UNION AND INDIA: TWO DEMOCRACIES
IN A MULTIPOLAR WORLD

Diplomatic relations between India and the European Economic Communities were established in 1963, but their development was hindered by
Cold War realities and economic underdevelopment and poverty-related
problems in India. Western policy makers did not recognize India as a
regional player and perceived it indifferently for several decades. After
the collapse of Soviet Union, India lost its most crucial strategic ally and
trading partner, and was faced with an urgent necessity of introducing
significant shifts in its foreign policy. The Indian political leaders realized
that economic growth and cooperation with other regional actors would
widen its influence in international affairs and place India where it de-
served to be among the influential rising powers[17]. The reforms introduced in the 1990s aimed at liberalization of the economy, and opening
India's vast market significantly contributed to reshaping India's position
in the new world order; subsequent plans for strengthening relations
with Europe were based on mutual recognition of both sides' aspirations
to play a more decisive role in global affairs. As a result, in 1996, the
Commission launched its Communication on an EU-India enhanced
partnership, where economic cooperation and expanding trade were the
main issues.

The first India-EU summit was held in 2000, and in 2004 at The
Hague, the EU-India strategic partnership was decided upon to upgrade
existing relations. The EU finally acknowledged that successful cooperation with emerging Asia could not exclude other Asian players such as
India and ASEAN. It is worth noting that in 2002, China, Thailand, and
Vietnam had protested against allowing South Asian states to join ASEM,
and India had been campaigning against this limited definition of Asia
since the 1990s, Indian Foreign Minister Pranab Kumar Mukherjee saying
in 1995 that 'Asia minus India is like Hamlet without the Prince of Denmark'[18]. The Helsinki ASEM summit of 2006 was important as far as EU
relations with India and South Asia are concerned because it was then
decided to enlarge membership to forty-five states, including India and
Pakistan. Some importance was therefore given by the EU to South Asia,
and not only to Northeast and Southeast Asia. Finland, a country with a

well-developed civil society, had held the rotating presidency of the EU Council, and this had a noteworthy impact on strengthening the image of the EU and its involvement in European and Asian civil society by engaging different civil society groups and NGOs in the dialogue developed within ASEM.

INDIA'S ASPIRATIONS AND COOPERATION WITH THE EUROPEAN UNION

Only just over six decades have passed since the end of European colonialism on the Indian subcontinent, and this short period of time has left a residue of resentment in the Indian subcontinent against economic exploitation and human rights abuses during British colonial rule. This has some impact on relations between Europe and India. The EU's goal is to act as a soft power and disseminate certain values globally; most of these values are already shared by India. Currently, however, India faces many regional security challenges, with terrorism and potential conflict with Pakistan uppermost. India does not pay much attention to the EU as far as strategic issues are concerned; in its security policy, India's purpose is to develop its bilateral relations with European key players such as Great Britain, France, and Germany[19]. Taking its threat perception into consideration, India's policy has a strong component of realpolitik, and one of the core elements of this is improvement in its relations with the United States. India significantly enhanced its relations with the United States through signing the nuclear deal, which enables civil nuclear energy cooperation. According to data published by Stockholm International Peace Research Institute in 2014, India is the world's biggest importer of arms, buying 'nearly three times as many weapons as its nearest competitors China and Pakistan over the last five years. . . . The volume of Indian imports of major weapons rose by 111 percent between 2004 and 2008 and 2009 and 2013, and its share of the volume of international arms imports increased from 7 to 14 percent'[20]. An element of Prime Minister Narendra Modi government's external policy is based on upgrading its strategic relations with Japan. These two countries might emerge one day as sheet anchors of Asian security to counterbalance Chinese aspirations. During Modi's visit to Tokyo in 2014 and meetings with Japan's Prime Minister Shinzo Abe, a decision was made to elevate the Japan-India strategic and global partnership to that of a 'special strategic and global partnership'. It may be noted that India has not conceded the appellation of 'special' to its strategic partnership with Europe. India's foreign policy indicates New Delhi's awareness of a regional security threat from Islamabad's political instability and incapability to deal with terrorist problems, and Beijing's East and South China seas maritime expansion claims.

Yet India presents itself as a peaceful soft power with a 'no-first use' nuclear policy, accenting its diplomatic, institutional, and cultural values; this is the major point of reference for upgrading its cooperation with the EU. Improving the standard of living is one of the major challenges for the Indian government: about one-third of its population lives in extreme poverty. The work force in India of seven hundred million might serve as an important factor against the declining demographics in European countries. India has to develop an industrial base for the needs of its growing population and transform itself into a knowledge-based society, and the EU's role might prove important in this process, because the quality and access to education has to be improved. The EU is also engaged in humanitarian assistance, a recent example being 249,000 euro provided by the European Commission for people affected by floods in the Odisha state. Another programme being conducted with Oxfam has the aim to increase access to information and services on human immunodeficiency virus and reproductive health for young people, especially for girls. These are examples of the EU's activities and engagement. EU-India cooperation in many fields may enhance India's prospects for stable and sustained growth on one hand and improve the perception of Europe as a region ready to provide assistance for vulnerable people in areas affected by disasters.

Comparing China and India with reference to the EU's external strategy, Europe's policy is focused mainly on Beijing, being EU's most important Asian economic partner. The EU's relations with India have gradually developed over the past two decades, and India's preeminent position in South Asia makes it an important partner for the EU's regional policy. Due to security challenges and political instability in some South Asian countries, cooperation between the EU and SAARC lags behind Europe's involvement in other parts of Asia, and the protracted conflict over Kashmir between India and Pakistan, the problem of human rights in Kashmir, and non-adherence to the Non-Proliferation and Comprehensive Nuclear Test Ban Treaties by India and Pakistan cause frictions in EU policy towards South Asia.

The strengthening of political, economic, and social cooperation with India should be one of high priorities for the EU's Asia strategy. There are more similarities in terms of respect for basic normative values between Europe and India than with China. It is often stated that EU and India, being the biggest democracies, share common interests as the rule of law, democratic culture, parliamentary democracy, support for market economy, and human rights, and they both face terrorism as a serious threat. There is some common ground for partnership as well as huge potential in strengthening and expanding bilateral relations in the future. The intensification of people-to-people contacts is a necessity if various projects are to be fully implemented. India aspires to enhance its legitimacy to play a greater role in world affairs through representation at various multilateral forums, and one of its aims is a permanent seat at the UN Security Council. The EU should support this campaign pursued by the world's biggest democracy. Annual summits and talks at ministerial level as well as enhanced people-to-people contacts are core elements in EU-India relations. The EU could and should use more efficiently the previously intense experiences of Central European countries, like Poland, the Czech Republic, and Hungary, which have a long, though lately interrupted, history of cordial relations with India.

CONCLUSION

After decades of political and strategic negligence resulting from Cold War determinants and poor economic performance by China and India, both Asian states are finally acknowledged by the EU as rising powers with global aspirations. This status was ascribed to China in the 1990s and then followed by recognition of India's similar aspirations at the turn of the centuries. Cooperation between the EU and these states has been significantly upgraded, but the three actors still need to make efforts to search for better relations and to strengthen their positions in contemporary multipolar world politics.

The EU's relations with China and India will undoubtedly remain a relevant element of foreign policy due to the already broad cooperation in various fields. The expansion of political, strategic, commercial, and cultural ties should be profitable for each side and based on mutual understanding of their differences. China and India have launched some economic reforms and have risen as major aspiring global powers. The EU is no longer a European Community consisting of nine Western European states; it comprises twenty-eight members, including many that regained their independence after the fall of the Iron Curtain. It has strengthened its capability to act as a single actor on the international scene by establishing the posts of president of the European Council and a high representative of the Union for foreign affairs and security policy. Drawing up common European foreign policy strategy is a very complex and difficult task, and there are criticisms that the EU's influence and coherence is limited due to strong individual positions taken by the leadership in the EU's major member-states such as France, Germany, and the United Kingdom, who want to retain control over external strategy.

The EU as a unified actor consists of two parts of Europe, which have different historical experiences with Asia in the twentieth century. This potential has been sadly neglected because the Central European states have not contributed significantly to the development of the EU's strategy or economic ties with emerging Asia. Rich post–World War II experiences of Central and Eastern European states, and the fact that they were never responsible for colonial conquest in Asia, should have served as an important input into the EU's Asia strategy, contributed to better mutual understanding, and brought a new quality to the dialogue. The Polish Prime Minister Donald Tusk's ascent to the post of the European Council's president is a great success for Poland and for Central Europe, and could contribute to an eradication of the East-West divide within the EU and strengthen the position of Poland and the whole of Central Europe within the EU to reshape its political power structure so that it will be less dominated by the economically powerful West European states. The security challenges arising from Russia's expansionist policy contribute to the fact that Europe faces a necessity to upgrade its international position and internal coherence in order to defend its interests and tackle new threats. Some analysts express an opinion that Europe is undermining its chance to influence world opinion by appointing Tusk as President and Federica Mogherini, former Italian foreign minister, who is rather unknown in the international arena, to the post of the EU's High Representative for foreign affairs and security policy. These critics claim that it signifies the unwillingness of member-states to choose high-profile political personalities to represent Europe. Such pessimistic forecasts may never materialize, but they have to be taken into serious account. All EU members must keep in mind that the involvement of post-communist and West European states in drawing up a coherent EU foreign policy has to be balanced and that each European country is too weak to exert any world influence alone. And the EU has to face many serious problems concerning its image in Asia — as an extremely bureaucratic monster where the conduct of any business requires many hours of painstaking and often fruitless paperwork. Only European unity and internal cooperation could enhance the EU's global reach, especially with reference to emerging Asia.

Gradual evolution and strengthening of the EU-China and the EU-India mechanisms of cooperation should positively contribute to enhance EU's capabilities to act globally as a single actor. Europe will remain a normative, civilian power, contributing to developing region-to-region peaceful relations. This role is especially important in the contemporary era in a conflict-prone world. These mechanisms should, however, be anchored in reality, and it must be acknowledged that Europe's capabilities to use its leverage and replicate its norms in Asia are totally limited. Europe should strengthen its engagement in intellectual and cultural exchange, as well as NGO activities, and respond to the important economic and social challenges of China and India.

Both Asian giants differ as far as economic progress and competitiveness are concerned. According to the Global Competitiveness Report 2014–2015, which was released by the World Economic Forum in 2014, China's economy belongs to the top thirty most competitive economies in the world. Ranked twenty-eighth out of 177 world economies, China stands approximately forty places ahead of India. China's political system is authoritarian in structure and ideology, whereas India shares democratic values with Europe; this will have some impact on the intensity and style of EU policy towards the two Asian powers. Economic cooperation, with special reference to trade and investment facilitation, remains the main platform for Europe-Asia ties, and combines political influence and practical knowledge with the experience of the business communities. Multifaceted civil society interactions and business-to-business contacts need to be promoted at the governmental and non-governmental level and constantly upgraded. The development of region-to-region strategic relations should be reinforced within the framework of regional structures in which China and India play dominant roles: the ASEAN Regional Forum and SAARC. The EU has already established cooperation with ASEAN, China, and Japan in various fields; with SAARC, its efficiency depends strongly on South Asian security issues, in particular the India-Pakistan conflict. European experience of integration will not serve as any model for China and India in their regions due to political and geostrategic reasons; regional organizations in Asia are based on completely different patterns of power politics. SAARC is dominated by India and is focused only on economic and social issues. Cooperation within this organization is hindered by the protracted Indo-Pakistani conflict and mistrust, and considering the deteriorating political and security situation in Pakistan, this will not change in the foreseeable future.

From the East/Central European perspective, Western European countries and institutions have thus far dominated the Europe-Asia dialogue, which is centred on the most powerful EU states, and where intra-European cooperation leaves much to be desired. It would be advisable to introduce joint projects with a common European agenda with enlarged participation of Eastern European experts who have their own experiences and can offer contributions in their fields of expertise. Improved intra-European cooperation by including the assets available in Central Europe could refresh the regional approach.

There is yet another problem when analysing the future role of the EU in international affairs. The high unemployment rate among young people results in disillusionment with the idea of European integration and in growing support for populist parties who offer no concrete solutions. In the worst-case scenario, it may lead to the gradual disappearance of European unity. The current economic and immigration-related challenges contribute significantly to the birth of a nationalistic attitude among young people. The eurozone crisis has not strengthened EU unity; on the contrary, it has proved that Europe has limited capabilities to face the crisis in a cooperative manner. It has ignited protectionism, showing that the pursuit of national interests prevail and only the major European economic nations play a leading role in dealing with the challenges. The Europeans have to consider whether, and if so to what extent, the key symbols of the EU's integration and its external policy manifesto, such as 'the mission', 'the ideals', and 'the European common identity', are meaningful values or parts of empty rhetoric repeated endlessly. The lack of integration may have a negative impact on strengthening the position of Europe in international affairs and on improving its image as a relevant element in the rapidly transforming world order, where the future significant position of Beijing and New Delhi seems already assured.

The EU's ambition is to strengthen its global position and upgrade its partnerships with China and India. In order to tackle this challenge successfully and take a proactive and enlightened policy towards China and India, it would be advisable for the EU to:

- Define more unambiguously the role and prerogatives of EU member-states and institutions in conducting the union's external actions;
- Inspire awareness and mutual respect about Europe-Asia cultural differences;
- Undertake more promotion activities to enhance people-to-people contacts;
- Upgrade cooperation within ASEM, a platform for interaction between governments and business communities; encourage family-owned small and medium enterprises from Europe, China, India, and other parts of emerging Asia to enhance their presence in region-to-region activity;
- Overcome passive multilateralism: Avoid endless mushrooming of political initiatives that turn out only to be diplomatic dialogue;
- Engage in economic and political cooperation with SAARC especially to enhance the EU's presence and active support in regional initiatives aimed at bringing development, peace, and stability to the region;
- Adjust EU-China human rights policy to the pace of Chinese reforms and the political/economic changes that China is currently going through; assume that changes come from within, and the affluent and more numerous middle class will assert their rights;
- Utilize the strategic partnerships based on traditional security (terrorism, weapons of mass destruction) and non-traditional elements of broadly defined security (environment, economy, trade, and energy);
- Enhance development cooperation in the sectors of education, public health, and protection of the environment with active engagement of think tanks, NGOs, and scientists from Western/Eastern Europe, China, India, and emerging Asia;
- Raise the connectivity of ideas by deepened, knowledge-based, people-to-people contacts and facilitate mutual, comprehensive ex-

change of experiences; develop the already existing networks and build new ones;

- Promote accountability, transparency, and greater involvement of civil societies;
- Activate specialists and scholars from 'new' EU states who should be engaged in sharing experiences and promoting their areas of Asian research; enhance intra-European cooperation between West, Central, and Eastern Europe with reference to Asia policy;
- Develop a common agenda aimed at promoting the need to up-grade Europe-Asia cooperation; propagate this cooperation at schools (lectures of experts, leaflets written in simple language) to awaken interest, eradicate prejudices, and enhance knowledge of emerging Asia;
- Avoid a preaching attitude to impart lessons; instead take a more egalitarian approach;
- Simplify EU bureaucratic procedures to the maximum possible extent.

NOTES

Work on this paper has been generously supported by the National Science Centre of Poland. Research Project no. 2012/05/B/HS5/00726.

1. As cited in Massouda Jalal, 'Women's Empowerment and Co-operative Development, Peace and Security in South and Central Asia', in *Perspectives on Bilateral and Regional Cooperation. South and Central Asia*, Rashpal Malhotra, Sucha Singh Gill, and Neetu Gaur (eds.) (Chandigarh: Center for Research in Rural and Industrial Development, 2013), 419.

2. *The CIA World Factbook*, www.cia.gov/library/publications/the-world-factbook/, accessed 1 September 2014.

3. *EU Connections. A Practical Guide to the European Union for Professionals* (Taiwan: European Economic and Trade Office, 2013): 12.

4. Juha Jokela, 'The European Union as an International Actor: Europeanization and Institutional Changesin the Light of the EU's Asia Policies', in *The Role of European Union in Asia. China and India as Strategic Partners*, Bart Gaens, Juha Jokela, and Eija Limnell (eds.) (Burlington: Ashgate Publishing Limited, 2009), 37.

5. *Regional Strategy for Asia 2007–2013*, European Commission, 31 May 2007, ec. europa.eu/external_relations/asia/rsp/07_13_en.pdf, accessed 28 August 2014.

6. *World Economy Outlook: Recovery Strengthens Remains Uneven* (Washington, DC: International Monetary Fund, April 2014): 58–59.

7. This analytical approach gained momentum in the post–Cold War era and was popularized in the works of Barry Buzan and Ole Waever, central scholars of the so-called Copenhagen School. See Barry Buzan, *People, States & Fear: An Agenda for International Security Studies in the Post Cold War Era* (New York: Harvester Wheatsheaf, 1991), 19–20; Barry Buzan, Ole Waever, and Jaap de Vilde, *Security: a New Framework for Analysis* (London: Lynne Riener Publishers, 1998), 8–9.

8. Bart Gaens, 'ASEM's Background and Rationale', in *Europe-Asia: Interregional Relations. A Decade of ASEM*, Bart Gaens (ed.) (Aldershot: Ashgate Publishing Company, 2008), 17–18.

9. Rajendra K. Jain, 'Engaging the European Superpower: India and the European Union', in Bart Gaens, Juha Jokela, and Eija Limnell (eds.), *The Role of European Union*, (Burlington VT: Ashgate Publishing Limited, 2009), 174.

10. Timothy Garton Ash, 'The Crisis of Europe. How the Union Came Together and Why It's Falling Apart', *Foreign Affairs* 91, no. 5 (September/October 2012): 11.

11. Siemon T. Wezeman and Pieter D. Wezeman, *Trends in International Arms Transfers, 2013, SIPRI Fact Sheet* (Stockholm: Stockholm International Peace Research Institute, 2014), 2.

12. Ummu Salma Bava, 'India–EU Relations: Building a Strategic Partnership', in *Europe-Asia Relations: Building Multilateralisms*, Richard Balme and Brian Bridges (eds.) (New York: Palgrave Macmillan, 2008), 243.

13. Frederic Lerais, Mattias Levin, Myriam Sochacki, and Reinhilde Veugelers, *China, EU and the World: Growing In Harmony?* (Luxembourg: European Commission, Office for Official Publications of European Communities, 2007), IX.

14. Nicholas Rees, 'EU-China Relations: Historical and Contemporary Perspectives', in Georg Wiessala, John Wilson, and Pradeep Taneja (eds.), *European Studies* 27 (2009): 31.

15. *China's Policy Paper on the EU: Deepen the China-EU Comprehensive Strategic Partnership for Mutual Benefit and Win-win Cooperation*, Ministry of Foreign Affairs, April 2014, www.fmprc.gov.cn/mfa_eng/wjdt_665385/wjzcs/t1143406.shtml, accessed 1 September 2014.

16. Stanley Crossick and Etienne Reuter (eds.), *China-EU: A Common Future* (Singapore: World Scientific, 2007), 221.

17. Walter Andersen, 'Recent Trends in Indian Foreign Policy', *Asian Survey* 41, no. 5 (2001): 765–76.

18. Bart Gaens, 'The Outcomes of the ASEM 6 Summit in Helsinki', in Bart Gaens (ed.), *Europe-Asia Interregional Relations. A decade of ASEM* (Aldershot: Ashgate Publishing Company, 2008), 151.

19. Madhavi Bhasin, 'The India-EU Partnership: Strategic Alliance or Political Convenience?' in *India's Foreign Policy*, Anjali Ghosh, Tridib Chakraborti, Anindyo J. Majumdar, and Shibashis Chatterjee (eds.) (New Delhi: Pearson, 2009), 221.

20. Siemon T. Wezeman and Pieter D. Wezeman, *Trends in International Arms Transfers, 2013* (Stockholm International Peace Research Institute), 6.

ELEVEN

Europe's Eastward Expansion

The Connotations for Emerging Asia

Hari Vasudevan

Emerging Asia has been held to centre on key economic indicators—the globally oriented economy of China, consistent growth in the Association of Southeast Asian Nations (ASEAN), and high growth rates in the Republic of Korea and India. A number of points of support include the slow but steady development of West Asia and Japan, resource contributions from the Russian Federation (RF), and investments and market support from the United States and individual states of Europe. The European Union (EU) as an entity has played its own role through partnership programmes with individual Asian states in a process that lacks a fixed centre. The Caspian-Central Asian region, meanwhile, independent of Soviet-era links to the RF, has been part of the processes that define emerging Asia, and has witnessed significant developments. This region comprises the nations of what are known as the Transcaucasus or South Caucasus and Central Asia: Georgia, Azerbaijan, Armenia (Transcaucasus), Kazakhstan, Turkmenistan, Uzbekistan, Tajikistan, and Kyrgyzstan (Central Asia). The area's hydro-carbon resources have figured in the energy strategies of China, South Korea, and India, and the region itself features as an important emerging market where investment from these countries has been established.

There is potential here for competition between Europe and emerging Asia for Caspian-Central Asian resources, competition that has dimensions that are understated but likely to assume new importance. Recent events indicate the probability that the character of the Caspian-Central

Asian region's institutions will become a target of competition, drawing strength from the economic interests involved. The new reach of the EU's association agreements into the Caucasus in 2013 and the determination shown by the EU to project and defend such agreements in Ukraine and Moldova show as much. A political shift in the EU's presence in the region has come about which coincides with the general continuity in the prevailing political orientation in the Caspian-Central Asian neighbourhood and in emerging Asia.

In this scenario, the political projection of Europe through the EU is significant. Profiles of emerging Asia seldom feature notions of political achievement, unless it is uneven and often doubtful achievement. In the global literature on governance, kudos for such achievement lies primarily with the states of the EU and the United States. The rhetorical tenor of EU documentation stresses an overall commitment to a special type of governance that is considered a cut above the processes and features that mark other parts of the world, and alternatives are seldom considered to have produced 'deliverables' in terms of guarantees of human rights, representative government, and transparency on a similar scale. The model of the erstwhile Soviet state is recognized to have had a poor record in this regard and also to have fallen short on growth orientation. This model has been reformed in China to provide the basis for growth, but does not address shortfalls in the non-economic deliverables mentioned above. The Euro-American model of political and administrative order has de facto become universal, with emerging Asia hardly contributing to it except to assert the value of sovereignty and the importance of cultural norms specific to a country, as part of a half-hearted and much debated sense of 'Asian values'. The tangible evidence of this model is the way in which a group of nations has assumed the right to intervene in fraught situations with the tacit or overt acceptance of the leadership of institutions of global governance. The background to major international interventions of the twenty-first century bear evidence of this, whether the Afghanistan crisis of 2001 and the constitution of the International Security Assistance Force, the Iraq crisis of 2003, the Somalia crisis after 2008, or the Libyan crisis after 2011.

This chapter examines the larger implications for emerging Asia of the initiative by the EU to move to association agreements with specific states within the framework of its Eastern Partnership Programme (EaP) since 2008. This initiative has drawn the EU deeper into the Caucasus-Central Asia region politically, with the signing of an association agreement with Georgia in 2013, and also generating the Ukraine crisis of 2013–2014. The initiative marks a new phase in a presence of the EU in its Asian periphery in states hitherto dominated loosely by the Commonwealth of Independent States (CIS). This presence began with EU partnership programmes with states of the Organization for Security and Cooperation in Europe (OSCE) that were once members of the former Union of Soviet

Socialist Republics (USSR) or its Eastern European alliance, the Council for Mutual Economic Assistance (CMEA) and the Warsaw Pact. To date, the OSCE sets the standard in areas of dispute ranging from electoral norms to the conflict between Armenia and Azerbaijan in the Nagorno-Karabakh region. It was from these general engagements with the EU that the inclusion of former CMEA members in the EU followed, and the European Neighbourhood Policy (ENP) developed after 2004[1].

The association agreement initiative within the EaP indicates the further maturation of a political process whereby the territories of the CIS are regarded as inadequately covered by political and economic regimes conducive to sustainable development and social welfare. EU regimes are considered as an ideal, and CIS states move to closer integration with them. The association agreement initiative also has major economic implications for the EU, potentially consolidating its energy security and extending its market reach. The consequences present a challenge to Russia, its security system, its global political postures, and the vision of growth pursued by its leadership. The consequences also present a challenge to major states of emerging Asia drawn to the region because the terms of commerce in this neighbourhood are being reset. This reset is through the establishment of a clear relationship between the political goals linked to governance and the processes that determine the domain of the state in economic matters, basically limiting that domain, and the reset also involves a close prescription of the manner of interaction between economic actors.

The EU initiative has a 'subversive' quality to it[2] since it uses the same terms of reference to which the post-Soviet states adhere, but holds them to different meanings and standards not usually linked to such terms. Unease has been noticeable in the neighbourhood: unease that will shape the way the EU will be viewed in the immediate future, that is, not only as a market and as source of financial support but also as a firmer competitor for resources and authority than in the past. The main issue here—the sense of EU competition at a political level—has already been a source of strong rhetorical opposition in the past in one major country of emerging Asia, when it was seen as part of a broader western strategy of regime change following the so-called colour revolutions in Ukraine, Georgia, and Kyrgyzstan, and an attempt at regime change in Uzbekistan. China vociferously objected to this at the India-Russia-China trilateral meetings and the Shanghai Cooperation Organization in 2005, establishing common cause with Russia[3]. The fact that European initiatives, in combination with the actions of US-based companies, are regarded in the Caucasus-Central Asia region as an opportunity, merely adds to the strength of the challenge.

The argument in this chapter is not to exaggerate the nature of this challenge, though the EU's resources, its strong presence in the past in the area, and its determination to stand by the association policy in

Ukraine indicates that the challenge should also not be underestimated. The argument acknowledges the domination of political systems in the region that far from accord with those of the EU. Local authorities are still fully in control in the shaping of relationships, dealing with criticism and engaging with the EU.

The chapter is set out in five sections. The first deals with the understatement of the importance for emerging Asia of the political dimensions of association with the EU in Asia, highlighting the lack of awareness in various countries of EU policy nuances—itself the result of some divided opinion in the EU. The second section points out the importance of the Caspian-Central Asian neighbourhood to emerging Asia. The third takes up the story of the relevance of the region to Europe, the nature of the EaP, and the authority of the EU in the area at various levels, based on transport corridors, migration patterns, and institutional and corporate structures. It deals with the distinctive features of the association agreements signed at Vilnius in November 2013 and after, and the factors that indicate that the agreements constitute a considerable departure in the EU's presence. The chapter then turns to the failure of the states of the region to achieve uniform socially and culturally acceptable political goals that accommodate changing interests, the inability of possible models of political organization to find traction, and the chaotic projection of alternative approaches to institution building. Focus also falls on specific matters (ethnic Georgian conflict and similar problems elsewhere) where the EU political model has been inadequate; such issues leave power in its least inclusive form the key determinant of institution building—a highly unstable situation. A new stage is clearly emerging in the region, however, where the many strong stakeholders in the Caspian-Central Asian region will be affected by a local European presence in a political and legal form. Such stakeholders will include the Eurasian community, the Chinese oil and gas sector, and Korean and Japanese investors in number, not to mention Europe's possible supporter in the region, the democratic, neo-liberal India.

The challenge before local stakeholders is not merely the example the EU sets. The local presence of the EU will generate engagements at more fundamental and practical levels (indicated in the terms of association agreements) that build on relations already in existence. Some of these themes are treated in next section, the nub of which is an explanation of the Russian response, the reorientation of Russian foreign policy in this area, and its possible meaning for emerging Asia. At issue is a serious sense of threat that association agreements with the EU represent which the crisis of 2013–2015 in Ukraine has demonstrated. At the end of the chapter, some implications of this general scenario for emerging Asia are drawn out.

Throughout the chapter, the Caucasus-Central Asia region and its independent states are treated as a whole, without a strong distinction between the South Caucasus and Central Asia. This reflects the general approach of Asian entrepreneurs and European policymakers, although there are many differences between the states making up the area. The region is interlinked by its energy distribution networks, distinguished from Iran by its membership of the OSCE, and has a distinct set of Soviet networks that run through it as well as a common concern with the resources of the Caspian shelf. All members of the neighbourhood also came, by the end of the 1990s, to assume a degree of distance from the main successor state of the USSR, the RF, even while they accept that country's exceptional importance.

THE LITERATURE AND THE PERSPECTIVES

Asian Academic Literature

Neglect of the aspects covered in this chapter is commonplace in the literature in Asian countries on Europe and the EU. The exceptions are general accounts of EU activities and the ongoing Ukrainian crisis, and tunnel vision in official circles has fixed on specific engagements; this is as true of China as of other parts of Asia. Despite the existence since the 1980s of a competent Western European Studies Institute (since 2011, renamed the European Studies Institute) at the Chinese Academy of Social Sciences, and the existence of the *Chinese Journal of European Studies*[4], broad evaluations of European intentions and policies are rare. The work in India at the School of International Studies and later the Jawaharlal Nehru University has been sparse. Japanese studies of Europe have been remarkable[5], but they have had few spin-off benefits in the rest of Asia. Other centres for European Studies in Asia are the result of EU initiatives and are relatively recent, concentrating on comparative frameworks for research and higher education in Asia, using categories and references that are common in Europe. They deal with Europe's integration process and are reinforced by the Erasmus Mundus and other similar programmes. These centres are part of a promotion of EU-based knowledge systems, such as the EU studies programmes at Chulalongkorn University in Bangkok, the unit located in the National Centre for Social Sciences and Humanities in Hanoi, and the European studies programme at the University of Malaya[6].

An understanding of the ramifications of the current expansion of Europe to its East requires an awareness of Europe's relationship with the territories of the former USSR. Since in most of Asia interest in this Soviet/Eurasian area was ideological at best, any discussion of the theme of this chapter is rare. China and Japan have been the exception, and despite a long isolation from the USSR and Eurasia, there has been a new professionalism in the specialist community. In Japan, the Slavic Institute at Hokkaido has led the way, but limited resources, both human and material, have been a handicap and long breaks in development in China have stunted study and research.

An immediate policy focus in literature on contemporary affairs in Asian countries has led to an emphasis on estimations of national resources and capabilities in discussions about global engagements. There is a lack of interest in the motivations that guide possible major economic partners, except in terms of economic goals as announced by the national government itself or the World Trade Organization (WTO). In the case of EU policies and intentions, neglect also follows from the absence in sites of emerging Asia of any direct EU political presence. EU diplomatic delegations may exist in many capitals, but the bulk of relationships with Europe are bilateral under specific programmes with individual European nations. The political challenge of the EU has been remote, even as the value of most European states' roles has been limited by the meagre spread of their individual resources.

The range of the activities of the EU itself has reinforced this situation. The orientation has been towards member-states and their neighbourhood along strict functionality such as support of trade, consolidation of economic sectors such as steel or agriculture, and so on. The main locales of emerging Asia have been distant from the proximate areas to Europe where such political as well as economic concerns operate. Such proximate areas have figured in the Barcelona Process (1994–2004) and the development of the Mediterranean and neighbourhood programmes since 2004, where the EU as a negotiator and actor has featured at political and economic levels. EU policy has been targeted to the benefit of the latecomers that require support for their economies, such as Spain, Portugal, and Greece in the case of the Barcelona Process. In such instances, subventions have been undertaken in Europe's name[7] to enhance the development of specific groups of nations, and through this, the functioning of the European market overall and the interests of EU members generally. Global strategy is part of the EU's common foreign and security policy, and it has been given a focus in the European External Action Service under the high representative, but this initiative is relatively recent, the European External Action Service having been formed in 2010, and its impact is restricted[8].

In Asian approaches to the EU, a long-term decolonization syndrome has been at play that has added to the neglect of the dynamics of EU expansion. This syndrome automatically rejects any interest in the former imperial power and the lacuna in research is one of the failings of a nation-centred approach to study that avoids the long-term value of connected histories[9] and which has been the product of a strong focus on decolonization. The syndrome has had broader ramifications. It has limited the understanding of the global range of former imperial entities and the power of their latter-day projections. Thus, Europe's periphery is considered to be the territory of the former states of the CMEA. Unlike the United States, which is recognized as a superpower with global range, the EU and its member-states are seen as capable of global strategy only in their immediate neighbourhood, and their political appeal is also delimited as such.

The corporate strategy of multinationals with a strong European profile (such as Siemens as opposed to the American Ford), and the investment of European banks such as the Banque Nationale de Paris are seldom associated with larger goals associated with political or legal regimes except those that are highly flexible or that require attention as in the case of the prescriptions of the WTO, or the international patents rights regime established by the WTO. At a broader level, association with the EU is primarily connected to access to European markets, as in the case of the EU–South Africa free trade agreement. Demonstrable instances of political interest in Asia by external actors have been primarily associated with the United States, as in the case of Iraq and Afghanistan, with other members of the North Atlantic Treaty Organization being included as supporting actors.

Such approaches have led to a serious blind spot in emerging Asia concerning the emergence of the EU as a so-called post-modern entity, acting both for and beyond the interests of its member-nations on a global scale. Globally, the phenomenon has been a matter of significance since the EU expansion of 2004 and the Treaty of Lisbon of 2007. Some of the ramifications have been evaluated seriously in the one country that has partnered the process but is actually external to it: the United States[10].

Eastern Orientation of the European Union: Uncertain Significance within the European Union

In Europe, meanwhile, in individual member-states the official literature on the Eastern orientation of the EU towards the Caspian-Central Asian neighbourhood as a part of the EaP has amalgamated such activity into policy statements or prescriptive suggestions. Policy itself is associated with bilateral partnership programmes between the EU and individual countries of the region. In academic circles, the focus is on the national discourse that takes shape in individual EU states. In the case of Poland and Lithuania, for instance, it is substantially focused on Ukraine; in Romania on Moldova[11], and so on. A swathe of arrangements for cooperation exists that cements the EU's relations with clusters of states indicating a variety of engagements that evade notions of a specific or well-defined direction. These arrangements involve a much larger number of states than those who accepted the standard association agreements that have led to EU membership at different times, and many diverse terms of engagement. They include association agreements that have not led to membership (with Turkey), stabilization and association agreements (with Macedonia, Montenegro, and Serbia), the Euro-Mediterranean association agreements where many North African and Levantine states are involved, free trade agreements, and finally the OSCE itself.

The Eastern Partnership associative agreements which have drawn the EU into the Caspian-Central Asian neighbourhood are not easy to distinguish from others, since they are also part of the European Neighbourhood Policy enunciated in 2004. Eye-catching statements comparable to those made by American pundits such as Zbignew Brzezinski are rare in discussions of the subject. This is especially true since each of the external initiatives of the EU has carried a subvention that has in turn generated its own range of interests, making the EaP apparently no more special than others. Because political developments, such as those associated with the Arab Spring, and institutional inertia have sustained EU Mediterranean and neighbourhood policies once they began, their significance is not to be ignored. Local bodies in the neighbourhood countries, European universities, non-governmental agencies, and corporate entities have been willing to use budgetary provisions provided by Brussels, giving the programmes a life of their own, which reinforces overall confusion regarding the value of any one programme over another. The interests of individual EU members in the business of the EU, and the importance attributed to the bilateral agreements they make, have led to further understatement of the emerging political authority of the association agreements in Europe's Eastern periphery.

SIGNIFICANCE OF THE CASPIAN-CENTRAL ASIA NEIGHBOURHOOD FOR EMERGING ASIA

Scale of the Significance

While the role of the EU in emerging Asia has been understudied in the countries of the area, the place of the Caspian-Central Asian neighbourhood in the robust development of emerging Asia has been clear. Plans of the period following the disintegration of the USSR have become the realities of the present, where Silk Route initiatives have taken solid form and the list of beneficiaries is large, including interests from emerging Asia.

By the time of the economic crisis of 1998 in the region, Russia's attempts to control developmental processes in the former USSR had tapered off. In the early 2000s, Russian aspirations in its 'near abroad' former Soviet republics had come down to specific points of interest other than ensuring the security of its territories through multilateral and bilateral arrangements. The focus of policy was on management of the country's specific interests as a purveyor of hydro-carbon resources, raw materials, and military equipment; handling migration from the former USSR; and dealing with the interests of Russian minorities outside Russia. This core aspect of Russia's global self-projection left former Soviet states overall with great room for manoeuvre, even if Russian interests intruded into policy, using former Soviet connections and points of dependence[12].

These developments saw the states of the Caspian-Central Asian neighbourhood evolve an independent economic momentum. Their hydro-carbon resources are now substantially outside the control of the RF's pipeline system (concentrated in the state company Transneft) that dominated distribution until 2006. Such resources are substantial, Turkmenistan figuring among the world's five major natural gas sources[13], and independence in the region has been reinforced by membership of the WTO in the case of Tajikistan and Kyrgyzstan—the result of a slow movement away from the former Soviet community. Among Soviet successor states, unlike Russia itself, these countries generated little capital for investment to improve their own resources and for a decade sought various formal and informal Russian inputs—inputs that were not forthcoming given Russia's own economic crisis. This inspired not only major investing agencies of Europe and the United States but also of emerging Asia to bridge the deficit and integrate the countries into their own growth paradigms.

In emerging Asia, China had logical advantages as a direct neighbour, and its technology had much in common with the Soviet technology that was common in the CIS of the region. Post-1991 China also had the advantage of a fast growing economy. China's interest in the area had begun to develop during perestroika, though its initiatives were few, with the normalization of relations with the USSR[14]. India had a large network of personnel on the ground even before 1991 in the form of businessmen operating from Moscow and managers from public companies who had interests in Soviet-era technology. After 1991, India was also in a position to use debt repayment funds to form the basis for new economic initiatives. The impact of Soviet disintegration and the currency crisis of 1992 on India were substantial, leaving its policy in a desperate state where it failed to evolve any perspective on new emerging markets and rapidly accepted the prescriptions set by Bretton Woods institutions and the WTO[15]. In ASEAN, the only country that had had a long-term connection with the former Soviet state was Indonesia, but its growth pattern in the post-1991 era was oriented regionally, and no attempt was made to build on past strengths. Otherwise, investment for the region was to come from Japan, which had no networks in the region, and South Korea, which was able to build on important community links, especially in Kazakhstan, to where many Koreans were deported in the 1940s[16].

Hence, in emerging Asia, it is the link between the Caspian-Central Asian neighbourhood and China that stands out, and this will play a crucial role in China's economic future. In a situation where the difficulties of integration of peripheral regions into coast-centred initiatives are acknowledged, the Caspian-Central Asian region is in a position to reinforce the production of China's Western regions, generating a varied network of stable energy resources and an enlarged market. Given the large trade and economic connections by China with emerging Asia, the importance of the region to China is most likely to have an impact on emerging Asia's growth as a whole.

Building on the China link, with its considerable strengths, has logically followed from the Chinese government's concerns to monitor this neighbourhood closely after Soviet disintegration. This was for security reasons, since centrifugal tendencies in the Soviet space affected independence movements among Uyghur in Xinjiang, and may have caused further problems in the region of Mongolia. Coinciding with Jiang Zemin's rapid economic expansion programme, these concerns led to considerable independence to provincial government in Heihe on the Russian border and Urumqi, the Xinjiang capital. Chinese companies, in the form of state-owned enterprises and others, utilized the opportunity to make inroads into the immediate neighbourhood during the decade 1992–2002, establishing nexus-centred relations involving business and administration across the borders which in turn led policymakers in China to a determination to use the border provinces for a resource build-up in the Western and Northern regions. Despite the centralization of the Russian state under the Putin and Medvedev administrations since 2002, this Chinese policy has continued, generating migration into its neighbourhood that benefits the Chinese economy[17]. Especially in the Western region, this has reinforced economic momentum that will contribute to the growth of China's interior beyond the Hwang Ho-Yang Xi region, growth that otherwise might have experienced short-term problems.

The overall increase in trade between China and the Central Asian region is made clear in Tables 11.1 and 11.2.

In general terms, trade has grown phenomenally between 2000 and 2013. The more dramatic consequences of the Chinese involvement in the Caspian-Central Asian neighbourhood have been associated with energy products. Integration into the Kazakh oil and natural gas systems linked to Tengiz, Karachaganak, and Kashagan oil and gas fields has been the motor of trade. This has been achieved through adjustment and marginal development of pipelines in the area, mainly working through the Atyrau-Alashankou oil pipeline and the Central Asia-Centre pipeline. The Chinese engagement with Kazakhstan has brought a pivotal section of emerging Asia to the Caspian shelf and into the competition for its resources as exploration proceeds. The off-take here reinforces the output of China's Western regions, and the Chinese uplift of natural gas from Central Asia is crucial to China and amounts to 45 percent of the country's needs. This is managed mainly from Turkmenistan and Uzbekistan,

Table 11.1.   China's Trade with the Caucasus-Central Asian States, 2000

Country	Exports	Imports
Kazakhstan	$598,749,358	$958,209,134
Kyrgyzstan	$110,173,636	$67,437,319
Uzbekistan	$39,432,215	$12,032,839
Turkmenistan	$12,102,480	$4,056,997
Tajikistan	$6,792,704	Below one million US$
Azerbaijan	$2,187,954	$3,979,866
Georgia	Below one million US$	$2,350,255
Armenia	$1,143,203	$4,210,218

with Kazakhstan acting as a transit state and supplying a small component in its own right. Central Asian supplies of oil to China, mainly from Kazakhstan, only make up 4 percent of the country's needs, but these constitute a supplement to that of Xinjiang for the growth of the country.

The dynamics of these developments have involved not only China's state-owned petroleum company, Sinopec. All other pipeline projects in the region, involving modernization and extension of Soviet era infrastructure, have drawn in investors from South Korea and Japan into substantial projects in Azerbaijan, Kazakhstan, and Uzbekistan[18]. Globalization of the region through financial means has involved parts of emerging Asia in the area other than by way of China. Of importance here is a possible Turkmenistan-Afghanistan-Pakistan-India pipeline or an Iran-oriented pipeline and further improvements in Caspian shipping.

Asian countries' activities are not solely linked to China-related projects. In the South Korean case, a prominent think tank points out that the South Korean interest in the Caspian/Central Asian region is seen as part of an overall strategy to project South Korea globally, where the republic could act as a go-between in areas where large powers are involved in competition. The government also projects itself as a democratic force that asserts Confucian values that are more acceptable in Asia than 'Western values'[19].

South Korea's prime focus in the post-disintegration period has been Uzbekistan. Investment has been targeted in the joint venture mode, encouraged by the Uzbek government. This has taken Daewoo into the Fergana valley for automobile production and engineering, telecommunications, and textiles. Daewoo further diversified into energy products and oil and natural gas exploration, joined in this by the Korean National Oil Corporation and the Korean Gas Corporation. These investments have ensured Korea a role in its negotiations with gas and oil majors, essential to the country since it has no reserves of its own. In the case of

Table 11.2.   China's Trade with Caucasus-Central Asia, 2013

Country	Exports To	Imports From
Kazakhstan	$12,545,123,569	$16,050,838,003
Kyrgyzstan	$5,075,346,113	$62,350,108
Uzbekistan	$2,613,355,048	$1,938,092,728
Turkmenistan	$1,137,643,740	$8,893,256,737
Tajikistan	$1,869,363,600	$88,751,269
Azerbaijan	$868,568,350	$233,583,286
Georgia	$862,092,297	$54,455,596
Armenia	$119,849,623	$73,138,531

Kazakhstan, South Korea has worked with a large group of ethnic Koreans settled in the area after deportation under Stalinist rule. This has generated many personal links and connections in the 1990s, leading to investments in the Kazakh financial sector, but it is in the past five years that heavy investments have begun in the energy sector and construction.

India has systematically built up its connections with the Caspian-Central Asian neighbourhood, but owing to transport logistics, most of its trade with this region is through third parties. A number of Indian business houses operate through Russia, where they were strategically positioned at the time of the repayment of the Soviet-era debt. Investments have been made directly in the textile industry in Uzbekistan and minor investments have been in the Kazakh energy sector. The Indian pharmaceutical sector has a major presence in Central Asian markets.

In all cases, the links are with the Caspian neighbourhood as well as Central Asia more broadly, albeit in varying ways. India and South Korea have businessmen on the ground in both areas as well as interests in energy resources. South Korean investments in Azerbaijan are large, running into construction and transportation, involving the corporate names of Samsung, Hyundai, and Halla Construction. China has energy interests in Azerbaijan and commitments to improvements in trade through the Kars-Baku railway project via Georgia, as well as the various interests in Central Asia mentioned above, most commitments being at the state-to-state level[20].

Character of the Engagement

The terms according to which many contracts have been signed and engagements made in states ranging from Azerbaijan in the Caucasus to Uzbekistan in Central Asia are habitually questioned for their transparency[21]. Clearly, rules exist here that are not part of the standard structure of dealings in the EU; even if EU companies have suitably benefited from these, their conduct abroad is justiciable at home and in practice requires suitable adjustment, but application of such strictures in the case of China, India, or Korea is almost unheard of. Emerging Asia's inroads into the Caucasus-Central Asian neighbourhood has consequently depended on state-to-state relations and construction of personal networks in a manner very different from those of EU agencies and companies. The approach of emerging Asia here is also governed by domestic assumptions that do not accord fully with EU terms of reference. This especially affects the political dimension of behaviour, where domestic legislation and debate in emerging Asia follows a rubric different from that prevalent in the EU. The coincidence of these attitudes with those prevalent in the Caucasus-Central Asia region varies from case to case; certainly, cultural and educational networks have proved to be powerful in the creation of bonds and business.

THE EASTERN PARTNERSHIP PROGRAMME OF THE EUROPEAN UNION AND THE ASSOCIATION AGREEMENTS OF 2013

The EU's documentation on its move from the ENP to the EaP emphasizes the voluntarism in the states that associated with the EU politically and economically. However, since the credentials of the regimes concerned have been considered suspect by EU standards, and since what specifically such aspirants had in mind has never been spelled out, who volunteered and for what is not clear.

European Stake in the Caspian-Central Asian Neighbourhood and the European Union's Eastern Partnership Programme

Members of the EU have definitely established a substantial stake in the Caucasus-Central Asia region. This has been through rail and shipping relays across the Black Sea, via Batumi and on to Baku or through Turkey. Comparable relays also operate from Kazakhstan, whose oil is hence sold independently of Russia. Major European and American investments in the region took shape in the 1990s, and these led to an exceptional outcome in the construction of the Baku-Tbilisi-Ceyhan (BTC) pipeline, which began operation in 2006[22]. The pipeline has been supervised by BP, while its security is the subject of special arrangements where the US government, the EU, and private players have a role, the so-called Caspian Guard[23]. The affairs of the BTC pipeline have been of importance to the EU's Energy Community, established in 2006[24], as a means of ensuring a stable supply of oil to the EU member-states.

Commercial self-awareness and corporatization locally, dominated by the state in Kazakh and Azeri country, led the state there to utilize government-led companies independent of the RF, namely the Kazmunaigaz and the State Oil Company of Azerbaijan, respectively. This process was the result of a substantial interest by global oil majors in the area, and these majors invested in specific fields and pipelines, the main companies being Chevron (in Kazakhstan the leading investor and pipeline constructor), Shell, Total, and ExxonMobil. The restructuring of the oil and gas industry in turn shaped the character of pipeline construction and the exploitation of new fields in the case of Kazakhstan, where the Russian Lukoil company had often to play second fiddle to international interests. The restructuring also provided the framework within which Azerbaijan's plans for the future of the Caspian shelf were established. Support activities in transport and shipping steadily developed as corollaries where Turkish and European companies were involved, in addition to Chinese and South Korean companies. In the course of the period following the construction of the BTC pipeline, a projected pipeline for the transport of gas from the Caspian to Europe has come to attract investment, a part of the transfer to be accomplished by the Nabucco pipeline linking Turkey and Southwest Europe and the projected Shah Deniz pipeline linking Turkey with Italy. These initiatives are in competition with the Russian South Stream project that was designed to strengthen Russia's presence in European energy markets, currently operating primarily the Druzhba pipeline and the North Stream link. In 2014, Russia abandoned the South Stream, citing obstruction from the EU.

The EU has played a special role in the Caspian-Central Asian region's development through the Technical Aid to Commonwealth of Independent States programme from 2000[25]. This among other projects has shaped communications improvements associated with the new Silk Route of the twenty-first century—the Transport-Corridor-Europe-Caucasus-Central-Asia (Traceca) initiative. This is intended to improve European links through the Caucasus to Central Asia and has featured investments in roads, port facilities, and other infrastructure since it was begun[26].

The EaP of the EU has raised the stakes further[27]. The target has been a group of non-EU CIS other than Russia. After the full integration into the EU from 2004 of the Visegrad and Baltic states, the outliers of the former CMEA (Bulgaria, Romania, and a number of the successor states of Yugoslavia), the EU's Eastern Partnership initiative of 2008–2009 examined the potential for associating states contiguous to the EU further to the East, states that were already part of the ENP initiative of 2004. The ENP itself drew in a large number of states, some in the Levantine and North African regions, but the majority was of countries to the east of the member-states that joined in 2004. The partnership programme itself covered Ukraine, Moldova, Belarus, Armenia, Azerbaijan, and Georgia.

The Eastern Partnership initiative and the agreements that were to be signed by those affiliating to it made no qualifications concerning goals, which were equally oriented towards the strengthening of a particular political profile, as well as the development of stronger cooperative structures with the EU and a tendency towards integration with the EU more broadly. The partnership's publicly stated objectives were 'to help promote political and economic reforms, and support efforts of the countries in the region to move closer to the EU'. This statement had an important rider that stressed its broader political character:

> At its basis lies a shared commitment to international law and fundamental values, including democracy, the rule of law and respect for human rights and fundamental freedoms, as well as to market economy, sustainable development and good governance[28].

Unexceptional as this may seem, it is clear that the determinants of political goals were to be measured by the standards of the EU and its institutional and legal framework.

The pivotal 'platforms' around which the partnership revolved were relatively general, as listed in objectives: democracy, good governance, and stability (Platform 1); economic integration and convergence with EU policies (Platform 2); energy security (Platform 3); and contacts between people (Platform 4). Here, Platform 2 was given pride of place within the overall framework, and it needs to be stressed that such a platform demanded the essentials of the political platform be met, that is, through agreement on the terms of the laws of contract, appeal and arbitration that guide commerce, investment, and allied economic activities, as well as rules concerning the treatment of minorities and safeguards for human rights. A number of EU directives and institutions were integrated into the 'platforms' to give the initiative a solid status. Crucial also is that Platform 3 had to be read in consonance with the Interstate Oil and Gas Transport to Europe initiative of the EU that sought to regulate and consolidate support to the EU from the resources of the Caspian-Central Asian region, beginning with projects in 1997[29]. The partners of the Interstate Oil and Gas Transport to Europe initiative are significantly the Black Sea littoral states of Ukraine, Moldova, and Georgia; the Caspian littoral states of Azerbaijan, Kazakhstan, and Turkmenistan; and the Central Asian states of Uzbekistan, Tajikistan, and Kyrgyzstan. Countries such as Russia and Iran were either ignored or included as observers.

The relatively general nature of the partnership, however well grounded in other initiatives, did not last long. By 2011, the Eastern Partnership initiative came to centre around a further move towards associative agreements and deep and comprehensive free trade areas agreements, where the pattern of commerce and investment procedures were to lead to accord with the laws and standards of the EU. These were intended to arrive at a framework for the migration of citizens of Partnership states into the EU space in a well-regulated, visa-free manner where the partner governments would be the main supervisors of procedures.

Association agreements that are more far reaching than partnership were taken up by members of the Georgia, Ukraine, Azerbaijan, and Moldova (GUAM) configuration[30]. There is no indication that the two initiatives were linked, but the overlap is worth noting. It is also notable that three of the states (Ukraine, Moldova, and Georgia) were associated with the CIS but had major differences with the RF, some of them severe, as in the case of Georgia and Moldova, where in South Ossetia, Abkhazia, and Trans-Dnestria the RF has supported positions opposed to those of the ruling regime in the state. GUAM itself is a grouping begun in 1997 and confirmed at Yalta in 2001[31]. From the time of its initiation, it sought to evolve transport corridors and institutions that differed from tradition-al reliance on Russia. It was encouraged by the EU, and from the mid-2000s the members shaped the Organization for Democracy and Econom-ic Development. This organization focused on trade agreements, political and judicial institutions, and norms. Ukraine, Moldova, and Georgia viewed the concept as the foundation for a future more appropriate to them than that provided by the CIS, and all took up the offer of associa-tion agreements except Azerbaijan, which, while a member of GUAM, was lukewarm and remained apart from the new initiative. EaP states that maintained links with Russia, like Belarus and Armenia, did not move towards association agreements.

The Range of Association Agreements of the Eastern Partnership

The association agreements that have been accepted by Ukraine, Mol-dova, and Georgia are a major advance on the general terms of Eastern Partnership and differ significantly from Euro-Mediterranean agree-ments. These association agreements were initialled after a prolonged period while the countries were evaluated for their capacity to fulfill the goals of association, and only later were they permitted to initial the agreements. The texts of the agreements are significant. While other part-nership agreements are dominated by trade data and feature general commitments to safeguard human rights, good governance, and action against terrorism, the association agreements of the Eastern Partnership deal not only with these but also indicate levels of control over the role of the state in the economy by stipulating limits on state action, including the nature of taxation. In general, the agreements require adherence to a larger sphere of EU directives that represent common practices of the EU members than do other partnership agreements that are more oriented to trade issues like reciprocal lowering of duties, nature of commodity pro-duction and packaging, and definitions of commodities and finished products.

Comparisons of the Euro-Mediterranean agreement with Algeria (2005) and other Mediterranean states with the association agreement with Georgia reveal this difference. The agreement with Algeria and others, beyond the political preambles and commitments concerning company formation and transport and legal cooperation, is concerned with trade issues centring on tariff adjustments and the bulk of the annexure material deals with such matters[32]. In the case of the agreement with Georgia, however, the major annexes to the general commitments indicate not only reiterations of OSCE safeguards concerning conflict (early warning systems and arbitration) but accords on trade in goods and services characteristic of other trade agreements right down to transcriptions of goods' names. There are various stipulations concerning standardization (voltage used and measurements) as well as timelines for their establishment, various restrictions on reservations on jobs, access to subsidies, and government role in privatization, often through enterprises that have a substantial state share, with sector-wise demarcations that accord with EU practice (Annexes I to XV) and timelines for when local legislation must be brought into line with EU legislation. The regulation of the local economy runs not only to matters of pollution and energy use, but also to adjustments of taxation and company and accounting procedures (Annex XXVIII). Clearly, there is more at work here than the corollaries of a deep and comprehensive free trade area: The agreement reshapes the economic practice of the state with social policy as a crucial component (Annex XXX)[33]. Integration of Georgia into the projection of an EU 'just society' is at issue here, not merely elements of cooperation.

THE IMPLICATIONS OF THE EASTERN PARTNERSHIP PROGRAMME'S ASSOCIATION AGREEMENTS FOR THE CASPIAN-CENTRAL ASIAN NEIGHBOURHOOD

In general, EU commentary has been negative concerning Caucasus-Central Asian political and institutional practice[34]. The following implications therefore can be foreseen.

Specific Implications

Given the regular movement of population in the South Caucasus/ Transcaucasus region, normal business enterprise and trade, and the importance of the BTC pipeline, the association agreement with Georgia is likely to have important consequences in the immediate neighbourhood[35], especially since finance from the EU is heavily present in the region and reinforces the initiative directly and indirectly. The adjustment of the economies of Azerbaijan and Armenia to the procedures that

Georgian-EU association introduces in the area will be a natural corol-
lary. Whereas traditionally adjustments between economies had been
mutual, varying a little with differences in strength, the adjustment with
the Georgian economy is likely to place other local Caucasus actors at a
disadvantage because Georgia is a transit state for both Azerbaijan and
Armenia to the larger Black Sea economy. The EU's authority is reinforced by the fact that the new procedures in Georgia accord with those
of the neighbouring state of Turkey, a long-term EU associate, which
offers a number of business opportunities in its own right. Hence, the
compulsions on Azerbaijan and Armenia to conform to European practices are substantially strengthened by the pivotal nature of Georgia's
geographical location. Pressures on Azerbaijan to conform are further
determined by its close association with the BTC pipeline and the oil and
gas majors with which the country does business.

The regional political implications are clear. In Azerbaijan, a country
where presidential power is almost untrammelled despite the existence
of a national assembly and regular elections, and where opposition parties such as the Musavat have limited freedoms, the presence of almost
continuous debate concerning the processes of representation bodes ill
for the regime in power. Geidar and Ilkham Aliev have successfully ruled
the country since disintegration without basic adjustments to any criticism, and suppressing with force the opposition against the BTC pipeline
is only one instance of such behaviour. Here, the changing atmosphere
across the border will undoubtedly be felt in future, and this is especially
true since Azerbaijan faces minority issues associated with the treatment
of Armenians, who have strong lobbies in Europe.

General Implications for the Larger Neighbourhood

The context in which the association agreements have been signed, in
the sense of the character of the states that abut on to South Caucasus
region, must be mentioned to understand the implications of such association outside the signatory country and its immediate neighbourhood. In
general, both Caucasus and Central Asian states privilege the notion of
expediting a transition to capitalism, where the model is the EU or the
United States. Yet, while all EaP signatories who did not sign association
agreements (Armenia, Azerbaijan, Belarus) have been marked by records
of privatization and investment management through banking, insurance, and other agencies, they have left the role of the state powerful and
with substantial continuity in the personnel of the state pre- and post-
Soviet disintegration. This has also been true of other states of the larger
Caspian-Central Asian area like Kazakhstan, Uzbekistan, Turkmenistan,
Tajikistan, and Kyrgyzstan. Despite a business environment that varied
considerably from what existed in the years after disintegration[36], this

overarching hold of the state and the importance of politics gave economic activity a flavour that was far removed from that of the EU.

The countries concerned have been marked by parliamentary systems that have either failed to find acceptance among sections of the population owing to the mismatch between the makeup of state personnel and the various interests that found means of expression, or where the power of the state has led to concentrations of authority in the hands of individuals and families. The former is true of Uzbekistan, Tajikistan, and Kyrgyzstan; the latter in Azerbaijan, Kazakhstan, and Turkmenistan. All states have accepted clan and regional affiliation as intrinsic to institutional building. Nominally, the states are republics and democracies with representative institutions and judicial bodies that support the rule of law, but in reality the range of interpretation of what this means is broad, allowing the state and individual presidents wide degrees of control as seen especially in Azerbaijan, Kazakhstan, Uzbekistan, and Turkmenistan[37]. Despite this, the main model that the countries of the neighbourhood approximate to in the realm of governance is that sponsored by the EU, and they apply many standards for such governance through the intervention of the OSCE. They stray far from the more practical aspects of governance when it comes to social policy or the notion of transfer of power, or separation of powers or an inclusive style of governance, but it remains the key reference point. In no state, it should be stressed, is the notion of an Islamic state held to be legitimate except among some opposition groups whose strength is difficult to measure, so great is the authority of the ruling establishment. The consequence is that despite institutional variation on a major scale from the EU model, its norms are held to be ideal, even if some states, as in the case of Kazakhstan, pride themselves on their institutional make up and even recommend it to others for emulation[38].

This in no way suggests that the modes advocated by the EU for institution building and negotiation have proved successful in complex situations. This is clear from the persistent refusal of South Ossetia and Abkhazia to come to terms with the Government of Georgia whatever the regime, and the failure of almost all EU peace-making attempts to resolve differences between Azerbaijan and Armenia in the Nagorno-Karabakh dispute. The repeated appeal to the EU and the OSCE in the circumstances, however, is an indication of the prestige they enjoy despite success or failure. In the circumstances, the presence of the EU in a more direct form than before in the Caspian neighbourhood will preserve the engagement with European norms, especially since it is backed by a strong desire in the EU to utilize the resources of this region for its energy security.

An Eye to Emerging Asian Enterprise in the Region

The prevailing regimes and processes, however, rather than EU-oriented reform regimes have shaped arrangements concerning contracts and rights that China and other emerging Asian countries have concluded within the Caspian-Central Asian neighbourhood. How far these will attract adjustment will be a question for the future that is dependent on the domino effect of EU presence. It is impossible, however, to wish away the possibility of such adjustments and already in the case of migration policy, states such as Kazakhstan face significant pressure from the EU to evolve fresh means of control and supervision.

RUSSIAN OPPOSITION TO EUROPEAN UNION INITIATIVES IN THE CAUCASUS-CENTRAL ASIAN NEIGHBOURHOOD AND IMPLICATIONS OF THE 'EURASIAN COMMUNITY'

The implications of these adjustments and other possible comparable shifts have antagonized Russia, which, according to the documentation on the EaP, is said to have been consulted as the EaP evolved. The initiative represented by the association agreements has encountered determined opposition from Russia, which sees this as a further strategy for the EU and North Atlantic Treaty Organization expansion. Russian opposition here, moreover, is not inspired purely by security considerations, but a sense of the necessity for policy regimes that are at variance with those of the EU. Notions of a possible 'Eurasian Community'[39] have been firmly promoted by Russian President Vladimir Putin. Putin has an eye to consolidating interests in the former Soviet space that accept notions of political and economic reform but advocate strict state by state control of the process, asserting 'sovereign democracy'[40], with a minimum agenda for a code of conduct. The extent to which Russia is willing to resist the development of EU strategies has been evident in the Ukraine crisis of 2013–2015, which originated in disputes over the Ukraine's intention to initial an association agreement at Vilnius in November 2013.

The Eurasian Community as a concept had its origins among early initiatives of the post-disintegration era when Russia, Kazakhstan, and Belarus signed an agreement to form a Customs Union (1995), extending this quickly to include Kyrgyzstan and bringing it into force in 1997, with Tajikistan being included in 1998. Owing to the circumstances of the time, the union was not important, especially following the crisis of 1998, but an agreement was signed by the above states to form a Eurasian Economic Community in October 2000, the terms to become valid from 30 May 2001.

A scheme of activity was worked out where three stages of cooperation were envisaged: the development of foreign trade zones in all member countries, the creation of a Eurasian Customs Union, and the creation of a Eurasian Economic Space. On 6 October 2007, Russia, Kazakhstan, and Belarus agreed to form the Customs Union in three stages (respectively effective 1 January 2010, 1 July 2010, and 1 July 2011). From 2012, following an agreement of the Customs Union members in December 2009, aspects of integration at the level of law and internal tariffs have evolved for the creation of a Eurasian Economic Space. Uzbekistan was associated with the organization between January 2006 and October 2008, Moldova and the Ukraine were observers from 2002 and were covered by the common aviation agreement and the Eurasian Bank for Development, and the same holds good for Armenia from 2003.

Faced with the support that the EU has provided through its association agreements in the Ukraine crisis of 2014, it is likely that the RF will use its foreign policy networks to resist the successful development of the EU initiative, placing pressure on sections of emerging Asia where it has influence. The significance of the relationship here, and especially in the case of the trade relationship with China, is evident from the growth in bilateral trade between 2000 and 2013 seen in Table 11.3.

Russia is likely to use its leverage at other levels. There is to be a strong energy ingredient in the development of future trade between the two states that will consolidate China's energy security through the construction of major pipelines from the Russian East. Common themes in policy approach are likely to be a factor: opinions concerning political organization and the relationship between the state and the economy are seldom congruent between the EU on the one hand and China and Russia on the other. In the case of the relationship with both China and India, there is a major RF arms component also: a component that is significant for the military forces of both Asian countries. This will also feature in Russia's search for a common platform with the important elements of emerging Asia.

CONCLUSION

A Perspective for Emerging Asia

It could be argued that some adjustment of the rules of the game may be a consequence of this encounter between varied forms of government and attitudes to the state. It is unlikely, however, that approaches for

Table 11.3.   China's Trade with Russia 2000–2013

Year	Exports	Imports
2000	$2,233,350,097	$5,769,892,360
2013	$49,591,171,963	$39,667,828,205

solidarity by Russia are likely to receive such broad-ranging support in emerging Asia that will eventually constitute a new paradigm or an international platform, unless confrontations over Caspian resources become the ultimate outcome of the Eastern Partnership's new twist. In the case of the EU's relationship with India, South Korea, and several members of ASEAN, there has been less divergence regarding the vocabulary of political organization, judicial process, and economic reform than there has been in the EU-Russia/China relationship. But even in China's case, Beijing is likely to find it possible to work with the terms of enterprise that may evolve in the region as a result of a general adherence to EU directives and procedures. This should be especially so when these terms do not fundamentally affect the working of the states of the EU neighbourhood other than those already inside the range of the EaP. Certainly, it is unlikely that the EU initiatives will evoke opposition from investors in emerging Asia since changes in regimes and rules are a norm of international financial practice, particularly in emerging markets of which the Caspian-Central Asian neighbourhood is but one. New rules are also unlikely to affect informed publics that have seldom seen in such issues a subject for concern or interest.

The mobilization of forces hostile to existing regimes around the new rules and their spirit, however, may undermine any such smooth transition, as the fate of Euro-Mediterranean agreements following the Arab Spring has shown. Whatever the chances of such an outcome, there are likely to be significant implications for the EU model and its general reputation. Caspian politics and various negotiations with China by EU-oriented states in the future may be on terms that China may set. As the Ukraine crisis has indicated, such engagements often lead to strange bedfellows and awkward commitments. The lines that have distinguished Asian political behaviour from that of the EU may be likely to blur in such circumstances, as the EU itself becomes embroiled in the complexities of the borderlands of emerging Asia and expanding Europe.

NOTES

1. This refers to the various initiatives associated with the ENP, termed 'instruments'. The ENP instrument indicates outlays and rubrics for operationalizing the ENP.

2. The term is used deliberately in the manner employed by Valerie Bunce, who pointed out that institutions throw up their own expectations from the terms they invoke and the ritual of the processes they involve. See Valerie Bunce, *Subversive Institutions* (New York: Cambridge University Press, 1999).

3. Declaration of Heads of Member-States of Shanghai Cooperation Organization (Xinhua), Updated: 12 June 2006, 15:15 (Astana, 5 July 2005), www.chinadaily.com.cn/china/2006-06/12/content_6020345.htm, accessed 12 October 2014. This stresses that 'Every people must be properly guaranteed to have the right to choose its own way of development'.

4. Institute of European Studies of Chinese Academy of Social Sciences, ies.cass.cn/en/cjes/Index.asp, accessed 12 October 2014.

5. For a recent example of this, see Kojin Karatani, *The Structure of World History: from Modes of Production to Modes of Exchange*, Michael K. Bourdaghs (trans.) (Durham, NC: Duke University Press, 2014).

6. Georg Wiessala, *European Studies in Asia. Contours of a Discipline* (Oxford: Routledge, 2014).

7. The tendency of an individual nation to use the notion of Europe has a history. It has been dealt with by Pascal Ory in *Les collaborateurs (1940-45)* (Paris: Editions de Seuil, 1976). The German use of the strategy in the 1960s and 1970s has been shown by Timothy Garton Ash in *In Europe's Name* (London: Vintage, 1994).

8. Information on the European External Action Service is to be found at www.eeas.europa.eu/, accessed 12 October 2014.

9. Georg Iggers and Edward Wang, *Global History of Modern Historiography* (New Delhi: Pearson Educational, 2008).

10. For more rhetorical literature, see Robert Kagan, *Of Paradise and Power: America and Europe in the New World Order* (New York: Alfred A. Knopf, 2003); and Peter Baldwyn, *The Narcissism of Minor Differences: How America and Europe are Alike* (New York: Oxford University Press, 2009).

11. A good example is Bohdan Hud, 'Eastern Policy of the European Union: Step by Step towards Ukraine', and Roman Kalytchak and Andriy Semonovych, 'European Union Enlargement—An Unfinished Business?' in *Introduction to European Studies: A New Approach to Uniting Europe*, D. Milczarek, A. Adamczyk, and K. Zajaczkowski (eds.) (University of Warsaw: Centre for Europe, 2013), 529–42.

12. The use of the integrated energy distribution system in the case of natural gas, and the early problems faced by Turkmenistan as an example, are graphically described in Valerii Pantiushkin and Mikhail Zygar, *Gazprom: Novoe Russkoe Oruzhie* (Moscow: Zakharov, 2008).

13. The most valuable collection on the Caspian appears to be Shirin Akiner (ed.), *The Caspian: Politics, Energy and Security* (London: Routledge, 2004). For fundamental information on the Caspian Sea's resources, see G. F. Ulmishek, 'Petroleum Geology and Resources of the North Caspian Basin, Kazakhstan and Russia', *US Geological Survey Bulletin* 2201-B (Washington, DC: USA Geological Survey, USA Department of the Interior, 2001). The USA Geological Survey has also published 'Assessment of Undiscovered Oil and Gas Resources of the North Caspian Basin, Middle Caspian Basin, North Ustyurt Basin, and South Caspian Basin Provinces, Caspian Sea Area' (Washington, DC: USA Geological Survey, USA Department of the Interior, 2010). See also World Energy Council, *World Energy Survey, 2013 Summary*, www.worldenergy.org/wp-content/uploads/2013/10/WEC_Resources_summary-final_180314_TT.pdf, accessed 12 October 2014.

14. For a fine account of normalization and perestroika perspectives on Asia, see Eduard Shevardnadze, *Moi Vybor* (Moscow: Progress, 1991).

15. See Hari Vasudevan, *Shadows of Substance, Indo-Russian Trade and Military Technical Cooperation since 1991* (New Delhi: Manohar, 2010), for the strategy of Indian business companies in the region.

16. See Georgii Kan, 'Koreitsy v Kazakhastane: deportatsiia is obreteniia novoi rodiny', in *Deportirovannye v Kazakhstan Narody: Vremia I Sudby* (Almaty: Arys-Kazakhastan, 1998), 109–21.

17. For details of this relationship, see Juan Pablo Cardinal and Heriberto Araujo, *China's Silent Army* (London: Allen Lane, 2013); and Marlene Laruelle and Sebastian Peyrouse, *The Chinese Question in Central Asia* (London: Hurst Publishers, 2014).

18. For China's energy information, see the USA Energy Agency at www.eia.gov/countries/cab.cfm?fips=ch, accessed 12 October 2014.

19. Balbina Hwang, 'A New Horizon in Korea-Central Asia Relations: The ROK joins the Great Game', *Korea Compass* (December 2012).

20. For China's relationship with Azerbaijan, see Fariz Ismailzade, 'China's Relations with Azerbaijan', *China and Eurasia Forum Quarterly* 5, no. 1 (2007).

21. www.fess-global.org/files/OilandGas.pdf (accessed 12 October 2014) is a document by the USA Agency for International Development that raises questions about the probity of oil and natural gas dealings in Kazakhstan and other states.

22. For information on the participants in construction, see www.bakuceyhan.org.uk. For the history of the pipeline, see S. Fredrick Starr and Svante E. Cornell, *The Baku-Tbilisi-Ceyhan Pipeline: Oil Window to the West* (Uppsala: Central Asia Caucasus Silk Road Studies Program, 2005), www.silkroadstudies.org/BTC.pdf, accessed 12 October 2014.

23. For cooperation between the United States and Europe in this venture, see Ariel Cohen 'Energy Security in the Caspian Basin', in *Energy Security Challenges for the 21st century*, Gal Luft and Anne Korin (eds.) (Santa Barbara, CA: Greenwood Publishing House, 2009), 109–27.

24. Energy Community, www.energy-community.org/portal/page/portal/ENC_HOME, accessed 12 October 2014.

25. Europa, 'Tacis Programme (2000–2006)', europa.eu/legislation_summaries/external_relations/relations_with_third_countries/eastern_europe_and_central_asia/r17003_en.htm, accessed 12 October 2014.

26. www.traceca-org.org, accessed 12 October 2014.

27. European Union External Action, 'Eastern Partnership', eeas.europa.eu/eastern/index_en.htm, provides all the documentation on the Eastern Partnership referred to in this essay. For some of the reflections, E. A. Korosteleva (ed.), *Eastern Partnership: A New Opportunity for the Neighbours?* (London: Routledge, 2011).

28. This is the representation at the European Commission's broader website for industry (ec.europa.eu/enterprise/policies/international/promoting-neighbourhood/eastern/index_en.htm#h2-1, accessed 12 October 2014). It accords with the *Communication from the Commission to the European Parliament and the Council* of 12 March 2008 concerning the Eastern Partnership at eur-lex.europa.eu/LexUriServ/LexUriServ.do?uri=COM:2008:0823:FIN:EN:PDF (accessed 12 October 2014). Platforms are indicated in this fundamental communication.

29. See www.inogate.org (accessed 12 October 2014) for the main documentation on this initiative.

30. See www.guam-organization.org (accessed 12 October 2014) for further information on the configuration.

31. L. M. Grigoriev and M. R. Salikhov, *GUAM, Piatnadsat' Let Spustia* (Moscow: Regnum, 2007).

32. EU Neighbourhood Library, 'EU-Algeria Association Agreement', www.enpi-info.eu/library/content/eu-algeria-association-agreement, accessed 12 October 2014. For implications of the Euro-Mediterranean agreements and their record, see Haizam Ahmira Fernandez and Richard Youngs, *The Euro-Mediterranean Partnership: Assessing the First Decade* (Madrid: FRIDE, 2005), www.fride.org/download/03_Libro_completo_ENG.pdf, accessed 12 October 2014.

33. For text of the agreement, see www.mfa.gov.ge/index.php?lang_id=ENG&sec_id=30&info_id=17015, accessed 12 October 2014.

34. This is normally evident in observers' comments during elections. A sense of the rhetoric is evident in comments of a writer with the Spanish think tank FRIDE. 'Central Asian legislators do not necessarily represent an electorate, but are "selected" based on their affinity with the incumbent regimes and often represent specific business interests'. See Tika Tsertsvadze, 'What Role for the European Parliament in Central Asia', *EUCAM, Commentary*, no. 25 (September 2014).

35. See Richard Giragosian, *Georgia's EU Alignment: Regional Repercussions*, www.aljazeera.com/indepth/opinion/2014/06/georgia-eu-alignment-regional-2014629123238966304.html, accessed 12 October 2014, for an assessment of the hegemony expected from Georgia in the Caucasus after the agreement.

36. See *Doing Business in Kazakhstan* for a sense of this, though the situation here was probably far more like the EU than that which prevailed in Uzbekistan and Turkmenistan. For the Internet edition of the volume, see www.bakermcken zie.com/files/Publication/7fcb0aa5-87d4-44d8-b13a7f00e11c1183/Presentation/Publicat ionAttachment/60fe2667-6097-480d-9b95dfef2dd28d2d/bk_dbi_kazakhstan_14.PDF, accessed 12 October 2014.

37. For an outsider's view of the foundations of the 'transition' and institution formation, which gives Islam and reform orientation a special place, see Ahmed Rashid, *The Resurgence of Central Asia* (New Delhi: Oxford University Press, 1994). For a CIS view, which avoids conclusions, see *Postsovetskaia Tsentral'naia Aziia. Poteri is obreteniia* (Moscow: Vostochnaia Literatura, 1998). The notion that institution building is a major problem is stressed in J. Ahrens and H. W. Hoen, *Institutional Reform in Central Asia: Politico-economic Challenges* (New York: Routledge, 2013).

38. The semiofficial history of Kazakhstan stresses statements by Nursultan Nazarbaev to this effect. See *Istoriia Kazakhstana*, vol. 5 (Almaty: Atamura, 2010), linking this with an overall European sensibility.

39. Russia's concerns about the Eastern Partnership are elaborated in Andrei Zagorski, 'Eastern Partnership from the Russian Perspective', *Internationale Politik und Geselleschaft*, no. 3 (2011). For basic information on the Eurasian Community, see www. evrazes.com/, accessed 12 October 2014.

40. For the range of support for these notions, see *PRO Suvrennyiu Demokratiiu* (Moscow: Izdatel'stvo Evropa, 2007).

TWELVE

American Bargaining, Pivoting, and Rebalancing

Implications for Europe and Emerging Asia

Philip I. Levy

The Obama administration has consistently proclaimed its turn towards Asia as a central feature of its foreign policy. This regional turn, sequentially known first as the 'pivot' and then as the 'rebalance', was intended to have multiple components: economic, diplomatic, and military. Given the prominence of the United States in crafting and maintaining global institutions and its significance for other alliances, a closer examination of the United States' intentions and policies in this area can have broad relevance to Europe and emerging Asian nations, and will be the focus of this chapter. Any new American initiative, especially one as potentially portentous as a pivot to Asia, can have broad ramifications.

One can pose the question about the depth of the American commitment to an Asia-focused policy in either absolute or in relative terms. In absolute terms, there is no doubt that President Barack Obama and his top foreign policy strategists consider the Asia region supremely important. In relative terms, the question is much more difficult to answer, and it is here that one finds a disconnect between rhetoric and results.

There are at least three dimensions in which the Obama administration has faced trade-offs with regard to the pivot. First is the geographical dimension. If the administration is pivoting towards Asia, from what is it turning away? The Middle East? Europe? These questions have proved uncomfortable. Not only was there a danger that allies in some key region of the world will feel spurned, but unsettled regions like Syria and

Ukraine have demanded American attention with an awkward insistence. Second, there is a basic budgetary trade-off. The American federal government has finite resources in terms of diplomatic personnel, and after a decade of military involvement in the Middle East, the Obama administration has been committed to reining in military spending. Thus, a draw-down of military resources in Iraq and Afghanistan does not provide much in the way of surplus to redeploy to the Asia-Pacific; this was true even before the recent conflict with the Islamic State in Syria and Iraq. Third, any administration has a limited amount of political capital. While the concept is somewhat nebulous, one can think about the amount of time that a president or his or her top officials spend importuning legislators or the limited number of actions an administration can take without annoying domestic supporters, before that support is exhausted. This third constraint has been particularly relevant in discussions of international trade.

This chapter will first briefly discuss the strategic origins of the pivot and break up the policy into its component parts. It will then delve into the most significant of those parts—the Trans-Pacific Partnership (TPP). While it would be difficult to identify any significant change stemming from the military or diplomatic facets of the Asian pivot, this is not true for trade. The TPP, if it were to meet its ambitions, could dramatically expand trade throughout the Asia-Pacific and establish new rules that could become global standards. As the most obvious and prominent manifestation of the pivot, the TPP serves as a useful guide to the depth of the administration's commitment in its turn to Asia as well as a demonstration of the obstacles the administration has faced in achieving it. The chapter will then conclude with a consideration of the implications of US policy for countries and regions outside the TPP negotiations, such as China and Europe.

To preview the conclusion, the administration has been sincere in its desire to emphasize American relations with Asia, but to date it has been consistently unwilling or unable to make the sorts of trade-offs that would give real substance to its rhetoric.

THE STRATEGIC ORIGINS OF THE PIVOT

From an American perspective, the Middle East could well be portrayed as a region of conflict, war, and terror, whereas emerging Asia could be portrayed as the region of the future, offering growth, investment opportunities, and promises of mutual prosperity. Who would not wish to turn from the former to the latter?

As a presidential candidate and before that, Obama had argued that the war in Iraq was unnecessary and unwise. Despite an initial surge of American troops in Afghanistan early in his first term, he was unenthusiastic about prolonged engagement there. The presumption was that his diplomatic focus would be driven by deliberate strategic choices rather than the imperatives of responding to events.

Meanwhile, Asia seemed to offer a great deal. In an initial and exuberant description of the origins of the pivot, Campbell and Ratner[1] describe the 'inescapable gravitational pull' of the Asian region, with its massive population and large and growing economies. They also note promising democratic change in countries of the region as well as a network of existing American military alliances and an important set of security challenges. China, of course, loomed large in American diplomatic sights and was to be a central part of the pivot. India, the second emerging giant in the region, was not a prominent part of the new strategic thinking regarding Asia and is usually treated separately in American foreign policy discussions. India is neither a major strategic competitor nor an ally, and American commerce with India is also relatively small. When India is the subject of diplomatic attention, this tends to be somewhat of a discrete nature (e.g., the civil nuclear agreement) from the pivot. But China was, and remains, a very important trade and investment partner. It also stirred concerns about its strategic intentions as a result of its territorial and maritime claims in the East and South China seas, some of which threaten the interests of American allies[2]. However one felt about China on balance, its uncertain trajectory contributed to a sense that this was a region that merited increased attention.

Five Asian nations—Brunei, Japan, Malaysia, Singapore, and Vietnam—are simultaneously negotiating the TPP and the Regional Comprehensive Economic Partnership (RCEP). The emerging Asian economies not included in the TPP do not expect to be invited anytime soon, and China has now secured endorsement at the Asia Pacific Economic Cooperation summit in 2014 for the importance of the Free Trade Area of the Asia-Pacific (FTAAP), which, despite its actual origins, may now be seen as a Chinese initiative.

In this extraordinarily layered and complex politicoeconomic situation in Asia, how, specifically, does the United States pivot?

COMPONENTS: DIPLOMATIC AND MILITARY

It was not hard to see how a country might pivot away from the Middle East at the beginning of Obama's term; that could be accomplished by decreased military commitments, of the sort the administration pursued in both Iraq and Afghanistan.

But what was required to show enhanced commitment to Asia? The easiest part appeared to be the diplomatic presence in Asia of top administration leaders. Both President George W. Bush and Secretary of State Condoleezza Rice had at various times missed summit meetings in Asia.

Their absences were due to pressing matters elsewhere, but this was portrayed in Asia as improperly relegating the Asian countries to secondary importance. The new Obama team in 2009 was determined to behave differently. It is not clear how much of a change this proved to be in practice, however. In 2013, President Obama had to absent himself when dealing with a budgetary impasse[3], and Secretary of State John Kerry has shown more inclination to attend to crises in the Middle East and Eastern Europe.

Campbell and Ratner note that below the level of top dignitaries, there are human capital resource challenges in effecting a regional pivot:

> After more than a decade of war and counterinsurgency, the United States has developed and promoted an entire generation of soldiers, diplomats, and intelligence specialists well versed in ethnic rivalry in Iraq, the tribal differences in Afghanistan, post conflict reconstruction strategies, and US Special Forces and drone tactics. But Washington has not made any comparable effort to develop a sustained cadre of Asia experts across the US government, and a surprising number of senior government officials make their first visits to the region only once they have reached high-level positions near the end of their careers.

This would be easier to address in expansionary budget times, and if the ranks of the US Foreign Service were growing rapidly. They are not.

Similar budget constraints limited the magnitude of the military pivot to Asia. Could there be a bigger American strategic response in Asia? There is certainly a political push for greater military strength, particularly from the newly expanded Republican majority in Congress. While hawkish political circles advocate a stronger navy to ensure a continuing role in Asian sea-lanes, for example, they simultaneously urge a more robust military presence in the Middle East and on the North Atlantic Treaty Organization's Eastern front. This stems not from an urge to bolster the pivot as such, but rather as part of a call for improved resources to strengthen the American armed forces to support the nation's global strategies. It remains to be seen how these impulses will be reconciled with budget constraints in a Congress displaying an aversion to higher taxation, growing entitlement spending, and fiscal deficits. Hypothesizing the way the pivot must look to Chinese observers (and adopting their imagined voice), the military analyst Kori Schake wrote:

> Good as its military is, fighting two wars has stretched America's capacity, yet they continue to cut it further. The Americans will send to the vast Pacific Ocean a greater percentage of a smaller Navy, amounting to fewer ships. They will rotate a few thousand Marines already assigned to their Pacific Fleet through Australia. They will add no military bases. . . . They force further cuts to their spending. Their defence budget is only 4 percent of GDP, so slight a burden they cannot feel it in so prosperous a country, and yet it plummets[4].

Therefore, in the case of both diplomatic and military pivoting, the Obama administration came up against resource constraints, whether they were the finite time of top diplomats, the limited ranks of junior diplomats, or the budget limitations on military spending and an unwillingness to emphasize defence spending over domestic projects. These constraints left the diplomatic and military components of the pivot looking more symbolic than substantial.

Yet, this did not doom the pivot to emptiness. After all, one common critique of Bush administration policy in Asia was an excessive focus on security matters, especially terrorism, in lieu of commercial matters. As Evan Feigenbaum, a State Department official in the Bush administration put it, 'the business of Asia is business'[5]. Even without new resources to deploy, the Obama administration had the opportunity to invigorate its Asian diplomacy through an emphasis on commercial policy, and new openings to trade and investment would have little budgetary impact. As it turned out, though, such approaches could impose other costs that the Obama team was reluctant to bear.

THE TRANS-PACIFIC PARTNERSHIP: MOTIVES

The TPP now is placed at the centre of the Obama administration's pivot to Asia. As a sprawling trade agreement encompassing twelve countries and promising to set new high standards for global trade regulation, it is easily the most significant component of the policy. It is the one part of the pivot that looks both momentous and new[6]. And yet it remains unfinished and, as of this writing, faces a rocky and uncertain path to completion.

The TPP actually originated before both the Obama administration and the pivot[7]. The agreement began as an undertaking among four countries (Brunei, Chile, New Zealand, and Singapore) in 2005, which set out to create a regional deal that was notable for two features: high standards and openness to new members, and the deal was pursued in stages. By the time the countries were taking on financial services and investment talks in March 2008, the United States asked to sit in. In September 2008, when the United States was engrossed in a presidential election and engulfed by financial chaos, the then US Trade Representative Susan Schwab announced that the United States would commence negotiations to join the TPP. The appeal was not the economic potential of the participants as trading partners. Aside from their small size, the United States already had free trade agreements (FTAs) with Chile and Singapore. Rather, it was the opportunity to push the case for high-standards trade agreements, particularly in the wake of the faltering Doha Round talks of the World Trade Organization (WTO) in summer 2008.

There was supposed to be a negotiating session in March 2009, but one of the Obama administration's early actions was to request a postponement. It wanted both to fill its trade posts and to conduct a review of what it hoped to accomplish in trade policy. The United States would not return to the agreement until November 2009, when Obama announced in Tokyo his intention to 'engage' with 'the goal of shaping' a regional agreement.

US TRADE POLITICS AND THE TRADE PROMOTION AUTHORITY

It is worth remembering that as a presidential candidate, Obama had expressed substantial scepticism about international trade[8]. He asserted that the North American Free Trade Agreement had cost the United States one million jobs and threatened to withdraw from the agreement if Canada and Mexico refused to renegotiate. This scepticism was not only retrospective; it applied as well to three American FTAs that were pending throughout 2008—with South Korea, Panama, and Colombia. Beyond opposition to the Korea-US FTA, the Obama campaign pledged to label China a currency manipulator and promised to reorient US-China policy towards increased enforcement actions against alleged Chinese trade malfeasance.

This distrustful approach to trade played well with organized labour and resonated in politically critical industrial states such as Michigan, Ohio, and Pennsylvania. However, it left the Obama administration in an awkward position once it came into office. How could one reconcile this suspicious approach with concurrent pledges to pursue multilateralism and raise America's standing in the world? If Obama were to embrace a liberal trade agenda in the classical sense, he would endanger his liberal domestic agenda in the modern American sense.

Turning from the TPP for a moment, the tension can be seen in the final congressional votes for the three pending trade agreements. Despite nominally enjoying the protections of the Trade Promotion Authority (TPA)—they were all negotiated before it expired in 2007—the agreements had languished under the Democratic leadership of the House of Representatives. They did not come to a vote until autumn 2011, after the Republican Party had recaptured the House in the 2010 midterm elections. The results of the votes were telling. The agreements that were voted upon had been renegotiated by a popular Democratic president and put forward with his endorsement. Even so, the Panama agreement drew 34.9 percent support from Democrats in the House, Korea drew 31.2 percent, and Colombia only 16.4 percent support. All three passed thanks to overwhelming Republican support (over 91 percent in each case)[9].

The fight over the passage of the three FTAs was highly contentious. In the midst of it, there was an effort by Senate Republicans to grant Obama a renewed TPA, although by then the Obama administration had plunged deep into the TPP negotiations without any mandate from Congress[10]. At the time, Senate Republican Leader Mitch McConnell said, 'Without trade promotion authority, there will be no other trade agreements. We all know that'[11]. Yet the amendment offering a TPA was defeated by the majority Senate Democrats on a fifty-five to forty-five vote, and leading Democrats explained that they needed more time to fashion new negotiating objectives for the TPA. Three years later, at the time of this writing, they are still working on acceptable TPA language. At the end of 2013, three of the four major trade leaders in Congress—Dave Camp, chairman of House Ways and Means; Max Baucus, chairman of Senate Finance; and Orrin Hatch, ranking member of Senate Finance—reached a consensus on a bipartisan TPA bill and seemed to have met White House calls for a TPA at long last.

Then in January 2014, everything fell apart[12]. The two body blows came in rapid succession: Obama dispatched Baucus to Beijing as the new American ambassador. Then in his State of the Union address, Obama devoted only a couple of lines to trade, and neglected to endorse the Camp-Baucus-Hatch TPA bill. The day after the address, Senate Majority Leader Harry Reid indicated that he did not want to take up the TPA before the November 2014 elections[13]. Similar reactions came from the Democratic minority in the House.

The point of this legislative history is to illustrate the third major budget constraint faced by the Obama administration as it contemplates delivering on its commitment to an Asian pivot. If Obama were to push a TPA bill, he would be likely to face the opposition of over 150 members of his own party in the House and would be opposing the wishes of his allies in the Senate. Not coincidentally, he would also incur the wrath of organized labour, a critical electoral ally and vocal opponent of trade agreements and the conventional TPA[14].

The president confronts a 'political capital' budget constraint. If he offends critical constituencies by pushing controversial trade agreements or bills, there could be serious repercussions for the rest of his agenda[15]. His approach has been to pursue trade initiatives as far as he could without drawing upon any political capital. So the negotiations have proceeded with high levels of secrecy. Whether or not this was the intent, secrecy has allowed the administration to assure multiple parties with conflicting interests that the ultimate agreement will be one that they will like. The administration has received ample credit for pursuing an ambitious agenda, but the costs will come if and when the administration tries to pass an actual agreement or bill. It remains to be seen whether any administration with a strong domestic focus would be willing to pay those costs.

THE TRANS-PACIFIC PARTNERSHIP: PROSPECTS

What does this mean for the TPP? While the United States was grappling unsuccessfully with its internal trade politics, the TPP was progressing though participants have been aware throughout about the difficulties of American electoral politics. For some time after the Obama administration rejoined the talks in 2009, there was a target date of November 2011 for the TPP conclusion. That was when the United States hosted the Asia Pacific Economic Cooperation summit in Hawaii, and the date seemed to offer both requisite deadline pressure to conclude a deal and sufficient distance from the 2012 US presidential election.

The deal did not conclude in 2011, of course. But a sense of momentum and excitement has been maintained through steady expansion. Most notably, Canada and Mexico joined the talks in 2012 and after long deliberation, Japan joined in 2013. Japan's entry in particular enhanced both the commercial significance of the talks and their centrality to American diplomacy with regard to Asia. Now the TPP was not just an attempt to set new global trade standards, but was the principal vehicle for resolving US-Japanese economic issues as well as a key element of Prime Minister Shinzo Abe's plans for economic reform. The United States and Japan have engaged in economic negotiations for decades, and these have often been frustrating. The latest version, embedded in the TPP talks, has had its share of disappointments. US-Japan high-level meetings over the last year, at both the head of state and ministerial levels, have concluded without agreement. The impasse has provided an excuse for the failure to conclude the broader talks among all twelve TPP members[16].

In fact, the impasse demonstrates the importance of the TPA battle described above. The Obama administration has steadfastly argued that the TPA is a technicality and its absence does not impede progress in concluding the TPP. It has even floated the idea that a concluded TPP agreement could successfully prod Congress to pass the TPA. The American argument is that each country in the TPP should trust the others to handle the domestic politics necessary to fulfill negotiating commitments.

There has long been an asymmetry in trade negotiations given the United States' distinctive political system. Countries with parliamentary systems are represented by trade ministers whose governing political formations have the votes to deliver on an agreement. In contrast, in the US system, the president does not have formal control over the legislature, and the closest the president can come to demonstrate the legislature's acquiescence is through a formal grant of the requisite negotiating authority. Absent such a grant, trading partners must rely on either a president's demonstrated mastery of the legislature or determine for themselves that the interests of the US president and the US legislature are clearly aligned. In the case of the TPP, neither of these applies. As just one example of the latter point, while the Obama administration has been negotiating the TPP, majorities of each branch of the US Congress have written to the executive demanding that the agreement include enforceable provisions dealing with currency manipulation[17]. Such a provision would be strongly opposed by other countries within the TPP, and there is no indication that the United States has itself raised it in negotiation. This serves as evidence that the administration and the Congress are not necessarily of one mind on trade.

Japanese Prime Minister Abe must be mindful of the experience of his South Korean neighbours. Even with the ostensible protections of a TPA, the Korea-US FTA lingered for four years before renegotiation and signature. Prime Minister Abe is being asked to open up five 'sacred' agricultural sectors in Japan: It would be politically disastrous were he to offer liberalization, only to see the agreement linger for years or be reworked through congressional amendments. Barring an extraordinary degree of trust on the part of the American TPP partners, it would seem that a TPA must precede any final agreement. That would push the TPP perilously close to the US presidential election season even if Obama can resolve political inhibitions about a TPA[18].

Trade policy was always going to be politically difficult for Obama, given the sharply conflicting views of key constituencies within his party. The TPP offered the administration a way to lend substance to an otherwise circumscribed pivot to Asia and to garner credit for an ambitious commercial and foreign policy agenda. But this was done on credit, in the other sense of the word. The enthusiasm was based not on the act of negotiation but on the promise of a successful conclusion and implementation. The TPP's central role in the pivot to Asia has dramatically raised the stakes on trade. In a landscape of competing trade agreements, such as the RCEP and the FTAAP, the costs to the United States of stalled or failed TPP negotiations would be likely to extend well beyond the commercial realm.

US POLICY TOWARDS NON-TRANS-PACIFIC PARTNERSHIP COUNTRIES

The TPP's role as the most salient feature of the Obama administration's Asian pivot policy begs the question of what it means when important Asian countries are excluded from the agreement. The most vigorous discussion has taken place in the context of China. There are two prominent reasons given for China's exclusion from the TPP: one geostrategic and one economic.

The geostrategic reason focuses on a perceived competition between the United States and China for the role of regional hegemon. In this narrative, the United States is manoeuvring to encircle China and to cement alliances with China's neighbours that ensure American primacy in Asia. Given the security aspects of the Asian pivot and the regional tensions that have occurred during the prolonged TPP negotiations, it can be difficult to separate the commercial and military prongs of the pivot[19]. Yet the Obama administration has consistently disavowed a strategic motivation behind China's exclusion from the TPP. There is a simpler, economic explanation. When asked why China was not in the TPP, US Trade Representative Michael Froman replied, 'Our goal is to have high standards. It's not worth it to have another country join just to lower the standards'[20].

This was a cost-benefit analysis that the United States had performed with each major new entrant into the TPP talks. When Vietnam joined, it offered a combination of an appealing large market against a daunting set of issues involving labour, human rights, and state-owned enterprises. When Canada joined, it offered the United States the opportunity to harmonize trade rules with its top trading partner, but that was set against anticipated difficulties in reaching agreement on dairy trade liberalization that was particularly important for New Zealand. Japan offered an enormous market and the potential for reaching long-standing reform goals, but at the cost of dramatically increased negotiating difficulty. Each of these decisions required prolonged deliberation in Washington. The length and the difficulty of those deliberations increased in proportion to the economic heft of the partners; it had little or no relation to the strength of the security relationship between the United States and the new applicants. Even South Korea, a close ally with whom the United States recently concluded an FTA, has been told to wait, given the complexities of adding a new member to the negotiations.

All of these new entrants to the TPP, it is worth remembering, essentially share the commitment of the United States and other TPP members to a 'high standards' trade agreement—that is, one that involves substantial commitments on topics such as investment, services, intellectual property, and regulation. China, on the other hand, was on the other side of this debate in the 2008 Doha Round talks, when it allied with India and backed the case for lesser obligations for developing countries.

It is fair to say that the TPP is targeted at China, but only in the sense that one of its central goals is to establish new ambitious standards to govern global trade, and there is a strong sense that China is not yet ready to adopt such standards at this time. If the TPP works according to plan, China would then be presented with a *fait accompli*—it would be welcome to join, as long as it is willing to sign up to the new rules. This is distinctly different from a strategic encirclement, a policy that would, in any case, be opposed by a number of other TPP participants and could alienate many non-TPP Asian nations as well.

There are at least two important issues concerning the possibility of eventual Chinese accession. The first and most basic is an accession protocol. As with other aspects of the TPP negotiations, this has not been publicly discussed. If it follows the WTO accession approach, it would portend a challenging discussion when China declares itself ready. The struggle to grant China so-called Permanent Normal Trading Relations in the United States in 2000 was significant and would indicate serious challenges for Chinese accession.

The second, more subtle, issue concerns the nature of the TPP agreement itself. If the vision is to establish a set of high standards to which future entrants must adhere, it will matter a great deal how uniform and transparent those standards prove to be. If, for example, there is a single set of market access rules, then it would be difficult for a new entrant to argue for a deviation from those rules. The challenge for the United States is that this runs up against the 'political capital' budget constraint. A uniform set of market access rules could involve granting the Australia sugar market access equivalent to that enjoyed by Mexico. This would dramatically increase the degree of difficulty of passing the TPP, and the United States has reportedly argued instead for leaving bilateral market access agreements in place where they already exist. While politically convenient, such a stance forgoes the potential benefits of harmonization and leaves it unclear just how any negotiations with China would proceed. If each of the TPP members end up enjoying individual carve outs, why would China not demand the same?

Of course, China has not simply waited for the United States to let it in, and it has worked to craft alternative trade configurations in Asia that favour its interests. The RCEP and the proposed China, Japan, and Korea agreement notably exclude the United States, while China's recent renewal of the push for a FTAAP seems an effort to supersede the TPP. These efforts have stoked arguments within the United States that may grow more heated over time. Those who take a more strategic view of Asian relations bemoan the potentially less-favourable configurations of East Asian architecture and argue for either leniency in TPP demands with existing partners, or the early admission of China into negotiations. Those who take a more economic view counter that the resulting dilution of the TPP would undermine the central purpose of the endeavour. Either way, the United States is highly cognizant of China's presence, even if China does not have a seat at the TPP negotiating table.

As for non-trade issues, of great concern to emerging Asian nations is the 'congagement' factor—a combination of containment and engagement towards China—that was believed implicit in the pivot policy. American strategic allies such as Japan, the Republic of Korea, and the Philippines welcomed the pivot; most of the other Asians are agnostic; and India, whatever its misgivings about China, is apprehensive of the reentry of a super-power in East Asia. These factors open up several questions about how any non-trade pivot will play across Asia.

US POLICY TOWARDS NON-TRANS-PACIFIC PARTNERSHIP COUNTRIES: EUROPE

Apart from the Asian region, the question of harmonization and standards applies as well to the European Union. After the TPP talks were well underway, the United States and Europe agreed to pursue their own mega-regional agreement, the Trans-Atlantic Trade and Investment Partnership (TTIP). In early and optimistic visions, the TPP would have concluded before the TTIP talks had advanced very far. Perhaps this is why relatively little attention seems to have been paid to coordinating the two, even though there are vast overlaps in the likely areas of coverage of the two agreements. As it has turned out, the talks are proceeding simultaneously but independently, though there is still an expectation on the American side that the TPP will precede the TTIP.

This would not be problematic if there was a binary choice between 'high' and 'low' standards and those favouring the former were always in agreement. The TTIP talks show very clearly that this is not the case. While both the United States and Europe strongly favour high standards, they differ with each other over important matters such as the treatment of financial services, the scientific basis for regulation, and investor-state dispute settlement mechanisms[21].

The United States certainly does not wish to exclude Europe from Asia, neither through its pivot nor through the TPP. There is a strong presumption that the United States and Europe share common goals in the region. In the WTO talks, the United States and Europe were together in pushing for a high-standard multilateral trade agreement that asked the developing world to offer substantial liberalization. When that effort faltered, the alternative approach was to persuade key developing nations of the virtue of ambitious and deep trade agreements. This means that American and European efforts can be complementary in a way that would not have been true in decades past. When tariffs were the key topic of discussion, preferential access for one region would generally be granted at the expense of the other. Now, while it is possible to grant preferential access through something like financial services regulation, it is more likely that a change in emerging market policies will benefit both the negotiating partner and others. This 'public good' aspect of high-standards liberalization dramatically lessens the extent to which the United States and Europe are competing through their commercial diplomacy in the region. The commonality of purpose is demonstrated, in part, by the simultaneous negotiation of the TTIP talks covering many of the same topics. However, achieving a common result through the parallel pursuit of two independent trade agreements will be a significant challenge.

CONCLUSION

The Obama administration was sincere in its desire to heighten the importance of Asia in American diplomacy. In practice, however, it has had difficulty taking actions commensurate with this wish. At each turn, it has encountered budget constraints of one sort or another. The limits on the time of the president and the secretary of state have meant that Asia has once again been pushed back in the face of domestic political battles or crises in other parts of the world. Resource constraints and a desire to deemphasize defence after prolonged military engagement in the Middle East have meant that the military component of the Asian pivot has been so far difficult to perceive. Finally, the 'political capital' constraint has forced Obama to choose between seeking trade negotiating authority, and thereby laying the groundwork for a path-breaking regional agreement or maintaining important domestic political alliances. To date, he has chosen to maintain the domestic political alliances. On the trade front, it is possible that in the future the political landscape could shift in such a way as to permit the successful conclusion of the TPP. The question is whether the United States' Asian partners in the TPP will have been patient enough to wait.

NOTES

1. Kurt M. Campbell and Ely Ratner, 'Far Eastern Promises: Why Washington Should Focus on Asia', *Foreign Affairs* (May/June 2014).

2. See, for example, the reports of the USA-China Economic and Security Review Commission.

3. David Nakamura, 'Obama Cancels the Rest of Asia Trip, Citing Difficulties of Travel During Shutdown', *Washington Post*, 4 October 2013.

4. Kori Schake, 'All Your Pivots Belong to Us', *Foreign Policy* (12 September 2014).

5. Evan Feigenbaum, 'America Risks Being Left Vehind in Asia', *Financial Times* (11 November 2009).

6. Note, though, that it is not a unique approach that distinguishes Asia from other regions. The United States is simultaneously pursuing the Trans-Atlantic Trade and Investment Partnership (TTIP) with Europe, an agreement with similar scope and ambition.

7. For an early recounting, see Claude Barfield and Philip I. Levy, 'President Obama and the Transpacific Partnership', *AEI International Economic Outlook*, no. 2 (December 2009).

8. See Philip I. Levy, 'Doing a Job on NAFTA', *The American* (6 March 2008).

9. See Philip I. Levy, 'With Dems Souring Further on Trade, Obama Unlikely to Push More Deals', *AEIdeas* (13 October 2011).

10. Under the USA Constitution, Article 1, Section 8, it is Congress that has the power to regulate trade. For decades, Congress has found ways to partially delegate this authority to the executive branch for both practical reasons and to avoid the sort

of parochial approach that can dominate a legislature. The TPA is the modern incarnation of this long-standing effort.

11. Doug Palmer, 'Senate Rejects Trade Promotion Authority for Obama', *Reuters* (20 September 2011).

12. See Philip I. Levy, 'Is Obama even Trying on Trade?' *Foreign Policy* (29 January 2014).

13. Richard McGregor and Geoff Dyer, 'Trade Backlash Leaves US "Pivot" to Asia on the Rocks', *Financial Times* (31 January 2014).

14. See Jackie Tortora, 'Trumka: Fast Track Trade Promotion is "Undemocratic" and "Bad for American Workers"', *AFL-CIO Now* (9 January 2014).

15. The three 2011 trade votes came only after strong pressure from Republicans in Congress.

16. See Krista Hughes, 'Mexico Sees U.S.-Japan Deal Key to Pacific Trade Pact Progress', *Reuters* (14 October 2014).

17. See Philip I. Levy, 'The Missing Trade Advance Team', *Foreign Policy* (18 November 2013).

18. See Philip I. Levy, (2014), 'The Trans-Pacific Partnership Isn't Going to Happen Any Time Soon', *Foreign Policy* (25 July 2014).

19. See Robert S. Ross, 'The Problem with the Pivot', *Foreign Affairs* (November/December 2012) for a partial description of the security tensions between the United States and China.

20. Emma Green, 'U.S. to China: Play by Our Economic Rules', *Atlantic* (13 November 2013).

21. On this last point, it is not even clear that Europe will pursue the same approach with the United States that it has just taken in its agreement with Canada.

Bibliography

Akiner, Shirin (ed.). 'The Caspian: Politics, Energy and Security'. Central Asia Research Forum. London: Routledge, 2004.

Andaya, Leonard. 'The Search for the "Origins" of Malayu'. *Journal of Southeast Asia Studies* 32-33 (2001): 315–30.

Andersen, Walter. 'Recent Trends in Indian Foreign Policy'. *Asian Survey* 41, no. 5 (2001).

Anthony, Ian. 'The European Union and a Nuclear-Free Korean Peninsula: A European Perspective'. *Jeju PeaceNet* (11 March 2013).

Ash, Timothy Garton. 'The Crisis of Europe. How the Union Came Together and Why It's Falling Apart'. *Foreign Affairs* 91, no. 5 (September/October 2012).

Asia Europe People Forum 2014. 'Examining the EU-ASEAN Free Trade Agreement (FTA)'. www.aepf.info/campaigns/eu-asean-fta/33-examining-the-eu-asean-free-trade-agreement-fta. Accessed 8 June 2014.

Association of Southeast Asian Nations and World Bank. 'ASEAN Integration Monitoring Report'. ASEAN Integration Monitoring Office and the Office of the Chief Economist—East Asia and Pacific Region on the World Bank. Jakarta: ASEAN Secretariat, 2013.

Association of Southeast Asian Nations Economic Community Chartbook 2012, quoted from Jayant Menon, 'PANEL – EU-ASEAN Relations in the Changing Global Economic Order.' Presented at the EU-ASEAN Economic & Policy Forum, ASEAN Secretariat, Jakarta, 18 April 2013.

Bae, C., et al. 'The Impact of Free Trade Agreements on Economic Performance in Korea.' *Research Report* 12-03. Seoul: Korea Institute for International Economic Policy, 2012.

Bainbridge, Mark, Philip B. Whyman, and Brian Buckitt. *Moored to the Continent? Future Options for Britain and the EU*. Exeter: Imprint Academie, 2012.

Balbina, Hwang. 'A New Horizon in Korea-Central Asia Relations. The ROK joins the Great Game'. *Korea Compass* (December 2012).

Baldwyn, Peter. *The Narcissism of Minor Differences. How America and Europe are Alike*. New York: Oxford University Press, 2009.

Balme, Richard, and Brian Bridges (eds.). *Europe-Asia Relations: Building Multilateralisms*. New York: Palgrave Macmillan, 2008.

Barber, James. 'Britain and India: A Continuing Relationship'. *The World Today* 42, no. 8-9 (August–September 1986): 133–36.

Barfield, Claude, and Philip I. Levy. 'President Obama and the Transpacific Partnership'. *AEI International Economic Outlook*, no. 2 (December 2009).

Basu, Shrabani. *Re-Imagine: India-UK Cultural Relations in the 21st Century*. London: Bloomsbury Publishing, 2014.

Berkofsky, Axel. 'The European Union in North Korea: Player or only Payer?' *Policy Brief No. 123*, Instituto per gli studi di politica internazionale (March 2009).

Bersick, Sebastian, and Paul van der Velde. *The Asia-Europe Meeting: Contributing to a New Global Governance Architecture. The Eighth ASEM Summit in Brussels*. ICAS Publications Series. Amsterdam: Amsterdam University Press, 2011.

Bhutan Foreign Policy and Government Guide. Global Investment and Business Center, Inc. Staff, Ibp USA. International Business Publication, 2000.

Bickerton, Christopher J. *European Union Foreign Policy*. Basingstoke: Palgrave Macmillan, 2011.

Black, Brian, Gavin Hyman, and Graham M. Smith (eds.). *Confronting Secularism in Europe and India: Legitimacy and Disenchantment in Contemporary Times*. London: Bloomsbury Publishing, 2014.

Blockmans, Steven, et al. 'Towards a Eurasian Economic Union: The Challenge of Integration and Unity.' *CEPS Special Report No. 75*. Brussels: Centre for European Policy Studies, December 2012.

Bond, Ian. 'Out of Range, Out of Mind: Is There a Role for Europe in the Korean Crisis?' Centre for European Reform, 12 April 2013.

Boulnois, Luce. *Silk Road: Monks, Warriors & Merchants*. Geneva: Odyssey Books & Guide, 2012.

Bull, Hedley, and Roger William Louis (eds.). *The Special Relationship and Anglo-American Relations since 1945*. Oxford: Clarendon Press, 1986.

Bunce, Valerie. *Subversive Institutions*. New York: Cambridge University Press, 1999.

Buzan, Barry. *People, States & Fear: An Agenda for International Security Studies in the Post Cold War Era*. New York: Harvester Wheatsheaf, 1991.

Cai, Fangbai. 'The European Situation and China-Europe Relations, 2008'. *Chinese Journal of European Studies*, no. 2 (2009).

Calleo, David P. *Rethinking Europe's Future*. Princeton: Princeton University Press, 2001.

Cameron, Fraser. *An Introduction to European Foreign Policy*. Abingdon: Routledge, 2012.

Campbell, Kurt M., and Ely Ratner. 'Far Eastern Promises: Why Washington Should Focus on Asia'. *Foreign Affairs* (May-June 2014).

Cardenal, Juan Pablo, and Heriberto Araujo. *China's Silent Army*. London: Allen Lane, 2013.

Casarini, Nicola. 'EU-Korea Cooperation in Northeast Asia Peace and Security'. Korea-EU Strategic Partnership and the Trust-Building Process on the Korean Peninsula. HUFS-HRI EU Centre, 25 April 2013.

Chareonwongsak, Kriengsak. 'Yuttasat Settakij Thai Su Settakij Raidai Sung' (Thailand's Economic Strategies Toward a High Income Country). Stock Exchange of Thailand, 23 April 2014.

Chen, Zhimin. 'The EU as a Limited Strategic Actor and China-EU Strategic Partnership'. *International Perspective*, no. 5 (2006).

Christiansen, Thomas, Emil Kirchner, and Philomena Murray (eds.). *The Palgrave Handbook of EU-Asia Relations*. Basingstoke: Palgrave, 2013.

Clutterbuck, Lindsay, and Richard Warnes. 'Exploring Patterns of Behaviour in Violent Jihadist Terrorists: An Analysis of Six Significant Terrorist Conspiracies in the UK'. RAND Corporation, 2011.

Cohen, Stephen P. *The Future of Pakistan*. Washington, DC: Brookings Institution Press, 2011.

Coker, Christopher. 'Post-Modernity and the End of the Cold War'. *Review of International Studies* 18, no. 3 (July 1992).

Collier, Paul. 'Why the WTO is Deadlocked: And What Can Be Done about It'. *World Economy*, no. 1 (2006): 1423–49.

Commission of the European Communities. *Towards a New Asia Strategy*. Brussels: Author, 1994.

Communication of the European Commission. *A Long-Term Policy for China-Europe Relations*. COM 279/final, 1995.

Conley, Heather A. 'The End of the West: the Once and Future Europe'. *International Affairs* 87, no 4 (2011): 975–84.

Constancio, Vitor. 'Growth Challenges for Asia and Europe'. *Asia Europe Economic Forum*, 15 May 2014.

Cooper, Robert. *The Post-Modern State and World Order*. London: Demos, 2002.

———. 'Britain and Europe'. *International Affairs* 88, no. 6 (2012):1191–203.

Council of European Union. *The EU-China Strategic Partnership: Council Conclusions*. Brussels, 11–12 December 2006.

————. *Guidelines on the EU's Foreign and Security Policy in East Asia*. Brussels, 20 December 2007.

————. *Report on the Implementation of the European Security Strategy: Providing Security in a Changing World*. Brussels, S407/08, 11 December 2008.

————. *Joint Statement of the 12th EU-China Summit*. Nanjing, 30 November 2009. www.consilium.europa.eu/uedocs/cms_Data/docs/pressdata/en/er/111567.pdf. Accessed 18 June 2014.

————. *Guidelines on the EU's Foreign and Security Policy in East Asia*. 15 June 2012.

da Silva, Jorge Tavares. *Europe Giving Shape to an Idea*. Gurgaon: Anthem Press, 2009.

Denninson, Susi, et al. 'Why Europe Needs a New Global Strategy'. *Policy Brief*, European Council on Foreign Relations. www.ecfr.eu/page/-/ECFR90_STRATEGY_BRIEF_AW.pdf. Accessed 17 July 2014.

Dettmer, Bianka, Fredrik Erixon, Andreas Freytag, and Pierre-Olivier Tremblay. 'The Dynamics of Structural Change'. *Chinese Economy* 44, no. 4 (2011): 42–74.

Dosch, J. 'Multilateralism and the European Role Towards the Korean Peninsula: Can European Experiences Serve asa Model for Conflict Resolution?' First Jeju Peace Institute-FNF-KF Joint Workshop, October 2007.

Duchâtel, Mathieu. 'The EU's Security Role in Northeast Asia'. Korea-EU Cooperation for Peace and Regional Development in Northeast Asia. HUFS-HRI EU Centre, 24 April 2014.

Dumbrell, John. *A Special Relationship: Anglo-American Relations in the Cold War and After*. Basingstoke: Macmillan, 2001.

El-Agraa, Ali M. *The European Union*. Cambridge: Cambridge University Press, 2011.

Elsig, M., and C. Dupont. 'European Union Meets South Korea: Bureaucratic Interests, Exporter Discrimination and the Negotiations of Trade Agreements'. *Journal of Common Market Studies* 50, no. 3 (2012): 492–507.

European Centre for Development Policy Management. 'EU, China and Africa: A Trilateral Partnership in Theory, a Bilateral One in Practice?' *EU-Africa E-Alert*, no. 9 (Maastricht: ECDPM) (2007). www.ecdpm.org. Accessed 9 January 2015.

European Commission. 'Towards a New Asia Strategy'. Communication from the Commission, COM (94) 314 final, Brussels, 1994.

————. 'Europe and Asia: A Strategic Framework for Enhanced Partnership'. COM (2001) 469 final, 4 September 2001.

European External Action Service. 'The EU-ASEAN Relationship in Twenty Facts and Figures'. (October 2013). eeas.europa.eu/asean/docs/key_facts_figures_eu_asean_en.pdf. Accessed 30 June 2014.

European Union. *The EU in the World 2013*. Brussels: Author, 2012.

————. *The European Union and the Republic of Korea—A Statistical Portrait*. Luxembourg: Publications Office of the European Union, 2012.

Eurostat External and Intra-EU Trade. *Statistical Yearbook*, data 1958–2008.

Fabius, Laurent. 'France's Policy in Asia'. Speech transcribed. ASEAN Secretariat, Jakarta, 12 August 2013.

Falkner, Robert. 'The Political Power of Normative Europe. EU Environmental Leadership in International Biotechnology Regulation'. *Journal of European Public Policy* 14, no. 4 (June 2007): 507–26.

Fawcett, J. E. S. *The Inters se doctrine of Commonwealth Relations*. London: Athlone Press, Institute of Commonwealth Studies, 1958.

Feigenbaum, Evan. 'America Risks being Left Behind in Asia'. *Financial Times*, 11 November 2009.

Feng Zhongping. 'The EU Adjusts its China Policy'. *Current Affairs Report*, no. 1 (2008).

————. 'China-Europe Relations: Co-existence of Opportunities and Challenges'. *Current Affairs Report*, no 12 (2006).

————. 'Partnership is not Doubted.' *Global Times* (13 February 2009).

Fernandez, Haizam Ahmiraand, and Richard Youngs. *The Euro-Mediterranean Partnership. Assessing the First Decade*. Madrid: FRIDE, 2005.

Fitriani, Evi. 'Asian Perceptions about EU in Asia-Europe Meeting (ASEM)'. *Asia-Europe Journal* 9 (2011): 43–56.
———. 'EU FTA Strategy and Southeast Asia: Indonesia Perspective'. International Conference on Proactive EU FTA Strategy and EU-Asian Economic Interactions. Taipei: National Chengchi University, 27 May 2014.
———. 'The Impact of the EU Crisis on EU-ASEAN Relations'. *Geopolitics, History, and International Relations* 6, no. 1 (2014): 78–93.
Foreign and Commonwealth Office. *The UK and China: A Framework for Engagement.* January 2009.
Fox, John, and François Godement. 'A Power Audit of EU-China Relations'. European Council of Foreign Relations, 2009. ecfr.3cdn.net/532cd91d0b5c9699ad_ozm6b9bz4. Accessed 3 August 2014.
FPRC Journal. India European Union Relations. E-book. New Delhi: Foreign Policy Research Centre, 2013.
Gaens, Bart (ed.). *Europe-Asia Interregional Relations: A Decade of ASEM.* Burlington: Ashgate Publishing Company, 2008.
Gaens, Bart, Juha Jokela, and Eija Limnell (eds.) *The Role of European Union in Asia: China and India as Strategic Partners.* Burlington: Ashgate Publishing Limited, 2009.
Gamble, Andrew. 'Better Off Out? Britain and Europe'. *The Political Quarterly* 83, no. 3 (2012): 468–72.
Ganon, Joseph E., and Ken Troutman. *Internationalization of the Remninbi: The Role of Trade Settlements.* Peterson Institute Policy Brief Number 14–15, 2015.
Garcia, Maria. 'Fears and Strategies: The European Union, China and Their Free Trade Agreements in East Asia'. *Journal of Contemporary European Research* 6, no. 4 (2010): 496–513.
———. 'From Bottom of the Pyramid to Top Priority: Explaining Asia in the EU's Free Trade Agreement (FTA) Strategy'. *Australia New Zealand Journal of European Studies* 4, no. 1 (2012): 42–58.
Geddes, Andrew. *The European Union and British Politics.* London: Palgrave Macmillan, 2004.
Ginsburg, Tom. 'Eastphalia as a Return to Westphalia'. University of Chicago Public Law and Legal Theory Working Paper No. 292, 2010.
Godement, Francois, 'A Global China Policy'. European Council on Foreign Relations, June 2010.
———. 'Divided Asia: The Implications for Europe'. *Policy Brief.* European Council on Foreign Relations, 2013.
Goh, Beng-Lan. 'Redrawing Centre-Periphery Relations: Theoretical Challenges in the Study of Southeast Asian Modernity'. In *Asia in Europe, Europe in Asia*, edited by Srilata Ravi, Mario Rutten, and Beng-Lan Goh, 79–101. Singapore: ISEAS, 2004.
Grant, Charles, and Katinka Barysch. *Can Europe and China Shape a New World Order?* London: Centre for European Reform, 2008.
Gratius, Susanne. 'Can EU Strategic Partnerships Deepen Multilateralism?' Madrid: FRIDE, September 2011.
Green, Emma. 'U.S. to China: Play by Our Economic Rules'. *Atlantic* (13 November 2013).
Grevi, Giovanni (ed.). 'Mapping EU Strategic Partnerships'. Brussels: FRIDE, 2011.
Grigoriev, L. M., and M. R. Salikhov. *GUAM, Piatnadsat' Let Spustia.* Moscow: Regnum, 2007.
Habermas, Jurgen. *The Divided West.* Cambridge: Polity, 2006.
———. *The Crisis of the EU.* Cambridge: Polity, 2012.
Hadi, Syamsul. *Strategi Pembangunan Mahathir and Suharto: Politik Industrialisasi dan Modal jepang di Malaysia and Indonesia.* Jakarta: Pelangi cendekia and Japan Foundation, 2005.
Han, Intaek. 'South Korea-European Union Security Cooperation: A South Korean Perspective'. *JPI PeaceNet*, no. 3 (20 March 2013).

Hellyer, H. A. *Muslims of Europe: The 'Other' Europeans*. Edinburgh: Edinburgh University Press, 2009.

Hennessy, Peter. *The New Protective State*. London: Continuum, 2007.

Hill, Christopher, and Sarah Beadle. *The Art of Attraction, Soft Power and the UK's Role in the World*. British Academy, 2014.

Hill, Christopher, and Michael Smith. *International Relations and the European Union*. Oxford: Oxford University Press, 2nd edition, 2011.

Hill, Christopher. 'The Capability-Expectations Gap or Conceptualizing Europe's International Role'. *Journal of Common Market Studies* 31, no. 3 (1993): 305–28.

———. *The National Interest in Question: Foreign Policy in Multicultural Societies*. Oxford: Oxford University Press, 2013.

Her Majesty's Government. 'Securing Britain in an Age of Uncertainty'. *The Strategic Defense and Security Review*, 2010.

House of Lords. *Stars and Dragons: The EU and China*. European Union Committee 7th Report of Session 2009–2010. London: The Stationery Office Limited, 2010.

Hud, Bohdan. 'Eastern Policy of the European Union: Step by Step towards Ukraine'. In *Introduction to European Studies: A New Approach to Uniting Europe*, edited by D. Milczarek, A. Adamczyk, and K. Zajaczkowski. Warsaw: Centre for Europe, University of Warsaw, 2013, 529–42.

Hughes, Krista. 'Mexico Sees U.S.-Japan Deal Key to Pacific Trade Pact Progress'. *Reuters*, 14 October 2014.

Hwee, Yeo Lay. 'Dimensions of Asia-Europe Cooperation'. *Asia Europe Journal* 2 (2004): 19–31.

Iggers, Georg, and Edward Wang. *Global History of Modern Historiography*. New Delhi: Pearson Educational, New Delhi, 2008.

Ismailzade, Fariz. 'China's Relations with Azerbaijan'. *China and Eurasia Forum Quarterly* 5, no. 1 (2007).

Jacques, Martin. *When China Rules the World: The Rise of the Middle Kingdom and the End of the Western World*. London: Allen Lane, 2009.

Jain, Rajendra K., and Shreya Pandey. 'The EU in the Eyes of India'. *Asia Europe Journal*. Published online (12 September 2010).

Jitsuchon, Somchai. 'Sources and Pro-Poorness of Thailand's Economic Growth'. *Thammasat Economic Journal* 24, no. 3 (2006): 68–105.

———. 'Thailand in a Middle-Income Trap'. *TDRI Quarterly Review* 27, no. 2 (2012): 13–20.

Johnson, Jo, and Rajiv Kumar (eds.). *Reconnecting Britain and India: Ideas for an Enhanced Partnership*. New Delhi: Academic Foundation, 2011.

Kagan, Robert. *Of Paradise and Power: America and Europe in the New World Order*. New York: Alfred A. Knopf, 2003.

Kalytchak, Roman, and Andriy Semonovych, 'European Union Enlargement—An Unfinished Business?' In *Introduction to European Studies: A New Approach to Uniting Europe*, edited by D. Milczarek, A. Adamczyk, and K. Zajaczkowski. Warsaw: Centre for Europe, University of Warsaw, 2013, 543–58.

Kamath, P. M. *Nuclear Disarmament: Regional Perspectives on Progress*. Bingley, United Kingdom: Emerald, 2013.

Kang Y. 'EU's New Trade Policy and Implications'. *World Economy Update* 11, no. 4 (2011), Korea Institute for International Economic Policy.

Kang, Yudeok, and Junyeop Kim. *KIEP World Economy Update* 13, no. 18 (27 August 2013), Korea Institute for International Economic Policy.

Kapur, H. *China and the EEC: The New Connection*. Dordrecht: Martinus Nijhoff, 1986.

Kawasaki, Kenichi. 'The Relative Significance of EPAs in Asia-Pacific'. *RIETI Discussion Paper Series* 14-E-009, January 2014.

Kelly, E. Robert. 'Korea–European Union Relations: Beyond the FTA?' *International Relations of the Asia-Pacific* 12 (2012): 101–32.

Keohane, R. 'Reciprocity in International Relations'. *International Organization* 40, no. 1 (Winter 1986).

Keukeleire, Stephan, and Jennifer MacNaughtan. *The Foreign Policy of the European Union*. Basingstoke: Palgrave Macmillan, 2008.

Khandekar, Gauri. *Mapping EU-ASEAN Relations*. Brussels: FRIDE, 2014.

Khosla, Inder Pal. *India and the New Europe*. Delhi: Konark, 2004.

Kibria, Nazli. *Muslims in Motion: Islam and National Identity in the Bangladeshi Diaspora*. New Brunswick, NJ: Rutgers University Press, 2011

Ko, Sangtu. 'Korea's Opportunity in the Crisis'. *Asia Europe Journal* 9, no. 2–4 (2012): 225–36.

———. 'Korea's Middle Power Activism and Peacekeeping Operations'. *Asia Europe Journal* 10, no. 4 (2012): 287–99.

Kojin, Karatani. *The Structure of World History: From Modes of Production to Modes of Exchange*. Durham, NC: Duke University Press, 2014.

Kongcharoen, Chalermpong. 'Rabob Settakij Thai Korn Wikridtakarn Karnngurn Por. Sor. 2540 (Por. Sor. 2530-2540)' [Thailand's Economic System before the Financial Crisis 1997 (1987–1997)]. Bangkok: Thailand Research Fund and Faculty of Economics, Thammasat University, 2010.

Korosteleva, E. A (ed.). *Eastern Partnership: A New Opportunity for the Neighbours?* London: Routledge, 2011.

Krotz, Ulrich. 'Momentum and Impediments: Why Europe won't Emerge as a Full Political Actor on the World Stage Soon'. *Journal of Common Market Studies* 47, no. 3 (June 2009): 555–78.

Kwa, Chong Guan, Derek Heng, and Tai Yong Tan. *Singapore, A 700-year History: From Early Emporium to World City*. Singapore: National Archives of Singapore, 2009.

Lamy, Pascal. *L'Europe en Premier Ligne*. Paris: Seuil, 2003.

Laruelle, Marlene, and Sebastian Peyrouse. *The Chinese Question in Central Asia*. London: Hurst Publishers, 2014.

Laurence, Jonathan. *The Emancipation of Europe's Muslims: The State's Role in Minority Integration*. Princeton Studies in Muslim Politics. Princeton, NJ: Princeton University Press, 2011.

Lee, M. 'A Step as Normative Power: The EU's Human Rights Policy towards North Korea'. *Asia Europe Journal* 1, no. 1 (2012): 41–56.

Lelieveldt, Herman, and Sebastiaan Princen. *The Politics of the European Union*. Cambridge: Cambridge University Press, 2011.

Leonard, Mark. *Why Europe will Run the 21st Century*. London: Fourth Estate, 2005.

Lerais, Frederic, Mattias Levin, Myriam Sochacki, and Reinhilde Veugelers. *China, EU and the World: Growing In Harmony?* Luxembourg: European Commission, Office for Official Publications of European Communities, 2007.

Levy, Philip I. 'Doing a Job on NAFTA'. *The American*, 6 March 2008.

———. 'With Dems Souring Further on Trade, Obama Unlikely to Push More Deals'. *AEIdeas*, 13 October 2011.

———. 'The Missing Trade Advance Team'. *Foreign Policy*, 18 November 2013.

———. 'Is Obama even Trying on Trade?' *Foreign Policy*, 29 January 2014.

———. 'The Trans-Pacific Partnership Isn't Going to Happen Any Time Soon'. *Foreign Policy*, 25 July 2014.

Li, Yonghui. 'Powerful China and Changing China-Europe Relations'. *Contemporary International Relations*, no. 12 (2007).

Lu, Chenyang. 'Analysis of the Recent China-Europe Difficulties'. *World Economics and Politics Forum*, no. 2 (2009).

Luft, Gal, and Anne Korin. *Energy Security Challenges for the 21st Century*. Santa Barbara, CA: Greenwood Publishing House, 2009.

Maddison, Angus. *Contours of the World Economy, 1-2030 AD*. New York: Oxford University Press, 2007.

Maier-Kanpp, Naila. 'The European Union as a Normative Actor and its External Relations with Southeast Asia'. *Journal of Contemporary European Research* 10, no. 2 (2014).

Malhotra, Rashpal, Sucha Singh Gill, and Neetu Gaur (eds.). *Perspectives on Bilateral and Regional Cooperation. South and Central Asia*. Chandigarh: Centre for Research in Rural and Industrial Development, 2013.

Malone, David M. *Does the Elephant Dance? Contemporary Indian Foreign Policy*. London: Oxford University Press, 2011.

Marquand, David. *The End of the West: The Once and Future Europe*. Princeton, NJ: Princeton University Press, 2011.

Marsh, David. *The Euro*. New Haven, CT: Yale University Press, 2011.

Marx, Axel, et al. 'EU–Korea Relations in a Changing World Project: Main Results and Recommendations'. *Asia Europe Journal* (December 2013).

Mayall, James (ed.). *The Contemporary Commonwealth: An Assessment 1946–2009*. Abingdon: Routledge, 2010.

Mayall, James, and Anthony Payne (eds.). *The Fallacies of Hope: The Post-Colonial Record of the Commonwealth Third World*. Manchester: Manchester University Press, 1991.

Mayall, James, and Krishnan Srinivasan. *Towards the New Horizon*. New Delhi: Standard Publishers, 2009.

McGregor, Richard, and Geoff Dyer. 'Trade Backlash Leaves US 'Pivot' to Asia on the Rocks'. *Financial Times*, 31 January 2014.

Mei, Zhaorong. 'New Perspectives on China-Europe Relations'. *Hongqi Wengao*, no. 4 (2009).

Meissner, Katharina. 'Unlocking the Potential of Interregionalism: Mutual Perceptions and Interests in EU-ASEAN Relations'. Policy paper from the working group on EU-ASEAN relations in the Young Initiative on Foreign Affairs and International Relations (IFAIR) think tank. www.euractiv.com/global-europe/practical-way-forward-eu-asean-. Accessed 16 March 2014.

Messerlin, Patrick. 'North East Asia Peace and Cooperation Initiative: A European Perspective'. Korea-EU Cooperation for Peace and Regional Development in Northeast Asia, hosted by HUFS-HRI EU Centre, 24 April 2014.

Ministry of Trade, Industry & Energy. '2nd Anniversary of Korea-EU FTA'. Seoul: MTIEP (21 June 2013).

Mishra, Vidya Nivas, and Rafael Argullo. *From the Ganges to the Mediterranean*. Gurgaon: Shubhi Publications, 2008.

Modwel, Suman, and Surendra Singh. 'The EU-India FTA Negotiations'. *ORF Occasional Paper*. New Delhi: Observer Research Foundation & Paris: GEM/Sciences-Po., February 2012.

Mohn, Liz. *Cultures in Globalization*. Gutersloh: Bertelsmann, 2006.

Møller, J. Ørstrøm. *European Integration: Sharing of Experiences*. Singapore: Institute of Southeast Asian Studies, 2008.

Mongsawad, Prasopchoke, and Niramon Ariyaarpakamon. 'Settakij Thai 15 Pee Lung Wikrid: Por Rue Young?' (Thai Economy between 15 Years after Crisis: Is It Sufficient?). Center for the Study of Sufficiency Economy, National Institute of Development Administration, Bangkok, 2012.

Moyo, Dambisa. *How the West was Lost*. London: Allen Lane, 2011.

Nakamura, David. 'Obama Cancels the Rest of Asia Trip, Citing Difficulties of Travel During Shutdown'. *Washington Post*, 4 October 2013.

Narine, Shaun. 'State Sovereignty, Political Legitimacy and Regional Institutionalism in the Asia-Pacific'. *The Pacific Review* 17, no. 3 (2004): 423–50.

Osborn, Milton. *Southeast Asian: An Introductory History*. Sydney: Allen & Unwin, 2013.

Ovendale, Ritchie. 'Britain, the United States and the Recognition of Communist China.' *Historical Journal* 26, no. 1 (1983): 139–58.

Pakpahan, B. 'Contemporary Trans-regional Cooperation between Europe and Asia in a Changing World'. *Journal of Contemporary European Research* 6, no. 4 (2010): 514–34.

Palmer, Doug. 'Senate Rejects Trade Promotion Authority for Obama'. *Reuters*, 20 September 2011.

Parker, Owen, and Ben Rosamund. 'Normative Power Europe Meets Economic Liberalism: Complicating Cosmopolitanism Inside/Outide the EU'. *Cooperation and Conflict* 48, no. 2 (June 2013): 229–46.

Palmujoki, E. 'EU-ASEAN Relations: Reconciling Two Different Agendas'. *Contemporary Southeast Asia* 19, no. 3 (1997): 269–85.

Pang, Zhongying. 'Crisis Increased the Mutual Demands'. *Global Times*, 13 February 2009.

Pantiushkin, Valerii, and Mikhail Zygar. *Gazprom. Novoe Russkoe Oruzhie.* Moscow: Zakharov, 2008.

Park, S., and S. Yoon. 'EU Perceptions Through the FTA Lens: Main Results of Interviews Among the Korean Elites'. *Asia Europe Journal* 8, no. 2 (2010): 177–91.

Park, Sung-Hoon, and Heungchong Kim. 'Asia Strategy of the European Union and Asia-EU Economic Relations: Basic Concepts and New Developments'. Revised version of paper presented at the international conference on *The EU-Asia Relations: Building Multilateralism?* Hong Kong Baptist University, 20–21 May 2005.

Park, Sung-Hoon. 'Quest for a Stronger Regional Leadership and an Upgraded Global Profile'. *Asia Europe Journal* 9, no. 2–4 (March 2012): 225.

Parry, J. H. *Europe and A Wider World.* London: Hutchinson's University Library, 1953.

Pathiyagoda, Kadira. 'India's Approach to Humanitarian Intervention and the Responsibility to Protect'. Working Paper, Oxford Institute for Ethics, Law and Armed Conflict, November 2013.

Patil, Reshma. *Strangers across the Border.* Noida, India: HarperCollins, 2014.

Patten, C. *Not Quite the Diplomat—Home Truths about World Affairs.* London: Penguin Books, 2005.

Penninx, Rinus, Maria Berger, and Karen Kraal. *The Dynamics of International Migration and Settlement in Europe: A State of the Art.* Amsterdam: IMISCOE Research, Amsterdam University Press, 2006.

Peters, Dirk. *Constrained Balancing: the EU's Security Policy.* Basingstoke: Palgrave Macmillan, 2010.

Poettering, Hans-Gert. 'Europe as a Global Player'. *Harvard International Review* 29, no. 1 (Spring 2007): 26–29.

Postsovetskaia Tsentral'naia Aziia. *Poteri I obreteniia.* Moscow: Vostochnaia Literatura, 1998.

PRO Suvrennyiu Demokratiiu. Moscow: Izdatel'stvo Evropa, 2007.

Rana, Pradumna, and W. M. Chia. *The Revival of the Silk Roads (Land Connectivity) in Asia.* Singapore: Rajaratnam School of International Studies, 2014.

Rashid, Ahmed. *The Resurgence of Central Asia.* New Delhi: Oxford University Press, 1994.

Reuter, E. 'A New Agenda'. In *China-EU: A Common Future*, edited by S. Crossick and E. Reuter, xi–xiii. Singapore: World Scientific, 2007.

Rocher, Sophie Boisseau du. 'The EU's Strategic Offensive with ASEAN: Some Room Left but No Time'. *GRIP Analis Note*, 8 January 2014.

Ross, George. *The European Union and its Crises.* Basingstoke: Palgrave Macmillan, 2011.

Ross, Robert S. 'The Problem with the Pivot'. *Foreign Affairs*, November-December 2012.

Sally, Razeen. 'Europe and Asia'. Institute of Economic Affairs. Oxford: Blackwell, 2008.

Saltmarsh, Matthew. 'EU Asian Relations in the Media'. *Asia Europe Journal* 2 (2004): 15–18.

Sandschneider, Eberhard. 'The Strategic Significance of China Partnership (Speaking Points)'. *Chinese People's Institute of Foreign Affairs, Foreign Affairs Journal, Special Issue* (November 2009).

Sarkozy, N. 'Speech at the International Aerospace Show'. *le Bourget*, 23 June 2007.

Schake, Kori. 'All Your Pivots Belong to Us'. *Foreign Policy*, 12 September 2014.

Seidelmann, Reimund, and Andreas Vasilache. *European Union and Asia*. Baden-Baden: Nomos, 2009.

Shambaugh, David. 'China and Europe: Development from Derivable to Independent Relationship'. In *China and Europe towards the 21st Century*, edited by Xinning Song and Xiaojin Zhang. Hong Kong: Hong Kong Social Science Press, 2007, 5–32.

———. *China Goes Global: The Partial Power*. Oxford: Oxford University Press, 2012.

Shen, Qiang. 'Why Does the Development of China-Europe Relations Face Difficulties?' *Party and Government Forum*, no. 1 (2009).

Shen, Yawen. 'Demands for Europe Have Been Sharply Decreased'. *Global Times*, 13 February 2009.

Shi, Yinhong. 'The US-Europe Adjacence, China-Europe Alienation and Chinese Strategic Demands'. *Contemporary International Relations*, no. 5 (2008).

Smith, Michael E., and Stephen McGuire. *The European Union and the United States: Competition and Convergence in the Global Arena*. Basingstoke, Palgrave Macmillan, 2008.

Solana, Javier. 'A Secure Europe in a Better World'. European Council, Thessaloniki, 20 June 2003.

———. 'Challenges for EU-China Cooperation in Africa'. *China Daily*, 7 February 2007. www.consilium.europa.eu/ueDocs/cms_Data/docs/pressdata/EN/articles/92678. pdf. Accessed 26 June 2014.

Song, Xinning. 'The Impact of Domestic Politics on Chinese Foreign Policy'. In *Leadership in a Changing China*, edited by Yang Zhong and Weixing Chen. New York: Palgrave Macmillan, 2005, 147–68.

———. 'China's View of European Integration and Enlargement'. In *China-Europe Relations: Perceptions, Policies and Prospects*, edited by David Shambaugh, Eberhard Sanschneider, and Zhou Hong. London: Routledge, 2008, 174–86.

———. 'The European Union and China: Partnership with Competition'. In *Challenges to Chinese Foreign Policy: Diplomacy, Globalization, and the Next World Power*, edited by Yufan Hao, C. X. George Wei, and Lowell Dittmer. Lexington: The University Press of Kentucky, 2009, 175.

———. 'The EU and East Asia: Economic Interests and Political Ambitions'. In *The European Union and the Rise of Regionalism: Source of Inspiration and Active Promoter*, edited by Christian Frank, Jean-Christophe Defraigne, and Virgine de Moriame. Louvain-La-Neuve: Academia Bruylant, 2009, 283–98.

Srinivasan, Krishnan. 'Asia as a Future Career'. The Swedish EU Presidency Conference, Lund University, 7 July 2009. www.vr.se/download/18.227c330c123c73dc58 6800011440/1340207479667/Krishnan%2BSrinivasan.pdf. Accessed 7 January 2015.

Starr, S. Fredrick, and Svante E. Cornell. *The Baku-Tblisi-Ceyhan Pipeline: Oil Window to the West*. Uppsala: Central Asia Caucasus Silk Road Studies Program, 2005.

Taylor, Paul G. *The End of European Integration: Anti Europeanism Examined*. Abingdon: Routledge, 2008.

Thomas, Daniel C. *Making EU Foreign Policy*. Basingstoke: Palgrave Macmillan, 2011.

Toje, Asle. *The European Union as a Small Power*. Basingstoke: Palgrave Macmillan, 2010.

Tortora, Jackie, 'Trumka: Fast Track Trade Promotion Is "Undemocratic" and "Bad for American Workers"'. *AFL-CIO Now*, 9 January 2014.

Tsuruoka, Michito. 'Defining Europe's Strategic Interests in Asia'. *Studia Diplomatica* 64, no. 3 (2011): 95–107.

Vasudevan, Hari. *Shadows of Substance, Indo-Russian Trade and Military Technical Cooperation since 1991*. New Delhi: Manohar, 2010.

Vaughn, Bruce. *Nepal: Political Developments and Bilateral Relations with the United States*. Darby, PA: DIANE Publishing, 2012

von Einsiedel, Sebastian, David M. Malone, and Suman Pradhan. *Nepal in Transition: From People's War to Fragile Peace*. Cambridge: Cambridge University Press, 2012.

Wasserstein, Bernard. *Barbarians and Civilization*. Oxford: Oxford University Press, 2007.

Wezeman, T. Siemon, and D. Pieter Wezeman. 'Trends in International Arms Trans-
fers, 2013'. *SIPRI Fact Sheet.* Stockholm: International Peace Research Institute,
March 2014.
Wiessala, Georg. *European Studies in Asia. Contours of a Discipline.* New York: Rout-
ledge, 2014.
Wiessala, Georg, John Wilson, and Pradeep Taneja (eds.). 'The European Union and
Democracy Building in South Asia'. *European Studies,* no. 27 (2009).
Wong, Rueben, and Christopher Hill. *National and European Foreign Policies.* Abingdon:
Routledge, 2011.
World Bank. *China 2030: Building a Modern, Harmonious and Creative High-Income Soci-
ety.* Washington DC: World Bank, 2012.
World Economy Outlook. 'Recovery Strengthens Remains Uneven'. Washington, DC:
International Monetary Fund, April 2014.
Wu, Jianmin. 'Dialogue and Cooperation are Still the Mainstream of China-Europe
Relations'. *China Today,* no. 2 (2009).
Wu, Liming. 'Looking at the EU: China Policy Papers from Rational Perspectives'.
Liaowang Newsweek, 30 October 2006.
Wu, Wenbing. 'Difficult Movement of China-Europe Relation During the Financial
Crisis'. Tsinghua University, 5 April 2009.
Wulbers, Shazia Aziz. *EU-India Relations.* New Delhi: Academic Foundation, 2008.
Yacob, Shakila, and Nicholas J. White. *The Unfinished Business of Malaysian Decolonisa-
tion: The Origins of the Guthrie Dawn Raid.* Cambridge: Cambridge University Press,
2010.
Yang, Jiechi. 'Oration'. *Chinese Journal of European Studies,* no. 5 (2009).
Yang, Yuanhua. 'Dual Faces of the EU Policy towards China'. *Party and Government
Forum* (December 2006).
Yoe, Lee Whee. 'Can the EU be a Serious Security Actor in Asia?' *Asia Europe Journal*
11, no. 4 (2013): 465–67.
Youngs, Richard. *Europe's Decline and Fall: The Struggle against Global Irrelevance.* Lon-
don: Profile Books, 2010.
Yu, Miaojie, and Wei Tian. 'China's Processing Trade: A Firm-level Analysis'. In *Rebal-
ancing and Sustaining Growth in China,* edited by Huw McKay and Ligang Song.
Canberra: Australian National University Press, 2012: 111–48.
Yuanlun, Q. 'The EU's Long-Term China Policy and the Sino-EU Economic and Trade
Relationship'. *World Economy* (Chinese periodical) 4 (1999).
Zhang, Jian. 'The Perception Change of the EU on China and Policy Adjustment.'
Contemporary International Relations, no 7 (2007).
Zhang, Weiwei. *The China Wave: Rise of a Civilizational State.* Hackensack, NJ: World
Century Publishing Corporation, 2011.
Zhang, Zhijun. 'Inheriting Past and Developing the Future: Creating a New Situation
for Sino-European Relations'. *Chinese Journal of European Studies,* no. 5 (2009).
Zhao, Chen. 'Current Situation and Development Tendency of China-Europe Rela-
tions'. *Expanding Horizons,* no. 2 (2008).
Zhao, Huaipu. 'Analysis of the Current China-Europe Relations'. *Foreign Affairs Review*
(October 2008).
Zhou, Hong. 'Sino-European Partnership: Symmetries above Asymmetries'. *Chinese
Journal of European Studies,* no. 2 (2004).
Zhu Liqun. 'China's Foreign Policy Debates'. *Chaillot Papers,* no. 121. Paris: European
Institute for Security Studies, September 2010.
Zielonka, Jan. 'Europe as a Global Actor: Empire by Example?' *International Affairs,* no.
3 (May 2008): 471–84.
Zimmermann, Hubert. 'Realist Power Europe?' *Journal of Common Market Studies* 45,
no. 4 (November 2007): 813–32.

Index

least developed country, 50, 58, 61
Liberation Tigers of Tamil Eelam, 54–55
Lisbon Treaty, 14, 47, 182, 188, 215, 239

Maastricht Treaty, 47, 212–213
Malaysia, 66, 68, 77, 96, 98, 133, 138, 163, 167, 261
Mandelson, Peter, 183, 187
Mao Zedong, 177; Middle Zone theory, 177, 179; Three Worlds theory, 177, 179
Medvedev, Dimitri, 242
mercantilism. *See* trade
Merkel, Angela, 73, 184
Mexico, 264, 266, 269
middle-income trap, 85, 86–88, 92, 97, 104, 150
Millennium Development Goals (MDGs), 49, 58, 60
Modi, Narendra, 57, 225
Mogherini, Frederica, 47, 137, 228
Moldova, 219, 234, 239, 246, 247, 248
multilateralism. *See* institutions
multipolar world, 2, 15, 19, 22, 43, 63, 179, 180, 186–187, 199, 201, 212, 216, 223

Nabucco pipeline, 246
Nepal, 56
New Development Bank, 152
New Zealand, 71, 122, 263, 268
non-government organization (NGOs), 26, 46, 49, 69, 219, 224, 228, 230
non-tariff barriers. *See* trade
normative principles, 7, 14, 61, 82–83, 126, 187, 226; in Asia, 11, 12, 14, 15–16, 25, 26, 73, 145, 179, 197, 217, 243; in the European Union, 14, 47, 49, 59, 68, 69, 78, 82–83, 131, 144, 182, 197, 198, 211, 215, 216–217, 230, 231, 234, 247, 248
North American Free Trade Agreement, 264
North Atlantic Treaty Organization (NATO), 8, 47, 108, 141, 146, 198, 239, 252, 262
North Korea. *See* Korea, People's Democratic Republic of

North Stream. *See* Russian Federation
nuclear proliferation, 4, 24, 51, 226
nuclear weapons, 2, 116, 119–120, 226

Obama, Barack, 259–260, 262, 263–264, 265, 266–267, 271; attitude to trade liberalization, 264; difficulties with Congress, 265, 267, 271; foreign policy, 259–260, 261, 263
Organization for Economic Cooperation and Development (OECD), 76, 87
Organization for Security and Cooperation in Europe (OSCE), 234–235, 237, 240, 249, 251

Pakistan, 23, 26, 49, 50–52, 62, 134, 218, 225, 226, 229; diaspora, 50–51; strategic dialogue with the European Union, 52
Park Guen-hye, 107, 113, 114–115, 117, 121, 124; Northeast Asia Peace and Cooperation Initiative, 117
Philippines, 66, 72, 76, 269
Pivot to Asia. *See* United States of America
plantation industry, 66, 67, 68
Plaza Accord, 91
Poland, 9, 211–212, 218–220, 226–227, 239; and Asia, 219–220; and China, 218–219; and India, 218–220; post-Soviet era ties with Asia, 218–220
Putin, Vladimir, 242, 252

rebalance to Asia. *See* United States of America
Regional Comprehensive Economic Partnership (RCEP), 71–72, 261, 267, 269
Responsibility to Protect (R2P), 25, 55–56, 145–146
Russian Federation, 30, 141, 195, 218, 219, 228, 233, 235, 236, 237, 240–241, 244, 245, 247, 248, 254; and emerging Asia, 253; North Stream, 246; South Stream, 246; trade with China, 253

Sarkozy, Nicolas, 182, 183, 187, 199

immigration, 130, 134–136, 139; importance of emerging Asia, 129, 131, 138, 146–147; and India, 131, 134; referendum on the European Union, 8, 132; reluctance to impose sanctions, 140; Scottish referendum, 130; and United States, 131, 141–143. *See also* European Union; Schengen Treaty

UK Independence Party, 130, 135

United Nations (UN), 3, 5, 54, 55, 57; Command in Korea, 122–123; Convention on Law of the Sea, 142; General Assembly, 25; Security Council, 2, 108, 122, 142, 145, 146, 196, 204, 226

United States of America (US), 5, 10, 16–17, 62–63, 69–70, 72, 108, 116, 150, 151, 154, 172, 183, 212, 223, 239, 241, 250, 259–271; and China, 72, 195, 198, 201, 203, 223, 261, 264, 267–269; common goals with Europe in Asia, 21, 63, 140, 142, 187, 201, 270; differences with Europe, 5, 131, 139, 140, 142, 195, 270; importance of Asia to, 262, 266, 271; and India, 225, 261, 268; and Middle East, 260; pivot to Asia, 10, 16, 23, 63, 72, 73, 116, 140, 141, 186, 189,

194, 198, 259–271; relations with South Korea, 117, 264, 267, 268; resource constraints, 259–260, 262, 263, 265, 269, 271; Trade Promotion Authority, 264–265, 266, 267. *See also* Trans-Atlantic Trade and Investment Partnership; Trans-Pacific Partnership

Uzbekistan, 233, 235, 242, 243, 244, 247, 251, 253

values. *See* normative principles

van Rompuy, Herman, 28

Vietnam, 66, 72, 77, 79, 98, 224, 261, 268

weapons of mass destruction, 29, 51, 114, 230

Wen Jiabao, 186, 194, 221

World Bank, 5, 37, 68

World Trade Organization (WTO), 12, 37–38, 38, 39, 68, 149, 160–161, 180, 181, 183, 238, 239, 241, 270

Xi Jinping, 14, 112, 116, 134, 189, 198, 222

Xinjiang. *See* China

Zhou Enlai, 175–176, 177

List of Contributors

Kriengsak Chareonwongsak is a former member of the Parliament of Thailand and presently a senior fellow at Harvard University.

Iftekhar Ahmed Chowdhury is a former ambassador and foreign minister of Bangladesh. He is currently principal research fellow at the Institute of South Asian Studies, Singapore.

Fredrik Erixon is director and co-founder of the European Centre for International Political Economy at Brussels. He has worked as adviser to the British government, and at the office of the prime minister of Sweden, in the World Bank, and at JP Morgan.

Evi Fitriani is head of the International Relations Department at the University of Indonesia and a senior lecturer at the European Studies Program. She is a co-founder of the ASEAN Study Centre at the Faculty of Social and Political Science, and Indonesian country coordinator of the Network of East Asian think tanks.

Agnieszka Kuszewska is assistant professor of political science at the University of Social Sciences and Humanities at Warsaw. She is a specialist on South Asia at the Poland-Asia Research Centre, and a member of the European Security Institute.

Philip I. Levy is senior fellow on global economy at The Chicago Council on Global Affairs and adjunct professor of strategy at Northwestern University Kellogg School of Management.

James Mayall is emeritus professor of International Relations at Cambridge University, member of the editorial board of The Round Table, and chairman of the advisory board of the Institute of Commonwealth Studies at London University. He is a fellow of the British Academy and Sidney Sussex College, Cambridge.

M. K. Narayanan is a former Indian national security adviser, minister of state, and governor.

Ana Palacio is a lawyer by training and a member of the Spanish Council of State. She was formerly Spain's minister of foreign affairs, and senior vice president and general counsel of the World Bank Group.

Jin Park is a former chairman of the Foreign Affairs, Trade and Unification Committee of the parliament of the Republic of Korea, and presently chair professor at the Hankuk University of Foreign Studies. He is the executive director of the Asia Future Institute, an independent policy think tank in Seoul.

Krishnan Srinivasan is a former Indian foreign secretary and deputy secretary-general of the Commonwealth. He is presently a visiting professor at the Administrative Staff College of India in Hyderabad and fellow at the Abul Kalam Azad Institute of Asian Studies at Calcutta.

Hari Vasudevan is professor of history at Calcutta University and is a specialist on modern Russian and European history. He has been a consultant to the Indian government on Russian trade and has published widely on Indo-Russian economic relations.

Zhang Xiaotong is a former Chinese diplomat at Brussels and presently associate professor in the department of international relations at Wuhan University.

Wang Yiwei is a former Chinese diplomat at Brussels and now professor of international studies at Renmin University, director of the Institute of International Affairs, director of the Centre for European Union studies, and director of the China-Europe Academic Network.

www.ingramcontent.com/pod-product-compliance
Lightning Source LLC
Chambersburg PA
CBHW021810270326
41932CB00007B/122